For Dr. Thompson

With good memories

Walter v. Lack

4/6/99

GENE TECHNOLOGY
AND SOCIAL ACCEPTANCE

GENE TECHNOLOGY

AND SOCIAL ACCEPTANCE

WALTER P. VON WARTBURG
JULIAN LIEW

UNIVERSITY PRESS OF AMERICA,® INC.
Lanham · New York · Oxford

Copyright © 1999 by
University Press of America,® Inc.
4720 Boston Way
Lanham, Maryland 20706

12 Hid's Copse Rd.
Cumnor Hill, Oxford OX2 9JJ

Library of Congress Cataloging-in-Publication Data

Wartburg, Walter P. von.
Gene technology and social acceptance / Walter P. von Wartburg,
Julian Liew.
p.   cm.
Includes bibliographical references.
1. Genetic engineering—Social aspects. I. Liew, Julian. II. Title.
QH442.W365   1999   306.4'6—dc21   98-52997 CIP

ISBN 0-7618-1325-X (cloth: alk. ppr.)

⊖™ The paper used in this publication meets the minimum
requirements of American National Standard for Information
Sciences—Permanence of Paper for Printed Library Materials,
ANSI Z39.48—1984

TABLE OF CONTENTS

TABLE OF CONTENTS

What is technology? A dictionary definition might say most broadly that it is the application of knowledge and skill to practical ends; more specifically today that it is the sum of knowledge, skills, tools, methods, processes, and systems developed from one or more scientific disciplines and is applied especially to industry. Neither definition explains the powerful reactions of admiration, curiosity, awe, fear, and anxiety that technology evokes. These conflicting reactions are even more pronounced with a new technology.

A new technology brings with it conflict, challenges, and uncertainty because it is a motor for change. The change is not just technical change but touches many aspects of society and the lives of most individuals. A new technology involves new knowledge, requires new skills, and demands new ways of thinking. It is a shift in **paradigm**.

Neil Postman, technology theorist, calls this shift the ecological effect of new technologies:

> A new technology does not add or subtract something. It changes everything. In the year 1500, fifty years after the printing press was invented, we did not have old Europe plus the printing press. We had a different Europe. . . . Therefore, when an old technology is assaulted by a new one, institutions are threatened. When institutions are threatened, a culture finds itself in crisis. (Postman, 1992, p.18)

The word *crisis* (from the Greek *krisis*, meaning "decision") refers to a turning point or a decisive moment. The term is appropriate in this context because the introduction of a new technology marks a turning point for society. "To call to mind the beliefs and attitudes that emanated from an ancient paradigm even a decade after it imploded is like looking at a city with the help of an ancient map. The world before has acquired a sepia tone" (Smith, 1992, p.61).

Among other consequences, a new technology leads to a redistribution of resources in society. As new skills and knowledge become more in demand, old skills and knowledge become obsolete, creating a ripple effect throughout society. Those with the new skills and knowledge form the new elite. A new structure is created with new legislation, new economic alliances, and new social dilemmas. This structure has an impact on the values and interests of different groups in society competing for those limited resources. The result is conflict.

The term *crisis* is also appropriate because the new technology creates a situation in which society has to make decisions in the midst of fast changes, usually without knowing for sure what the consequences will be. Decision makers have to rely on existing knowledge about the technology, which is often incomplete. They may also have to extrapolate from similar experiences with other technologies. But by definition, a new technology does not follow previous paradigms. Therefore, they also need trust. In addition, they are torn between the desire to maximize the benefits and opportunities, and the desire to avoid the risks and costs of the new technology.

At the end of the twentieth century, technologically driven (or postindustrial) society faces tremendous technological change, even if it is premature to call it a crisis. Gene technology—also called genetic engineering or recombinant DNA technology—is the motor behind this change, which raises concerns, provokes conflicts, and leads to a redistribution of resources. Gene technology sparks fears about unknown risks, fears that can be linked to disasters in past human experience. Because of the uncontrollable spread of diseases and epidemics in the past, and the crop failures that have led to massive starvation, people are alarmed by the very idea of genetic alteration to microorganisms or plants. Gene technology also raises ethical issues born of existing conflicts in values in Western society. Most of these conflicts touch on the way individuals, or groups look at the world, especially the living world. These conflicts existed before gene technology, which as it emerged, provided the spark that set off an ethical powder keg.

This book is not about gene technology but about the introduction of a new technology in society. It uses the gene technology issue to illustrate the concerns, conflicts, and controversies that a new technology raises. The book is interested in the mechanisms and circumstances that provoke economic, legislative, environmental, social, and ethical issues.

The book also tries to understand what social acceptance of a new technology means in concrete terms. The premise is that social acceptance is really a decision-making process that provides an opportunity to clarify ambiguities in social values and priorities. A paradigm shift forces society to set priorities and to redistribute resources. This shift forces different segments of society to articulate their values and interests, which are not always compatible or self-evident to others. The process of setting priorities requires a process of negotiation—where compromise may not always be possible—to decide which sets of interests and values are compatible with those of society as a whole.

Finally, this book is interested in how individuals and institutions deal with change. Depending on their response, they fall into one of three categories. Those who see new opportunities in the new situation tend to be vocal advocates of change and risk. Those who see new dangers tend to be the vocal defenders of the status quo or even of an ideal past; they resist change and advocate prudence. Most people, however, are chiefly concerned with how the new technology or distribution of resources will affect them. This third group will perhaps support genetic research for new medication but will reject the creation of transgenic animals. They want to maximize the benefits—to themselves or to society—while minimizing long-term risks.

To achieve a broad, unbiased perspective of the complex issues, the book uses a dialectic approach. It does not champion any particular cause or advocate a particular stance on issues. It favors critical analysis and tries to understand the underlying motivations and principles of the different groups whose interests are affected by the introduction of the new technology. The authors' perspective of curious observers allows a broad grasp of issues in different areas.

The book also relies on a contextual approach. The authors maintain that a technology does not develop in a vacuum but in response to existing needs and as an attempt to address specific problems. This approach allows a new technology to be seen against the background of existing problems and previous solutions, providing a sense of continuity with the past. For example, the creation of transgenic crops is seen in the context of the ongoing need to control pests, and previous attempts to achieve sturdier varieties of crops.

In addition, a contextual approach allows a new technology to be placed in relationship to other technologies. How people perceive a new technology will be influenced by their experience with other technologies. Gene technology, for example, will always be compared with nuclear technology and, to a lesser degree, with information technology. The book analyzes the impact of such comparisons on people's perception of gene technology.

In many ways, this is a book written by generalists for generalists. It is intended for students, managers, legislators, or other decision makers who are interested in how a new technology affects society directly or indirectly as it creates a paradigm shift. It suggests ways for a society to resolve a common dilemma when the disputants are full of anxiety in the face of change and the solution will inevitably create winners and losers. It explains why it is important to understand gene technology and its resulting changes in the context of other technologies and as a phenomenon taking place in a particular society at a particular time and place.

REFERENCES

Postman, N. 1992. *Technopoly: The Surrender of Culture to Technology.* New York: Vintage Books.

Smith, A. 1996. *Software for the Self: Technology and Culture.* London: Faber and Faber.

1 FACTORS THAT DETERMINE SOCIAL ACCEPTANCE OF A NEW TECHNOLOGY

The arrival of a new technology signals the beginning of a period of change, conflict, and uncertainty. It is also the beginning of a process in which individuals and society as a whole struggle to understand the new technology and cope with the implications of the accompanying changes. The outcome of that effort determines the degree of society's acceptance of the technology. This chapter examines the factors that make for acceptance of gene technology. The aim is to offer a broad view of the surrounding conflicts and arguments.

Inherent in anything new is a challenge to old concepts, traditional methods, and established frameworks. Implicit in change are risks involved with moving toward the unknown. The need to take risks in an unfamiliar and shifting environment results in conflicts between the advocates of change and risk taking and the defenders of stability and risk avoidance. At the center of these conflicts are individuals who try to figure out what the new technology means and how it will affect their lives.

This process of conflict and argument is part of society's evaluation of the risks and benefits of a new technology. It is a process that society has experienced many times in the course of history. The degree to which society accepts a new technology depends in part on two types of factors: rational and emotional.

Rational factors include the degree of public understanding, the amount of social control over the technology and the decision-making process behind it, and the conviction that the technology will be of practical use to society as a whole and to people as individuals.

Emotional factors—which in this context include lack of knowledge, level of anxiety, and degree of aversion to risk—all play a more subtle but equally important role in whether or not there is acceptance. Emotional factors are a response to the uncertainty that the technology will bring and that both individuals and society must deal with.

The synthesis of rational and emotional factors results in society's acceptance of a new technology. But that acceptance also requires another element: trust. Trust depends on the public's perception of the people and the institutions involved with the technology. Building trust requires three elements: openness, truthfulness, and willingness to share knowledge and experience. Trust also depends on balance in science communication. Here, the scientific community and the media share a special responsibility in ensuring that the public receive factual and balanced scientific information.

RATIONAL FACTORS

Rational Factors contributing to social acceptance of new technology include public understanding, social control, and social utility.

PUBLIC UNDERSTANDING

In talking about understanding scientific and technological matters, it is perhaps useful to distinguish between factual knowledge and general awareness. Surveys in various countries seem to confirm that there is indeed a difference between the two (Macer, 1994). In a survey carried out in New Zealand in 1990, about 73 percent of those surveyed said that they had heard of gene technology; about 20 percent of all respondents said they could explain it to a friend. (The figure is slightly higher for biotechnology, a science that includes gene technology, which was treated as a separate item.)

About three years later, the same questions about biotechnology and gene technology were used in a Japanese survey. About 94 percent said they had heard of gene technology, but only about 26 percent felt that they could explain it to a friend.

A 1993 survey (Eurobarometer 39.1) in the European Community (EC, now the European Union, or EU) also points to a noticeable difference between what the researchers consider *elementary* knowledge and *thorough* knowledge of biotechnology and gene technology among those surveyed (Marlier, 1993). Using a range from 0 to 6 for each type of knowledge, the index across all twelve countries of the EC was 4.1 for elementary knowledge and 1.97 for thorough knowledge. This finding suggests that while those interviewed are familiar with either biotechnology or gene technology, they do not have a thorough knowledge of either one.

The difference between factual knowledge and general awareness may appear to be interesting but not very important. The Eurobarometer survey went one step further by looking at the correlation between objective knowledge (based on answers to questions dealing with facts of biotechnology and gene technology) and the degree of optimism that gene technology "will improve our way of life" (Marlier, 1993, p. 27).

The results suggest that there is a positive relationship between knowledge about the technology and optimism about its impact. The ratio of optimists to pessimists increases with greater thorough knowledge. The report warns, however, that this positive correlation does not necessarily indicate cause and effect:

> It is nevertheless important to specify that, on average, the level of objective knowledge for "pessimists" (those who think that "biotechnology/genetic engineering will make things worse") is only slightly lower than that of the "optimists" (6.53/12 versus 6.73/12 respectively).

> This clearly highlights that one should not look for automatic links between cause (knowledge) and effect (optimism) in these knowledge/optimism relationships. (Marlier, 1993, p. 30)

E. Marlier's comment echoes observations in the report on the surveys in Japan and New Zealand. For comparison, these surveys used subsamples drawn from biology teachers in secondary schools and scientists at universities; additional subsamples included students and nurses. "The greater familiarity of these groups with science and technology was not found to be associated with lower concern about science and technology" (Macer, 1994, p. 24). Thus, one useful lesson in these findings is that it should not be assumed that a policy of public education would almost automatically lead to optimism about gene technology or its acceptance.

At the same time, one should not ignore the clear link between depth of knowledge and attitudes toward particular scientific applications. From their research in this field, G. Evans and J. Durant came to this conclusion: "Thus knowledge appears to be important, both because of its effect on the consistency of general attitudes to science and because it is associated with support for particular areas of scientific activity—and opposition to others" (1995, p. 70). This finding seems to imply that greater depth of knowledge or real understanding enables people to deal with the complexity of a new technology. It will be suggested here that knowledge is important for meaningful, broad (nonexpert) participation in the social control of technology in at least two ways.

First, on the one hand, better knowledge seems to lead to consistency in public attitude. This consistency may help policy makers (such as legislators and regulatory officials) in formulating guidelines for a new technology and its applications, guidelines that will better reflect the position of large segments of a well-informed public. At the same time, as Evans and Durant say, a knowledgeable public may also provide a useful counterbalance to policy decisions about the control or the direction and growth of particular areas of scientific research or technological development.

Second, on the other hand, although public understanding is important, it should not be forgotten that other factors, such as social control and the usefulness of a technology or the degree of public anxiety and the level of risk aversion in society, also help determine acceptance of a new technology. These factors are one reason that knowledge or understanding by itself is not enough to guarantee social acceptance or even public optimism. In fact, there are suggestions that when other needs of the public are not met or when relationships are confrontational, an information or educational campaign will actually backfire (Greber, Frech, and Hillier, 1994, p. 134, citing Sandman 1990). This observation seems to underline the subtle and ambivalent but powerful role of knowledge in social acceptance, of new technology.

SOCIAL CONTROL

Another rational factor determining social acceptance is the degree to which technology is under society's control. An important concept behind technological progress is that technology and its products will bring some degree of good to society or serve particular social needs. This is one of the underlying concepts of societal instruments that promote research in science and innovation in technology. Thus, social acceptance depends on the perception of benefits to individuals, society, and the environment. More precisely, a decisive factor is the perceived or actual *net value* of benefits in relation to risks.

It will be argued here that many people in the industrialized world probably do not think of technology in absolute terms—either as benefits or risks. Instead, most people probably tend to see technology in relative terms. Thus, the question is whether the benefits truly justify the costs. This question is especially true of gene technology, which was born in the 1970s—in the age of the cold war, the peace movement, and the birth of the environmental movement. In the 1990s, gene technology started to come of age in a period of dramatic political restructuring, increasing environmental concern, and rapid technological changes. More important, gene technology has also come of age at a time when many people in industrialized society are questioning the *true* benefit-to-cost ratio of earlier technologies.

Unforgettable examples on television screens and in newspapers showed clearly the high costs of technologies. Within the twenty-five-year period since the development of gene technology, the world witnessed major accidents that were unforeseen, that involved key technologies, and that have long-term, unknown consequences for human beings and the environment. They involved some of the most important technologies, industries, and countries of the world:

- the accident at the nuclear reactor on Three Mile Island, N.Y., U.S.A.
- the release of toxic gases in Bhopal, India
- the oil spill caused by the *Exxon Valdez* in Prince William Sound, U.S.A.
- the meltdown at the nuclear facilities in Chernobyl, Ukraine
- the chemical spill into the Rhine River near Schweizerhalle, Switzerland
- the explosion at the Westray coal mine, Plymouth, N.S., Canada
- the derailment of the Intercity Express train in Eschede, Germany

Within the same period, many people in the industrialized world saw technology being directed at military ends, a process leading to stockpiles of weapons and the brink of nuclear war. At the same time, more and more people felt alienated from the institutions that produce and use these technologies.

Many people were no longer satisfied with the promises of technology or of the institutions in charge of it. Many of these institutions had dismissed public anxiety. They told concerned members of the public that their fears were irrational or that the experts had everything under control. The technological accidents were evidence that the public had reason to worry and that technical experts are human beings who can—and will eventually—make errors of judgment.

With each technological accident, industry and government lost more and more of their credibility with the public. Because they have been told repeatedly that all is under control in technological paradise, people became cynical when yet another accident proved otherwise. Two key lessons of the last twenty years of industrial and technological history are, first, to expect the unexpected where technology is concerned and, second, to recognize that technological solutions to the problems of humanity will create other problems for humans and the environment.

It is against this social, political, and technological backdrop that gene technology has come under the spotlight of public scrutiny. This background may also partially explain why society feels a strong need to ensure that gene technology (and, to a lesser extent, other new technologies) is under control *from the start*.

In discussions on new technology, it is important to make a distinction between *technical control* and *social control*. These are independent but connected concepts; both are critical to social acceptance.

Technical Control

In technical control, the emphasis is on the quantifiable—the measurable and statistically predictable. Technical control focuses on two aspects: risk prevention and damage control. Key to risk prevention is the ability to anticipate situations that would result in damage to, or loss of, health, life, property, or the environment, and to understand the consequence of such events. Thus, prevention usually takes the form of precautionary measures, such as safety standards, emergency planning, and guidelines for handling dangerous products or processes.

If risk prevention fails, that is, if precautionary measures are unable to prevent something from happening, the other aspect of technical control comes into play. Measures need to be taken to control damage, to ensure that it can be limited. Such measures must contain the damage in the short term and possibly repair it in the long term.

Control by Society

Traditionally, risk assessment focused on the technical aspect of control. Since the mid-1980s (or perhaps even earlier), there has been growing attention to the role of social control. While taking into account the technical aspect, social control also gives weight to the concerns of the nonexpert public and to factors that are not necessarily quantifiable.

There are several ways for society to control technology. At the formal level and on a day-to-day basis, social control is exercised by elected officials and the civil service acting on behalf of their fellow citizens. At their disposal are a range of legal mechanisms and institutions that can promote or limit the growth of technology: at least, these measures are aimed at encouraging growth in certain directions while curbing its tendencies in other areas. Social control can also be exercised directly by the people. Direct public participation can take many forms, including public consultation panels, parliamentary commissions, citizen forums, plebiscites, and referendums.

Legislative and nonlegislative measures that governments use to promote a technology include funding to encourage research in certain technical areas, patents for inventions, and subsidies for the development of expertise or incentives for the use of the technology. Restrictive legislative measures include rules, guidelines, laws, and regulations, governing health, safety, or other issues of public interest. In rare and extreme cases, a government could enact legislation to prohibit a technology or particular areas of its use. For example, many nations prohibit the export of military material or expertise to certain other nations. In such situations, of course, political and military considerations are involved.

Depending on the technology, its perceived importance, and the political jurisdictions involved, technologies and the industries that use them could be subject to social control at the international, national, or regional level. For example, technology developed for the civil aviation industry must conform to both the regulations of national transport commissions and the international safety standards of the International Civil Aviation Organization (ICAO).

At the national or regional level, as W. Edwards and D.v. Winterfeldt describe in detail, there are three main bodies responsible for creating and enforcing control on behalf of society. Generally, legislative assemblies define broad rules and mechanisms for dealing with the risks of a technology and other matters of public concern. Because legislatures are not made up of technical experts, legislation tends to be general guidelines that set objectives and principles to be followed in specific instances.

Usually, legislative assemblies delegate the task of formulating more specific guidelines to agencies designated to oversee a particular technology or industry. Depending on the authority derived from the legislature, such an agency may set standards, grant permits, enforce compliance, and issue penalties in case of noncompliance. Finally, courts interpret and enforce the rules. More often, they act as an agent of recourse or appeal in case of dispute between government agencies (or sometimes the government) and a third party.

Beyond the national jurisdiction examined by Edwards and von Winterfeldt, there are also cross-border agreements and a few international agencies that can affect the use of technology. With the move toward globalization and the formation of international political-economic blocs, there may be more agreements and agencies establishing guidelines for certain areas of technology. Examples include the ICAO (mentioned above), the European Patent Office (EPO), and the International Organization of Standardization (ISO). While the EPO and ISO do not set regulations or measures of control as such for any specific technology, both agencies do make decisions in areas related to technologies that affect more than one legal or political jurisdiction.

These instruments and agents are means for society to retain formal and legal control over technologies and their impact on society. Sometimes, such institutionalized control may also incorporate ways for ordinary people to change policy or offer their input in decisions on the use of a technology. For example, in Canada, the Canadian Radio-Television and Telecommunications Commission (CRTC) will issue a notice of hearing when an organization applies for a broadcasting license or when a broadcaster wishes to change the status of its license. This practice allows the public—and especially those who may be affected—to contest the application.

In German-speaking countries, where there is greater emphasis on public participation in political processes, ordinary citizens can also voice their opinions through citizens' initiatives, plebiscites, or referendums. Examples include a referendum in Austria on a nuclear power plant and a referendum in Switzerland on biotechnology and new reproductive technology. The Swiss held a plebiscite on biotechnology in June 1998.

Social control, however, goes beyond citizens having a say about the legal technicalities concerning a technology or the direction of its growth. Another dimension of social control is control over the decision-making process where technology is concerned. In the past, those making the decisions were seen as being isolated—perhaps even aloof—from the community at large. The history of nuclear technology (a comparison often made in discussions about gene technology and one used frequently in this chapter) provides a good example.

Supported by technical specialists and risk analysts used to working with statistical probabilities of injuries and fatalities, the nuclear industry initially failed to take seriously the concerns of the lay public. The dominant way of thinking was that industry and government had the *risk experts* on their side and their opinions should be good enough for everyone (Greber et al., 1994; Otway and Wynne, 1989; Slovic, 1987). Industry and government sited facilities where *they* felt best: the community involved was expected to agree and accept the decision. The community often had little say over the operations of facilities, especially over decisions to shut down operations in case of problems or failure.

The lesson that the nuclear industry has learned is that communities resent the superior attitude of industry and want to be involved in decision-making processes as intelligent and legitimate partners (Greber et al., 1994). As P. Slovic says, while capable of rationally assessing the risk of injuries or fatalities, the lay public often has a richer conceptualization of risk and tends to include factors that experts ignore. Studies show that the public judgment of risk involves a complex of eighteen factors. These include, among others, questions about whether

- the risk is observable
- the risk is known to those exposed and to science
- the effects are controllable
- the consequences are fatal
- exposure is voluntary
- the effects are reversible
- the risk to future generations is high

It is not a question of one assessment being better than the other. Rather, the key point is that technology assessment and risk management must take into consideration both the assessment of the risk experts and the evaluation of those who have to live closely with the risks.

> As a result, risk communication and risk management efforts are destined to fail unless they are structured as a two-way process. Each side, expert and public, has something valid to contribute. Each side must respect the insights and intelligence of the other. (Slovic, 1987, p. 285)

Communities should be involved throughout the various stages of decision making: from siting a facility near a community to dealing with technical problems that will inevitably arise in the operation of the facility and the disposal of hazardous waste. The people living near a facility are the ones most directly affected by the technology: they enjoy economic benefits from the operations (for example, jobs and spin-offs for the local economy), but they also carry a greater share of the risks—to family, to health, and even jobs, should the operation be shut down.

When dealing with an emerging and rapidly changing technology (such as gene technology), there will be lots of unknown factors. These must be acknowledged candidly and discussed openly. As H. J. Otway and B. Wynne point out, the stereotypical image of a naive public demanding zero-risk is probably not realistic: "People are all too familiar with uncertainty and lack of control in their daily lives" (1989, p. 143).

Researchers in the field of risk management (Greber et al., 1994; Leiss and Chociolko, 1994; Otway and Winterfeldt, 1982; Slovic, 1987) suggest that voluntary acceptance of risks and uncertainty is important to the social acceptance of technologies. People are more willing to accept those risks if they think they have some degree of control over decisions that inevitably will affect their lives and the lives of their families.

This willingness would be especially appropriate to gene technology—given the legacy of previous major technologies and the social-cultural context in which gene technology has emerged. Perhaps because of this background, there is a greater need for those involved with gene technology to bring the lay public into the decision-making process. "If the community and other members of the affected public are involved as full partners in program decisions, they will be asked, in effect, to trust themselves" (Greber et al., 1994, p. 132).

UTILITY TO SOCIETY
Although social control improves the social acceptability of a technology, it is probably not enough in itself. Gene technology has been called a revolution because of its ability to alter living organisms at the molecular level. Although a revolution implicitly promises a new and better future, it also entails many uncertainties. If the risks are perceived to be great, the advantages to be gained must be even greater. Individuals in society must be able to see concrete benefits for themselves and for those around them.

Medical Benefits
So far, some of the biggest benefits of gene technology are in the field of human medicine and pharmacy. For the pharmaceutical industry, gene technology represents a key biological tool in the area of research and development (R&D). The pharmaceutical industry has long relied on the natural world for ideas and new products. Both folk medicine and modern medi-

cine have derived medicinal products from microorganisms (penicillin from a mold), plants (many pain relievers contain salicin, a substance derived from certain willows), and even animals (insulin from the pancreas of cows or pigs).

Yet these drugs are only a tiny fraction of the healing substances available. The methods of gene technology will allow researchers to reproduce quickly and relatively inexpensively these natural substances in the quantity needed. For example, the transfer of human genes into yeast cells has allowed the production of human proteins that were previously available only from cadavers (human growth hormone for treating dwarfed children), through animal substitutes (human insulin replacing animal insulin for treating diabetes), or else were simply not available at all (interferons, human proteins that activate or reinforce the body's immune system against viruses or abnormal cell growth). Many of these products (for example interferons) are aimed at the treatment of dread diseases such as cancer or acquired immune deficiency syndrome (AIDS). It is expected that by the year 2000, most if not all medication will involve gene technology in at least one stage of R&D.

In addition to pharmaceutical products, applications of gene technology in human medicine have already provided doctors with new methods of treatment and given hope to many patients. Mapping the location of genes and studying their sequences have already provided medical science with a better knowledge and understanding of the role of genes in many human diseases.

Genetic research has also opened up new doors. For example, the location of defective genes linked with diseases has proven to be a powerful diagnostic technique. Early detection—even before birth—may enable doctors to start treatment early enough for it to be effective. In some cases, early diagnosis allows doctors to recommend a program of prevention. This could be as simple as a special diet that takes into consideration the body's deficiencies (see "Genetic Diagnostics," chapter 2).

Not only has work in gene technology provided better diagnostic methods, it now offers the possibility of a cure for some genetic disorders. In the past, conventional medicine was unable to offer any hope for treatment, let alone a cure. Although somatic-cell gene therapy is still at the stage of clinical trials, it is already proving to be an effective weapon for some disorders caused by single genes. Progress in the field is providing further insight into more complex diseases, where the link between the influence of genes and the influence of the environment is not yet clear.

Economic Benefits
Beyond medical benefits, individuals and segments of industry can expect economic benefits from gene technology. One of the hopes is that production methods using gene technology will be less expensive than more con-

ventional methods. A technology is likely to be more acceptable if consumers can enjoy more benefits for the same amount of money, or if they pay less to enjoy the same benefits as before.

Although it is still early in the development of gene technology, the outlook is promising in some fields. For example, researchers are working with genetically altered dairy animals (cows, sheep, and goats) that will produce human proteins and hormones for less than more traditional means of production. So far, this method of production (or gene pharming) has remained on an experimental scale and the number of such animals limited. If work in this area proves successful, it may *possibly* even replace (or at least become an alternative to) current biotechnological methods, which use cell cultures of yeast or other microorganisms requiring expensive investments in equipment. With large-scale gene pharming, the savings in cost of production would be passed on to patients.

There are additional economic benefits to consider. A new technology represents job opportunities, in both direct employment and job spin-offs. Gene technology not only means jobs for scientists and researchers but also opportunities for administrators, support staff, and other nonscientific personnel. These may include jobs for those in the building industry as laboratories and production facilities are built; for the public sector, notably in administrative departments dealing with technology, health, or safety regulation; and for service industries, including providers of food service.

On a broader economic scale, gene technology is seen as a form of competition for countries and companies in specific sectors of industry. Many countries have decided to invest in research in the fields of biotechnology and gene technology because these technologies are seen as key to international competitiveness in the next century. New technologies eventually spawn new industries, which create employment and national prosperity, resulting in economic and political stability. Governments have actively provided grants to academic and research institutions for work in this area, as well as funding work in government research programs and laboratories.

Some industries, notably the pharmaceutical and health-care industries, have also taken a keen strategic and commercial interest in the new biotechnology industry. In the United States, this interest has in part led to the rapid growth of small firms clustering around leading university research facilities (especially in California and Massachusetts). Long-established companies in the pharmaceutical and health-care industries have either invested in their own biotechnology R&D departments (for example, DuPont, Eli Lilly, and SmithKline Beecham) or else formed strategic alliances with younger biotechnology companies (for example, Roche of Switzerland and Genentech of the United States; and the Swiss-based Ciba-Geigy [now Novartis] and Chiron in the United States).

Some of the economic interest on the part of government and industry comes from the drive to stay competitive through innovation and technological excellence. In many countries, the recession (and high unemployment) of the late 1980s provided a strong reason to look for alternatives that would restore economic prosperity. The United States, in particular, linked long-term economic prosperity and international competitiveness with investment in technologies of the future, such as biotechnology, gene technology, and information technology (especially software and electronic networks). Other countries, such as Japan and many of those in the European Union, held similar views. Gene technology is a promising field with the potential to become a leading industry of the future. By investing in the technology and in the expertise of its people, these nations expect to reap economic benefits in the next century: new jobs, economic stability, and international competitiveness.

Industry had similar considerations. In particular, the pharmaceutical sector needed new products and new ideas for R&D. For many companies, gene technology is a logical and natural continuation of their experience in working with microorganisms to develop vaccines and antibiotics. The techniques of gene technology offer companies new tools for research, development, and production. At the same time, these techniques are a pipeline to innovative products that may provide an answer in the search for cures for life-threatening diseases.

The farming sector also needed new methods to improve production to respond to a growing urban population. Previous agricultural technologies, notably mechanization and the introduction of chemicals, offered some solutions but at a high cost to the environment. Other sectors looked at what gene technology has to offer in areas such as pollution control, waste cleanup, and repair of damaged sites. All of these will help industry respond to the needs of being in business today: environmental sensitivity, product innovation, market competitiveness, and source of employment.

An additional consideration for many governments is health care. This interest has been sparked by the awareness of an aging population that requires increasing medical attention, the issue of access to universal health care, and in some countries, the closure of hospitals and other medical facilities due to a shortage of funds. Through the media and through the awareness campaigns of nonprofit organizations (especially in North America), attention was increasingly focused on the search for cures to cancer, AIDS, cystic fibrosis, muscular dystrophy, and other life-threatening diseases.

It was in the middle of these issues that gene technology emerged, promising new pharmaceutical products and medical procedures. The fact that a new technology offers new jobs in a poor economy was lost on very few leaders in government or industry: this was clearly a technology that would respond to the needs of the present and economic interests in the longer term as well.

Environmental Benefits

Gene technology could also respond to the ecological concerns of many individuals in industrialized society, especially in areas related to the farming industry. Public attention has been drawn to studies linking health risks to the widespread use of pesticides in crop protection and of antibiotics in the care of meat- or milk-producing animals. At the same time, there has been a growing awareness of the negative, long-term effects of chemical products (that is, herbicides, pesticides, and insecticides, as well as chemical fertilizers) on soil and water. This awareness has led to various attempts to reduce the use of chemicals in farm production. The source of the problem, however, lies in the fact that a small agricultural population is trying to support a comparatively large urban population. This situation implies continued reliance on technology to sustain large-scale farming.

Various developments in gene technology in the area of crop protection and veterinary care hold the potential for a solution. If successful, they would include effectively reducing chemical use and at least maintaining the level of production necessary to satisfy demand. A recent development in crop protection is the activation of certain genes to increase the plant's own defense against disease or pests. Other efforts have been directed at the introduction of foreign genes that will produce substances harmful only to specific types of insects or microorganisms. Such efforts would help reduce the need for chemical products in crop protection. At the same time, they could be the key to saving millions of tons of grains lost to insects and diseases every year. At the individual level, the ecological benefits to consumers would be fruit and vegetables with fewer chemical residues. At the environmental level, there would be a lower concentration of chemicals in soil and ground water.

In addition to the different applications of gene technology to the farming industry, there are also applications for use in environmental cleanup (see "Environmental Engineering," chapter 2). Microorganisms have long been used in the elimination of waste. Using gene technology, researchers have been able to enhance the ability of microbes to reduce hydrocarbons found in various industrial waste products. These genetically altered microorganisms can become a new tool in the cleanup of contaminated storage sites or industrial spills and leaks. Together with a continued effort to increase safety and environmental performance, these efforts would contribute to better pollution control and a cleaner environment.

Social Benefits

Health-care, economic, and environmental problems are not the only concerns that gene technology could address. Early on, gene technology was linked with solutions for other world problems, especially those requiring urgent attention in developing countries, for example, food shortage and hunger. Sometimes the problem with crop shortage or crop failure stems from overuse of chemicals or of the land itself; in such cases, the solution must entail a change of production methods.

There are times, however, when the problem lies with nature itself: a short growing season, frost or extreme cold, an arid climate, or other harsh environmental conditions. In these situations, part of the solution may come from research in gene technology in the area of plants. Some of such work includes efforts to improve the nutritional values of vital crops (such as rice, wheat, and maize), to boost yield, and to shorten the growth period (thus speeding up harvest cycles).

A new technology becomes more acceptable if large segments of the population can see benefits for themselves as individuals and for society as a whole. However, the history of technology since the beginning of the Industrial Revolution has shown that there are costs attached to all technology. Today's technological society has come to understand acceptability in terms of net benefits. Gene technology, even at this early stage, offers the hope of net benefits for individuals and society in the medical, economic, and environmental areas. No matter how persuasive such intellectual arguments are, however, social acceptance of a technology depends on emotional factors as well.

EMOTIONAL FACTORS

In this book, emotional factors are considered to include not only such obvious emotions as fear or anger but also such nonintellectual factors as lack of knowledge, anxiety, and aversion to risk. The fact that they cannot be easily explained, or changed, by a rational process does not make them any less valid, less legitimate, or less important. On the contrary, they deserve at least equal consideration.

LACK OF KNOWLEDGE

It may be surprising that lack of knowledge is considered an emotional factor affecting social acceptance. But, in the absence of knowledge or understanding, people rely on their individual or collective experience in similar situations. Past lessons—often internalized to such a point that we are no longer aware of them—provide a framework for how we should behave in a new environment where there is no other point of reference.

There is a general lack of knowledge about gene technology. One report (Macer, 1994) provides some figures that seem to support this statement: a telephone survey done in 1992 in the United States suggests that 25 percent of those interviewed had never heard of biotechnology. The same report compares that figure with figures from surveys conducted in New Zealand and Japan in the early 1990s: about 44 percent of those asked in New Zealand had never heard of biotechnology; 26 percent said they had never heard of gene technology (or genetic engineering, the term used in the survey). In Japan, about 3 percent said they had never heard of biotechnology, while 6 percent said they had never heard of gene technology.

Lack of Knowledge versus Lack of Information

It must be made clear that the lack of *knowledge* is not the same as the lack of *information*. On the contrary, there is probably an information overload on gene technology, as biotechnology companies, the media, special-interest groups, and government agencies release booklets, brochures, and special supplements to explain what gene technology is and how it works. Often, the story is one sided, with a focus on the positive elements only or on the negative elements only. Nevertheless, as one technology commentator writes: "It is a mistake to suppose that any technological innovation has a one-sided effect. Every technology is both a burden and a blessing; not either-or, but this-and-that" (Postman, 1993, pp. 4-5).

Despite this plethora of information, most people are probably not conscious of the presence of science and technology in their everyday lives. Only when something happens—an accident, a failure, or a sabotage—do they realize how much of an influence science and technology have on them as members of an industrialized society. The popular image of biotechnology or gene technology is probably of something done in labs by people in long white lab coats. Few people would associate biotechnology with the beer they drink in pubs, the cheese they eat in their sandwiches, or the polio vaccine in the sugar cubes they took as children. These are products of the brewery, the dairy, or the doctor's office.

For that matter, many people probably do not associate telephones, computers, or traffic lights with, respectively, telecommunications technology, information technology, or road technology. Most people probably think of them as part of common experience rather than encounters with technology. These items do not match the popular images that the word *technology* calls up. Thus, it is hardly surprising if more recent developments in gene technology, such as bovine growth hormone and gene therapy, seem even further removed from the average person's daily existence.

The gulf between gene technology and reality for most people exists for a number of reasons. On the one hand, there is a high degree of scientific illiteracy in the general population: many people, especially in North America, do not have a good foundation in science. Most are not as well informed as they could be in a world where science and technology have such a large influence on personal-health choices, public-policy decisions, products on the market, industrial competitiveness, and job opportunities. Without a firm grasp of basic scientific concepts, they find it difficult to understand complex technological advances or the impact they could have. Such an understanding would enable people to make choices that better reflect their needs or the long-term interests of society.

In the case of gene technology, that illiteracy is partly compounded by the fact that the field is a relatively recent development. Even now, some twenty-five years after the first successful experiment, scientists are still learning about genes, the way they work, and their role in the lives of organisms. It is a new area of science and one that is not easy to present. It is difficult to explain how four tiny molecules could be found in every organic life form—from a bacterium to a whale—and how different combinations of these molecules could help determine the size, sex, or shape of an organism. It becomes even more difficult to explain how a change in those combinations could kill or heal. Furthermore, because there are relatively few people working in this area, gene technology may seem even further removed from day-to-day reality. All of these factors lead to a lack of familiarity with the science and its applications.

On the other hand, scientists must learn to communicate information about science and technology to a wide audience in a way that is clear and understandable. They have to do it without using technical language and without making the readers or listeners feel like children. For example, it is commonly said by way of introduction that biotechnology goes back thousands of years to the first production of beer, bread, or soy sauce. Yet, the highly technical, controlled, and sophisticated, modern biotechnology production facility very likely does not resemble the simple kitchens where the Sumerians brewed their first beer.

The intelligent reader may find it hard to accept seriously the information that follows. Besides, while most people know about bread, soy sauce, or alcohol, few know much about hormones, amino acids, or gene sequences. Yet all these products are supposed to be derived from the *same* biotechnology. The quantum leap in technology causes a break in associative links in the reader's mind. That gap becomes the first stumbling block in communication and understanding.

This gap may in turn lead to the perception that science is shrouded in secrecy or that scientists are isolated from the real world in their ivory towers; and that every now and then, a scientist will emerge to explain on the evening news in thirty seconds or less how a scientific innovation will revolutionize our lives—perhaps in technical terms that few understand. Some may argue that this is a misperception. That may very well be true, but the fact is that this perception exists. So long as broad segments of the population continue to believe that, then science and technology will continue to be seen as a secret shared by an enlightened but isolated and remote minority.

As a result, people tend to believe that society has little control over the development or use of technology. When this belief becomes a political issue, it leads to the imposition of public control of a technology—in the form of legislation or regulation—before there is public understanding. Current examples of this trend include legislative proposals to curb rapid innovation in human reproductive technology, information technology, and gene technology; and increasing pressures on legislators to limit certain developments in these same technologies. Switzerland offers an example of such proposals. A citizens' group has proposed changes (the so-called Genschutz-Initiative) to the Swiss constitution to prohibit a broad spectrum of activities involving gene technology. The government rejected the proposal and referred it to a plebiscite. In June 1998, 67 percent of Swiss voters rejected the proposal.

When social controls are put in place *before* there is full public understanding, it implies that the new technology has mostly negative consequences and few merits. Such timing does not allow society the chance to weigh carefully the inherent risks against the inherent benefits of a new technology. This is not to say that society should not proceed with caution on new and relatively unexplored technological territory.

Nevertheless, there is a difference between timidity and prudence. In the context of new technologies, timidity results in rigid controls being set before the benefits and risks have been carefully weighed in the light of recent and emerging understanding of the technology. A policy of prudence allows broad segments of society the opportunity to make an informed choice about a new technology while respecting the right of society to retain control over it.

Conflicting Scientific Models
Adding to the confusion of the public debate is the conflict of traditions and worldviews within the scientific community. The various scientific disciplines see the world differently and use different paradigms (that is, working models for approaching a new problem or an unfamiliar situation). To some degree, the heat of the public debate on gene technology is intensified by the process of assessing technology in general and risk in particular. Both assessments look at the positive and negative effects of technology in different areas—for example, technology itself, health and safety, people as individuals and society, and human beings and the environment. This broad view and the focus on systems as a whole fit within the paradigm of ecology.

Molecular genetics, one of the bases of gene technology, has strong roots in physics, which is by nature a predictive scientific discipline. Physicists can study natural phenomena in controlled environments. Natural laws can be expressed in mathematical terms using statistical analysis. In contrast, ecology has its roots in biology and rests on principles and traditions different from those of physics. As a result, ecology requires a different approach to the natural world. The emphasis is on observation and explanations of what happens rather than predictions of what will happen. The focus in ecology is on whole systems rather than just individual elements.

In the ecological tradition, the emphasis is on *interactions* rather than *reactions*, a subtle but important difference. In physics, causes and effects may be more closely linked and, thus, more easily established. In ecology, events in one area may trigger a whole chain of events in the ecosystem because of the (sometimes less evident) links between different parts of the system. The links between causes and effects may be long and complicated. Life, in the ecological view, is a system of closely intertwined parts. One image used is a pond: disruptions in one part of the pond will send ripples to other parts.

In the technological assessment of gene technology, conflict arises when the physical traditions of molecular genetics confront the biological traditions of ecology. This confrontation results in disagreements between geneticists and ecologists on the nature and degree of risks. For those outside the scientific community who turn to experts for clarity and explanations, such disagreements lead to even more confusion. In the absence of consensus from scientists, many people become disenchanted with expert opinions and distrustful of experts themselves. They rely instead on their own experience and judgments.

ANXIETY

Anxiety, another emotional factor that affects social acceptance of a new technology, has a positive function as a survival mechanism: it provides guidance and direction in uncertain or unfamiliar situations (Röglin, 1994). During the period of change, conflict, and uncertainty that accompanies the introduction of a new technology, anxiety is a healthy response on the part of individuals and society as a whole.

Anxiety is a phenomenon that may be seen whenever society is confronted with new technologies—from the introduction of the movable-type printing press in the fifteenth century to the introduction of information networks in the twentieth century. W. Edwards and D. von Winterfeldt offer a brief overview of the fears and concerns about previous technologies: the steamboat, the automobile, the zeppelin, among others.

Paradigm Shift

One reason for this anxiety is that the new technology changes everything, including the way we see reality and the way we deal with the world. This radical change is called a **paradigm shift**. N. Postman provides a good example in the story of an invention by the French physician F. Laënnec, who realized that his instrument would allow physicians to diagnose chest diseases without surgery.

> But it should not be supposed that all doctors or patients were enthusiastic about the instrument. Patients were often frightened at the sight of a stethoscope, assuming that its presence implied imminent surgery, since, at the time, only surgeons used instruments, not physicians. Doctors had several objections, ranging from the trivial to the significant. (Postman, 1993, p. 98)

As Postman goes on to show, the stethoscope changed the practice of medicine in ways that Laënnec could not have imagined. The old paradigm suggested that medical instruments belonged to surgeons and that instruments meant surgery. But Laënnec's stethoscope did not fit into this paradigm. Instead, it changed the paradigm altogether: hence, a paradigm shift.

Lack of Experience

Anxiety comes not only from the *change itself* (that is, physicians using an instrument) but also from the *lack of experience* with the new paradigm (that is, patients not knowing why a physician would need an instrument, because experience suggested that medical instruments meant surgery). This general anxiety resulting from lack of experience can also be seen to follow from the introduction of other technologies, especially gene technology. The way these concerns are addressed will have a strong impact on the social acceptance of gene technology. This section will examine some of those concerns individually. First, there has been no experience with actual cases of damage. In the past, legislation and regulation came *after* evidence of damage—an accident or discovery of a malfunction. In the case of gene technology, legislation and regulation are being proposed *before* there is any actual harm. This point that will be discussed again later in this chapter.

The lack of experience with actual damage is partly because gene technology is a new development and partly because the earliest scientists in this field took the initiative to put in place security measures for experiments and laboratory work. (With greater knowledge and understanding of the technology, there is now a consensus in the scientific community that some of those measures were in fact unnecessarily strict.) The lack of experience means that it is to some degree unclear what the nature of the damage might be or how it should be contained. Of course, scientists could put forward theories based on current knowledge of biological functions and living systems. But in an open system, different factors come into play, making prediction even more difficult.

Lack of Consensus About Risk

In addition, there is a lack of consensus among members of the scientific community about prospective risks and negative effects. There is still some discussion about which risks and negative consequences are realistic and which are not. As documented by M. F. Cantley, this disagreement goes as far back as the mid-1970s in the United States.

> Scientists were often angered by the misrepresentations [by journalists and politicians] and by the strident and hostile tone of the attacks they encountered—in some notable cases from major environmental movements. But a few eminent scientists supported the

critics, in their calls for intense security provisions or a total moratorium on all rDNA research. (1995, p. 513)

Concern About Safety

In hindsight and with more experience, scientists are realizing that some of the early security measures proposed did not have to be as stringent as they were; nor were some of the risks as great as scientists originally thought. No one will argue with the fact that there are risks involved with different applications of gene technology, just as there are in any technology. The discussion now centers on which risks are real and in which contexts and what measures can be taken to contain these risks. There is a growing shift from a narrow and immediate focus to a wider and long-term perspective. More and more, attention has moved from scientific issues, such as laboratory safety, to broader issues, such as the impact on the ecosystem as a whole, on the relationship between human beings and the natural world, on society, and on people as individuals. The outcome of discussions about the impact of the technology in these areas will be critical to social acceptance.

Concern About Irreversibility of Damage

In light of this move toward long-term perspective, it is easier to understand why there is growing concern over the irreversibility of damage, or negative side effects. People are no longer willing to believe that technology carries no potential for harm. To a greater or lesser extent, all technologies in the past have included both obvious benefits and hidden costs. A pragmatic person would say that there is no reason to expect gene technology to be any different. The fear is that some application of gene technology will unleash irreversible and unstoppable damage. If, on the one hand, there is little evidence that such effects can be reversed, corrected, or at least halted, then there is a greater likelihood of the technology being rejected. On the other hand, if applications of gene technology include a way of repairing or limiting subsequent damage or negative side effects, the chances of social acceptance are likely to be greater.

Concern About Misuse of Knowledge

There is also concern that the emerging knowledge, especially in the field of human medicine, could be misused or abused. In the past, medical information meant the record of a patient's past or current health conditions—for example, diseases suffered or reactions to medication. In contrast, DNA information reveals the patient's predisposition to a disease or medical condition *before* there is any incidence of it. There have already been cases where ignorance or prejudice has led to discrimination against individuals based on their genetic predisposition.

Confidentiality, in this context, refers to the individual's right to decide who should know or have access to information relating to genetic conditions or predisposition. The debate focuses in particular on the right of health insurers and employers to such information. This debate is especially relevant and particularly sensitive in countries where there is no publicly funded health care and where employers bear some or all of the costs of their employees' healthcare.

Confidentiality of genetic information (and the potential for misuse) is of real concern, especially to carriers and people with genetic disorders. For example, if employers decide to require mandatory genetic screening, the fear is that employees may face job discrimination if they happen to have a disposition to cancer or some other medical condition when exposed to certain agents or situations. Some human-rights advocates worry that such testing and the resulting information would be an excuse for employers not to improve worksite safety: it would be simpler to hire workers who are not predisposed to negative health conditions.

Some employers, however, may be motivated by a genuine concern with legal liability for workers' health. In the past, employees were often left to fend for themselves if they suffered illness as a result of their job (Leiss and Chociolko, 1994). Even in the earlier part of the twentieth century, workers had little or no legal or financial recourse. Today, however, and especially in a litigious society, employers may find themselves in court over questions of workers' health and safety. By screening out those who may be genetically predisposed to adverse health effects, some employers may be hoping to avoid costly court battles or expensive medical bills.

At the heart of this debate is equity. On the one hand, large segments of society benefit from certain products or processes of industry. On the other hand, workers and perhaps their families bear a greater share of the health risks. Who should be responsible for the health of those involved: the individuals concerned or society (as represented by an employer health plan or a publicly funded health care)? How can society's scarce resources (medical, financial, or otherwise) be fairly distributed?

Independent of the issue of equity but closely intertwined with it is the concern for the right to privacy, the protection of privacy, and the individual's right to consent. Today, many people feel alienated from institutions that seem remote and yet have the power to make seemingly arbitrary decisions about people's lives. In a society based on information, government, business, and employers already have access to many details of an individual's private life—health record, income level, insurance policies, credit rating, and even purchasing habits.

Information about genetic predisposition is one more way in which institutions can gain access to an individual's life and place it under scrutiny. With electronic storage systems, electronic networks, and other developments in information technology, information about an individual can be easily stored. By the same token, this same information can be just as easily retrieved and perhaps even shared without the person in question ever knowing about it. Confidentiality about genetic information is essential in protecting the privacy of the individual and his right to make informed choices about personal matters.

There is also some concern that genetic knowledge could once again be misused for eugenic purposes. In the last ten years, with media attention on discoveries in genetic research, there has been renewed interest in the origins of complex human characteristics, such as intelligence or behavior. Are individuals the result of nature (genes) or nurture (the environment)?

In the first half of the twentieth century, several countries passed laws that allowed the enforced sterilization of particular groups of people, starting with those labeled "mentally defective." The premise was that such traits are hereditary and should be eliminated because they are socially undesirable. In Europe, eugenic laws, mixed with the politics of racism, led to genocide. In 1995 a woman in Canada brought the province of Alberta to court for ordering her to be sterilized without her knowledge or consent in the mid-1950s on the bases of a single intelligence test and a sexual sterilization law from the 1920s. The province is not contesting her right to compensation (Feschuk, 1995). Amidst the nature-or-nurture debates, such stories serve as a reminder that genetic information is vulnerable to misinterpretation and misuse and that human understanding of the role of genes is constantly evolving.

Concern About Pushing Natural Boundaries

People are also afraid that science and technology may go too far in pushing the boundaries of nature. The dream of Western society is a perfect world where technology will help human beings recover paradise lost. In the seventeenth century, in *New Atlantis*, Sir Francis Bacon describes a biological utopia where scientific knowledge transforms plants and animals to suit human needs and desires (Krimsky, 1991). In the twentieth century, in *Brave New World*, Aldous Huxley describes a technological utopia where human beings are conceived in laboratories and programmed to perform certain tasks in society. Gene technology holds the key to both the dream of Bacon and the nightmare of Huxley.

For some people, the fear of the Huxleyan nightmare seems to prevail. They feel alienated from decision-making bodies—industry, which often promotes the technology, and governmental agencies, which are supposed to keep it under control. In addition, people have become disenchanted with, and even more wary of, the promises of technology. Gene technology has inherited the legacy of previous "technology revolutions": better medicine is accompanied by chemical spills, fast automobiles by air pollution, cheaper fuel by tanker spills, cleaner energy by the threat of nuclear war. Given this unenviable record, there is no reason to believe that the biological utopia of Bacon would not also include the hellish society of Huxley.

Experience with Nuclear Technology

Many of the specific causes for anxiety discussed—lack of experience, lack of consensus about risks, concerns over safety, the fear of irreversible damage, potential misuse of knowledge, and questions about crossing natural boundaries—suggest a link to an older paradigm. This paradigm was formed through experience with previous technologies, especially nuclear technology. Some people would argue that gene technology and nuclear technology are not the same. However, it is not hard to find similar benefits and, more important, parallel concerns.

- Both technologies offer the promise of medical benefits for those suffering life-threatening diseases. For example, radiation therapy and gene therapy both offer hope to cancer patients.
- In both technologies there are important differences in the way the experts and the public view and evaluate risks. In both areas, the debate is intensified by disagreements between specialists working with the technology and ecologists concerned about its wider impact.
- Safety is a key issue for both technologies. Experiments are carried out in contained areas that require varying degrees of security measures. In both technologies, accidental release of dangerous material and accidental contamination of the environment are specific issues of concern.
- There are similar concerns over long-lasting negative effects on future generations: the risk of genetic mutations, the fear of irreversible damage, and the potential for large-scale damage from a single accident.
- Misguided use of both technologies could place all life on earth under serious threat. There is the fear of the military potential of nuclear and biological weapons. The invisible nature of radiation and genetic mutation greatly adds to this fear.
- There is concern that human beings may have crossed natural boundaries with the alteration of molecular structures of inert matter and the alteration of genetic structures of life forms.

There is more than just parallel fears and concerns about the technology itself. There is likely to be just as much unease with the mechanisms, structure, and agents in the decision-making process. In the introductory phase of both technologies, those making the decisions—the scientists developing the technology, the industry using it, and the officials regulating it—seem far removed from "ordinary" people and their concerns. A good example is the gap between *expert assessments of risks* and *public perception of risks*. Yet while the experts themselves have not reached consensus and sometimes openly disagree with one another, they seem to be telling people that the public's perception is wrong, exaggerated, or unrealistic. Society's experience with nuclear technology set the backdrop for how people think that industry is likely to behave and how government will respond.

There are too many similarities between nuclear technology and gene technology for people to believe that history will not repeat itself. These specific fears and concerns add to the general anxiety, which in turn shapes public perceptions of gene technology. Earlier in this chapter, it was pointed out that gene technology faces demands for regulation even though it does not have a history of accidents. Other technologies face regulation only after an accident or some catastrophe. It will be suggested here that the similarities between nuclear technology and gene technology are so strong that people might also start to make links between actual accidents in the nuclear industry and potential risks in gene technology.

This point is precisely where paradigms sometimes fall short. Paradigms depend on past patterns. So long as a situation follows those patterns, paradigms provide excellent guides for decision making. Sometimes, however, a new situation is sufficiently different that it creates a paradigm shift. There are a number of significant differences between nuclear technology and gene technology (see Table 1.1).

In their analysis of the controversies surrounding nuclear technology and gene technology at similar stages of development, Edwards and von Winterfeldt note strong similarities but also important differences. They conclude that while the nature of the conflict and the concerns over risks were very similar, "The debates were about different issues, and the institutions and regulatory processes differed" (Edwards and Winterfeldt, 1986, p. 91). For example, concerns about nuclear energy initially came from unions concerned with workers' health and safety. In contrast, geneticists were the first to raise concerns and initiated a voluntary moratorium on research in the area until these concerns were addressed.

Furthermore, one of the earliest products of nuclear energy was the atomic bomb. In contrast, from the start, the effort in genetic research has been to improve medical knowledge and pharmaceutical products. One of the earliest applications of gene technology was gene therapy, which literally saved a child's life.

This difference would suggest that, like Laënnec's stethoscope, the anxiety surrounding gene technology stems from two sources. The first is the change itself from similar patterns (that is, a new technology, which raises concerns about risks similar to those of nuclear technology). The second is the lack of experience with the new paradigm (that is, the lack of a regulatory agency that differs significantly in composition and history from the one overseeing the nuclear industry).

AVERSION TO RISK

The degree of aversion to risk is yet another emotional factor with a strong impact on social acceptance. An intrinsic element of risk is the potential for loss or damage. Risk aversion comes from an instinctive desire to reduce the potential for damage or to minimize the potential loss. However, as mentioned at the beginning of this chapter, risk is an intrinsic element of progress. A new technology holds the potential for both risks and benefits.

Table 1.1 Partial List of Significant Differences

	Nuclear Technology	Gene Technology

Main field of science	• Physics:
	   - predictive theories suggesting what might happen
	   - laws of physics fairly predictable
		• Biology
		   - descriptive models explaining what is seen
		   - no laws of biology: nature highly variable and difficult to predict

Initial interest	• Military defense	• Medicine

Main areas of application (in order of importance)	• Military defense
	
	• Energy production
	
	• Health care
	   - radiation therapy
	   - analysis
		• Health care
		   - pharmaceutical production
		   - diagnostics
		   - therapies
		
		• Agriculture
		   - protection of plant and animal health
		   - new breeds of plants and animals
		
		• Industrial use
		   - new processes in research, development, and production
		   - products, e.g. reagents, enzymes, and proteins
		
		• Environmental care
		   - diagnostics
		   - prevention
		   - remediation

Disaster record	• Three Mile Island • Chernobyl	• No record of disaster

Accepting one necessarily implies accepting the other. In commenting on its decision to grant a patent for the so-called Harvard onco-mouse (see "Animals," chapter 3), the Examining Board of the EPO writes:

> The development of new technologies is normally afflicted with new risks: this is an experience mankind has made many times in the past. The experience has also shown that these risks should not generally lead to a negative attitude vis-à-vis new technologies but rather to a careful weighing up of the risks on the one hand and the positive aspects on the other, and that the result of this consideration should be the determining factor in whether a new technology should be used or not. (1992 p. 591)

With gene technology, the risks are not clear—and, frankly, may never be clear. Perhaps more so than with previous technologies, there is a lot of uncertainty about potential risks and long-term impact even within the scientific community. This uncertainty makes the process of carefully weighing risks and positive aspects very difficult, especially as new information emerges. No decision, however, is ever perfect: there is never complete information or limitless time to make perfect decisions. Yet individuals and society continue to make routine decisions about risks. If they did not, society would stagnate. Hence, the opposite of a risk-averse attitude is a risk-taking attitude; more precisely, they are two sides of the same coin.

It will be argued here that risk aversion is simply taking the smallest risk possible or taking the greatest risk necessary. Most people would accept the risk of doing something (for example, heart surgery or vaccinating young children), if the risk of *not* doing it is even greater.

The same consideration applies as society struggles with the risks of a new technology. The new technology is likely to be more acceptable if the costs to individuals and society for not making the technology available are higher. Despite the risks of accidents and the greenhouse effect of exhaust gases on the ozone layer, millions of people still use cars, motorcycles, and airplanes on a daily basis. By not using transportation technology, they risk limiting the range of their mobility and perhaps their career opportunities. Their choices of products, leaders, employment, and ideas are limited to what is available in the immediate surroundings. This analogy is simplistic, but it shows that technological costs cannot be seen merely in terms of risks inherent in a technology; one must also take into account the costs of not having the technology.

There are certainly risks involved in gene technology. There is lack of experience with accidents and a lack of information. Moreover, as time moves on, sooner or later, a choice will be made. One cannot forget that not taking a decision is in itself a decision taken. It might be useful to consider some factors that could make gene technology more acceptable as applied to medical, economic, and environmental problems.

Medical Concerns

In the medical area, gene therapy (see "Gene Therapy," chapter 2) offers hopes of a cure for some genetic disorders. Some critics fear, however, that certain genes might be accidentally activated or deactivated in the process, with long-term negative impact on health, for example, the activation of cancerous genes. Some patients may choose to accept this risk if they think that their situation can be no worse or that the possibility of good health is worth the risk of long-term bad consequences.

This attitude is not uncommon among cancer or AIDS patients who volunteer to try experimental drugs or alternative treatments. In disorders such as Huntington's disease or cystic fibrosis, some patients (or even carriers) might feel that they want to try to halt the disease before their conditions deteriorate. Based on experience (for example, with family members who suffered from the disease), they may be more inclined to accept any reasonable risk from gene therapy.

Society may have similar considerations. There are times when society will decide that the well-being of the large majority is worth some risks to a small number of individuals. For example, it decided to introduce universal vaccination (using deactivated live microbes) of young children against childhood diseases (such as smallpox or polio) despite possible adverse reactions in a very small number of children.

Similarly, society may decide that the health and well-being of a community is worth the risks inherent in novel vaccines (using genetically altered microorganisms). For example, geneticists have deactivated certain harmful enzymes in a certain intestinal bacterium but added genes that would trigger the body's immune system against infections such as influenza or malaria (BMA, 1992). Such a vaccine might be of importance to Mediterranean countries and in the tropics, regions where it is estimated that a million or more people die each year from malaria. When such a vaccine becomes available for human use, some countries may decide to introduce it as part of a general health-care program. Even if there is a risk of limited side effects, given the current loss of lives to malaria, the overall benefits for society may be worth the risk.

Economic Concerns

So far, there have been no concrete arguments about negative economic impact directly caused by an application of gene technology. On the one hand, it has been argued that there will be a loss of jobs in certain industry segments. That, however, is true of any new technology that replaces an older one. The introduction of word processors meant the gradual disappearance of the card punch operator. On the other hand, the new technology also meant the introduction of jobs for those with skills in word processing, creating opportunities for secretaries, junior managers, computer technicians, and computer programmers. Similarly, it is conceivable that certain jobs in industries adopting gene technology will no longer be needed. However, this loss happens over time. During that same period, the next generation is acquiring the skills and knowledge (at school, at university or technical institutes, or in apprenticeships) to use the new technology.

In the socioeconomic area, critics have raised concerns about the distribution of wealth among nations. The argument flows from the ability to transfer genes across species and even biological kingdoms. Some commonly used flavors in food processing come from tropical plants—for example, banana or vanilla (extracted from an orchid growing predominantly in Madagascar). Such plants are frequently the main exports from industrializing countries to industrialized countries.

If flavor is controlled by a single gene, then it would be possible for geneticists to transfer such a gene into any plant or other organism used in food preparation (for example, yeast). If they did so, it would be a serious threat to the livelihood of individual producers in these industrializing countries and would upset the balance of trade between countries. The result, so goes the argument, would add to the unequal distribution of economic wealth and worsen living conditions in developing countries.

Such an argument deserves serious consideration. Before looking at the situation from a risk perspective, however, two points deserve comment. First, given the current state of knowledge, the scenario described remains for the moment hypothetical. It is not certain that genetic science will ever be able to reproduce complex traits like food flavors. Second, it must be said that the situation of developing countries is more a question of world politics and economics than it is of technology. A satisfactory answer to the problem must, therefore, include political and economic solutions—which are beyond the scope of this discussion.

As for social acceptance of gene technology, it will be suggested here that acceptability depends on other aspects of the technology itself. The premise is that risk aversion means people tend to accept certain risks for doing something if the risks for not doing it are higher. Thus, even if there is a risk of upsetting the economic balance in certain countries or even in larger regions, there are two conditions under which society and individuals may be willing to take that risk.

First, most applications of gene technology would be acceptable if the benefits of the technology for industrializing nations (for example, in improved health care, in needed pharmaceutical products, in better agricultural production, in fewer stresses on the environment) outweigh even the risk of economic and social costs in some areas . Second, the technology would be deemed acceptable if the costs of not having it would be even greater (for example, measured in loss of local crops to poor growing conditions, in loss of human lives to infections and other illnesses, in nutrient-poor diets leading to ill health).

Environmental Concerns
Critics have often raised concerns about the impact of microorganisms on the environment. This concern is based on an ecological perspective. The ecosystem is seen as an integrated whole, where equilibrium must be maintained. Normally, the system will contain self-control mechanisms, which adjust to or account for the slight imbalances and changes that occur. However, if one element is seriously off balance or if a previously unknown element enters the system, it will disrupt the entire system. For example, when a plant or animal is introduced into a place where it has no natural predators, it will end up killing other plants or animals or else destroying the ability of soil and water to support life.

Opponents of gene technology say there is a risk that genetically altered microorganisms released into the environment will upset the natural balance because they have no known natural predators. This argument formed part of the controversy over the ice-minus bacteria (see "Agriculture," chapter 2). The natural (ice-plus) variety plays a role in the formation of frost on plant surfaces and *possibly* has an influence on rain formation. Critics were worried that the ice-minus variety, which has been disabled from helping form frosts, would end up affecting weather patterns in a region. If that happened, it would of course have serious consequences for farming.

The risk of ice-minus bacteria might be more acceptable if weighed against the risks of existing alternatives. Traditional methods focused on keeping the air warm by "burning smudge pots, watering the soil, utilizing wind machines . . . and applying foam-like insulation around the plants" (Krimsky, 1991, p. 115). Another method was to use chemicals to destroy the bacteria themselves. But smudge pots, foam, or bactericides also take a toll on the environment.

For example, long-term use of foam or bactericides may lead to the buildup of chemical residues in the soil and possibly to contamination of ground water. Bactericides also kill other bacteria that might be useful to the plant itself. The buildup of carbon particles in the atmosphere and the increase in air pollution may also affect weather patterns not only over a region but also globally. Thus, if a study of comparative impact finds that these costs are greater (especially to the environment and to the livelihood of farmers), then ice-minus bacteria may become an acceptable or perhaps even desirable option.

Thus gene technology poses risks in the medical, economic, and environmental areas. But there are also benefits in these areas. As this discussion tries to show, on the one hand, society must weigh the risks and benefits of gene technology. On the other hand, it must also weigh the risks of the new technology against the risks of existing alternatives. In discussions about the risks of a new technology of any kind, people must not forget that all technologies—even older ones—carry risks. Social acceptance means weighing the benefits and costs against one another and all available options.

TRUST AS A SPECIAL FACTOR
In addition to a synthesis of rational and emotional factors, social acceptance also requires another element: trust. Communities and society at large must be able to trust the people and the institutions involved with the technology. In accepting a technology, a society makes a commitment to live with the technology and its consequences. Acceptance also implies that society has given a certain legitimacy to the people and institutions behind the technology.

Seen in this light, social acceptance may be said to be the beginning of a long-term relationship. In this exchange, it is understood that society will accept the inherent risks of the technology as long as those responsible for producing the technology continue to provide benefits to society. As in any agreement, trust means that each side can expect the other to live up to its part of the bargain.

Trust cannot be assumed. It cannot be demanded. It must be *earned*. In the context of introducing a new technology, earning trust requires three conditions: openness, truthfulness, and the willingness on the part of those working with the technology and especially its advocates to share knowledge and first-hand experience. There must also be balance in the presentation of new information.

OPENNESS
In technology, openness means that the scientific and industrial communities have to be frank with the lay public about what they know and what they do not yet fully understand. Earlier it was said that the uncertainties of dealing with an emerging and rapidly changing technology must be candidly acknowledged. Managers in industry and scientists have an obligation to acknowledge to the public how much they know of a problem or how little they know about certain risks. The most compelling reason is that the people who may be affected have a right to know. In a free society, individuals must have the necessary information to make an informed personal choice.

If that is not reason enough, then the following points should be considered. First, mistakes, problems, and controversies within a company or the scientific community will eventually become evident to the community at large. In the age of information technology, it is futile to try to hide knowledge of problems or to cover up ignorance about risks. Even without electronic networks, information filters through.

For example, for years, miners at the Westray coal mine in Nova Scotia, Canada, complained of violations of safety regulations, technical problems left unsolved, and unsafe working conditions. When a fatal explosion killing twenty-six miners occurred in 1992, no one in the town was surprised. Three years later, criminal investigations were still going on, key managers of the company involved were brought to trial, and the future of the company was uncertain. The bitterness and the resentment of the town were still strong.

Second, if an organization or a person is trying to hide something, the media will catch on sooner or later. The greater the effort to cover up a situation, the more suspicious the media will become. If management or those in authority cannot or will not provide a satisfactory answer, the media will turn to other sources for information—former employees, unions, outside experts, or people living near a site. Chances are that they will find someone willing to talk such as a disgruntled employee, someone seeking recognition, or someone with the truth.

For example, in the mid-1980s, just as the California firm Advanced Genetic Sciences was facing a controversy over proposed field trials with ice-minus bacteria (see "Agriculture," chapter 2), a dissatisfied employee "blew the whistle on the company by disclosing that ice minus had been injected into trees located on the roof of the facility" (Krimsky, 1991, p. 131). It must be stressed here that the media do not necessarily have an agenda to destroy an organization or to make up damaging stories. It is sufficient to spark their interest and they will raise questions. Once those questions are publicly asked, the organization will have to answer in the court of public opinion—or in a court of law.

Finally, a policy of openness makes sense because people are not stupid. As pointed out earlier, people are used to uncertainty in their day-to-day experience. Common sense suggests that a young technology will produce some unexpected surprises. Scientists do not have all the answers to many questions about gene technology at this point and may never have them. No one has a monopoly on knowledge.

In addition to the ethical and practical reasons for it, openness makes communication easier. Being candid about doubts, misgivings, and uncertainty also demonstrates a willingness to talk and to listen. Sometimes the experts may be found outside the scientific community. As specialists in risk management and those in the nuclear industry have learned, sometimes the nonscientific public can have a richer and broader understanding of the problem than scientists and technical experts. Openness can lead to mutually beneficial exchanges for experts and nonexperts.

Of course, openness does not mean revealing all the secrets of an organization. There are organizational plans, strategies, tactics, and projects that must remain confidential. Most people can understand that an organization may have valid reasons for not giving out certain kinds of information. Openness means acknowledging such limitations while cooperating with those seeking other kinds of information. Nevertheless, these limits should not become an excuse for not sharing information that is of no strategic or competitive importance to the organization.

TRUTHFULNESS

The concept of openness is closely linked with the idea of truthfulness. In organizational communications, truthfulness rests on two essential components: the information itself and its source. Both must be reliable and credible.

Truthful information is based on facts and is verifiable. The information reveals what has happened (or is happening) rather than speculating about possibilities. More important, the information must be provided in the appropriate context. A young technology is characterized by rapidly emerging knowledge, which quickly changes the way scientists view a problem or situation. For example, in gene technology, the last ten years have seen some remarkable discoveries in the area of human medicine. Researchers have located the genes for a number of dread diseases, including cystic fibrosis and Huntington's disease. These discoveries are an important step forward in the search for a cure. But medical science is still a long way from finding a cure for these and other diseases where genetic links have been established. Reports must thus place these discoveries in the context of the ongoing search for a cure. Otherwise, there is danger of giving false hope to patients and their families.

Truthful communication admits gaps in knowledge. It is only to be expected that scientists will not know all there is to know about a new technology. There are areas that have not been explored. Scientists will not agree on how to interpret certain pieces of data. It is doubtful if the lay public expects unanimous agreement or omniscience from the scientific community. Perhaps the most important task for scientists is to explain that there is no consensus and possibly give the reasons why. The goal of communications is *not* to provide information. Truthful communication—or authentic information, as Otway and Wynne call it—is part of a genuine and integrated effort to sustain a mutually beneficial relationship between those responsible for a technology and those who live with the consequences of it.

> Authenticity, for example, would entail open recognition of the unavoidable uncertainties and difficulties of managing technological risks. This would normally be regarded as a threat to credibility, but credibility depends less on the quality of information than on the quality of relationships. (Otway and Wynne, 1989, p . 144)

Rather than destroying the credibility of the source of information, admitting uncertainties, difficulties, or even failure demonstrates good faith and a willingness to acknowledge limitations. It shows a serious commitment to the tacit agreement between the technology producer and society. In the future, when there is good news, people will be more likely to believe it. This is the point where credible information becomes intertwined with the second component of truthfulness: the source of the information. The credibility of the source depends on a record of consistency between words and action.

For example, during the Tylenol crisis, Johnson and Johnson took three steps to acknowledge public concern. First, it admitted that it did not know what happened. Second, it simultaneously initiated a company recall of all Tylenol products. Finally, the company cooperated with public authorities in their investigations. After the crisis, the company promised to improve security on its product packaging and followed through on that promise. The fact that there was no significant decline in sales a year after the scare underscores the reputation of the company as a credible source. (It should be remembered that from a business perspective, a good reputation is an important asset.)

Although the details and the circumstances are significantly different, there is an important lesson from the Tylenol experience for advocates of gene technology. At this stage of gene technology, there is still no experience with risks and damages. Instead of reassuring the public that the risks are limited, the absence of a disaster is actually a *source* of concern for large segments of the population. In addition, disagreements in the scientific community over potential risks places even more focus on the problem. Experience suggests that the longer the delay, the greater the potential for catastrophe.

Rather than deflecting public concerns about risks, advocates of the technology should be willing to acknowledge the limitations of scientific knowledge and the lack of experience with it. This willingness not only encourages reciprocal behavior, but also demonstrates openness towards constructive cooperation. "In risk management, as elsewhere, information only becomes an authentic attempt at communication when a corresponding social commitment is implied" (Otway and Wynne, 1989, p. 144).

By being frank about unknown risks and by listening carefully to the interests of other stakeholders, advocates of gene technology demonstrate their commitment to a long-term relationship. Such an attitude indicates a willingness to participate in finding solutions for problems that affect the interests of large and diverse segments of society. Without this commitment from the advocates of change and risk taking, there is little basis for building trust.

WILLINGNESS TO SHARE KNOWLEDGE AND EXPERIENCE

For trust to develop, more is required than just openness and truthfulness in communications. There has to be a willingness to share knowledge and experience, however limited this experience is. Where society is confronted with a new technology, those in industry and the scientific community have to take an interest in public opinion. After all, it is not simply whether a technology is acceptable or not: their own livelihood is at stake. As the main proponents of the new technology and the stakeholders in it, they have a responsibility to initiate a dialogue with the public, who also have a stake in it.

In particular, leaders in science and industry need to understand the concerns and interests of other stakeholders. Such understanding may shed some light on the differences between the concerns of science and industry and those of the nonscientific public. It may also help all parties involved to find grounds of common interest. Finally, such understanding would allow leaders in science and industry to develop policies and programs that take into account the concerns and interests of society.

An important part of this willingness to share knowledge includes providing the information that large segments of the public truly want and need to form a clear opinion of the technology and to make appropriate choices. Often this information goes beyond the technical details and the technical assessment of risks. Many people want to know the impact of technology on their lives, society in general, and the environment. Perhaps more so than in the past, many people today are wary of technology or the institutions behind it. To earn their trust, leaders in science and industry need to show that they have considered the wider context of technology and its long-term consequences.

Along with the sharing of knowledge, there should also be a sharing of experience. Relatively few people have seen, or even know, how a gene is spliced or how cells are cultured to produce biological substances. The nuclear industry has found, for example, that employees of nuclear power stations and residents near these stations are not as fearful as those living farther away (Greber et al., 1994). To overcome this problem, the AECL (and others in the nuclear industry) have proposed demonstration disposal vaults for nuclear wastes. The goal is to allow those who have had no background in the field "to become more familiar with the technology and to form personal judgments based on actual experience" (Greber et al., 1994, p. 133).

This lack of experience is also true for gene technology, where cells, chromosomes, and nucleotides remain vague concepts for the majority. The movie *Jurassic Park* probably did more to focus attention on gene technology than any communications effort on the part of the scientific community or industry in the last twenty-five years. A visit to a laboratory where genetic work is carried out would allow many people to see for themselves what they would otherwise learn about only through the media. Familiarity may not lessen public concern over the magnitude of risks or the potential for damage, but it would at least reduce or perhaps even eliminate the fear of the unknown.

In addition, actual contacts between lay people and scientists working in the field give names, faces, and context to the scientific community. Conversely, scientists are given an opportunity to meet members of the *general public*—a vague, all-encompassing phrase that means little in human terms. Meeting face to face brings home the message that each group is made up of individuals who have much in common at the human level—families, friends, dreams, and concerns.

Such contacts are important for other interested parties as well, from special-interest groups to government officials to industry managers. It is not easy to trust a faceless group or organization. Trust is a human need that requires a human response. The proponents of a new technology ignore the human element to their own cost and at the risk of society's rejection of the technology.

COMMUNICATION OF SCIENTIFIC KNOWLEDGE

Trust also depends on balance in communication of scientific information. Scientists, as well as the media (in particular, science reporters), have a special responsibility. Disagreement over the interpretation of discoveries and new data is nothing foreign to the world of science and technology. "It should be noted that uncertainties are not unusual in a scientific context; it is uncertainty that drives all of science. In fact all scientific results are only provisional, subject to better data, better methods and better frameworks" (Leiss and Chociolko, 1994, p. 137). Conflict, however, becomes a problem when it becomes divisive.

ROLE OF THE SCIENTIFIC COMMUNITY

The conflict in scientific opinion is often intensified as it spreads to the general public. Legislators, government officials, the courts, special-interest groups, the media, and the lay public often look for answers or at least an *informed* opinion from members of the scientific community—who are, of course, supposed to stay scientifically neutral or disinterested from the wider social debate. As groups jostle to have experts on their side, it is hardly surprising when the usual disagreements in the scientific community suddenly become entangled in the larger social conflict. Differences in scientific opinion quickly become polarized into extreme positions, for example, the public controversies over the effects of electric and magnetic fields from power lines on people's health.

> Technical expertise was used by all parties to form, support and alter their own and others' views on the PF E/MF [power frequency and electric and magnetic fields] health effects issue.
> . . . Because of the state of scientific understanding about the issue, it did appear that studies were lined up on either side of the public debate about regulations or, at least, that evidence could be found to support any value position in the regulatory debate. The

credibility of the experts was questioned, in both their roles as researchers (because studies were "rigged") and as expert witnesses or advisers (because of "selective" use of studies). (Leiss and Chociolko, 1994, p. 138)

Scientific debate and differences of opinion are inevitable and, indeed, necessary for the advancement of scientific knowledge. But polarization in scientific debates tends to destroy the credibility of the scientific community as a whole. The watching public may conclude that perhaps the *experts*, in fact, do not know what they are talking about. In case of doubt, the safest route is prudence. This attitude may in turn lead to or reinforce an aversion to risk where science and technology are concerned.

A constructive scientific debate allows for differences in scientific opinion but accepts the points in opposing views that are valid. For example, it would be counterproductive to claim that the different applications of gene technology are either tremendously risky (with no benefits) or wonderfully useful (with no risks). Such rigid positions, especially if they come from the scientific community, do not contribute to the broader debate on the acceptability of a technology.

In the early stages of a technology, existing data may be inadequate, knowledge incomplete, or experience insufficient to exclude any error in judgment. The social acceptance of any technology, as this chapter argues, has to take place in the context of trust. The scientific community can help create that trust by acknowledging the limits of its knowledge—the limits of *scientific* knowledge.

A constructive scientific debate involves explaining why one might come to a certain conclusion while accepting that missing information may change or reinforce it. In addition, scientists have a responsibility to point to the limits of science, especially in the context of making social and political decisions. For example, they can provide useful information for determining emission level in cars or factories, but the acceptable level of emission can only be set by legislators and regulators.

ROLE OF THE MEDIA

The media (in particular, editors and science reporters) also have a responsibility to ensure that reporting is factual and balanced, especially in the field of gene technology. Research on the human genome and other genetic research in human medicine have produced key findings that offer hope for a cure for many diseases. Often these discoveries are the result of years of slow and careful work. In the excitement of a breakthrough, it becomes too easy to focus on one aspect and forget the broader implications.

It is the job of the media to put such events in perspective for the general public. This task applies as much to reports about triumphs and discoveries as to reports on risks and problems. Given limited space for a written article or little air time for a broadcast report, journalists often can take only one or two examples to illustrate a point. They must make sure, however, that such examples give a truly representative view of a generalized situation rather than a glimpse at a particular instance.

Because conflict makes an event or situation newsworthy, public controversies usually become news stories. When the media are caught in the controversy, reporting among different media agencies becomes divided along political-editorial lines (MacLeod, 1995). In social and technological conflicts, the media are not, contrary to what one might believe, an *objective* third party—no more than are the scientific community and government agencies. The media cannot be, simply by the fact that, as *mediators* of information, they shape the information that large segments of society receive and the way they perceive events. By choosing to focus on certain aspects, to emphasize specific angles, or simply to give attention to a situation, media agencies affect the content of news and public information. In addition, as H. M. Kepplinger found in the German media, reporters and editors introduce their own biases through their own comments and through their selection of experts. This is probably true of the media in other countries as well.

There are several ways in which the decisions of editors and journalists influence what the public reads, hears, or watches. Large segments of the population depend on the media for information and analysis to make sense of complex issues such as those in science and technology, which can affect broad areas of society, and the lives of individuals. People need information as well as opinions from those who have access to events and people. Clearer distinctions between news reporting and editorial perspective would help people to have both factual information and informed perspectives to help them make personal and social choices as further discussed in chapter 6.

KEY POINTS

- Social acceptance of a new technology depends on rational factors (public understanding, social control, and utility of the new technology) and emotional factors (lack of knowledge, anxiety, and aversion to risk). Trust in the institutions promoting the technology is also important.

- Public understanding alone is not sufficient for social acceptance, but it does lead to consistency in public attitudes and may provide a useful counterbalance to the decisions of public officials.

- Control over technology falls into two categories: technical control (focusing on risk prevention and damage control) and social control (which uses legislative measures and public decision-making processes to control the nontechnical aspects of a technology).

• New technology changes the way people see the world, that is, causes a paradigm shift.

• A new paradigm causes anxiety because it is a change and because people lack experience with it.

• Most people will probably accept the risk of doing something if the risk of not doing it is even greater.

• Trust, an essential element in the social acceptance of a new technology, must be earned.

• Building trust requires openness, truthfulness, and the willingness to share knowledge and experience. Trust also depends on balance in presenting new information.

• At the center of the public debate on gene technology stands the individual. The challenge of an emerging technology is not in controlling the technical risks but in dealing with the changes that the technology unleashes and their impact on people's lives.

REFERENCES

British Medical Association. 1992. *Our Genetic Future: The Science and Ethics of Genetic Technology*. Oxford: Oxford University Press.

Cantley, M. F. 1995. The Regulation of Modern Biotechnology: A Historical and European Perspective. In *Biotechnology,* edited by D. Brauer. 2d ed. rev. Vol. 12, *Legal, Economic and Ethical Dimensions*, pp. 508–681. Weinheim, Germany: VCH.

Edwards, W., and D. v. Winterfeldt. 1986. Public Disputes About Risky Technologies: Stakeholders and Arenas. In *Risk Evaluation and Management* edited by V. T. Covello, J. Menkes, and J. Mumpower pp. 69–92,. New York: Plenum Press.

European Patent Office. 1992. Decisions of the Examining and Opposition Divisions: Grant of European Patent No. 0 169 672 (Onco-mouse/Harvard). *Official Journal EPO* 10: 588–593.

Evans, G., and J. Durant. 1995. The Relationship Between Knowledge and Attitudes in the Public Understanding of Science in Britain. *Public Understanding of Science* 4: 57–74.

Feschuk, S. 1995. Woman Suing Province over Forced Sterilization. *Globe and Mail*, 6 April, pp. A1, A11.

Greber, M. A., E. R. Frech, and J. A. R. Hillier. 1994. T*he Disposal of Canada's Nuclear Fuel Waste: Public Involvement and Social Aspects* (AECL-10712, COG-93-2). Pinawa, Canada: Atomic Energy of Canada Ltd. Research.

Kepplinger, H. M. 1995. Individual and Institutional Impacts upon Press Coverage of Sciences: The Case of Nuclear Power and Genetic Engineering in Germany. In *Resistance to New Technology: Nuclear Power, Information Technology, and Biotechnology*, edited by M. Bauer, pp. 357–378. Cambridge: Cambridge University Press.

Krimsky, S. 1991. *Biotechnics and Society: The Rise of Industrial Genetics*. New York: Praeger.

Leiss, W., and C. Chociolko. 1994. *Risk and Responsibility*. Montreal: McGill-Queen's University Press.

Macer, D. R. J. 1994. Perception of Risks and Benefits of In Vitro Fertilization, Genetic Engineering, and Biotechnology. *Social Science and Medicine* 38 (1): 23–33.

MacLeod, R. 1995. Resistance to Nuclear Technology: Optimists, Opportunists, and Opposition in Australian Nuclear History. In *Resistance to New Technology: Nuclear Power, Information Technology, and Biotechnology*, edited by M. Bauer, pp. 165–188. Cambridge: Cambridge University Press.

Marlier, E. 1993. *Biotechnology and Genetic Engineering: What Europeans Think About It in 1993*. Survey Report Eurobarometer 39.1: The European Commission.

Otway, H., and B. Wynne. 1989. Risk Communication: Paradigm and Paradox. *Risk Analysis* 9 (2): 141–145.

Otway, H. J., and D. v. Winterfeldt. 1982. Beyond Acceptable Risk: On the Social Acceptability of Technologies. *Policy Sciences* 14: 247–256.

Postman, N. 1993. *Technopoly: The Surrender of Culture to Technology*. New York: Vintage Books.

Röglin, H.-C. 1994. *Standorstsicherung - Auch eine Frage der Öffentlichkeitsarbeit*. Düsseldorf: Institut für Angewandte Sozialpsychologie.

Slovic, P. 1987. Perception of Risk. *Science*, 236: 280–285.

2 APPLICATIONS OF GENE TECHNOLOGY

It may be easy for the interested but uninitiated observer to gain the impression that gene technology consists of a single uniform application. In reality, it encompasses a broad range of applications. Making a clear distinction between these applications is important because they do not affect all forms of life in the same way or have the same impact on society. As a result, these applications raise different concerns and levels of anxiety. This difference is key to understanding the concerns underlying the debates on gene technology. Such understanding may also provide a better approach to social control of the new technology.

This chapter focuses on the diverse areas of application of gene technology and the degree of social acceptance apparent in each area. This section aims to clarify some uses of the terms *biotechnology* and *gene technology*. The following four sections compare traditional methods for altering life forms to obtain desired characteristics with modern techniques using gene technology. The last section looks at the level of acceptance that industrialized society has shown toward these different applications of gene technology.

The terms *biotechnology* and *gene technology* can mean a lot of things to different people. One reason for the ambiguity lies in the broad field of biotechnology itself. The uses of biotechnology range from traditional methods of production to modern industrial techniques. Gene technology is a relatively recent development since the 1970s. Like the broader field of biotechnology, it also comprises a wide spectrum of applications. What sets gene technology apart from earlier developments of biotechnology is the ability to control and direct changes in living things at the molecular level.

Many terms are used to describe gene technology. Other sources may prefer *genetic engineering* or *recombinant DNA (rDNA) technology*: direct quotations throughout this book will retain the terms used in these sources. This book uses the term *gene technology* because of the emphasis on the concept of technology and because it focuses attention on the relationship to the broader field of biotechnology.

In a very broad sense, **biotechnology** includes all uses of living organisms for human purposes and deliberate human intervention in the process of natural selection—the fermentation of food and drinks using microbes, the cultivation of crop plants, the breeding of domesticated animals (SGCI, 1989; US OTA, 1989). In a special way, human medicine as an application of life sciences is also a form of human intervention in the natural selection process. In a narrower use, biotechnology includes any set of techniques that apply both natural genetics and molecular biology to the modification of microbes and cells for use in production. In that sense, biotechnology has ancient roots, going back thousands of years to the first recorded uses of yeast in making food.

Nevertheless, the biotechnology that first produced beer or bread has as much in common with modern biotechnology as flying a kite has with aviation technology. In both biotechnology and aviation technology, human beings have used their understanding of the forces of nature in large-scale industrial applications. Although the underlying principles of fermentation and modern biotechnology—or of kite flying and modern aviation—remain the same, there is an important difference in the scientific extrapolation of these principles and the techniques of application.

Today, biotechnology may be more specifically defined as the use of living organisms, biological systems, or biological processes in the integrated application of various disciplines of science to industrial products and processes. This definition captures four essential characteristics of modern biotechnology: the use of living systems, the scientific base, the multidisciplinary approach, and the industrial aspect. Some key disciplines of modern biotechnology are biochemistry, chemical engineering, process engineering, medicine, cellular biology, and microbiology (Bu'Lock, 1987; Higgins, 1985).

In industrialized society, a number of segments rely on biotechnology, including the health-care industry (production of medication, vaccines, and other substances), veterinary medicine (vaccines and other substances), the agriculture industry (from the production of fertilizers to the improvement of animal feed), the food industry (for protein or flavor enhancement, and food preservation), and other large industrial processes (Bu'Lock, 1987; Higgins, 1985; WHO, 1982).

Gene technology, which arose from molecular biology, is the application of that and other scientific disciplines to the selection and improvement of genetic traits for research, industrial, environmental, agricultural, or medical purposes through the isolation, characterization, and recombination of genetic material, as well as the insertion of this material into new living cells.

The ability to direct genetic changes at the molecular level marks the shift from traditional biotechnology to gene technology. Traditional breeding methods rely on crossing organisms with observable physical traits to produce the desired characteristics in the offspring. "Results are often unpredictable and lengthy back-crossing may be necessary to remove undesirable traits introduced together with the desirable ones" (FAO/WHO, 1991, p. 3).

In contrast, gene technology allows scientists to guide the selection process at the molecular level by identifying and isolating genes that are linked to specific traits. The advantage is that gene technology offers a more precise selection process, replacing the labor-intensive and time-consuming screening procedure used in traditional breeding methods (FAO/WHO, 1991; Hardy and Oliver, 1985). This precision does not mean that unexpected results and negative side effects can be eliminated completely, but it has reached a higher degree than ever before possible in the selection process. Furthermore, new knowledge and discoveries have greatly enhanced and refined the ability to transform living organisms at the molecular level.

AN OVERVIEW OF MOLECULAR BIOLOGY AND TECHNIQUES OF GENETIC ALTERATION

The basic information for cellular life is contained in genes, molecular segments that code for proteins necessary for sustaining life. Genes form the biochemical basis for what an organism is and how it functions. Found in every living cell, genes are organized into single molecules called chromosomes. In most life forms, chromosomes form strands contained in a little membrane-surrounded core of the cell called the nucleus. In some single-cell organisms, there is only a single chromosome organized into a circular core called a plasmid.

In 1953 Francis Crick and James Watson discovered the structure of deoxyribonucleic acid (DNA)—the chemical substance making up the genetic information of life. That structure is a double helix of four units called nucleotides. Each nucleotide has one of four nitrogenous bases—adenine (A), guanine (G), cytosine (C), and thymine (T). What is important for the double-strand structure is that A will pair with G only, and C with T only. This complementary pairing, which binds the two chains together, is essential to the ability of DNA to split and self-replicate. The pairing also explains how DNA divides to create a template for ribonucleic acid (RNA) in the production of proteins (Wagner, 1994; Watson, Gilman, Witkowski, and Zoller, 1992)

RNA is very similar to DNA. But unlike DNA, RNA consists of a single strand of nucleotides made up of adenine (A), guanine (G), cytosine (C), and uracil (U). As in DNA, the nucleotides will only form complementary pairs, with U linking to C only. Both this complementary pairing and the single-strand structure of RNA are important for a key stage of protein production called transcription. To make a protein, the DNA splits down the middle of the double helix. Each side of the helix thus forms a mold, or template. From the DNA template, RNA forms a complementary template, which picks up amino acids free in the cell and places them in particular orders to create different proteins (Wagner, 1994; Watson et al., 1992).

The work of Crick and Watson eventually led to various key findings: the discovery of DNA-cutting enzymes (called restriction enzymes), the decoding of the genetic information itself, the isolation of specific enzymes called ligases (which fuse DNA fragments together to form the double strand of DNA), and the understanding of polymerase chain reaction (or enzymatic replication of DNA) (Davis, 1991a; Ryser and Weber, 1990).

With the new discoveries, scientists were able to reproduce changes that naturally occur in all living beings. In nature, changes in genes (leading to variations, mutations, and evolution) are the result of the replacement, deletion, or insertion of a nucleotide (or a chain of nucleotides) or even the total transposition of whole blocks of DNA. For the first time, scientists were able to isolate specific genetic material, characterize it, and put it back together to obtain specific traits, that is, recombine the genetic material. In the early 1970s came the first successful recombinant DNA experiment (Davis, 1991a; Ryser and Weber, 1990). This event was the beginning of gene technology.

Although there are several approaches to directing genetic changes in the laboratory, the following is a summary of the basic procedure, more fully described in various sources (BMA, 1992; FAO/WHO, 1991; Suzuki and Knudtson, 1990; Watson et al., 1992). A sample of DNA having been removed from donor cells, the first step is to isolate the gene of interest using a type of enzyme generally known as a restriction enzyme (or more specifically called restriction endonuclease). The second step is to create a vector, a vehicle for carrying the isolated gene into the living target cell or cells. One commonly used vector is a plasmid from a bacterium. To make a plasmid into a vector, it is necessary to use a restriction enzyme, which cuts or splits the plasmid at a specific site. The isolated gene is then spliced into place using a DNA ligase, another kind of enzyme.

The third step in the process is to insert the vector into the nucleus of the host cell or cells using microinjection or other techniques. Once in the nucleus, the gene of interest is integrated with the rest of the host genetic material. It will be replicated during normal cell division. The final step is to make sure that the gene is expressed, or activated. This can be done by adding the proteins or enzymes that activate the gene promoters, nucleotide sequences controlling the production of specific proteins (BMA, 1992; FAO/WHO, 1991; Suzuki and Knudtson, 1990).

With one exception, all cells in the body of a complex organism contain the full complement of genes; these kinds of cells are called somatic cells. The exception is the germ line, the group of cells that produce sperm and eggs—in scientific language, germ cells or reproductive cells—which have only a half set of genes (BMA, 1992; Wagner, 1994; Watson et al., 1992). The genetic information in both types of cells can be subject to natural or human-directed changes. However, there is one important difference. Changes in somatic cells affect only the organism in question. Changes in germ-line cells affect both the organism and all offspring produced after the changes.

APPLICATIONS USING MICROORGANISMS
This section will discuss traditional uses of microorganisms and applications of gene technology that use microorganisms.

TRADITIONAL INDUSTRIAL USES OF MICROORGANISMS
Since early times, humans have used yeast, molds, and bacteria for producing staple food items (bread, cheese), brewing beverages (wine, beer), preserving food (sauerkraut, pickles), and enhancing flavors (soy sauce, vinegar). These techniques have been known in many cultures for thousands of years. Early microbial fermentation did not, however, use a scientific approach. Without knowing the biological functions, early practitioners probably selected strains of organisms displaying favorable traits and brought them together to create hybrids expressing a combination of desired characteristics (Hardy and Oliver, 1985). Through generations of deliberate selection, practitioners improved production by speeding up the fermentation process or increasing product yield.

In the second half of the nineteenth century, Louis Pasteur discovered that microbes were the real key in fermentation, and he showed that different types gave different products (Higgins, 1985). He thus laid the foundation for what has become biotechnology today. With the beginning of the twentieth century came the first industrial-scale application of biotechnology. An important element is the selection and culture of one or more specific microbial strains. The microbes are then allowed to multiply into the mass necessary for large-scale processes. Such processes rely on the mechanisms that microorganisms use to grow and reproduce in the absence of oxygen—converting carbohydrates into other chemicals in the process. Examples of large-scale application of traditional biotechnology include the use of microbes in producing industrial chemicals and in sewage-treatment facilities (Bu'Lock, 1987; Higgins, 1985).

Perhaps the most significant contribution of biotechnology is in the field of medicine. At the end of the 1920s, Alexander Fleming, while working in London, discovered penicillin, the product of a mold with antimicrobial properties. This discovery led to a breakthrough in drug therapy and launched the antibiotic industry in the 1940s (Corbett, 1987; Higgins, 1985; SGCI, 1989).

Today, many industries, individual sectors, and processes rely on the large-scale application of biotechnology and further advances in the innovative use of microbes. Although it is beyond the scope of this book to go into technical details, an overview is perhaps useful as background to later discussions. The following is a list of industries, processes, products, and services that rely on traditional biotechnology—in the narrower sense of using microorganisms.

- The food and drink industry relies on microbes in the production of cereal products (such as bread), dairy goods (such as cheese), alcoholic beverages (such as beer), preservatives (such as vinegar), and additives (such as flavor enhancers).

- Microorganisms are also part of the fermentative production of various industrial and medical chemicals: from solvents and acids to steroids and antibiotics (Best, 1985). Perhaps the most important of these is penicillin, the first antibiotic to be isolated. The discovery and production of other antibiotics followed, radically changing not only human medicine but also veterinary medicine. They even play an important role in the control of plant disease. The value of antibiotics lies in their antimicrobial activities. The systematic screening of microorganisms has helped increase efficacy, decrease toxicity and other negative effects, and improve ways of administering antibiotics (Best, 1985). In the early 1980s, the World Health Organization (WHO) estimated that various kinds of penicillin accounted for roughly 25 percent of worldwide sales of antibiotics (WHO, 1982).

- The copper and uranium sectors of the metallurgy and mining industry make use of microorganisms in a process called leaching. The microorganisms, living in an acidic pool, break down the compounds to produce a solution from which the metals can then be purified and recovered (Brierly, Kelly, Seal, and Best, 1985).

- Environmental engineering has long used microorganisms. Since the late nineteenth century, microbes have played a key role in municipal sewage-treatment facilities. Today, with greater environmental awareness, the focus is shifting from mere waste treatment to resource recovery (Best, Jones, and Stafford, 1985). One of the by-products of anaerobic waste processing is the production of methane gas, which can be used as a source of energy (Best et al., 1985; Bu'Lock, 1987; Hall, Coombs, and Higgins, 1985). More recently, researchers are exploring the use of microorganisms in destroying dangerous chemicals and in restoring sites and cleaning up pollution. A German newspaper reported that scientists in Stuttgart were doing research on the microbial deactivation of the explosive chemical trinitrotoluene (TNT) in contaminated storage sites.

- In agriculture, there is a complex relationship between microorganisms and plants. On the one hand, the effects can be devastating. For example, wet soil encourages the growth of a number of fungi, which, if left unchecked, will destroy seedlings. On the other hand, the introduction of various species of the fungus Trichoderma helps reduce the harmful effects of these parasitic fungi (Skinner, 1985). The role of the bacterium *Rhizobium* in converting nitrogen for plant use is also well known. Various methods are used to introduce rhizobia into soil for crop planting and encouraging bacterial growth in root nodules (Miller, 1991; Skinner, 1985).

- In veterinary and human medicine, the role of microorganisms is not limited to the production of antibiotics. Vaccines—suspensions of microorganisms—have also had a revolutionary impact on medicine. Inoculation is a preventive measure in which these microbes are injected into the body, activating the immune system against these microbes or their more harmful relatives (Miller, 1991; Spier, 1987). In the eighteenth century, Edward Jenner developed the world's first vaccine for human use—against smallpox. Today, in many countries, vaccines have successfully eradicated such diseases as polio, measles, and mumps. In veterinary care, vaccines have helped prevent outbreaks of foot-and-mouth disease and rabies, among other viral infections (Spier, 1987).

GENE TECHNOLOGY AND MICROORGANISMS
Through gene technology, various industries are exploring the potential in microorganisms and tapping into the resources that they represent. Products arising from the use of microorganisms in gene technology are already available in the fields of environmental engineering, agriculture, and medicine.

Environmental Engineering
There is increasing awareness of the need for cleaning up the environment. Oil spills and tanker accidents along coastlines, chemical spills in river systems, and contamination of soil and ground water by toxic waste are some of the environmental problems facing industrialized society. As discussed in

the previous section, microorganisms have certain mechanisms that enable them to break down hydrocarbons such as petroleum and petrochemical products.

There are limits and obstacles, however, to what microorganisms can do. One problem is that microorganisms are fragile by nature: they require the right environment (for example, certain temperature and nutrients) to multiply or even survive. Another difficulty is that many synthetic chemicals contain complex structures that microorganisms do not often find in nature. So they have limited natural abilities to break down these chemical structures. Genetic alteration can enhance these abilities by reinforcing their production of those enzymes that actually change or degrade these structures.

One example is a genetically altered bacterium that was of potential use in cleanups of oil pollution. In 1980 the General Electric Company developed a bacterium that could degrade crude oil components in laboratory conditions. For publicly unknown reasons, the company did not bring this innovation to market (see also "Gene Technology and Microorganisms," chapter 3).

Agriculture

Different needs in agriculture have led to diverse uses of genetically altered microorganisms. One important area of research is disease control and, more generally, crop protection. Gene technology offers an alternative to chemical pesticides and insecticides. One of the problems with chemical products is that their effects are indiscriminate, killing off both harmful organisms and ones that are either harmless or even beneficial to the plant. Gene technology provides a more selective option and may even capitalize on positive relationships between microorganisms and plants.

For example, an interesting relationship exists between the environment, plants, and a soil bacterium called *Pseudomonas syringae*. For water to crystallize at 0°C, there must be ice-forming centers, for example, bacteria or particles of matter. Otherwise, freezing will not take place. The formation of ice on plant tissues leads to frost damage, resulting in crop loss. "Frost damage accounts for losses estimated at up to $3 billion per year in the United States" (OECD, 1988, p. 19). To prevent frost damage, farmers either keep the area around their crops above 0°C or else they use a pesticide to kill bacteria that help form ice particles.

For scientists, the bacterium *Pseudomonas syringae* was interesting. Research showed that some strains of it form ice crystals at higher temperatures (between -1.5°C and -5°C) than other strains of the same bacterium, most microbes, or even inanimate matter. The reason is a gene producing a protein that becomes a center for ice crystals to form. Research also showed that if this activity could be controlled, then frost damage on crops could be reduced. The most effective solution is to remove the gene producing the protein. Although scientists explored several methods (including chemical mutagenesis), the most effective was using rDNA techniques (Campbell, 1991; Krimsky, 1991).

The genetically altered variety ("ice minus") would then be sprayed on the plants, where they would compete with the ice-producing variety ("ice plus") for food, thus keeping the ice-plus population in check. The result would be a reduction in frost buildup (and hence frost damage). Critics were worried, however, about the impact of ice minus on the formation of snow and rain in the atmosphere once the bacteria were released; and they were equally concerned about the bacteria's impact on the ecology of the region. In the United States, where this work was being done, proposals for field trials led to protests and court challenges from a number of ecologists, environmentalists, and different opposition groups (Campbell, 1991).

In the United Kingdom, proposed field trials with a genetically altered insect virus encountered similar opposition. According to the journal *New Scientist* (Coghlan, 1994), scientists at an institute in Oxford genetically altered a virus to carry the scorpion gene making a venom that is lethal to several insect pests. The unaltered virus came to Britain in a moth native to the United States; it is also a natural insect-killer, but it does not work fast enough to prevent crop damage. With the scorpion gene, the virus kills the caterpillars before they cause any serious damage to the plant.

Laboratory experiments already indicated which of seven moth species the virus would kill. The proposed field experiments were to be carried out in net-enclosed fields: the goal was to confirm these findings in more natural settings. Opponents raised three areas of concern and objection:

- The virus might also kill the caterpillars of butterflies and moths native to Great Britain (especially given that the test site was near a reserve with rare moths). There was also some disagreement among virologists as to the range of host butterflies and moths susceptible to the unmodified virus. The researchers used fine netting to prevent the virus from spreading through wind, burrowing animals, birds, or other animals.

- The virus might be able to trade genes with other viruses. In theory, two different viruses could end up invading the same cell, which would then recombine DNA fragments at random. For that to happen, however, both viruses must be close relatives. In this case, there was only one close relative of this particular virus in Britain.

- How long would the virus survive in the environment? The field trials were intended to answer that particular question. Experiments in the United States indicated that the altered virus multiplied at only one third the speed of the unaltered variety and that no virus was found on plant leaves after three months or in the soil after six months.

As these two examples illustrate, the use of genetically altered microorganisms in agriculture raises concerns about impact in two areas: the environment and human health. Although laboratory tests can provide some answers, field trials are necessary to complete an environmental-impact study. Trials in enclosed fields show the effect of factors that scientists might not be able to simulate in the laboratory, for example, competition from other microorganisms or the effects of chemicals in the air. As for safety, it must be remembered that field trials would normally follow laboratory experiments. An important goal of field experiments is to *confirm* the results of laboratory experiments. In both the cases described above, for the experiments to proceed to the stage of field trials, tests in the laboratory would have to have shown that these genetically altered microorganisms are harmless. In addition, such experiments would have to have been conducted on a scale that would have made sure that the accidental or intentional impact of the experiment on the natural environment would be limited—hence the wire mesh and other containment measures.

The concern with human health comes from the theory that harmless microorganisms could be accidentally converted into harmful ones. Risk-assessment studies, however, have not confirmed this theory. In addition, experiments in the last few years have also failed to demonstrate that host organisms have gained new and unexpected properties as a result of genetic alteration (OECD, 1988). It must also be remembered that factors such as pathogenicity (that is, the ability to cause disease) result from a combination of several unrelated genes. In addition, the long history of microorganisms used in food production provides important information and experience that can be used in evaluating pathogenicity and other factors of microorganisms (FAO/WHO, 1991; OECD, 1988; WHO, 1982).

Medicine

Using genetically altered microorganisms (such as yeast or bacteria specially bred for laboratory use), the pharmaceutical industry can now produce sufficient amounts of the human proteins and other substances that the health-care industry requires. Although this section focuses on human medicine, genetically altered microorganisms play similar roles in the production of vaccines and monoclonal antibodies for the prevention of diseases in animals (FAO/WHO, 1991). The following is a partial list of new products in human medicine manufactured with the help of genetically altered microorganisms.

- **Human insulin** replaces the insulin of cows or pigs, which has a similar but not identical structure. The problem with bovine or porcine insulin is that some patients develop an allergic reaction to it. The problem is now being solved by using human insulin produced in bacterial culture. Because this insulin is now identical in structure to what the patient's body would produce, allergic reactions can be avoided. Human insulin was the first protein produced using genetically altered microorganisms (Pickup, 1985; Unternährer-Rosta, Carbonare, Manzoni, and Ryser, 1994).

- **Hirudin** (also called eglin C) is a substance that the medicinal leech produces. Its ability to inhibit blood coagulation makes the substance invaluable in the treatment of emphysema, arthritis, and thrombosis and in freeing clogged blood vessels that might otherwise lead to stroke or heart attacks. Scientists have been able to synthesize the hirudin gene and insert it into a plasmid. The plasmid is transferred into yeast cells, which then produce the substance in the self-multiplication process. Using traditional methods, it would require approximately 62, 000 leeches to produce one gram of hirudin, and it would take about six months to extract and process the substance for medical use. The use of genetically altered yeast cells allows the production of several kilograms of the substance (Unternährer-Rosta et al., 1994).

- **Human growth hormone**, before gene technology, had to be extracted and purified from cadavers. The new process involves the insertion of the human gene coding for the substance in bacteria and letting them produce the substance as they multiply in a growth medium. It eliminates the risk of the transfer of certain fatal diseases associated with traditional extraction methods (see "Emotional Arguments for Gene Technology Patents", chapter 3). Using bacteria that have been programmed with the gene coding for the hormone, biotechnologists are able to replicate this hormone and produce it in the quantities required for medical use (Unternährer-Rosta et al., 1994).

- **Interferons** are a group of proteins that cells produce in response to viral infections. Interferons have several important characteristics. First, they make neighboring cells or even the whole immune system resistant to viruses. Second, their effectiveness is specific to each species of organism. Third, they inhibit cell proliferation and they play a role in the way the immune system functions. All these factors make interferons potential weapons in the fight against cancers, especially in slowing down the spread of cancerous cells and reinforcing the effects of chemotherapy. They are not, however, "the cure" for cancer that many had hoped they would be. Gene technology has made it possible to produce several kinds of interferons (Pickup, 1985; Unternährer-Rosta et al., 1994).

Besides the production of medication, genetically altered microorganisms now provide further options in the search for cures and remedies in human and veterinary medicine. Viruses, for example, make effective vectors (that is, shuttles for delivering a gene to a cell) in gene therapy (see

"Medicine" above). Because viruses have evolved to target very specific cells and to transfer their genes into a host cell without killing it, genetically altered viruses can bring gene sequences containing "corrections" for genetic "errors" into defective genes (Plummer, 1995).

One of the concerns with the use of genetically altered microorganisms in medicine is their potential for accidental release into the environment or of their becoming epidemic. This is unlikely, however, for different reasons. First, microorganisms used in bioproduction (whether medication or other substances) are stored and cultured in secure containers (BMA, 1992) to prevent accidental release and, even more important, to prevent contamination of the batch. If foreign microbes entered, they could just as easily multiply (after all, the culture medium promotes microbial growth), possibly killing the desired strains of microorganisms and certainly spoiling the quality of the substance being produced.

Second, release of the microorganisms is highly unlikely because they are killed after production. It must also be remembered that microorganisms used in bioproduction or laboratory experiments have been genetically altered for that purpose. In other words, they were developed to live in very special environments: for growth, they often require—as a minimum—controlled temperature and a culture medium with sustaining nutrients. They would thus be very unsuited to survive outside that environment. Furthermore, in the wild (the "natural" environment), microorganisms face competition from other microbes and setbacks from the environment itself, for example, harsh temperature (BMA, 1992; Campbell, 1991).

> Micro-organisms in general have well-controlled metabolic sequences for optimal growth in their natural environment. The development of organisms for commercial exploitation usually involves eliminating those properties which in an industrial context are undesirable and amplifying those considered useful and beneficial. Such modification also lowers the probability of multiplication of the organism outside the production plant. (WHO, 1982, p. 15)

There is also concern because some patients experienced side effects or were allergic to certain medication produced by gene technology. On the one hand, for example, some patients experienced an increase in low blood sugar attacks on switching from the insulin of other animals to human insulin produced by gene technology. "Whether there is a link between human insulin and the frequency of attacks is currently under fierce debate with studies finding conflicting results" (BMA, 1992). On the other hand, it must be remembered that allergic reaction is a possible risk of any medication—whatever the methods of production. For example, some individuals are allergic to antibiotics such as penicillin. As with medication produced using other methods, data from clinical trials (and information from a patient's medical background) should indicate if doctors and patients should expect any allergic reactions and if so under which conditions.

At the same time, human insulin produced using microorganisms may also reduce the side effects of using certain animal insulins. Bovine insulin, for example, differs slightly in its amino acid sequence from human insulin. As a result, patients using bovine insulin develop anti-insulin antibodies. Because human insulin produced by gene technology does not differ in its structure, there should be no response from the immune system in this respect (Pickup, 1985).

Finally, special concerns are raised by the use of viruses as vectors in gene therapy. In theory, it is possible for viral vectors to cause target cells eventually to mutate into cancer cells. The main concern is that the body's immune system may become activated against viral vectors, either causing rejection of the vector and the gene it contains or else reducing the benefit of such therapy. Such a situation may develop if the therapy requires the gene to be administered several times (Plummer, 1995).

APPLICATIONS TO PLANTS

Agriculture is in essence the continued domestication and cultivation of certain plants for food—preserving desired traits and preventing undesired ones. One of the goals of agriculture is the improvement of quality, nutritional content, taste, and often yield. One of the challenges is the reduction or eradication of pests, weeds, diseases, and crop failure (Davis, 1991a; FAO/WHO, 1991; Skinner, 1985).

TRADITIONAL PLANT-BREEDING TECHNIQUES

In the past, because little was known of plant reproduction, plant breeding (especially of staple crops such as rice, wheat, barley, and maize) relied on open pollination. Wind or flying animals would carry pollens from one plant to another. Farmers saved the best or biggest seeds for the next planting season (Skinner, 1985).

At the beginning of the twentieth century, two contributions gave a genetic basis to the selection process. The first was the rediscovery of the works of the Augustinian monk Gregor Mendel, who in the mid-nineteenth century was the first to recognize the fundamental principles of genetics. Studying the inheritance of peas, he realized that parents pass traits on to offspring in almost separate units. Today, these units are called genes (Davis, 1991a). This work became the foundation of genetics as a discipline and provided better understanding of heredity in breeding.

An equally important contribution was George Shull's work in identifying the role of hybrid vigor in plant productivity. For example, a breeder can create purebred lines of maize showing uniform kernel traits. But these plants are so weakened that they cannot easily multiply. Crossing two purebred lines, however, produces plants with the uniform characteristics of the parents and yields higher than those of open-pollinated strains. Later, Donald Jones showed that crossing two hybrids—double crossing—improves productivity and vigor. This was probably the first application of genetics to the field of agriculture (Micklos and Freyer, 1990).

Hybridization resulted in new varieties of crops with improvements in selected traits, such as higher yield. This technological success is often called the Green Revolution. However, in the fight against pests and diseases, crop protection has relied mainly on the use of chemical pesticides and herbicides in the twentieth century. There are still no viricides or chemical weapons against viruses (Knight and White, 1994). Earlier sections in this chapter have already looked at other options of crop protection, including inoculation to prevent viral and fungal infection. Although most herbicides and insecticides can be degraded by microorganisms, they present other ecological problems. One problem is that they are not necessarily species specific: a herbicide cannot tell the difference between a crop seedling and a weed. Nor can an insecticide distinguish between a beneficial insect and a pest. Another problem is that pesticides can get into animals higher up on the food chain when these animals eat plants that have been sprayed or insects that have been poisoned. The side effect is the disruption of the whole web of the food chain (Hobbelink, 1991).

GENE TECHNOLOGY AND PLANTS

Advances in gene technology brought new tools to the world of agriculture. The goals and challenges of the agricultural industry remain unchanged: better quality of content, greater yield of harvest, and fewer losses to pests and diseases. The genetic alteration of plants, however, brought its own challenges. A key challenge—more specifically, in introducing foreign genes into host plant cells—is that plant cells differ from microbial or animal cells in structure and function in several ways. Perhaps the most important difference is that each plant cell is surrounded by a thick, rigid cell wall, which makes it difficult to penetrate when inserting genes. There are now two successful solutions for overcoming this barrier.

The first is the use of *Agrobacterium tumefaciens*, a species of bacteria living in the soil and known to be very effective in causing a type of plant cancer commonly called crown gall. *A. tumefaciens* has a tumor-inducing (Ti) plasmid. When the bacterium enters a plant cell, it transfers this plasmid into the cell's genetic material, causing uncontrolled cell growth (that is, cancer). By removing the tumor-causing sequence from the plasmid and splicing in a foreign gene sequence, scientists create a highly effective vector by taking advantage of the bacterium's natural ability to penetrate the cell walls of plants (Arntzen, 1991; BMA, 1992; Hobbelink, 1991).

One drawback of using agrobacteria as vectors is that they infect certain kinds of plants and not others (including cereals—among the most important crop plants). This drawback led to the development of another effective alternative: particle bombardment using the so-called gene (or particle) gun. Microprojectiles of metal are coated with the chosen DNA sequences and fired from a particle gun directly into the plant cell, where the foreign DNA integrates with the host genome (Arntzen, 1991; Frey, 1992; Hobbelink, 1991; Odenwald, 1995).

Research in gene technology and plants currently concentrates on four areas:

- improved nutrient content (for example, protein)
- greater resistance to pests (insects) and diseases (bacteria, viruses, and fungi)
- tolerance of chemical herbicides and pesticides
- better tolerance of the elements (for instance, extreme heat or drought)

These areas show the importance of crop protection in gene technology research. Every year, pests, diseases, and weeds result in serious damage or losses to crops. The Max Planck Institute for Breeding Research gives the following estimates for damages and losses in worldwide crop production:

- Insects were responsible for the loss of about 13 percent of production (Steinbiß, 1992).
- Weeds were responsible for the loss of another 10 to 15 percent of crops produced (Logemann, 1992).

Similar figures were not available for damage by microbial agents. For a long time, viruses presented an especially difficult problem because there were no effective chemical controls. As a result, farmers traditionally relied on prevention, which offers limited protection. Gene technology now offers the first tools for reducing or eliminating the effects of viral infection in plants.

Besides insect pests and harmful microorganisms, crop plants also face competition from wild plants that compete for nutrients and space. One solution has been the use of chemical controls. Such protection has its costs, however. Prolonged use of chemical products for controlling pests, diseases, and weeds can lead to various environmental and ecological problems, including the contamination of air, soil, and ground water.

Both pesticides and herbicides create an additional problem in that their action can be indiscriminate. Pesticides can lead to the unintentional killing of symbiotic life forms, such as insects that might be harmless to the crops or even useful to the farmer elsewhere (for example, in pollinating flowers). Birds and other animals sometimes become victims of pesticides because they prey on pests that have digested pesticides.

Herbicides pose similar problems. On the one hand, a herbicide is essentially a plant killer and its action can be indiscriminate, killing useful plants as well as weeds. Inappropriate use of a herbicide could do more harm than good for the crops that it should protect. On the other hand, weeds (like other life forms) will naturally, occasionally, and spontaneously mutate; that is, the genes develop in random uncommon combinations. Some of these mutations prove to be resistant to the herbicides used (see "Tolerance of Chemical Herbicides" below). For these different reasons, scientists have sought alternative protection in direct genetic alteration of seeds and plant tissues.

Improvement of Nutritional Content

To maintain a balanced diet, human beings require twenty essential amino acids. Because the human body cannot produce many of these by itself, a balanced diet is important. But in places where a single crop (for example, potatoes, beans, or lentils) forms the larger part of the diet, it becomes difficult, if not impossible, to obtain all the necessary nutrients. Nutrient deficiency leads to diseases: people who rely on lentils as the main source of food often become susceptible to diseases of the liver.

Through gene technology, it will be possible to supply such staple crops with the missing amino acids by transferring genes from plants that do produce these substances. Brazil nuts, for example, are rich in certain amino acids missing from beans, an important part of people's diets in certain places. By transferring a gene from the Brazil nut, researchers at the Free University of Berlin have developed a nutrient-enriched bean plant, which will allow people to maintain a balanced diet despite their reliance on a single staple crop (BMA, 1992; Odenwald, 1995; WHO, 1982).

Although such developments may be promising, they should not prevent society from asking critical questions. In the twentieth century, the Green Revolution promised higher yields and better-quality crop plants. Although it achieved these ends, the social consequences are more debatable (BMA, 1992; Hobbelink, 1991; Mieth, 1995). "Frequently the introduction of Green Revolution varieties increased agricultural productivity and total crop yields, but also increased the total number of hungry and starving people" (BMA, 1992, p. 152). The main reason is that such crops often require a lot of water, fertilizer, herbicides, and pesticides—all of which make such crops more expensive for both farmers and consumers. In areas where there was no wide gap between rich and poor farmers, the Green Revolution was generally beneficial; in areas where disparities already existed, the situation became aggravated. "As a consequence, relatively wealthy farmers increased their harvests and incomes, while the standard of living of poorer farmers declined steeply to the point where a large proportion of them lost their farms and joined the ranks of the homeless in search of an income" (BMA, 1992, p. 153).

The British Medical Association suggests learning from the lessons of experience and makes the following recommendations:

- Take into account the range of impact of Green Revolution plants (and secondary products, such as higher use of chemical herbicides). If asked at the beginning of a project, this question could help determine the focus of research efforts and help set research objectives. This factor would also be of use to farmers and governments for making decisions.

• Ask what the risk is of transferring to weeds those genes intended to give crop plants an advantage. "Although such questions should not prevent research on genetic modification of plants [from] going ahead, it is important for those working in this area to ask themselves whether or not these concerns are realistic" (BMA, 1992, p. 154).

• Take into consideration the fact that gene technology may offer benefits to both industrialized countries and developing ones, but the social impact could widely differ. This difference is of particular importance in using gene technology to replicate certain flavors, such as coffee or vanilla. In some countries these plant products are of economic importance.

Accidental gene transfer (from crops to weeds) is a problem that often arises in discussions surrounding gene technology and plants. The concern is based on the fact that some weeds are closely related to crop plants. Therefore, it may be possible for genes from two plants to be exchanged, for example, through natural cross-pollination. In that event, a gene introduced into a crop plant to give it an advantage will likely have the same effect in a related plant that is a weed (OECD, 1988). One result would be a hybrid weed that is difficult to eradicate and that would have the novel characteristic, such as resistance to pests.

One precautionary measure would be extensive testing under both laboratory and field conditions to determine the extent of such a risk. Laboratory conditions provide only some of the answers that scientists need. In the farmer's field, different factors come into play to produce situations not possible to simulate in a laboratory. It is therefore necessary to use field trials, which try to approximate open conditions and provide a more complete picture. Field testing itself faces controversy. Some critics are concerned that natural elements—wind, insects, or other animals—may carry pollens or seeds from these plants beyond the confines of test areas. However, a field trial would include safety precautions such as a fenced enclosure, mesh netting, and a protective perimeter outside the immediate testing area.

Such safety measures must be taken in the context of what is known about plants and the likelihood of accidentally producing a weed. "It is likely that a large number of genes must interact appropriately for a plant to display the properties of a weed. . . . In any event, the chances of introducing 'weediness' into a crop by rDNA techniques is far less likely than the introduction of such a characteristic by conventional plant breeding methods, in which weeds are often used as a source of genetic material for desirable traits such as disease and insect resistance" (OECD, 1988, p. 30).

Resistance to Pests and Diseases

As well as using genetically altered microorganisms in crop protection, scientists can genetically alter the plant itself in the fight against insects and microorganisms. Since the 1910s, biologists have been producing pesticide compounds using protein crystals produced by a bacterium, *Bacillus thuringiensis*, against certain insect pests. The crystals are toxic to certain species of insects but not to other insects, humans, and other vertebrate animals. One of the drawbacks of the toxin is that it is short-lived. This limitation requires frequent production of small amounts of such pesticide compounds. With the tools of gene technology, biologists have been able to transfer the gene coding for the protein into crop plants. Because the level of protein produced in such plants is very low, the toxin works against only those insect larvae that are sensitive to it (Steinbiß, 1992; Watson et al., 1992).

Plants genetically altered to fight insect pests offer at least two distinct advantages over chemical pesticides. First, the defense mechanism is localized and target specific (Steinbiß, 1992). Unlike chemical pesticides that have to be sprayed over a relatively wide area, the gene producing the toxin against the pest is located only in the plant. In addition, because the toxin is specific to one or several species of insects, its effects in the ecological habitat will be limited to these insects. However, the specificity of transgenic plants also has its drawbacks:

Transgenics could never replace all uses of chemical insecticides. Where a crop is attacked by a diverse pest complex, the grower will usually need to resort to chemical spraying. Transgenics will come into their own where a crop is vulnerable to a single serious pest. For example, a corn rootworm-resistant maize would be a very attractive alternative to conventional insecticides. (Knight and White, 1994, p. 143)

Genetically altered plants with built-in self-protection have a second advantage over the use of chemicals. Promoters are nucleotide sequences controlling the synthesis of RNA (see "A Quick Overview . . ." above) in the expression of a gene and the production of proteins (Watson et al., 1992). The use of such promoters allows transgenic plants to activate their defense once a pest starts attacking the plant and to produce the amount of toxin necessary to rid itself of the pest (Steinbiß, 1992).

In addition to protecting plants against insect pests, gene technology is also providing an effective weapon against microorganisms, in particular, viruses. An important mechanism in dealing with viruses is cross-protection, which works in a similar way to inoculation in animals or human beings. The exact functioning of the mechanism of cross-protection is still not fully understood. Once a weakly virulent strain of virus has infected it, a plant will become immune to infection by a more virulent strain. Experiments have shown that viruses contain a gene that codes for the coat protein (CP) surrounding the virus. When this gene is transferred into plants and they are able to produce the CP, the transgenic plants are able to resist infection by viruses. Cross-protection also results in prolonged resistance against viral infection and related viruses (Rohde, 1992; Watson et al., 1992).

Two concerns associated with this application must be addressed. First, as with all food products, there is concern about the impact of genetically altered plants on human health. From an emotional standpoint, this concern is understandable. After all, food is one of the most basic needs of any living organism, and any changes to food products could affect an individual directly. From a rational perspective, however, the use of genetic techniques does not increase health risks, as compared to other techniques. A joint report of the FAO and the WHO explains: "The DNA in all living organisms is structurally similar. For this reason, the presence of transferred DNA in produce in itself poses no health risk to consumers" (1991, p. 31).

The second concern focuses on plants with introduced toxin-producing mechanisms. It is imaginable that a vegetable with a toxin against microbes or insect pests could have negative side effects on human beings as well. However, as the FAO and WHO joint report points out, many plants used for food have natural toxins, which are present at different levels depending on the variety and environmental factors (such as climate, season, and location). In addition, in a small number of cases, conventional breeding methods have also produced vegetables with unacceptably high levels of toxin.

In this context, the report includes in its recommendations the following considerations:
- The modified plant should not produce substances that are toxic at the levels found in the finished food product.
- The safety of the modified plant should be assessed with respect to possible deterioration in the nutritional value of the consumed product. (FAO/WHO, 1991, pp. 48–49)

Tolerance of Chemical Herbicides
Because the use of chemicals in crop protection is likely to continue, one of the aims of gene technology in agriculture is the breeding of crop plants with greater tolerance to these chemicals, especially herbicides. One of the challenges in weed control is that through spontaneous mutations and other ongoing changes, some weeds develop a resistance to herbicides that would otherwise have been effective. Similar mutations explain the development of antibiotic-resistant strains of bacteria in human and veterinary medicine.

This ability of weeds to mutate into herbicide-resistant strains caught the attention of scientists. Logically, if these genetic mutations occur in nature, they can be replicated as well in crop plants in a directed way using gene technology. Studies of the mechanisms behind such phenomena have led to the isolation of the genes responsible and provided options for transferring such genes into crops. Herbicides contain active agents that disrupt vital functions of the plants, such as the production of certain enzymes. In herbicide-resistant plants, there is a gene that creates herbicide resistance by one of the following methods (Logemann, 1992):

- producing an enzyme that detoxifies the active agent in the herbicide
- changing the structure of the target enzyme to such an extent that the herbicide has no further effect
- increasing the amount of the target enzyme to such a point that there is more of it than of the herbicide, reducing or eliminating the effectiveness of the herbicide

From a molecular point of view, there is no difference in the composition of genes, whether they are in a bacterial or a plant cell: every gene is made up of the same four units (see "An Overview of Molecular Biology" above). This structure has allowed the transfer of genes from bacteria to plants in crop protection. For example, scientists found a gene in bacteria that effectively degrades a chemical herbicide. The gene responsible for the enzyme was isolated and transferred into crop plants. In the plant, "the bacterial enzyme destroys the applied herbicide without harming the plant" (Arntzen, 1991, p. 112). Such built-in tolerance overcomes the problems of using herbicides on weeds coming from the same family as the crop plants themselves.

One of the concerns specific to this application is that herbicide-resistant crop plants would allow or even encourage farmers to use more chemical herbicides, adding to existing environmental problems. "By failing to replace herbicides, the biotechnology industry greatly restricts its potential for reducing overall chemical use" (Mellon, 1991, p. 72). However, this argument misses an important point. Pesticide-resistant crops will not necessary eliminate pesticide chemicals; they simply offer new options to weed control. The true value of herbicide-resistant crop plants comes to the fore when the weed in question is closely related to the crop in question. In that event, a herbicide that will kill the weed would be likely to have the same effect on the crop plant. Nevertheless, the central argument that M. Mellon makes is still important: in developing such plants, researchers and the companies that support them must take into account strategies for long-term environmental development. The genetic alteration of crop plants has its place *alongside* other approaches in such a framework.

Tolerance of the Elements

Besides increasing plant resistance to insect and microbial attacks, gene technology is also enhancing plant tolerance of extreme conditions—excessive heat, cold, dryness, water, or salt content of the soil. These conditions have a negative impact on the plant, resulting in either limited growth or death. To survive, plants growing in harsh environments have developed strategies for coping with or adapting to them (Bartels, 1992). Most crop plants, however, do not have these resistance mechanisms to deal with extreme environment conditions (such as frost or drought) or with conditions caused by changes of human origin (such as climate changes from the effects of pollution).

One area of research focused on seeds and plants with mechanisms to deal with drought or extremely dry environments. In particular, one family of plants (Scrophulariaceae) provides an interesting model to study. In the absence of water, the leaves will dry out but remain intact until the plant is watered again. Researchers found a number of proteins that are likely to help preserve the structures of cells and tissues, thus preventing irreversible damage to the protective membranes of plant cells in the absence of water (Bartels, 1992). If the genes for these proteins could be transferred to important crop plants, this transfer could be an important part of a strategy to help crops survive in extremely dry conditions.

Other research studies are providing scientists with a better understanding of how certain plants cope with frost, high salt content, and heat. Gene technology has given researchers the tools to look at the function of these coping mechanisms at the molecular level. It is hoped that these studies will lead to the development of strains of crop plants that will survive harsh environments.

Those kinds of applications will be important to farmers in regions with naturally harsh conditions. It should be recognized, however, that not all harsh conditions are natural. Some are the result of overproduction leading to soil depletion; excessive chemical use resulting in soil erosion; or other careless use of the land leading to extreme dryness, flooded lands, and high salt content (Hobbelink, 1991). In such situations, the root of the problem lies not with the harsh conditions themselves but more likely with the methods of cultivation and production that led to these conditions. The development of stronger, more resistant crop plants will only deal with the symptoms without reaching the heart of the problem. Therefore, it will be important to take environmental needs and ecological factors into consideration while improving the tolerance of plants to extreme conditions.

APPLICATIONS TO ANIMALS

Like agriculture, animal husbandry continues a long process of domesticating organisms for human purposes.

TRADITIONAL ANIMAL-BREEDING TECHNIQUES

In the past the selection and preservation of desired traits and the elimination of undesirable ones depended to a large extent on selective breeding—that is, "the enforced mating of parents with superior characteristics" (Micklos and Freyer, 1990, p. 169). Through millennia of selective breeding, farmers and herdsmen developed pure breeds and crossbreeds of animals for food, clothing, companionship, and recreation. In the last few centuries, with the growth of scientific investigation and the development of experimentation, animals played an increasingly important role in science and industry.

Perhaps one of the most important functions of animals is providing humans with food. On a worldwide basis, it is estimated that more than 50 percent of the proteins that humans consume come from meat and animal products (Geldermann and Momm, 1995). (This figure is likely much higher in some regions and cultures and depends to a large extent on the availability of meat and alternatives to meat products.) This difference highlights the commercial importance of farm animals, which, to some degree, provided the driving force for the development of veterinary medicine, modern reproductive technology, and gene technology in this field. Because other sections of this book deal with veterinary medicine, the current discussion will focus on breeding techniques.

Modern reproductive technology is a continuation of traditional breeding practices, and it paved the way for gene technology in animal husbandry. One of the first developments of modern reproductive technology, in the 1940s, was **artificial insemination** (AI). For commercial, veterinary, or other reasons, AI offers an alternative to enforced mating. The technique, often used with the larger animals (especially cattle but also pigs and horses), allows farmers and breeders to obtain sperm from a selected male and plant them in a chosen female (Geldermann and Momm, 1995).

Another significant method of reproductive technology in animal husbandry is **in-vitro fertilization** (IVF), which requires sperm and eggs to be obtained from the selected parent animals. The successful union of sperm and eggs in a laboratory results in embryos, which can be transferred into either the female donor or a surrogate mother animal (Geldermann and Momm, 1995). Among other purposes, IVF allows the screening and selection of sperm according to sex, an important criterion in various areas of the farming industry. The technique is also of prime importance in conserving or increasing pedigree breeds.

One of the most recent developments in animal reproduction is **cloning**, a term full of connotations—mental associations that people make with words. Apart from these associations, cloning refers to the development of several offspring from one embryo. Unlike gene technology, cloning techniques arose not from molecular biology but from microbiology and cellular biology. There are two approaches to cloning: embryo splitting and nuclear transplant.

After the fusion of the sperm and egg, the resulting embryo begins a process of cellular division. Every cell arising from this division contains a nucleus, carrying a full complement of chromosomes made up of DNA. Each cell and each set of genetic information is exactly the same as the others. In embryo splitting, a technician uses the techniques of microbiology to split the embryo into two (or, in certain animals, four) separate parts. These are implanted in the female donor or foster mothers, where they will continue cellular division and develop into two genetically identical entities (BMA, 1992; Geldermann and Momm, 1995).

The second approach, nuclear transfer, is a more recent innovation. In this approach, the embryo is allowed to divide up to the eight-cell, sixteen-cell or thirty-two-cell stage. Again using the techniques of microbiology, a technician separates the cells from one another, removes the nucleus from each cell, and transfers the nucleus into an unfertilized egg from another donor female. Alternatively, the nucleus is transferred into an embryo (taken from a donor female) at the one-cell stage with its own nucleus removed. The new embryos are then implanted into the donor females, who carry them to term as foster mothers (BMA, 1992; Geldermann and Momm, 1995).

Cloning involves the alteration of cells, cellular matter, and the process of cellular division. Thus, cloning is not an application of gene technology (which involves direct intervention in the genetic material using molecular techniques). At the same time, however, because the more recent technique of nuclear transfer includes the removal and transplant of the nucleus, cloning may be considered as a bridge between modern reproductive technology and gene technology.

GENE TECHNOLOGY AND ANIMALS

For the sake of convenience and clarity, it has been useful in this chapter to treat veterinary medicine, reproductive technology, and gene technology separately. Nevertheless, as may be apparent to some readers already, this separation is to some degree arbitrary. First, both the health of an animal and its reproductive capacity are essential to its commercial value. Second, gene technology has provided more options in veterinary medicine and animal reproductive technology.

In a similar way, it was useful to draw a line between the use of animals in science and industry and the use of animals on farms and in breeding. That is also, however, an arbitrary distinction. Techniques used for animals in research are likely to be developed for use with animals on the farm— and vice versa. For example, cloning was first developed for the reproduction of laboratory animals but was later adopted for the reproduction of cattle and eventually other farm animals (Loew, 1991).

If there were ever any real differences between animals used in the laboratory and on the farm, gene technology has certainly closed that gap today. Experiments and initial trials show that transgenic farm animals can produce proteins and other substances for medical use. In addition, transgenic animals may be an important source of organs for transplants in human medicine. These are ways in which gene technology has continued and expanded the domestication of animals for human purposes. The next four sections look at these and other technical developments as they affect farm animals, laboratory research animals, animals in pharmaceutical production, and animals as transgenic organ donors.

Farm Animals

An on-going challenge in animal husbandry (like agriculture) is maximizing yield and increasing nutritional content—of meat and milk. Equally important is the animal's speed of growth: the faster it grows, the sooner the farmer can bring it to market. One of the earliest experiments with laboratory animals (mice) showed that the stimulation of growth hormone made the animals grow faster and bigger. Subsequent experiments with farm animals showed that growth hormone also plays an important role in producing animals that require less feed, have leaner meat, and give more milk—commercially important aspects.

Gene technology offers two alternatives for increasing the amount of growth hormone in an animal. The first approach entails injecting the animal with growth hormone produced in a bacterial culture. The method of production is the same as the one used in producing human growth hormone and other proteins, as described earlier. The second approach is to transfer the gene for the growth hormone directly into the cells of the animal. **Gene transfer**, as this technique is called, was first developed for experiments with laboratory animals. The technique was later modified for trials with farm animals (Geldermann and Momm, 1995; Loew, 1991; Watson et al., 1992).

Early experiments with farm animals used human growth hormone for two reasons. First, initial experiments with laboratory animals also used human growth hormone, producing transgenic mice twice the size of their nontransgenic relatives. Scientists thus expected the same results with other animals. In that case, size alone would give a preliminary indication of gene expression. Second, the foreign hormone can be identified quickly in tests, making confirmation of gene expression easier (Geldermann and Momm, 1995; Loew, 1991; Watson et al., 1992).

In addition to increasing the economic value of farm animals, gene transfer is also a tool for improving their disease resistance. Because modern farming methods often entail raising many animals close together, the spread of bacterial and viral infection is a real risk. Experiments suggest that it is possible to create chickens with viral resistance by integrating the gene coding for the viral coat protein into the zygotes. Such a technique would be key to protecting animals that are prone to certain diseases (BMA, 1992; Geldermann and Momm, 1995; Loew, 1991; Watson et al., 1992).

Gene-transfer experiments with farm animals (mainly rabbits, sheep, goats, pigs, and cows) show that it is possible to integrate foreign genes into the genomes of animals (that is, the animals' own complete set of genes). Nevertheless, with current techniques (originally developed for laboratory mice), there are a number of drawbacks and negative side effects:

- low frequency of the genetically altered eggs developing into transgenic farm animals: approximately one in two hundred—about ten to fifteen times lower than the success rate in mice (Watson et al., 1992)
- unexpected physical and metabolic defects, such as arthritis (Loew, 1991)
- infertility in certain animals, in particular the female (BMA, 1992; Geldermann and Momm, 1995)
- the activation or deactivation of other genes (Geldermann and Momm, 1995)

On the one hand, "such findings reinforce the realisation that biological systems are rarely as simple as they might first appear" (Micklos and Freyer, 1990, p. 178). On the other hand, it is important to remember that unexpected and undesirable side effects—such as infertility and physical deformities—occur in many ways, not simply through genetic alteration. Some defects occur naturally. Environmental factors—some better understood than others—can affect the developing embryo and result in a "freak" of nature (Loew, 1991). Other defects are the result of human intervention, for example, through traditional breeding methods. S. Krimsky (1991) gives the example of turkeys bred with such large breasts that they could not mate. Infertility is one of the side effects observed in mules, the result of a cross between horses and donkeys (two different species) using traditional breeding methods.

Gene transfer is only one of several developments in gene technology as applied to farm animals. Other developments offer new tools for the prevention, diagnosis, and correction of genetic diseases. The result of such diseases account for some of the losses in animal husbandry—loss of embryos, aborted pregnancies, stillbirths, and birth defects. It is possible to reduce such losses by screening out carriers of these genetic diseases, that is, those animals that carry the defective gene but do not have the disease. Another possibility is the direct intervention in the DNA code to correct the error using an approach called gene therapy (BMA, 1992; Geldermann and Momm, 1995). (Applications such as genetic diagnosis, genetic screening, and gene therapy are described in more detail in the sections below on gene technology and human beings.)

Behind these developments in animal husbandry there is a range of economic and social implications that deserve consideration. First, from an economic standpoint, both producers and consumers benefit from fast-growing, disease-resistant animals that produce leaner meat and more milk. For the modern producer, such animals could represent greater efficiency because of

- lower costs—meat-producing animals leave the farm sooner; less feed is required
- decreased risks—animals are more resistant to disease, lowering the risk of spreading an infection among the livestock
- higher yield per animal—leaner meat and more milk translate into greater return on investment for the producer

Leaner meat will undoubtedly appeal to today's more health-conscious consumer. The consumer could also benefit from potentially lower prices in the long run. Perhaps, when this method of production is new, the prices of these meat and milk products will be higher than products from animals raised by more traditional methods. However, it is usually true with most new products that in the beginning there are few producers, which means that competition in the market place is limited. Marketing costs may be higher also as producers introduce the product to consumers. Prices start to fall, however, when more consumers buy more of the product and when more producers start to offer the same product. To take an example from a "new" technology, computers were initially out of the price range of the average consumer; today, computers are becoming more and more affordable. This process is part of the cycle that new products go through.

From a social and ethical perspective, the impact of genetically altered farm animals is more problematic. On the one hand, many opponents often argue that the methods of gene technology ignore or even violate the integrity of the creature. A frequently cited example is one of the first transgenic pigs produced: it was indeed bigger and had less fat, but it was also lethargic, had a deformed skeletal structure, and suffered from arthritis. In other words, this early "scientific success" was also an animal that suffered continually and was unable to live "normally" like the rest of its species without pain. On the other hand, proponents (especially those with a scientific background) point out that more recent techniques are more accurate than those used in initial experiments and that researchers have been able to reduce or eliminate undesirable side effects. Since the first transgenic pig, researchers have gained greater understanding about the complex interaction between genes and between genes and the environment.

This kind of scientific (rational) counterargument misses two essential value-based points implicit in the original argument: all living things have a right to live without undue human interference; gene technology promotes a mechanistic viewpoint, which reduces life forms to biological machines to be exploited. Those with such a perspective do not necessarily exclude the agricultural domestication of animals. What they do reject is the concept that animals (or other living things) have no inherent value outside an economic or technological, human-defined framework. This view is reinforced by a growing unease with the alienation of industrialized society from nature or creation.

In addition to this concern about the animal's integrity, opponents raise questions about the value of transgenic farm animals to society. Previous technologies (based primarily on physics or chemistry) had also promised improvements, but such innovations have come at a price. On the one hand, health-care and living standards have indeed risen in many countries partially because of technological innovations. On the other hand, the gap between the "haves" and the "have-nots" has also increased—not only between industrialized countries and developing countries but also within individual countries. There is a surplus of food in industrialized nations as a result of the Green Revolution in the 1970s, which increased the yield of crop plants; but it also increased the number of hungry and starving people in areas where there had already been a disparity between rich and poor. At the same time, hunger is still a major world problem. Against this background, proponents say the question of genetically altering farm animals to improve production quickly becomes one of choice rather than necessity. Opponents ask if industrialized countries need, and if developing countries can afford, a new technology (based primarily on biology) that, echoing the past, promises to increase food production.

Laboratory Research

Beyond the farm, animals are invaluable to the laboratory as well: rodents and other mammals are living models of biological systems. As such, animals are often used in experiments in university, government, and industry laboratories for models for research and product testing. Transgenic laboratory animals are used as models for disease or therapy. They allow researchers to study closely the genetic causes of diseases and perhaps develop strategies for diagnosis, prevention, or even therapy.

To test a medication or treatment for a human disease using animal models implies that these animals must also have that disease. Before the development of gene technology, such conditions had to be induced in healthy animals through different kinds of agents—biological (microbial infection), chemical (injection of substances), or physical (irradiation). All of them involve a certain degree of stress and suffering for an otherwise healthy animal. Gene transfer and the genetic alteration of embryos offer an alternative to such methods.

The first transgenic laboratory animal was created for cancer research. In 1985 two scientists at Harvard University inserted a gene associated with various kinds of human cancer into the eggs of a mouse. Offspring expressing the gene were the first transgenic animals bred with the human onco-gene; they also became the first mammals to receive a patent (see "Gene Technology and Animals," chapter 3). These mice are easily susceptible to developing cancer, making them of value in both studying the genetic cause of cancer and testing drugs against human cancer. Not only are there genes in the body predisposed to becoming tumorous, there are also genes that keep these onco-genes in check. Researchers also found that several factors occurring in various stages are needed to transform the cells affected into cancerous ones.

In addition to their role as disease models, "onco-mice" also serve as models to test treatment for cancer (BMA, 1992; Watson et al., 1992). The onco-mice raised two areas of concern in particular: patenting and violating the integrity of laboratory animals. Because the next chapter deals in depth with the issue of patenting, this section will concentrate on the second area. Before looking more closely at this concern, it is necessary to stress a key distinction between animals on the farm and animals in the laboratory. Consumers expect farm animals to be as well treated and as humanely slaughtered as possible; most people would probably oppose deliberately or unnecessarily inflicting suffering on farm animals. In contrast, implicit in using animals as models for disease or therapy is the concept of suffering from a particular disease. For example, to study the effects of a medication or a therapy for arthritis, animals used as models must have arthritis, which means painful, swollen joints. One way to achieve this state has been the injection of clay or other substances in joint areas.

Through gene technology, it is possible to ensure that certain laboratory animals are born with specific medical conditions. Opponents argue that this procedure is inhumane because it involves deliberately making animals suffer. Proponents counter that it is in fact more humane than previous methods, where an otherwise healthy animal is inflicted with physical pain and mental stress *before* it even develops the conditions necessary for research. In that sense, it can be said that the suffering of transgenic animal models is reduced overall. Proponents also argue that health authorities require data from animal tests before allowing a medication or therapy even to be tried on human beings. It is a question of balancing the suffering of animals against the benefits to human beings. What constitutes *humane treatment* in a situation where it is implicit that the animal will suffer? At the heart of the issue is animal testing in general. For the sake of finding a cure, is it justifiable to make animals suffer (regardless of the means)? One could argue that society must first answer this question before dealing with the concerns surrounding transgenic laboratory animals.

Gene Pharming

One of the most innovative areas opened through gene technology, **gene pharming** is the use of transgenic dairy animals to manufacture human and other substances needed in human medicine. It relies on the procedures of gene transfer.

In gene pharming, one takes a gene coding for a human protein and splices a milk-protein promoter into it. Milk contains a number of proteins whose production is strictly regulated by promoters (that is, specific nucleotide sequences). Milk-protein promoters limit the production of these proteins to the cells of the mammary glands. The altered gene is injected into the zygote of a milk-producing animal such as a goat, sheep, or cow. If the resulting embryo is female, it is transferred into an adoptive mother to carry to term (BMA, 1992; Geldermann and Momm, 1995; Helmy and Siefer, 1994; Watson et al., 1992).

The milk from the resulting offspring will contain the human protein, which can be isolated from the milk through a purification process. Researchers in the United Kingdom have already successfully created transgenic sheep that produce Factor IX, a blood protein, in their milk. Despite high yields of protein in trials with laboratory animals, early experiments with Factor IX have yielded less protein than anticipated (BMA, 1992; Watson, 1990).

A similar approach is currently being tried. Instead of using genes regulating milk-producing cells, this approach uses genes controlling the production of blood proteins. One experiment used transgenic pigs to produce human hemoglobin, which are responsible for transporting oxygen to tissues in the body. Hemoglobin can also be used as a blood substitute (Helmy and Siefer, 1994; Watson et al., 1992). "A large pig can donate 20 pints of blood over the course of a year without detrimental health effects, thereby yielding 500 to 1,000 g of purified human hemoglobin" (Watson et al., 1992, p. 480).

Although both methods are still at the experimental stage, it is expected that gene pharming will be fully developed by the beginning of the twenty-first century. As previously mentioned, the techniques of gene transfer have yet to be fully developed for farm animals. By 1994, about twenty biological substances had been produced by gene pharming. It is hoped that gene pharming will eventually provide a steady supply of needed human proteins: a single cow could yield more than 10,000 litres of milk and about 300 kilograms of proteins per year (Helmy and Siefer, 1994).

The biological products of gene pharming are purer than those obtained from human sources or animal substitutes using conventional methods. Gene pharming may even offer an equally safe but less expensive alternative to the use of genetically altered microbial culture, which requires costly equipment. In addition, many human proteins have sugar molecules attached, but those produced using bacterial culture lack these molecules, resulting in faster elimination of the protein from the body. Because farm animals (as mammals) are closer in terms of evolution to human beings (also mammals) than to bacteria, this problem is not expected in human proteins produced using transgenic farm animals (BMA, 1992).

Gene pharming has met with little resistance. It is likely that the concept of it is close enough to dairy farming that most people already have a degree of familiarity and comfort with animals being used this way. More likely, though, the reasons for the lack of resistance are more complex. For one thing, there is little or no harm to the animal itself. For another, the benefits for human sufferers are clear to most people. In addition, gene technology that is applied to human medicine tends to be more acceptable. This fact would explain why there is resistance to enhancing the milk or meat production capacity of farm animals but more acceptance of gene pharming.

Transgenic Organ Donors

A shortage or, in some cases, a decrease of human organ donors has led to long waiting lists for transplant organs. The Eurotransplant International Foundation, which coordinates organ exchanges in Austria, Belgium, Luxembourg, Germany, and the Netherlands, provides the following figures for the year 1994 in the participating countries. Over the course of 1994, nearly 3,000 patients received a kidney transplant; about 400 patients died while waiting for a transplant. At the beginning of the year, there were about 12,000 patients on the waiting list for a kidney; by the end of the year, there were about 12,900. During the same period, nearly 700 patients received a new heart and about 280 died while waiting. The waiting list for a heart at the beginning of the year had 1,100 patients; by year end, there were about 870. There were more than 890 liver transplants during the same year; and more than 120 died on the waiting list. The waiting list at the beginning of 1994 had about 310 patients; at the end of the year, that list had roughly 330.

In the absence of more donors, one viable alternative would be **xenotransplantation**, which involves the grafting of animal organs, including those of pigs and primates closely related to human beings. One major technical problem with using primates as a source of organs is that many of these animals are either from scarce and protected species or else their organs are too small for human use. From a physiological standpoint, pigs are ideal organ donors: not only are they easy to raise and have large litters of offspring, but they also have organs very similar in size and shape to those of humans.

Whether the donors are humans, primates, or pigs, there is another technical problem with transplanting organs—hyperacute organ rejection induced by the immune system (Eberhard-Metzger, 1995; Fletcher, 1994; Staff, 1993; White and Wallwork, 1993). The introduction of immunosuppressing medication has somewhat reduced this risk with human organs, making transplantation possible. But, organ rejection still poses a barrier for xenotransplants. Because animal organs are foreign tissues (with different genes and protein structures), the human immune system reacts by bombarding the new organ with antibodies. Under this attack, an ordinary pig's heart would not survive for more than fifteen minutes in a human body.

There is no conventional mechanism to overcome this reaction (Fletcher, 1994; James, 1993; Staff, 1993).

In 1992, using the techniques of gene transfer, a team in the United Kingdom successfully created the first transgenic pig that could potentially provide organs for transplants. The team injected into a zygote the isolated gene coding for the decay accelerating factor (DAF), which allows the immune system to recognize and accept the body's own tissues. The offspring of this pig had cells whose surface was coated with DAF. Because of this protective coat, the human immune system did not react to the transgenic organ as a foreign intruder. In initial laboratory experiments, there was no evidence of the rejection process taking place (Fletcher, 1994; Staff, 1993). In 1995 the number of offspring from the first transgenic pig had reached two hundred. Although there are now enough pigs to allow scientists to carry out the first laboratory experiments, it is likely to be a long while before the first transgenic organ transplant in humans will be conducted.

Beyond technical challenges and compliance with legislation, there are ethical implications to transgenic organ transplants that deserve attention (Fletcher, 1994). An important question is what negative side effects donors of transgenic animal organs might experience. Closely related is the question to what degree human needs and suffering outweigh those of animals (transgenic or otherwise). An equally important ethical question is what real alternatives exist to transgenic animal donors as a compensation for the lack or decrease of human organ donors. In the view of the creators of the first transgenic animal organ donors (White and Wallwork, 1993), the shortage of organs makes it necessary to continue research on transgenic xenotransplantation.

At the time of writing, this application is still relatively new and has not yet reached the stage of clinical trials. As it has had little attention in the mass media, there has been little public reaction on record. One might assume, however, based on the concern with animal testing in medical or industrial laboratories in general and on the resistance to transgenic laboratory animals in particular, that this application is likely to meet with resistance or, at the very least, considerable public debate.

Like gene pharming, the creation of transgenic organ donors will have clear medical benefits: these animals will help save many human lives. But, there is one important difference: the animal donor will likely die in the process. Can we justify killing an animal or causing it to suffer in order to obtain benefits for human beings? It might be argued that human beings have always killed animals for their own benefit, for example, for food. Does that justify killing an animal to save a human life?

Unlike laboratory animals, animals as transgenic organ donors are likely to lead a healthy life. This fact makes it hard to reject them as transgenic organ donors. Animal-rights activists are still likely to protest that requiring the animals to live in sterile conditions in total isolation from their kind, is contrary to the nature of social animals, such as pigs, which tend to live together in groups. On balance, because the welfare of transgenic animal donors is otherwise attended to, they will probably not be rejected outright.

APPLICATIONS TO HUMANS

The applied science that most directly affects human lives is perhaps medicine, in which gene technology plays an important part.

MEDICINE

Medical interventions range from reproductive medicine to disease control. Since the 1950s, better understanding of human genetics and the development of other technologies have led to the development of genetic screening to predict congenital diseases in fetuses. For example, amniocentesis allows doctors to check for Down's syndrome using the chromosomes of cells in the amniotic fluid surrounding the fetus (Bayertz, 1994; BMA, 1992). Although such chromosomal screening does not rely on molecular genetics techniques, it was an early form of genetic testing. Today, DNA diagnosis plays a key role in applications of gene technology in human medicine.

Although genetic information may be desirable to some parents, the combination of genetics and reproductive medicine more often raises the specter of eugenics as propagated and practiced by the Nazis in the 1930s and 1940s. The concept of eugenics and its implications will be examined later in this chapter.

As discussed elsewhere in the chapter, the broad field of biotechnology has provided various methods and substances for the prevention or cure of viral and bacterial infections. Not all diseases, however, have a microbial cause; some are hereditary. Hereditary diseases were known before scientists discovered the role of genes in inheritance or the genetic cause of these diseases. Perhaps one of the best-known, well-documented hereditary disorders is hemophilia, which occurred in a number of royal families in Europe.

Although Sir Francis Galton and others in the nineteenth century had proposed theories about the role of genes in inheritance, the first understanding of the genetic causes of hereditary diseases dates from the beginning of the twentieth century. About 1910, Sir Archibald Garrod put forward the idea that genetic errors in enzyme production were the cause of hereditary defects. This theory was confirmed in the late 1940s, when Linus Pauling and his colleagues found the mutation in hemoglobin (a protein) responsible for sickle-cell anemia. Almost a decade later, in the late 1950s, more than four hundred genetic disorders had been identified. By the mid-1980s, that figure reached about four thousand. "While most of these diseases are individually very rare, each having a frequency of only one in several thousand births or even tens of thousands births, together they affect roughly 1-2 per cent of all live-born babies" (BMA, 1992, pp. 183-184; Friedmann, 1991).

It must be made clear, however, that not all genetic disorders are the result of deficiencies of a single gene (monogenic diseases). Multifactorial diseases are the result of deficiencies in several genes or even a combination of genetic and environmental factors (BMA, 1992; Friedmann, 1991).

GENE TECHNOLOGY AND HUMANS

Health being a fundamental human need (according to Abraham Maslow's hierarchy of needs), it is perhaps not surprising that much of gene technology in the human area is being applied to the study, prediction, prevention, and treatment of diseases. Studies of the human genome (see "The Human Genome" below) and other research have shown the link between genetic disposition and literally thousands of human diseases. Human curiosity—the need to know—and progress on finding genes linked with diseases have combined to give particular emphasis to genetic diagnosis (see "Genetic Diagnosis" below).

For doctors and patients, once the defective gene has been identified, the next step (if the option exists) is therapy—either correcting the defect in the gene or replacing it altogether. Because gene therapy using molecular genetic techniques changes the "chemical underpinnings of human existence" (Watson, 1990, p. 44), questions are raised as to how far therapy should go, especially if the genetic error—and the "genetic correction"—can be passed on to future generations (see "Gene Therapy").

From genetic intervention for medical reasons, it is perhaps not that big a step to enhancement (see "Gene Enhancement" below) and, some fear, eugenics based on gene technology (see "Eugenics" below). The results of human genome studies are likely to add to scientific and eventually medical understanding of genes and the role they play in human health. This newfound information will influence existing applications and lead to the development of other methods. At the same time, the technology will raise complex and challenging legal, ethical, and social questions.

The Human Genome

The human genome is made up of twenty-three pairs of chromosomes (or forty-six individual chromosomes) and is estimated to contain between fifty thousand and a hundred thousand genes. With one exception, all cells in the body contain the full complement of forty-six chromosomes; these are somatic cells. The exception is the germ line, the group of cells that produce sperm and eggs (in medical language, germ cells or reproductive cells) (BMA, 1992; Wagner, 1994; Watson et al., 1992).

As previously noted, genetic disorders lie at the root of many human diseases and even influence a person's disposition to developing certain diseases. Studying the human genome can shed some light on the genetic causes of such diseases and perhaps lead to more effective ways of preventing, treating, or curing them. Comparisons of the human genome with the genomes of other organisms (such as *E. Coli*, a bacterium often used as a research model in microbiology) will give greater understanding of how organisms—and perhaps life itself—function at the genetic level and how complex mechanisms and processes interact (Lee, 1991; Nowak, 1995; Watson et al., 1992).

As explained at the beginning of the chapter, genes are made up of pairs of nucleotides. It is estimated that there are about 3 billion base pairs in the full human genome. Out of those, only an estimated 2 to 5 percent are known to code for a protein. In other words, 95 to 98 percent of human DNA serves no *obvious* function and, at this point, does not give any *usable* information on the cell. Understanding genes will lead to a better understanding of how human life functions and how genetic diseases develop. To reach that goal, scientists need to know where genes are located on the chromosomes, what they do, and how they work. Acquiring such knowledge is part of an international effort* to map the human genome and characterize its genetic sequences (Cooper, 1994; Kahn, 1993; Lee, 1991; Watson et al., 1992).

One major part of human genome research is the development of two kinds of maps. One is a **genetic linkage map**, which shows the positions of genes in relation to one another and measures the *frequency* with which two different traits are inherited together. Linked genes (that is, close to one another and inherited together) give the relative positions of all known sites of genes. The other is a **physical map** of all the chromosomes showing the position of genes in the *order* in which they appear on the chromosome. Such a map would give scientists a better picture of the way the genome is organized and a more precise fix on where genes are located. Both maps are needed: the genetic linkage map shows genes in relation to one another; the physical map shows genes as they relate to a segment of chromosome (Davis, 1991a; Kahn, 1993; Lee, 1991; US DHHS, 1991).

The other major part of human genome research is the characterization of nucleotide sequences making up genes. Because the sequence is specific to a gene, knowing its sequence will lead to better understanding of how the gene works. More important, in identifying the link between DNA sequences and specific diseases, scientists hope to gain an insight into the role that genes play in these disease (Davis, 1991a; Lee, 1991).

One of the challenges in characterizing the human genome is its sheer size. Both technical innovation (for example, polymerase chain reaction) and technological developments (for example, sequencing machines) have

---

* Various sources refer to the numerous groups around the world working on the human genome as the Human Genome Project. While HUGO aims to foster collaboration, there are really many (frequently independent) human genome projects—with varying degrees of collaboration and different combinations of public or private funding. For this reason and to avoid confusion with the U.S. Human Genome Project, this book prefers the terms human genome research projects or simply human genome research.

allowed rapid progress on the job of sequencing the approximately 3 billion base pairs—or 6 million bases—of the total human genome.

Analyzing a sequence of DNA requires multiple copies of a DNA segment. The polymerase chain reaction (PCR) is a method for selectively duplicating short regions of DNA (ranging from a hundred base pairs to six thousand base pairs). For genome analysis, PCR has become an indispensable tool. It replaces the time-consuming and complex process of cloning—that is, the nonselective replication of longer DNA segments (ranging from several hundred base pairs to a million base pairs) in bacterial or yeast cells. Automation of this and other processes has led to the mapping of sizable areas of the human genome. The use of robots, for example, has helped one group in Paris, Généthon, to finish mapping more than 25 percent of the human genome and most of one chromosome within three years of the center's beginnings in the early 1990s (Doggett, 1994; Kahn, 1994; Lee, 1991; Watson et al., 1992).

New mapping-sequencing techniques and automation technology have resulted in rapid progress in human genome research and produced a flood of new information. This information has led to the development of electronic databases for storage, retrieval, analysis, and communication of findings. Electronic information systems are instrumental in constructing a comprehensive picture of the human genome based on the results of different groups working around the world—using different methods and approaches (Murray et al., 1994; Watson et al., 1992).

In the United States, the National Institutes of Health and the Department of Energy funded such research projects in the mid-1980s; a number of other organizations in the States had similar programs. By 1990, many of these had coalesced into the U.S. Human Genome Project (HGP). By 1995, other national governments were also funding human genome research in Australia, Canada, Denmark, France, Israel, Italy, Japan, the Netherlands, Russia, Sweden, and the United Kingdom. Several developing countries are involved in or supporting genome research, as are supranational bodies such as the European Union, the United Nations Educational, Science and Cultural Organization (UNESCO), and the World Health Organization (WHO), an organization of the UN (Davis, 1991a; HUGO, 1995; Kahn, 1993; Lee, 1991; Watson, 1990).

In early 1995 the French government announced plans to take over direct control of all publicly funded research on the human genome in France. Until then, funding for all genome research came under the umbrella of the Groupement de Recherches et d'Études sur les Génomes (GREG). That year, the ministry of higher education and research took direct charge of funding for programs on genetic function, medical genetics, and genetics and the environment (Butler, 1995). In the same period, the Samuel Lunenfeld Research Institute at Mount Sinai Hospital in Toronto announced that it had received grants from both government and industry for what will be the largest genome research center in Canada (Spurgeon, 1995).

It soon became clear to scientists working on human genome research that different countries needed to "work together instead of indulging in costly competitive races for the same chromosomal objectives" (Watson, 1990, p. 48). This realization led to an effort to coordinate the multinational projects to map the structure of the human genome and characterize gene sequences, in particular the foundation of an independent international body to facilitate the exchange of information and foster collaboration (Bodmer and Evans, 1991): "The Human Genome Organisation (HUGO) is the international organisation of scientists involved in the Human Genome Project. . . . HUGO was established in 1989 . . . to promote international collaboration within the project" (HUGO, 1995, p. 1).

It must be emphasized that HUGO's role is one of facilitating rather than directing. It enables individual scientists or research groups to exchange information or to build links between specific projects; HUGO coordinates international workshops and meetings focusing on work and issues in human genome research. Projects remain under the direction of various public or private organizations. "The [international] Human Genome Project is not under the central control or direction of any individual, group or organising committee" (HUGO, 1995, p. 2).

The same situation can be seen at the national level in most countries as well, where research programs are funded, directed, or carried out by both public and private research organizations. In addition, there are various joint programs, with participation between public institutions (such as universities) and private interests. This multiplicity makes it difficult to obtain a complete overview of projects underway around the world or even in individual countries. Table 2.1 lists some of the human genome research projects taking place in different countries with public or private funding. There are two important remarks about the table. First, although HUGO does not carry out genome research, it is included in this list. Second, with two exceptions (both international), projects are shown in alphabetical order according to country.

Those working on human genome projects and their proponents are expecting the results to have a significant impact on the field of medicine. One anticipated outcome will be a better understanding of how genetic diseases develop. Indeed, much of the effort in mapping and sequencing focuses on finding genes linked with diseases. Practical applications from human genome research to medical science rely on the discovery and understanding of what genes do. As mentioned, researchers have linked about four thousand diseases (possibly more) to genetic causes.

Some of these disorders are **monogenic**—the result of a defect in one gene (for example, sickle-cell anemia, cystic fibrosis, and hemophilia). Others are **polygenic** (or multigenic)—the result of a failure in several genes

Table 2.1 Partial List of Human Genome Research around the World

Name of Project or Organization	Sources of Funding	Country or Region	Founded	Area of Work
Human Genome Organization (HUGO)	various governmental, industrial, and nonprofit organizations	international/world-wide(coord-nated from the UK)	late 1980s	functions as coordinator and facilitator for international co-operation in exchanging research data
Human Genome Diversity Project (HGDP)	regional committees	international (coordinated from the US)	about 1991	aims to create a collection of cell lines and DNA prepared from blood, hair, or saliva samples from anonymous donors in different populations, especially those that are geographically isolated or have distinct language and cultures; material to be available for research on human history and biology
Women's and Children's Hospital (Adelaide)	U.S. Department of Energy	Australia	1990	focuses on mapping human chromosome 16
Canadian Genome Analyses and Technology Program (CGAT)	the Government of Canada and National Institute of Canada	Canada	1992	offers funding for the analysis of the genome of humans and other organisms; the development of related technolo-gies; and the study of medical, ethical, legal, and social issues

Table 2.1 Partial List of Human Genome Research around the World

Name of Project or Organization	Sources of Funding	Country or Region	Founded	Area of Work
Centre for Human Genome Research and Human Medicine	Bristol-Myers, Squibb, and three levels of government to fund the building of the center	Canada	proposed in 1995	does research into the genetic factors responsible for human development and the molecular basis of a number of diseases; possibly the diagnosis and treatment of these diseases
Groupement de Recherches et d'Études sur les Génomes (GREG)	government of France	France	1993	originally funded research on all types of genomes (human, animals, plants, and microorganisms); in 1995, was limited to model animals and plants
Centre d'Étude du Polymor-phisme Humain (CEPH)	private foundation with some funding by le Centre National de la Recherche Scientifique (CNRS)	France	1993	promotes development of a genetic linkage map by making DNA samples from selected families available
Généthon	CEPH and Association française contre les myopathies (AFM)	France	1991	has established a physical map; aimed to complete a genetic map by the end of 1995; aimed to localize certain disease genes by end of 1995

Name of Project or Organization	Sources of Funding	Country or Region	Founded	Area of Work
The Human Genome Center	Ministry of Education, Science, and Culture	Japan	N/A	serves as the base for material and information relating to human genome analysis
Scientific research programs	Ministry of Health and Welfare	Japan	N/A	does research on human genome relating to ageing and to diseases
Various institutes	Science and Technology Agency	Japan	N/A	does different projects relating to human genome analysis
Human Genome Mapping Project	Medical Research Council	United Kingdom	1992	works in two areas: Resource Centre (independent, nonresearch centre); directed program with focus on physical mapping
Human Genome Project	U.S. National Institutes of Health and the U.S. Department of Energy	United States	1990	focuses on mapping and sequencing the human genome by the beginning of the 21st century

Table compiled from various sources. (Cooper, 1994; Kahn, 1993; Kahn, 1994; Murray et al., 1994; OECD, 1995; Spurgeon, 1995; Watson, 1990; Watson et al., 1992). Additional information provided by the Adelaide Women's and Children's Hospital, CGAT, GREG, HUGO Europe, and HUGO Pacific.

(for example, diabetes, breast cancer, and acute nonlymphocytic leukemia may all be polygenic disorders). Many disorders are **multifactorial**, resulting from genetic disposition and environmental conditions (for example, coronary heart disease, alcoholism, and various types of cancer). Because polygenic and multifactorial genetic disorders are complex and relatively few, more attention has been given to monogenic disorders. Nonetheless, researchers are hoping that human genome maps will result in predictive tests for polygenic disorders and perhaps even multifactorial ones (BMA, 1992; Friedmann, 1991; Lee, 1991; Watson et al., 1992).

"Although the ability to obtain health information from human DNA is not a direct outcome of the Human Genome Project, technology developed as part of the project will increase the amount and kind of information obtainable from DNA" (US DHHS, 1991, p. 17). Some anticipated state-of-the-art applications arising from this new information include more accurate and more effective methods of genetic testing, screening, and possibly therapy. Such applications will also reveal more information about an individual's genetic background and predisposition: genetic diseases carried, tendency to developing illnesses, or even risks of developing them. Thus it becomes clear that human genome research will have broad social, ethical, and legal implications.

Aware of these implications and of the possibility for abuse of genetic information, prominent scientists working on the project have spoken out for the need to address these nonscientific aspects of human genome studies. The U.S. Human Genome Project, for example, has set aside about 3 to 5 percent of its budget to address these concerns and has established the working group Ethical, Legal, and Social Implications (ELSI) to focus on them (Friedmann, 1991; Lee, 1991; Watson, 1990). In 1990 the European Community authorized the initiation of a three-year human genome program. From its total budget, the EC set aside 7 percent for studying the ethical implications of the program (Kevles, 1994).

One of ELSI's goals is to identify key issues and fund research that will contribute to policy decisions in the area of gene technology. By the mid-1990s, ELSI had placed priority on the following four issues (themes that reappear in the last section of this chapter and indeed throughout this book):

- freedom from genetic discrimination in the absence of laws in this area—for example, from employers or private health insurers
- genetic confidentiality, or an individual's ability to control personal genetic information
- practices in the health-care sector regarding the collection, storage, handling and release of genetic information
- education of broad cross-sections of society on genetic knowledge, as well as the challenges and opportunities that it provides (Friedman and Reichelt, 1994)

Few of those in ELSI and other ethicists see any ethical problems with the human genome research itself. In their book *Justice and the Human Genome Project*, T. F. Murphy and M. A. Lappé (1994) concur with this supposition. "In an age entirely comfortable with the promises and priorities of science, we do not have the sense that science (in contrast to its uses) is morally problematic" (1994, p. 5). The U.S. Genome Project and other human genome projects are based, at least in part, on the premise that genomic information will lead to better understanding of genetic diseases and, it is implied, will perhaps help eliminate them.

Thus, the question of the genome project may be put into relief this way: what is the moral argument to be offered that the suffering of people here and now can be sacrificed to expected benefits in the future? In this vein, it is also worth considering whether and to what extent the genome project may amount to an evasion of contemporary social and medical problems, problems that we could address and possibly overcome if only we so chose. (Murphy and Lappé, 1994, p. 3)

On the one hand, Murphy and Lappé acknowledge that society may never be able to help some of the "genetically disadvantaged" (1994, p. 4). Their point is that there is an ethical responsibility to discuss the implications of the underlying assumptions of human genome research itself, as distinct from the uses of the information generated. It is important to ask about the hidden costs of the research and the resulting applications to society.

On the other hand, for some like Nancy Wexler, chair of ELSI, "the question is not whether we can afford to do this project, but rather whether we can afford *not* to do this" (Cooper, 1994, p. 318, original emphasis). Wexler is internationally known for her research on Huntington's disease, a degenerative disease that has directly affected her family. For her, human genome research is already stimulating ethical discussions.

The high visibility of the Genome Project is, in effect, throwing a spotlight on existing problems of discrimination and social stigmatism. People are beginning to realise that almost all of us are at risk in some fashion or another, and that knowledge can give us a new impetus toward solving these problems. (Cooper, 1994, p. 319)

Genetic Diagnosis

The early detection and timely identification of a disease is important for options for treatment. Applications of gene technology have enhanced the ability of the medical profession to screen for and detect genetic diseases long before any symptoms appear. This success is largely due to the location of defective genes or at least sequences linked to the suspected gene site. Genetic disorders are the result of abnormal mutations of the genes. Genetic diagnosis—or DNA-based diagnosis—before or after birth can indicate if a person has a genetic disorder or is predisposed to develope it.

Prenatal Diagnosis — Diagnosis before birth involves the genetic analysis of fetal tissue sample or sometimes amniotic fluid for biochemical or chromosomal abnormalities. If parents are carriers or have a family history for a particular genetic disorder, prenatal diagnosis offers both information and choices (BMA, 1992; Friedmann, 1991; Watson et al., 1992). If the fetus has not inherited the disease, there is probably a sense of relief. Even if the fetus is a carrier or has inherited the disease, the information might offer peace of mind to parents. They can start looking for options on which to base a decision—carry the fetus to term if therapy is available, end the pregnancy if therapy is not available, or carry the fetus to term despite the lack of an existing therapy.

It must be stressed that not all genetic disorders are fatal or disabling, and there can also be a wide range of expression for some disorders. For example, Tourette syndrome causes involuntary movement, ranging from mild twitches that disappear early on to more severe muscular contractions that last a lifetime; but the life expectancy of a person with the syndrome is the same as that of the general population (Friedman and Reichelt, 1994).

Such gray zones make decisions especially difficult, and they highlight the particular importance of **genetic counseling** before and after genetic tests. Genetic counselors are specially trained professionals who can "interpret tests, answer questions, provide counselling and direct people to treatment services" (BMA, 1992; Friedman and Reichelt, 1994, p. 311). They help explain to the patient what the test is meant to show and discuss the results.

Postnatal Diagnosis—Diagnosis after birth takes two main forms: neonatal screening (of new-born babies) and carrier screening (of adults). In both situations, the aim is to detect the presence of a disease before the onset of any symptoms and to effect a course of prevention (if possible) or therapy (if available). Neonatal screening has become established practice for some disorders, such as phenylketonuria (PKU) (BMA, 1992; Friedman and Reichelt, 1994). In the case of PKU, prevention means a diet with very low amounts of the amino acid, which the baby cannot process properly. Screening of carriers (healthy people who carry a gene for a disease but in whom the gene does not express itself) is important because if a carrier marries another carrier, their children are likely to inherit the gene, which will express itself in them. In such marriages, prenatal diagnosis of the fetus will indicate the presence of the disease. The couple may prefer, however, to avoid this risk by using in-vitro fertilization (that is, having the sperm fertilize the ovum outside the body under laboratory conditions). The advantage of IVF is that it allows **preimplantation diagnosis**. In other words, cells from the embryo (the fertilized egg) would be screened for the disease, ensuring that only unaffected embryos would be implanted in the woman and that the child would be free from the genetic disorder (BMA, 1992).

Eugenic Implications—Genetic diagnosis, genetic screening, and even genetic counseling raise concerns about their eugenic implications (see "Eugenics" below). The identification and selection of the "healthiest" or "the most desirable" human being is not simply an echo of past eugenic practices; some critics fear that it is the same concept under new forms. For society today, these practices have tremendous implications about attitudes towards the sick, the disabled, and the "genetically disadvantaged."

These practices are also raising questions about society's understanding of the concepts of "health" and "sickness." Genetic testing will give a probability only that an adult, a child, or a fetus will develop a certain disease—or perhaps estimate the degree to which the person is at risk. In nature, there will always be a wide range of variation of genetic characteristics. In a genetically "healthy" society, when does a variation become a disorder? Of course, there is still too little understanding of the relationship between genetic and nongenetic factors in human diseases (Murphy and Lappé, 1994; Watson et al., 1992).

> Individuals may be stigmatised by their genetic constitution, irrespective of their actual health or behaviour. . . . Will an increasing understanding of the genetic components of our mental and behavioural characteristics lead to biological determinism, that is, to the assumption that these characteristics cannot be shaped by our environment and culture because they have an inherited component? (Watson et al., 1992, p. 559)

With the current state of genetic knowledge and technology, one of the biggest ethical problems is the gap between diagnosis and therapy. It is one thing to be able to diagnose a genetic disorder; it is another thing to be able to offer therapy for it. For a few genetic diseases, gene therapy (see "Gene Therapy," below) is already available; for some, gene therapy is at the stage of clinical trials. For patients with such diseases, they are at least secure in the knowledge that "something" can be done.

For most genetic disorders, which have complex origins that combine genetic predisposition and environmental influences, the possibility of gene therapy may never exist, or it may be available too far in the future to be helpful to patients today. For these patients, being diagnosed as having a predisposition to a particular disease is the hell of knowing they are at risk without knowing the cure. For example, every time something happens—a slight lump, a bruise, a cough, a memory lapse—the person is likely to ask: Is this *it*? Wexler explains: "Genetic diseases are like deadly assassins. If you are in a family at risk, you know the assassins are there, but you have no way of finding them and no way of hiding from them" (Cooper, 1994, p. 318).

An important question must be asked: What is the social and legal difference between someone *definitely* having a disease *now* and someone who may *possibly* develop the disease in the *future*? This question is quickly becoming urgent. With more awareness of genetic information obtained from tests, a growing number of public institutions (police departments and the courts) and private companies (employers and health insurers) have an interest in obtaining such information. Should they be able to do so and, if so, under what conditions? (One condition may be that the information released has to be analyzed and interpreted by at least one competent third party.) Is consent from the individual concerned required? What are the ramifications for all parties if the individual refuses to give consent? Are there circumstances where the individual is required to release genetic information? The increasing use of databanks for storage and retrieval (along with the absence of specific legislation governing this area) makes private genetic information vulnerable to access by other individuals or organizations without the person's consent. Thus a doctor may willingly or inadvertently end up providing health insurers with information about a patient's genetic disposition or current condition.

The implications are even more serious when it comes to prenatal diagnosis. The results of a genetic test may show that a fetus has a given probability of either developing a disease or becoming a carrier. In such a situation, the number of dilemmas increase exponentially. Is abortion an alternative? Some couples may make a religious or personal moral decision not to have an abortion. They can then go on to decide whether they are financially or emotionally able to keep the child or if they should give it up for adoption. If the child is indeed born with a genetic disorder, would the parents be allowed to obtain comprehensive health insurance for their child? If health care is publicly funded, is it an equitable use of public resources? If it is private, would the parents or their physician be obliged to provide the genetic information to insurance companies? If the parents are not allowed comprehensive coverage for the child, is this not genetic discrimination?

For couples who contemplate abortion, to what extent should they rely on the results of a genetic test? After all, a test does *not* offer certainty; it only indicates a possibility or at best a probability. There is always a chance of statistical and human error in the results as well. What should a couple decide if this is their last chance of having a child?

It may be easy to insist that genetic counseling be nondirective. That implies that the full responsibility of the final decision rests on the patient as an individual. What moral and psychological support should the person receive before *and* after making a decision? In Jonathan Tollin's play *Twilight of the Golds*, a couple has to decide whether to carry to term or abort a healthy fetus that has a high probability of becoming a homosexual. As the wife points out to the husband, it is fine for everyone to say that the decision is hers; but in the end, she alone carries the responsibility for the decision—for the rest of her life. This is an important consideration not only for genetic diagnosis but also for other applications of gene technology to humans. Gene technology offers more choices for individuals, but individual choices imply the burden of responsibility.

Gene Therapy
Gene therapy is the use of a functional, wild-type gene (that is, a "normal" or "healthy" gene) to replace a mutant gene (that is, a "defective" or "malfunctioning" gene), which causes a genetic disease. There are currently three approaches to gene therapy, all relying on specific gene targets (BMA, 1992; Wagner, 1994; Watson et al., 1992). The first is gene replacement, in which a defective gene is removed and a healthy one is spliced in. The second approach is gene correction, which aims to alter the problem gene, which has caused a "mistake." The third is gene augmentation, which is *comparatively* less difficult than the first two. It involves the introduction of a healthy gene into the target cell without removing or changing the defective one (BMA, 1992).

Because gene therapy focuses on specific genes and because of the current level of knowledge, monogenic disorders have been the main focus for gene therapy. It must be underlined, however, that gene therapy is still at an early stage, most efforts being in clinical trials. Even gene therapy for monogenic disorders faces many hurdles, the first being the safe and efficient delivery of modified genes to target cells. Another problem is avoiding immune-system resistance to vectors (shuttles used for delivering a gene to the cell). These and other difficulties are compounded in the cases of polygenic or multifactorial disorders. Finally, one should distinguish between somatic-cell gene therapy and germ-line gene therapy. The distinction is important because they raise different kinds of concerns and receive different degrees of acceptance.

Somatic-Cell Gene Therapy— As explained earlier, somatic cells are those containing the full complement of genes. In somatic-cell gene therapy, cells containing genes that have been corrected are transferred back into the affected tissues (for example, blood) or organs (for example, bone marrow and skin). The genetic correction will not be carried to descendants of the patient because it does not affect the reproductive cells in the body.

The first attempt at somatic-cell gene therapy in human beings took place in September 1990. The targeted disorder was severe combined immunodeficiency disorder (SCID), which results from a deficient gene coding for a particular enzyme. The rare disorder (two thousand reported cases worldwide) leads to a weakened immune system and the inability of the body to resist diseases. W. French Anderson and his team developed a process for correcting the defect in a four-year-old patient. They took a sample of white blood cells from the girl, introduced a healthy gene into the cells, and transferred the cells containing the healthy gene back into the patient. Within a year of the therapy, the girl's bloodstream showed normal amounts of white blood cells, which are responsible for resisting infections (BMA, 1992; Elmer-Dewitt, 1994). But because the team also used conventional methods of treatment, it remains unclear to some critics in the scientific and medical communities whether gene therapy alone was responsible for the increase in blood count.

At this point, because gene therapy is "still essentially experimental, diseases to be tackled by genetic modification are also likely to be very severe conditions for which there is no effective alternative treatment" (BMA, 1992, p. 129). Moreover, as one scientist notes, even though the first trials have started with blood or bone marrow tissues, "for many hereditary diseases somatic gene therapy will be difficult because the abnormalities are present in multiple, highly organised tissues, such as secretory cells in the lungs and the pancreas in cystic fibrosis" (Davis, 1991b, p. 257).

Because somatic-gene therapy is still at an early stage, there are still no concrete data on the long-term consequences. For this reason, the British Medical Association recommends a realistic perspective of risks and acceptance of informed individual choices:

> While the immediate benefits of successful somatic cell gene therapy may be obvious, the long-term effects of the therapy may be less easy to predict. . . . It is important therefore that in the excitement of developing new treatments the possible long-term health hazards of tampering with somatic cells should not be overlooked. Nevertheless, it should also be recognised that people may choose to accept the long-term risks of a treatment if it enables them to attain better health in the short term." (BMA, 1992, p. 185)

Government, religious, medical, and other bodies in both the United Kingdom and the United States have concluded that somatic-cell gene therapy, in comparison to germ-line gene therapy, poses few ethical problems. Because the modifications are effected on medical grounds and because they affect only the person concerned, somatic-cell gene therapy is in principle no different from other therapies such as organ transplants (BMA, 1992; Friedmann, 1991). As with other new medical treatments, however, one concern focuses on the risks implicit in clinical trials. For treatment to be attempted with human patients, the potential benefits of such treatment must outweigh potential risks (BMA, 1992).

Germ-line Gene Therapy— In contrast to somatic cells, germ-line cells have only twenty-three chromosomes, that is, half the complement of genes. More important, the germ line produces sperm and eggs. Germ-line gene therapy seeks to correct serious genetic errors by eliminating them permanently from the germ line. Because the therapy affects the very source of genetic material in reproductive cells, its results will carry on to future generations (BMA, 1992; Friedmann, 1991).

For this reason and because the long-term implications are still unclear, germ-line gene therapy has not been allowed in human medicine. Although there are both ethical and technical reasons (the former often outweighing the latter) for this restriction, the development of the technology is such that the issues it raises will one day no longer be academic. Germ-line therapy has been performed in laboratory animals such as mice, for example, in the creation of transgenic animals. The rest of this section will look mainly at some of the practical problems with germ-line therapy, as well as medical and ethical objections to it.

A key scientific argument against germ-line gene therapy for human beings *at this stage* is that it is not well enough developed. This argument is based on current knowledge of laboratory work with animals: "The efficiency of production of transgenic mice is low, with many more failures than successes and an occasional new defect—obviously an impermissible situation in work with human beings" (Friedmann, 1991, p. 147).

Some people question the necessity of germ-line therapy as a method for eliminating genetic disorders, pointing to the alternative of embryo screening in preimplantation diagnosis after in-vitro fertilization (see "Genetic Diagnosis" above). Embryo screening would not involve alteration of the embryo's genetic material. But, IVF is expensive and is thus not necessarily available to all couples (BMA, 1992; Friedmann, 1991). This argument, however, ignores the fact that germ-line therapy, if available, would also probably be an expensive procedure. The alternative to both IVF and germ-line therapy is prenatal diagnosis, which would lead, depending on the couple's decision, to the abortion of an affected fetus. At the same time, it must be recognized that abortion is itself still the subject of controversy.

One of the most compelling medical reasons against germ-line gene therapy *at this point* is that there is still limited scientific and medical understanding of genetic disorders, the role they play in human health, and their long-term effect. Only now are scientists beginning to understand why some genetic disorders occur with higher frequency among some populations than among others.

> A classic example . . . is the gene for sickle cell anemia. This gene is particularly prevalent in tropical Africa and the Mediterranean. It is now known that the gene protects carriers (i.e. those who have one disease gene and one normal gene) from malaria and as a result they have a survival advantage over both the individuals who have two normal genes and those who have two disease

genes—the former being more susceptible to malaria and the other suffering from a fatal disease. Because of this advantage, carriers are more likely to survive to have children and the disease gene will be passed on to future generations, thereby maintaining it in the population. (BMA, 1992, p. 186)

As the BMA points out, the eradication of this disease would also have eliminated the benefits of the gene in these regions of the world. Even in the United States, where the mosquitoes are not malarial, the BMA does not see any need to use germ-line therapy to remove the gene: "Statistics are showing that the incidence of the gene in the US is declining naturally because the advantage conferred to carriers no longer exists" (BMA, 1992, p. 186). Work on human germ-line gene therapy has been rejected on more than just practical, technical, and medical grounds. There is concern that it would possibly lead to gene enhancement and perhaps even to eugenics, as discussed below.

From an ethical point of view, it has been argued that human beings have a moral obligation to future generations. Germ-line gene therapy implies possibly irreversible changes to the genetic code of the patient and all descendants. Where one or two individuals are concerned, the consequences for the human race may not be all that important. But, should germ-line gene therapy become available, it will affect broad segments of society. Because the long-term effects cannot possibly be known before hand, there is a moral imperative to refrain from making changes that may irreversibly affect society.

Implicit in this line of thought is the concept of accountability: as human beings, we have to be responsible for the consequences of our decisions and actions. At the end of the twentieth century, we can see clearly the unforeseen negative impact of past technologies: pollution of the air, land, and water. This impact is perhaps sufficient reason for industrialized society today to realize that human activities can have lasting negative impact. Germ-line gene therapy has great potential to eliminate some dread diseases but at what cost now or in the future? We are coming to realize that it is extremely shortsighted to see only the benefits of technology and not the costs or harm.

Yet one may argue that it is just as shortsighted to see only the costs and not the benefits. Without knowing the consequences (positive or negative), should society forbid germ-line gene therapy? A prohibition is one way of not dealing with the consequences. At the same time, it must be remembered that avoiding a decision is in itself a decision. If society is morally accountable for its actions, then it is just as morally accountable for its lack of action.

By forbidding germ-line gene therapy, society has already made a decision that will also have unknown consequences for future generations. If this prohibition cannot be lifted under any condition in the future, society has effectively closed one option to coming generations. Circumstances may change: medical understanding of germ-line gene therapy may increase. Ways of reversing the effects of gene therapy may be developed. Future generations may either disagree with the prohibition or find compelling reasons to turn to germ-line gene therapy. Does society not have an obligation to leave options open to those in the future?

One possible alternative would be to place a conditional moratorium on germ-line gene therapy. In the meantime, resources would be focused on developing other applications of gene technology to human medicine (for example, somatic-cell gene therapy or using genetic information for prevention). This delay would allow the benefits of gene therapy in general to be better understood and evaluated. When that happens, the moratorium would be lifted.

Gene Enhancement

In human medicine, gene enhancement is the hypothetical use of gene technology on grounds other than medical necessity. Though not yet a reality, the applications previously described could conceivably be used to "improve" physical and nonphysical traits, or perhaps even "to introduce novel genes into people" (Davis, 1991b). In contrast to gene therapy, enhancement of genetic traits would not be for the elimination of a life-threatening genetic disorder but for removing "unwanted" medical or non-medical traits.

One example of medical gene enhancement would be the correction of a mildly expressed genetic disorder such as Tourette syndrome (see "Genetic Diagnosis" above) through somatic-cell gene therapy. A second example might be the correction of a disease gene in a carrier (one who has the gene but does not suffer from it). Strictly speaking, gene therapy is not a necessary medical procedure for carriers, but it is conceivable that if the technique were available someone might wish to use it to eliminate all possibility of transmitting the gene to future generations.

The point must again be made that most diseases have complex origins. As the discussion on somatic-cell gene therapy noted, gene therapy for even monogenic disorders faces many technical barriers and for many fatal genetic disorders remains at the experimental stage. Medical gene enhancement thus remains even further in the future, although there will come a time when it will no longer simply be theory.

Nonmedical gene enhancement would involve genetic intervention for social or aesthetic reasons. Genes play a role in defining physical traits of social value—such as great height or slender body build, or particular physical features, hair, or eye color. They may even play a part in defining non-physical qualities of social value, such as intelligence, inclination toward sports, predisposition to developing artistic or musical talents. If they do, and if such genes were located and their functions understood, parents wishing a "good future" for their children might decide to have their own germ lines (or those of embryos) altered. This possibility is for some people the dream—and for others the nightmare—of "designer genes." It is still unknown, however, which genes contribute to defining physical characteristics or how they do it, so it is still a long way to determining the influence of genes on nonphysical attributes.

If diseases have complex origins and if it is difficult to locate and correct the defective genes responsible, it must be even more difficult to locate and enhance genes that determine aspects of social value, whether physical features or nonphysical qualities. Realistically, for the present, there are technical barriers to both nonmedical and medical gene enhancement (Davis, 1991b; Kevles, 1994). "While the human genome project will undoubtedly accelerate the identification of genes for physical and medical traits, it is unlikely to reveal with any speed how genes contribute to the formation of those qualities—talent, behaviour, personality—that the world admires" (Kevles, 1994, p. 19).

Given human nature, there will always be a desire to discover secrets and push back the boundaries of knowledge. The concern is that gene enhancement, especially for nonmedical reasons, would lead to eugenics: "If gene therapy can be practised successfully on the ill, perhaps it can enhance the lives of the healthy by enriching their intelligence or physical strength; if somatic cells can be genetically manipulated, perhaps reproductive cells can be made to pass selected enhancements on to offspring" (Kevles, 1985, p. 295). This possibility has tremendous implications when it comes to the mix of enhancement and germ-line gene therapy because in such therapy, the changes will be carried on to succeeding generations: "The critics argue that we are not wise enough to know which, if any, human traits can be modified without dire social or evolutionary consequences" (Friedmann, 1991, p. 147).

Eugenics

Initially it was feared that governments might misuse germ-line gene therapy and gene enhancement for political ends. After all, eugenics was a part of public policy, not only in Nazi Germany but in other countries as well (Kevles, 1994). Today the worry is that "the greater danger would probably be the free market, with parents wishing to purchase—and hucksters willing to promise—beauty, athletic prowess or intelligence for future offspring" (Davis, 1991b, p. 257).

The modern concept of eugenics dates from Sir Francis Galton, who, as noted, first proposed it in the United Kingdom in the 1860s. After examining books on eminent men whose lives collectively spread over two centuries, he found that a large number had been blood relatives. He concluded that "nat-

ural ability," defined as eminence of reputation, is a factor of heredity. Therefore, through state-sponsored marriages of individuals with "hereditary
merit," it would be possible to produce a race of highly gifted people with
natural ability. From this concept Galton later coined the term **eugenics**,
meaning "good in birth" or "noble in heredity" (Kevles, 1985; Kevles, 1994,
p. 15). "In his writings, Galton defines eugenics—with a candour seldom
encountered among adherents of modern eugenics—as the science of
improving the human condition through 'judicious' matings . . . to give the
more suitable races or strains of blood a better chance of prevailing over
the less suitable" (Suzuki and Knudtson, 1990, p. 21).

It is important to place Galton and his concepts within the framework of
the time, place, and society from which they came. Galton lived in the same
period as Gregor Mendel, Charles Darwin (who, incidentally, was a cousin of
Galton), and Jean Lamarck, all of whom contributed to the study of inheritance. This period was characterized by interest in the sciences and technology, which had led to the Industrial Revolution of Great Britain and
elsewhere in Europe at the end of the eighteenth century.

> All around him [Galton] the technology of the industrial revolution
> confirmed man's mastery over inanimate nature. To be sure, in
> the mid-Victorian era, heredity in plants and animals was less a
> science than a body of lore based on empirical practice. . . . Never-
> theless, it was well known that by careful selection, farmers and
> flower fanciers could obtain permanent breeds of plants and ani-
> mals strong in particular characters. "Could not the race of men be
> similarly improved?" Galton wondered. "Could not the undesirables
> be got rid of and the desirables multiplied?" (Kevles, 1985, p. 3)

By the end of the nineteenth century, Galton's ideas gained attention and
became the focus of discussions among scientific and social circles. By the
1920s and 1930s, eugenic groups started to develop in several countries.
Many of the early proponents of eugenics were biologists and geneticists,
including prominent and respected figures from the United Kingdom, Sweden, Germany, and the United States (Kevles, 1994; Paul and Spencer, 1995;
Suzuki and Knudtson, 1990).

> Eugenicists declared themselves to be concerned with preventing
> social degeneration, whose abundant signs they found in the social
> and behavioural discordances of urban industrial society. For
> example, they took crime, slums and rampant disease to be symp-
> toms of social pathologies, and they attributed them primarily to
> biological causes—that is, to "blood," to use the term of inheritable
> essence popular at the turn of the century. (Kevles, 1985, p. 15)

Out of this mix of biology and sociology—the data for which were dubious at best—came government policies based on eugenic principles with eugenic aims. These policies could be positive or negative. **Positive eugenics** involves the manipulation of human heredity, breeding, or both to develop a superior type of individual (for example, family allowances as an incentive for those considered to have "desirable" genes or traits). **Negative eugenics** means eliminating or discouraging the birth of those deemed unfit (for example, sterilization of those with "undesirable" genes) (BMA, 1992; Kevles, 1985; Paul and Spencer, 1995).

In the 1930s a number of countries and regions enforced existing legislation or enacted new legislation requiring compulsory sterilization of "feebleminded" or "mentally defective" people: about thirty states in the United States (mainly affecting institutionalized individuals), the province of British Columbia in Canada, Denmark, Norway, Sweden, Finland, Iceland, Estonia, and Germany (BMA, 1992; Paul and Spencer, 1995).

In the Germany of the 1930s, the policies of the Nazi government went beyond state institutions to sterilize "all people, institutionalised or not, who suffered from allegedly hereditary disabilities, including feeblemindedness, schizophrenia, epilepsy, blindness, severe drug or alcohol addiction, and physical deformities that seriously interfered with locomotion or were grossly offensive" (Kevles, 1985, p. 116). The Nazis also enacted a program of positive eugenics by providing special loans and subsidies to couples whose children would add to an "Aryan elite." At the height of their power, in 1939, the Nazis merged their policy of negative eugenics with their racial policy. They moved from sterilization of the physically and mentally disabled to genocide in the form of death camps where whole classes of "social deviants" and other "undesirables" were killed.

> Nazi Germany exhibited the most offensive and ruthless commitment to eugenicist ideas. The rationalisation which the Nazis invoked for their appalling treatment of Jews, gypsies, homosexuals, and people with mental illnesses or handicaps relied heavily on eugenicist theories. (BMA, 1992, pp. 208–209)

The horror of the Nazi death camps brought about a strong backlash against eugenic ideas and policies. But as D. I. Kevles (1985) points out, this backlash started long before the Nazis came to power. The driving force was a coalition of religious and secular groups: Catholics, Protestants, and Jews, as well as humanists, academics, social workers, and the political left. This coalition also included biologists and "eugenicists who had never been part of the mainline . . . and mainliners who had become apostates" (Kelves, 1985 p. 118). Among them were J. B. S. Haldane, Julian Huxley, Lancelot Hogben, and Herbert S. Jennings, all of whom contributed to the advancement of genetics and evolutionary biology. They were also all leading critics of eugenics (Kevles, 1985).

The involvement of so many people from the scientific community—doctors, biologists, and geneticists—has left an indelible association among genetics, eugenics, and genocide (Paul and Spencer, 1995). In the second half of the twentieth century, the ghost of eugenics still haunts the field of human genetics, as is evident from the many calls for public discussions about research and developments in gene technology, especially where human beings are concerned. These reminders come from both humanists and scientists, including well-known geneticists such as James Watson and Bernard Davis and scientists known as outspoken social critics such as David Suzuki. For example, in his reflections on the ethical, legal, and social implications of the human genome research project, Watson writes:

> We must be aware of the terrible misuses of the incomplete knowledge of human genetics that went under the name of eugenics during the first part of this century. . . . We have only to look at how the Nazis used leading members of the German human genetics and psychiatry communities to justify their genocide programmes, first against the mentally ill and the Jews and the Gypsies. We need no more vivid reminders that science in the wrong hands can do incalculable harm. (1990, p. 46)

On assuming the associate directorship of the HGP, Watson asked that at least 3 percent of its funding be set aside for exploring broader, nonscientific implications of the HGP.

The memory of eugenics forms a conscious and subconscious backdrop for much of the concern surrounding work in human genetics. For some people, any of the various applications of gene technology in the human area could be the start down the slippery slope toward a new era of eugenics. One example is preimplantation diagnosis, which involves embryo screening and embryo selection: those with gene defects are filtered out and only the "healthiest" embryo is implanted. For these critics, this procedure is not the start down the hill: it is already eugenics in practice. Another example follows: "One objection [to germ-line gene therapy] is that it sets the dangerous precedent of interfering with human evolution. I would note that we already do so by the accepted practice of negative eugenics (i.e., genetic counselling to avert serious defects)" (Davis, 1991b).

Some may differ in opinion. Genetic counseling and embryo screening may be the last hope for a couple to have a healthy baby, especially if both partners are carriers and the risk is significant that their child will have a crippling or life-threatening genetic disease. In-vitro fertilization and preimplantation diagnosis would be an even more likely option if the couple is financially or otherwise unable to give adequate care to a child with such a disease. Would that procedure still be considered eugenics?

DNA Typing

The discussion in this chapter has focused mainly on gene technology as medical treatment or in areas related to human health and welfare. One application of gene technology in the human area is not health-care related. DNA typing, also called genetic fingerprinting, DNA fingerprinting, or DNA profiling, refers to the use of DNA information to identify individuals, especially in criminal and legal cases.

In principle, DNA typing is based on the same concept as DNA diagnosis. Along a strand of DNA there are sites that have certain numbers of nucleotide sequences joined together in a series. Such a site is called a variable number tandem repeat (VNTR) locus. When techniques break off the nucleotide sequences on either side of such a locus, the resulting fragments have a specific length and a specific sequence of nucleotides. The chances of two persons having the same nucleotide pattern are very low (Watson et al., 1992). However, there are suggestions that a *random* match may be more likely in certain genetic subgroups than in the general population (Annas, 1992).

Nonetheless, DNA typing has tremendous implications for forensic medicine and criminal investigations as well as for criminal and civil court cases, such as paternity suits (BMA, 1992). In theory, to identify a criminal suspect, all it requires is a small amount of DNA material from the suspect. Then the sample can be compared with biological evidence—hair, semen, blood—taken from the scene of the crime. "There is general agreement that DNA profiling or fingerprinting can accurately exclude individuals from being possible suspects of specific crimes, and it should continue to be so used" (Annas, 1994, p. 80).

Despite the consensus on the use of genetic typing in such cases, there are problems with the lack of standards (that is, generally accepted principles and procedures) in laboratory practices (Annas, 1994). Without such standards, the validity or accuracy of genetic evidence submitted for court proceedings will be open to challenges. This possibility could lead to prolonged disputes about validity of evidence rather than speeding up a case. In addition, there is considerable concern with the issue of consent (BMA, 1992). Without the individual's informed consent, there is a risk of taking away a person's right and will to choose. Such action would amount to invasion of privacy. After all, a genetic fingerprint contains much more information than an actual fingerprint: it includes all of a person's genetic history and disposition.

In both the United Kingdom and the United States, there have been proposals (from police officials among others) to maintain a national databank of DNA fingerprints from criminals (especially sex offenders) or even wider segments of the general population (Annas, 1994; BMA, 1992). In the absence of any laws governing the use of such information by the state, there is unlimited potential for abuse of this information. Furthermore, as

G. J. Annas points out, if the state were to maintain generic databanks for the purpose of identifying suspects, it implies that everyone in the nation is a suspect.

DIFFERENCES IN SOCIAL ACCEPTANCE OF DIFFERENT APPLICATIONS OF GENE TECHNOLOGY

At the time of writing, there is limited documented scientific research on social acceptance of applications of gene technology in different countries. But a few countries and supranational organizations have commissioned research on public attitudes in this area. This chapter relies on three works covering such research. The first is a review by B. Zechendorf (1994) analyzing different opinion polls around the world. His work provides many points of comparisons for countries outside the European Community. The second is an article highlighting some of the results of a survey conducted in Japan (also in 1991) on three areas of biology-based technology. The third is the European Commission, which in 1991 made a survey (Eurobarometer 35.1) of a number of issues, including biotechnology and gene technology. The survey was carried out at the same time in all twelve member states of the European Community (EC) (Marlier, 1992). In 1993 the Commission took another survey (Eurobarometer 39.1) to examine changes in attitude in the same areas (Marlier, 1993).

For various reasons, this section uses the European survey in 1991 as a point of reference (see Table 2.2, p.96). First, the data were easily accessible, which is not always true with other surveys. Second, the 1991 survey was a useful point of comparison for a follow-up survey in 1993. Finally, the European surveys are the most recent surveys on biotechnology or gene technology on a national or supranational level.

The Eurobarometer survey results suggest that, in the EC, the level of support for gene technology depends to a large extent on the area of application. Respondents tended to support most areas of gene technology. A high percentage supported gene technology involving microorganisms for environmental engineering (87 percent) and involving the production of medication for humans (88 percent) (see Table 2.2). They gave least support to research involving genetically altered farm animals (only 42 percent). Respondents also gave low support (58 percent) to research for improving the quality of food.

Another part of the survey (see Table 2.3, p.97) asked respondents about their perception of gene technology and the risk to human health or to the environment in each area of application. The gap between respondents who agreed and disagreed about risks was narrower than the gap between those who agreed and disagreed on support. At the same time, the results overall showed an inverse relationship to the support in each area. For example, a high proportion of respondents associated a risk to human health or the environment with gene technology applied to farm animals (68 percent) and

Table 2.2 Summary of Areas of Gene Technology Research Considered Worthwhile in the EC (1991)

Areas of Research and Application	Agree	Disagree	Don't Know or No Answer
Microorganisms altered to improve performance for making traditional or new products	78	12	10
Microorganisms altered for environmental engineering	87	5	9
Plants altered for resistance to biological attackers or nonbiological stress	74	18	9
Farm animals altered to improve disease resistance or quality of meat and milk	42	48	9
Food improved using gene technology	58	32	10
Medicine (for human health) produced using gene technology	88	4	7
Human body or tissues altered for medical purposes	74	16	10

Based on Eurobarometer 35.1 (Marlier, 1992, p. 75). Figures are percentages (rounded off to the nearest whole number—totals do not necessarily add up to 100).

to the improvement of food quality (62 percent). Fewer respondents associated a risk with the production of medicine (48 percent) and with microorganisms altered for environmental engineering (49 percent).

From these two tables, one may draw a number of conclusions. First, the level of acceptance for gene technology varied according to the area of application, and within each area, according to specific applications. For example, there was more support for genetically altering microorganisms for environmental cleanup than for improving their production performance. "Of course, the degree of risk perceived varies much with the applications" (Zechendorf, 1994, p. 873). This is consistent with survey results from other regions of the world and from other periods (Macer, 1994). Thus, in discussions on gene technology, one should avoid making generalizations about gene technology as if it were a uniform and indivisible whole.

The second conclusion from these two tables is that there was a general decrease in support as the areas of application affected more complex life forms. For example, moving from microorganisms to plants and then to animals, there was a decrease in the percentage of people in the EC who considered these areas of research worthwhile—from 87 percent for microorganisms in environmental engineering to 74 percent for plants to

Table 2.3 Summary of Different Areas of Gene Technology Applications
Perceived as Risky (1991)

Areas of Research and Application	Agree	Disagree	Don't Know or No Answer
Microorganisms altered to improve performance for making traditional or new products	54	29	18
Microorganisms altered for environmental engineering	49	34	17
Plants altered for resistance to biological attackers or nonbiological stress	57	28	16
Farm animals altered to improve disease resistance or quality of meat and milk	68	19	14
Food improved using gene technology	62	24	15
Medicine (for human health) produced using gene technology	48	36	16
Human body or tissues altered for medical purposes	58	25	17

Based on Eurobarometer 35.1 (Marlier, 1992, p. 83). Figures are percentages
(rounded off to the nearest whole number—totals do not necessarily add up to 100).

42 percent for farm animals. In Japan, 73 percent found the genetic alteration of microorganisms to be acceptable (Zechendorf, 1994). Surveys in
other countries showed a similar ranking: "In Japan, New Zealand and the
USA, genetic manipulation of plants was most acceptable, with genetic
manipulation of microbes next, then animals and human cell genetic manipulation was least acceptable" (Macer, 1994).

There is an important exception to this gradation from simple to complex organisms—at least in the EC results. Although human beings may be
considered a "higher," or more complex, life form than farm animals, the
Eurobarometer results showed considerable support (74 percent) for the
genetic alteration of the human body for medical purposes. In contrast, there
was considerable resistance to genetically altering farm animals: 48 percent disagreed (42 percent agreed) that this kind of research is worthwhile,
and 68 percent agreed (19 percent disagreed) that there is a risk to health
and environment. This was one of the lowest levels of acceptance of any area
of gene technology. One may speculate that most people are likely to reject
the genetic alteration of food—a basic human need. This rejection can be
seen in the responses to questions about it: 58 percent agreed that it is
worthwhile (one of the lowest levels of support to a gene technology appli-

cation), and 62 percent thought that there are risks to human health or the environment.

This supposition seems to be confirmed by findings from other countries. In 1989 a science magazine in Japan received three hundred responses to a survey of its readers. Because participants had not been randomly selected from the population, the responses may not be an accurate reflection of what the general public in Japan thinks. However, the results are still interesting: "39.5 per cent would not accept vegetables from cell culture, 33.3 per cent say 'no' to genetically altered wine, and 73 per cent reject transgenic fish" (Zechendorf, 1994, p. 875). It is also worth noting that the rejection of transgenic fish was higher than the rejection of genetically altered wine or vegetables. This finding is again consistent with findings in the EC, where more respondents reject the genetic alteration of farm animals than any other area.

There may be another possible reason for the high resistance to genetically altered farm animals. Again, acceptance seems more likely when it is a question of necessity rather than desirability. Thus, there tends to be more support for an application when its aim is to correct a negative situation than when it intends to improve something that is perceived to be already positive. Hence, altering human tissues to cure diseases seems to be more acceptable than altering farm animals to improve disease resistance or the quality of meat and milk.

It might have been revealing if the survey had made a distinction between altering farm animals for disease resistance and altering them to produce better quality meat and milk. Following the current line of thought, one would expect at least slightly greater support for improving disease resistance. The criterion of necessity or desirability would also explain the relatively high acceptance for the alteration of human tissues for medical purposes. The same logic may also partly explain the general acceptance of somatic-cell therapy in humans and the resistance to germ-line therapy. (It is a necessity to cure a sick person; but it is not strictly necessary to "interfere" with the future—especially when the consequences are unforeseeable.) The same difference can be seen in attitudes toward the use of gene technology for producing food (58 percent agreed this is worthwhile) and medicine for human use (88 percent). Although both are for human consumption, curing a disease (correcting a negative situation) was seen as being more of a necessity than enhancing the quality of food (improving positive traits). It is important to remember that the Eurobarometer surveys were done in Europe, a region where hunger or famine is not a problem for the majority of those surveyed.

The third conclusion from the two tables is that there is a strong correlation between acceptance and the perception of risks. Although most Europeans were supportive of different kinds of gene technology applications, even more associated these applications with risks to people and the environment. "The perception of any kind of risk (real or imaginary) related to biotechnology is a crucial point in biopolls, because the degree of risk perceived heavily influences the acceptance" (Zechendorf, 1994, p. 873). Despite the overwhelming support (87 percent) for genetically altering microorganisms for environmental engineering, nearly half the respondents (49 percent) agreed that this application might involve risks to human health or the environment. Significantly, only 34 percent disagreed. These results are very similar to those for gene technology used for the production of medicine. However, "several polls show that even when people assume high risks, they don't necessarily reject biotechnology/genetic engineering altogether" (Zechendorf, 1994, p. 873). These results are similar to those found elsewhere. For example, in Japan, 59 percent those surveyed expressed concern about genetically altered microorganisms; yet, 73 percent said that the application of gene technology to microorganisms is acceptable (Zechendorf, 1994).

From all these data, one may conclude that for discussions on gene technology to be focused, they have to take into consideration different aspects of the issue. Generalization and simplification should be avoided. For example, one may say that applications of gene technology are more likely to be accepted the less directly they affect human beings. But it would be necessary to add that other factors appear to modify that conclusion, for example, when the application is perceived to have a remedial effect (that is, to turn a negative situation into a positive one).

Although the Eurobarometer surveys are important, they (like all surveys) have their limitations. First, they did not treat the different areas of gene technology to the same depth in the 1991 and 1996 surveys: a distinction was made for applications relating to microorganisms but not for applications relating to plants, animals, or human beings. Because the surveys show different responses to two different applications to microorganisms, there may be similar differences between specific applications *within* other areas as well. For example, the 1991 and 1996 surveys raised questions about farm animals but not about animals as disease models. Not only is disease an important area of gene technology research, but the results may show interesting and possibly significant differences in attitudes.* Furthermore, questions relating to new medicine produced using gene technology did not distinguish between use of microbes and use of farm animals (that is, gene pharming). If the distinction had been made, there might have been an interesting point of comparison for the different uses of microorganisms and farm animals. The Eurobarometer studies consequently offer only a partial picture.

---

*The 1996 study did, in fact, raise a question about the use of genetically altered animals as research models, with 58 percent of respondents agreeing that "this application benefits society" (Eurobarometer 46.1, 1996, p. 31). However, the 1996 suvy did not repeat the question on farm animals. So the basis for comparison remains limited.

A second limitation is that the Eurobarometer surveys dealt only with EC/EU countries at particular points in time. The surveys showed significant differences in responses in different countries and cultures. One should therefore exercise caution in making inferences to other geographical or cultural areas, especially outside of the EC/EU. As different authors (Cantley, 1995; Marlier, 1992; Zechendorf, 1994) emphasize, perceptions of risk in relation to different areas of application and the degree of concern expressed vary from country to country and from culture to culture. Nevertheless, these variations are consistent with findings from other surveys from different countries, regions, and time frames. For example, the first ever national opinion survey on biotechnology and gene technology was commissioned by the U.S. Office of Technology Assessment (OTA)—completed between 1986 and 1987. Commenting on the results of this survey, M. F. Cantley writes: "The OTA study foreshadowed similarly divided views in other countries and times. The relative rankings, e.g., of different applications, are very similar from country to country, although the numbers vary enormously between countries" (1995, p. 660).

There is a danger in interpreting any survey outside its temporal or geographical contexts. For example, there may be lurking variables (that is, hidden factors) that have a significant impact on responses in various countries or regions. In the Eurobarometer studies, one may reasonably ask if there is a correlation between the issue of farm subsidies in Europe (resulting in overproduction) and the degree of support for applications of gene technology that would enhance production of meat and milk. Such factors are important in interpreting the results of such surveys. These caveats notwithstanding, the Eurobarometer surveys show that different areas and purposes of applications of gene technology enjoy different degrees of support and the perception of risk varies also according to the area and purpose of the application.

KEY POINTS
- Broadly defined, *biotechnology* refers to the use of living organisms for human purposes and deliberate human intervention in the process of natural selection. In a narrower sense, the term refers to the modification of microorganisms and cells for use in production.

- *Gene technology*, as a part of biotechnology, may be defined as the use of molecular biology and other scientific disciplines in the selection and improvement of genetic characteristics for research, industrial, agricultural, environmental, or medical purposes. It involves the isolation, characterization, and recombination of genetic material, as well as the insertion of this material into new living cells.

- Modern biotechnology, especially gene technology, developed in response to existing needs. It is the result of increasing sophistication in the search for technological solutions to existing problems.

- The ability to direct genetic changes at the molecular level marks the shift from traditional biotechnology to gene technology. Whereas traditional breeding methods rely on crossing offspring with observable traits, gene technology allows greater precision than ever before in the selection and breeding process.

- Gene technology is not limited to any particular field but may be applied to a wide range of areas. These include environmental engineering, agriculture, and medicine.

- Surveys in the EC/EU and elsewhere strongly suggest that people's support for gene technology and their perception of the associated risks vary according to the applications in question.

- Survey results also seem to point to a correlation between support for applications and the complexity of the organisms involved. There is low support, however, for research involving food destined for human consumption. There also seems to be a correlation between the degree of support for a particular application and the risk associated with it.

REFERENCES

Annas, G. J. 1994. Rules for Gene Banks: Protecting Privacy in the Genetics Age. In *Justice and the Human Genome Project*, edited by T. F. Murphy and M. A. Lappé, pp. 75–90. Berkeley: University of California Press.

———. 1992. Setting Standards for the Use of DNA-Typing Results in the Courtroom—The State of the Art. *New England Journal of Medicine* 326: 1641–1644.

Arntzen, C. J. 1991. Plant Agriculture. In *The Genetic Revolution: Scientific Prospects and Public Perceptions*, edited by B. D. Davis, pp. 105–117. Baltimore: Johns Hopkins University Press.

Bartels, D. 1992. Streß bei Pflanzen unter besonderer Berücksichtigung des osmotischen Stresses. In *Pflanzenproduktion und Biotechnologie*, edited by W. Schuchter and C. Meyer, pp. 161–173. Cologne: Max-Planck-Institut für Züchtungsforschung.

Bayertz, K. 1994. *GenEthics*, translated by Sarah L. Kirkby. Cambridge: Press Syndicate of the University of Cambridge.

Best, D. J. 1985. Chemistry and Biotechnology. In *Biotechnology: Principles and Applications*, edited by, I. J. Higgins, D. J. Best, and J. Jones, pp. 111–162. Oxford: Blackwell Scientific Publications.

Best, D. J., J. Jones., and D. Stafford. 1985. The Environment and Biotechnology. In *Biotechnology: Principles and Applications*, edited by I. J. Higgins, D. J. Best, and J. Jones, pp. 213–256. Oxford: Blackwell Scientific Publications.

British Medical Association. 1992. *Our Genetic Future: The Science and Ethics of Genetic Technology.* Oxford: Oxford University Press.

Bodmer, W., and L. Evans. 1991. HUGO's There! *Science and Public Affairs,* autumn, pp. 35–38.

Brierly, C. L., D. P. Kelly, K. J Seal, and D. J. Best. 1985. Materials and Biotechnology. In *Biotechnology: Principles and Applications,* edited by I. J. Higgins, D. J. Best, and J. Jones, pp. 163–212. Oxford: Blackwell Scientific Publications.

Bu'Lock, J. D. 1987. Introduction to Basic Biotechnology. In *Basic Biotechnology*, edited by J. Bu'Lock and B. Kristiansen, pp.3–10. London: Academic Press.

Butler, D. 1995. France Takes Control of Genome Programme. *Nature* 373: 650.

Campbell, A. 1991. The Laboratory and the Field. In *The Genetic Revolution: Scientific Perspectives and Public Perceptions,* edited by B. D. Davis. Baltimore: Johns Hopkins University Press.

Cantley, M. F. 1995. The Regulation of Modern Biotechnology: A Historical and European Perspective. In *Legal, Economic, and Ethical Dimensions,* edited by D. Brauer, vol. 12, pp. 505–691. Weinheim, Germany: VCH Verlags Gesellschaft mbH.

Coghlan, A. 1994. Will the Scorpion Gene Run Wild? *New Scientist,* 24 June, pp. 14–15.

Cooper, N. G., Ed. 1994. *The Human Genome Project.* Mill Valley, Calif.: University Science Books.

Corbett, K. 1987. Production of Antibiotics. In *Basic Biotechnology*, edited by J. Bu'Lock and B. Kristiansen. pp. 425–448. London: Academic Press.

Davis, B. D. 1991a. From Classical to Molecular Genetics. In *The Genetic Revolution: Scientific Prospects and Public Perceptions*, edited by B. D. Davis, pp. 9–27. Baltimore: Johns Hopkins University Press.

————. 1991b. Summary and Comments: The Scientific Chapters. In *The Genetic Revolution: Scientific Prospects and Public Perceptions*, edited by B. D. Davis, pp. 239–265. Baltimore: Johns Hopkins University Press.

Doggett, N. A. 1994. The Polymerase Chain Reaction and Sequence-Tagged Sites. In *The Human Genome Project*, edited by N. G. Cooper, pp. 128–134. Mill Valley Calif.: University Science Books.

Eberhard-Metzger, C. 1995. Der Club der toten Spender. *Bild der Wissenschaft* 4: 26–31.

Elmer-Dewitt, P. 1994. The Genetic Revolution. *Time,* 17 January, pp. 32–39.

European Commission (Directorate General XII—Science, Research and Development, Biotechnology). 1996. Eurobarometer 46.1: European Opinions on Modern Biotechnology. Brussels: European Commission.

Fletcher, D. 1994. Donor Pigs Could Supply Transplant Organs by 1996. *Daily Telegraph,* 30 March, p. 5.

Food and Agriculture Organization/World Health Organization. 1991. *Strategies for Assessing the Safety of Foods Produced by Biotechnology: Report of a Joint FAO/WHO Consultation.* Geneva: World Health Organization.

Frey, M. 1992. Genübertragung. In *Pflanzenproduktion und Biotechnologie,* edited by W. Schuchert and C. Meyer, pp. 103–114. Cologne: Max-Planck-Institut für Züchtunsforschung.

Friedman, G., and R. Reichelt. 1994. ELSI: Ethical, Legal and Social Implications. In *The Human Genome Project: Deciphering the Blueprint of Heredity,* edited by N. G. Cooper, pp. 302–313. Mill Valley, Calif.: University Science Books.

Friedmann, T. 1991. Molecular Medicine. In *The Genetic Revolution: Scientific Prospects and Public Perceptions,* edited by B. Davis, pp. 132–151. Baltimore: Johns Hopkins University Press.

Geldermann, H., and H. Momm. 1995. Biotechnologie als Grundlage neuer Verfahren in der Tierzucht. In *Biotechnologie Gentechnik: Eine Chance für neue Industrien,* edited by T. v. Schell and H. Mohr, pp. 244–287. Berlin: Springer-Verlag.

Hall, D. O., J. Coombs, and I. J. Higgins. 1985. Energy and Biotechnology. In *Biotechnology: Principles and Applications,* edited by I. J. Higgins, D. J. Best, and J. Jones, pp. 24–72. Oxford: Blackwell Scientific Publications.

Hardy, K. G., and S. G. Oliver. 1985. Genetics and Biotechnology. In *Biotechnology: Principles and Applications,* edited by I. J. Higgins, D. J. Best, and J. Jones, pp. 257–282. Oxford: Blackwell Scientific Publications.

Helmy, M. M., and W. Siefer. 1994. Pillen vom Bauernhof. *Focus*, May, pp. 160–162.

Higgins, I. J. 1985. What Is Biotechnology? In *Biotechnology: Principles and Applications* edited by I. J. Higgins, D. J. Best, and J. Jones, pp. 1–23. Oxford: Blackwell Scientific Publications.

Hobbelink, H. 1991. *Biotechnology and the Future of World Agriculture*. London: Zed Books.

Human Genome Organization. 1995. The Human Genome Organisation (HUGO). Human Genome Organization Europe.

James, A. 1993. Transplants with Tansgenic Pig Organs? *Lancet*, 3 July, p.45.

Kahn, P. 1993. Genome on the Production Line. *New Scientist*, 24 April, pp. 32–36.

———. 1994. Genetic Diversity Project Tries Again. *Science* 266: 720–722.

Kevles, D. J. 1994. Eugenics and the Human Genome Project: Is the Past Prologue? In *Justice and the Human Genome Project*, edited by T. F. Murphy and M. A. Lappé, pp. 14–29. Berkeley: University of California Press.

———. 1985. *In the Name of Eugenics: Genetics and the Uses of Human Heredity*. Berkeley: University of California Press.

Knight, B. E. A., and R. White. 1994. *Transgenic Crops*. Richmond, England: PJB Publications.

Krimsky, S. 1991. *Biotechnics and Society*. New York: Praeger.

Lee, T. F. 1991. *The Human Genome Project: Cracking the Genetic Code of Life*. New York: Plenum Press.

Loew, F. M. 1991. Animal Agriculture. In T*he Genetic Revolution: Scientific Prospects and Public Perceptions,* edited by B. D. Davis, pp. 118–131. Baltimore: Johns Hopkins University Press.

Logemann, J. 1992. Genetische Erzeugung von herbizidresistenten Pflazen. In *Pflanzenproduktion und Biotechnologie,* edited by W. Schuchert and C. Meyer, pp. 175–180. Cologne: Max-Planck-Institut für Züchtungsforschung.

Macer, D. R. J. 1994. Perception of Risks and Benefits of In Vitro Fertilization, Genetic Engineering, and Biotechnology. *Social Science and Medicine* 38 (1): 23–33.

Marlier, E. 1993. *Biotechnology and Genetic Engineering: What Europeans Think About It in 1993*. Survey Report Eurobarometer 39.1: The European Commission.

————. 1992. Eurobarometer 35.1—Opinions of Europeans on Biotechnology in 1991. In *Biotechnology in Public,* edited by J. Durant, pp. 52–108. London: Science Museum.

Mellon, M. 1991. An Environmentalist Perspective. In *The Genetic Revolution: Scientific Prospects and Public Perceptions,* edited by B. D. Davis, pp. 60–76. Baltimore: Johns Hopkins University Press.

Micklos, D. A., and G. A. Freyer. 1990. *DNA Science: A First Course in Recombinant DNA Technology.* Burlington, N.C.: Carolina Biological Supply Company.

Mieth, D. 1995. Ethische Evaluierung der Biotechnologie. In *Biotechnologie-Gentechnik: Eine Chance für neue Industrien,* edited by T. v. Schell and H. Mohr, pp. 505–557. Berlin: Springer-Verlag.

Miller, H. I. 1991. Regulation. In *The Genetic Revolution: Scientific Prospects and Public Perceptions,* edited by B. D. Davis, pp. 196–211. Baltimore: Johns Hopkins University Press.

Murphy, T. F., and M. A. Lappé, eds. 1994. *The Genome Project and the Meaning of Difference.* Berkeley: University of California Press.

Murray, J. C., K. H. Buetow, J. L. Weber, S. Ludwigsen, T. Scherpbier-Heddema, F. Manion, J. Quillen, V. C. Sheffield, S. Sunden, G. M. Duyk, J. Weissenbach, G. Gyapay, C. Dib, J. Morrissette, G. M. Lathrop, A. Vignal, R. White, N. Matsunami, S. Gerken, R. Melis, H. Albertsen, R. Plaetke, S. Odelberg, D. Ward, J. Dausset, D. Cohen, and H. Cann. 1994 A Comprehensive Linkage Map with Centimorgan Density. *Science* 65: 2049–2065.

Nieren aus dem Saustall. 1993. *Der Spiegel* 30 August, pp. 208–214.

Nowak, R. 1995. Getting the Bugs Worked Out. *Science* 267: 172–174.

Odenwald, M. 1995. Superreis gegen den Welthunger. *Focus,* 20 March, pp.152–161.

Organization for Economic Cooperation and Development. 1995. *The Global Human Genome Programme.* Paris: Organization for Economic Cooperation and Development.

————. 1988. *Recombinant DNA Safety Considerations—Safety Considerations for Industrial, Agricultural and Environmental Applications of Organisms Derived by Recombinant DNA Techniques.* Paris: Organization for Economic Cooperation and Development.

Paul, D. B., and H. G. Spencer. 1995. The Hidden Science of Eugenics. *Nature* 374: 302–304.

Pickup, J. C. 1985. Medicine and Biotechnology. In *Biotechnology: Principles and Applications,* edited by I. J. Higgins, D. J. Best, and J. Jones, pp. 283–304. Oxford: Blackwell Scientific Publications.

Plummer, E. 1995. Gene Therapy: Pipe Dream or Reality. *Scrip Magazine,* March, pp. 29–31.

Rohde, W. 1992. Induzierte Virusreistenz: Strategien gentechnologischer Veränderungen an Ertragspflanzen. In *Pflanzenproduktion und Biotechnologie,* edited by W. Schuchert and C. Meyer, pp. 129–134. Cologne: Max-Planck-Institut für Züchtungsforschung.

Ryser, S., and M. Weber. 1990. *Genetic Engineering: A Chronology.* Basle: Editiones Roche.

Schweizerische Gesellschaft für Chemische Industrie. 1989. *Biotechnologie: Eine Stellungnahme der Schweizerischen Chemischen Industrie.* Zurich: Schweizerische Gesellschaft für Chemische Industrie.

Skinner, F. A. 1985. Agriculture and Biotechnology. In *Biotechnology: Principles and Applications,* edited by I. J. Higgins, D. J. Best, and J. Jones, pp. 305–345. Oxford: Blackwell Scientific Publications.

Spier, R. E. 1987. Processes and Products Dependent on Cultured Animal Cells. In *Basic Biotechnology,* edited by J. Bu'Lock, pp. 509–524. London: Academic Press.

Spurgeon, D. 1995. Canada to Set Up Genome Research Centre in Toronto. *Nature* 373: 274.

Steinbiß, H.-H. 1992. Resistenz gegen Insekten. In *Pflanzenproduktion und Biotechnologie,* edited by W. Schuchert and C. Meyer, pp. 155–160. Cologne: Max-Planck-Institut für Züchtungsforschung.

Suzuki, D., and P. Knudtson. 1990. *Genethics: The Clash Between the New Genethics and Human Values.* Cambridge, Mass.: Harvard University Press.

Unternährer-Rosta, S., B. D. Carbonare, C. Manzoni, and S. Ryser. 1994. *Gentechnik: Worum geht es?* Basle: Editiones Roche.

U. S. Department of Health and Human Service. 1991. *The Human Genome Project: New Tools for Tomorrow's Health Research.* Washington D.C.: U.S. Department of Health and Human Services, National Center for Human Genome Research.

U.S. Office of Technological Assessment. 1989. *New Developments in Biotechnology: Patenting Life,* no. 5. Washington D.C.: U.S. Congress, Office of Technological Assessment.

Wagner, R. P. 1994. Understanding Inheritance: An Introduction to Classical and Molecular Genetics. In *The Human Genome Project: Deciphering the Blueprint of Heredity,* edited by N. G. Cooper, pp. 1–6. Mill Valley, Calif: University Science Books.

Watson, J. D. 1990. The Human Genome Project. *Science*, 248: 44–49.

Watson, J. D., M. Gilman, J. Witkowski, and M. Zoller. 1992. *Recombinant DNA*. 2d ed. New York: Scientific American Books.

White, D., and J. Wallwork, 1993. Xenografting: Probability, Possibility or Pipe Dream? *Lancet* 342 (8876): 879–880.

World Health Organization. 1982. Health Impact of Biotechnology: Report on a WHO Working Group, Dublin, 9-12 November 1982. *Swiss Biotech*, 2 (5): 7–32.

Zechendorf, B. 1994. What the Public Thinks About Biotechnology. *Bio/technology*, 12 September, pp. 870–875.

3 PATENTS AND GENE TECHNOLOGY

Much of the debate on gene technology focuses on the question of patenting. This chapter takes certain key patent cases in gene technology and shows how decisions in these cases influenced later considerations. The goal is to provide not a detailed legal discussion but quick sketches as context for the challenges facing patents of innovations arising from gene technology.

To understand the debate on the patenting of gene technology, it is important first to comprehend key concepts and principles of the patent system.

PATENTS

After a brief survey of the development of patents, this section discusses patent law in the twentieth century.

A HISTORICAL OVERVIEW

Patents for inventions were introduced in the fifteenth century Italian city-states as inventors' privileges. They became an instrument for promoting industrial development in England in 1623–1624 with the passing of the Statute of Monopolies (Beier and Straus, 1985). Further comprehensive laws dealing with patents did not appear until the end of the eighteenth century—in the infant United States of America (1790) and in the early days of republican France (1791). In both republics, patents were an expression of democratic action and the assertion of the rights of the individual, in particular, the natural right of the inventor to the exclusive right of his or her invention (Krimsky, 1991).

Most other countries introduced patent statutes toward the second half of the nineteenth century. F. K. Beier and J. Straus make the following observation, which one should remember when considering patent law in the context of modern technologies, especially biotechnology:

> In spite of all subsequent amendments, judicial developments and administrative refinements, our national patent laws, even those which have been harmonised and modernised recently, cannot conceal that many of their basic conceptions and principles are still determined by the state of science and technology prevailing at the time of the first industrial revolution. (Beier and Straus, 1985, pp. 18–19)

The Industrial Revolution of the nineteenth century gave rise to mechanical inventions. The biotechnological revolution of the twentieth century has given rise to biological (that is, self-reproductive) inventions. This difference has led to a "gap between the state of the art and the state of the law" (Beier and Straus, 1985, p. 15), which in turn has led to challenges to our concept of "invention" and to the very values of industrialized society.

PATENT LAW IN THE TWENTIETH CENTURY

Today, a patent of invention is a grant of exclusive rights either to make something or to exclude others from doing so for a limited period of time, generally about twenty years, although sometimes shorter.

An invention is a technical creation. It may be a product, a method, a conversion, an arrangement, or a task. To qualify for a patent, an invention must satisfy three criteria. Although these criteria are legally defined and may thus vary in specifics from jurisdiction to jurisdiction, they are generally the same key prerequisites in most countries with patent laws. The criteria are as follows:

- novelty, which ensures that patent protection is given to something that has not been done before

- nonobviousness, which encourages innovations that will advance the state of knowledge in a particular technology
- utility, which promotes inventions that have a practical application and will be of use to society

Not everything is patentable. The utility requirement thus excludes scientific discoveries from patent protection, because though interesting for further research, they have no practical applications for society. As will be seen later in this chapter, the utility criterion plays a decisive role in whether a patent is granted or withheld. Also excluded from patentability are scientific theories and mathematical methods; rules and methods for performing mental acts, playing games, or doing business; methods for diagnosis or treatment by surgery or therapy; plant or animal varieties as such; and essentially biological processes for the production of plants or animals (Beier and Straus, 1985).

An invention is a form of intellectual property and is the result of human endeavor. Because industrialized society considers such intellectual property to be essential, it has accorded the inventor an exclusive right to control and benefit from the commercialization of products resulting from the invention for a limited time. Based on this premise, the patent system promotes technical, economic, and social progress by the following means:

- rewarding inventors, thus stimulating inventive activity
- encouraging the disclosure of the subject matter so that knowledge is in the public domain
- offering an incentive to produce the item
- offering incentives for disclosing and disseminating technical knowledge (Beier and Straus, 1985)

The exclusive right of the inventor is aimed at encouraging the inventor to manufacture the item and make it available for use, as the person is protected from competition within the period granted. As a by-product of the system, competition in inventions is introduced. Again, the utility criterion plays a vital role.

One important benefit of the patent system is that it places knowledge in public hands. In a way, the patent system is a kind of barter arrangement between the inventor and society. The inventor produces something of use, value, and interest to society. Society grants the inventor a limited monopoly on the benefits arising from the invention. In exchange, the inventor reveals the "secrets" of the invention, so that others may be able to gain new knowledge and reproduce the invention or improve on it. This disclosure serves three purposes:

- preventing the inadvertent infringement of the patent during the period granted
- placing the inventor's secret in public hands when the patent expires
- preventing patents from being given for known inventions (Beier and Straus, 1985)

The patent system ensures disclosure through two requirements. When applying for a patent, the inventor must make a detailed description of the invention and deposit a sample in a publicly accessible location (for example, the patent office or an official depository). The disclosure must be such that those "skilled in the art" could reproduce the invention. As the next section shows, both requirements, especially the deposit, pose special problems for innovations in biotechnology.

Although a patent grants an inventor the right to exclude others from making, selling, or using the invention, a patent does not grant that person the right to make, sell, or use the invention. This distinction is important. Although an inventor may receive a patent for a particular innovation, the invention must still satisfy the law of the land governing its use, sale, or production. For example, a patent for a new drug may allow a company the right to exclude competitors from making it, but the company must still satisfy national or international legislation governing the testing, production, distribution, and use of that drug.

The time-limited monopoly, as noted above, is usually for twenty years. In some countries, this period may be shorter. For example, in the United States, a patent was traditionally valid for seventeen years from the date of issue. In December 1994, new legislation brought the United States in line with international practice: patents are now valid for twenty years as of the date of application (Browning, 1994). This limited monopoly is the inventor's reward.

It is important to make two observations about this monopoly. First, the exclusive protection of the invention does not include academic research purposes (Adler, 1992); this exclusion is in keeping with the principle of patents advancing the state of technology. Second, if abused, the monopoly can be curbed through various measures, such as compulsory licensing. If the patent holder has not produced anything after a certain period, the patent office or a court may force him or her to grant a licence to a third party who is able to produce the invention. Several countries have provisos in their patent legislation for compulsory licensing in the area of medicine. Thus, as with any system, the patent system can be subject to abuses, but there are legal mechanisms to discourage, prevent and, if necessary, punish them.

Several categories of patents are available. The following sections will concentrate on utility patents, which cover processes, machines, articles of manufacture, and compositions of matter. A subcategory of utility patents is the process patent, which covers the steps for applying a particular method. In other words, an inventor may apply for a patent for a process, a product (resulting from the new process), or both (Gregory, Saber, and Grossman, 1994). For example, someone invents a method of recycling using genetically altered microorganisms. The inventor could patent the process of changing the organisms, the organisms themselves, the method of recycling, and even the final recycled product. It could be advantageous to obtain patent protection for processes using biological material to make end products, especially if the products themselves are not patentable.

PATENTING OF LIFE FORMS

The debate on the patentability of life forms is not recent. In 1873 Louis Pasteur received a U.S. grant for a patent for purified yeast as part of a manufacturing process. Courts in the United States, however, later rejected the grant on the basis that such yeast is the "handiwork of Nature" (EFB, 1993; Krimsky, 1991).

The Plant Patent Act of 1930 was the first time legislation was passed for patenting living matter.

> In the 1920s plant breeders sought the same opportunity to reap the benefits of the patent system as those innovators in mechanical arts. Congress responded by passing the Plant Patent Act of 1930 and thereby removed the distinction between plant developers and industrial inventors. . . . As a sign of the public support or indifference, the 1930 Plant Patent Act was passed within three months of the time the bills were first introduced. (Krimsky, 1991, p. 46)

As Krimsky points out, the Plant Variety Protection Act "made possible the patenting of major food crops" (Krimsky, 1991, p. 46). It must be made clear, however, that the Plant Patent Act and the Plant Variety Protection Act (1970) in the United States were enacted in the context of traditional breeding methods. It was only in the early 1980s that patenting in the context of gene technology became the focus of public debate.

In Europe, patent law was originally not considered suitable for new plant varieties developed through traditional methods. Instead, in the 1960s, special laws were enacted in some countries; and in 1961, the Union for the Protection of New Varieties of Plant (UPOV) was formed to protect plant-variety rights (PVR). To avoid legal confusion, plant varieties were subsequently excluded from patentability in Europe. "However, it is now generally recognised that patent law is better suited to the protection of recombinant methods for producing transgenic plants and the resulting products" (EFB, 1993, p. 2). Patents are now granted for methods and products in this area.

Because patenting in biotechnology deals with life, which is constantly evolving, it poses special challenges to laws created during the Industrial Revolution. One special problem is the requirement to deposit a sample. *"Biotechnology presents a unique administrative issue in that it is the only art known where words alone may be incapable of describing an invention*

sufficiently to enable one skilled in the art to make and use it in a repro-
ducible manner" (US OTA, 1989, p. 18, italics in the original). It is thus useful to support the written description with a deposit.

The practical question is: How does one deposit a living being? Till now,
one solution has been the use of a culture depository.

> A culture depository accepts, maintains and distributes cultures of
> micro-organisms, viruses, cells or other genetic-type material. A
> depository may be public or private; non-profit or for-profit. The
> main function of a public culture depository is the preservation and
> distribution of reference cultures that serve as standards for users in
> the scientific and educational communities. (US OTA, 1989, p. 141)

The patentability of animals having been established in the United States,
attention is now focused on animal deposits. The deposit requirement for
the first patented transgenic animal was fulfilled with the deposit of the
genes intended for transfer into the animal (US OTA, 1989).

As the OTA in the United States points out, however, there could be problems if deposit of animals is required. Costs of facilities and expert staff for
maintaining an animal depository would be too high to make the idea feasible. A depository could not provide samples without growing more animals,
which raises other problems, such as maintaining progeny and disposing of
animals no longer needed. It would not be practical to maintain an animal
deposit for the current required period of thirty years, since most animals
have shorter life spans. One practical solution has been the deposit of animal
embryos that are frozen for later recovery (US OTA, 1989).

This section has provided an overview of the broad debate on the
patentability of life forms and the attendant problems. The following sections deal more specifically with patents for various levels of life forms.

MICROORGANISMS

The U.S. Congress did not initially pass legislation for patenting single-celled
organisms, only for their role in a process. In 1980 the U.S. Supreme Court
set a precedent for patenting living things (Krimsky, 1991). Ananda
Chakrabarty, working for the General Electric Company (GEC), developed
a bacterium that would break down crude oil. His patent made claims in
three key areas: 1) on the process of making the microbe, 2) on the method
of dispersal, and 3) on the organism itself. The U.S. Patent and Trademark
Office (PTO) accepted only the first two claims. It denied the third claim—on
the bacterium itself—on the grounds that microorganisms are the products
of nature and, as living things, are not patentable. The PTO Board of Appeals
overturned the first decision, arguing that this particular bacterium did not
occur in nature and therefore qualified as human invention. It accepted the
second decision (namely, that living things are not patentable). However, the

Court of Customs and Patent Appeals, the next highest level, decided that "the living status of an entity is not grounds to exclude a patent claim" (Krimsky, 1991, p. 48).

The case (*Diamond* vs. *Chakrabarty*, #206USPQ 193) was finally appealed to the Supreme Court. In a five-to-four decision (16 June 1980), a patent was awarded for the bacterium. Writing for the majority, Chief Justice Warren Burger said that the issue was not whether the entity was living or dead but whether the entity was a product of nature or of human invention (EFB, 1993; Krimsky, 1991).

This case had three important outcomes:

1. It was a precedent-setting grant of patent for a microorganism as such (regardless of how it was used). Previous grants in this area had always been for the organism as part of patents granted for a process.

2. It set a precedent by defining the all-important criterion for patentability as "human invention." It paved the way for patents for higher life forms of human invention.

3. It set a precedent for the patenting of all genetically modified life forms (except humans). In 1987 the PTO issued a policy statement based on this case stating that the office considers all "non-naturally occurring non-human multicellular living organisms, including animals, to be patentable subject matter" (Krimsky, 1991, p. 48; US OTA, 1989)

There are two important footnotes to the case. First, although GEC finally won, the company never developed or marketed the oil-degrading bacterium. Although GEC never publicly explained why, Krimsky proposed three plausible explanations. The first reason is technical: although the bacteria were able to do their job efficiently in controlled laboratory settings, they might not be efficient in large-scale cleanups. The second explanation is that it might not have been financially viable to develop and market the bacteria. After all, oil spills from offshore drilling had decreased as a result of a drop in world oil prices and better drilling practices. The third explanation is that the company feared too much public resistance. This was a period when liability insurance for deliberate release was not certain and there was no regulation for such releases (Krimsky, 1991).

The second footnote is that the case went through without public outcry. Indeed, ironically, at the end of the 1980s, the *Exxon Valdez* spill in Prince William Sound, an ecologically diverse area, sparked interest in microbial cleanups of oil spills and leaks. As Krimsky points out, with tens of thousands of chemical sites around the world, there could well be market interest in microorganisms genetically modified for cleaning sites. For a summary of objections and responses, see Table 3.1 (p.116).

Table 3.1 Summary of Arguments Against and For Patenting
Microorganisms

Objection	Reply
Microorganisms are products of nature. Life forms made by rearranging genetic material and modifying the life forms do not qualify as products of manufacture.	The bacterium does not exist in nature in this form and therefore is of human invention. Argument was upheld in three higher-level appeals after initial rejection.
Living things as such do not qualify for patents because they are not human invention.	Living things can qualify for patents if they do not exist as such in nature. Argument was upheld in three higher-level appeals after initial rejection.
Decisions for patentability should be based on the criterion of living or non-living.	The living status of an invention is not grounds for rejection. Argument was upheld in two higher-level appeals after rejection at two lower levels.

PLANTS

Four scientists in the United States—Timothy Hall, John Kemp, Jerry Slightom, and Dennis Sutton—developed a method for modifying a plant cell with foreign plant genes using a bacterial vector. The result was a plant with certain desired characteristics of another plant—for example, higher protein or lectin content; tolerance to environmental factors; specific flavors; or resistance to pest, disease, or herbicide.

In April 1983 Lubrizol Genetics Inc. filed a patent application with the PTO in the United States, which eventually granted a patent. A year later, Lubrizol applied for a patent with the European Patent Office (EPO). The claims were for the vector, the bacterial strains containing the vector, methods for modifying the plant cell, the plant cell itself, and the resulting plant tissue or plant as a whole. Five years later, in March 1989, the EPO granted a patent (EP-B-01-22791).

The Opposition Division of the EPO subsequently received notice of opposition from eleven parties ranging from opponents of gene technology to multinational corporations. The grounds of opposition were as follows:

• insufficient disclosure
• lack of inventive step

- an exception of patentability because the invention went against morality or public order
- the exclusion from patentability of plant varieties and essentially biological processes
- lack of novelty

In June 1992, three years after the opposition was filed, the EPO Opposition Division rendered its decision (Interlocutory Decision against EP-B-0122791). Regarding insufficient disclosure, the opposition alleged that the term *bacteria* was too broad, possibly including unsuitable strains. The Opposition Division judged that this objection was irrelevant. What was important was that suitable strains were known to one skilled in the art. Another protest was that in certain cases, the expression of a desired gene was not obtained and that there was no known reason for it, hence constituting insufficient disclosure. On examining the arguments, the EPO ruled that the only evidence the opposition had provided was that trial and error might be necessary for success in this technical field. It was also clear that the invention taught for the first time the use of plant promoters for regulating a plant gene in another plant. It was equally clear that a skilled person could apply the new knowledge not only to examples provided but to other areas as well.

The opposition said the application did not meet the criterion of inventiveness but was merely a discovery. They requested a revocation of the patent for Lubrizol's claims on the vector, the method for genetically altering the plant cell, the plant cell itself, and the resulting plant or plant tissue.

The EPO ruled in favor of Lubrizol's claims, based on the following line of reasoning. According to existing EPO guidelines, finding the property of a known material constitutes a discovery, as is finding a freely occurring substance in nature. However, if a substance found in nature has to be isolated first and has no previously recognized existence in this isolated form, it qualifies as a patentable invention. In the Lubrizol case, to obtain what was claimed, technical intervention was necessary on at least three levels: alteration of the DNA sequences themselves, of the plant cell, and of the plant. Further, the resulting plants, plant tissues, and plant cells did not occur in this form in nature. The naturally occurring plant did not have the particular combination of genes as claimed.

According to Article 53(a) of the European Patent Convention (EPC), the statute creating the EPO and governing patent matters in most countries in Europe, no patents would be granted for inventions whose exploitation would be contrary to public order or morality. It was this article that some opposition members invoked against the Lubrizol patent. They argued specifically that the patent was in violation of a resolution by the Food and Agricultural Organization of the United Nations (FAO) that plant genetic resources as a common heritage of humankind should be freely available for use. Further, since most of these resources come from developing countries, the patenting of plant genetic resources failed to recognize or reward the farmers in these countries and was contrary to the FAO resolution. Finally, patenting of plants would lead to a decrease in the number of existing plant varieties and the loss of plant genes.

In its rulings, the EPO reiterated certain principles of patent law. A patent does not give its holder the right to use the invention but only the right to exclude others from doing so during a limited period. The patent system is intended to promote research and technical advancement; it is not intended to suppress research that is dangerous or unacceptable to certain groups for whatever reason. If legislators think that certain technical knowledge should be restricted to particular conditions, it is up to them to enact the appropriate legislation outside the framework of patent law. "Patent law would be rather unsuitable for this as such legislation always would have to take into account the most recent state of the art in a particular technology and thus would have to be changed quite frequently" (EPO, 1992, p. 13). Finally, the article cited set the condition for withholding patents: the exploitation of *the invention* must be immoral, *not* the exploitation of the *rights gained through a patent.*

The EPO responded to the specific points before coming to the general ruling on the morality of the patent. First, the patent was not in violation of the FAO resolution. To qualify as the common heritage of humankind, these genetic resources would have to have been known to the public; otherwise they would not be *common* heritage. Since patentable subject matter must always be new, it follows that no valid patents could exist on the common heritage of humankind. In the Lubrizol case, there was a new (previously unknown) combination of genes created through human intervention.

Second, farmers in developing countries are not directly affected by patents in member countries of the EPC, as these patents do not extend to their countries. Furthermore, the question of compensation to such farmers lies outside the scope of patent law.

Third, patenting for plants cannot be blamed for genetic erosion. Indeed, patents are an incentive for inventions, which in the area of plant biology would normally create new combinations of genes. Thus, contrary to the arguments from the opposition, patenting would only increase the amount of genetic combinations in the plant world. Nevertheless, it is possible that improved varieties would lead to fewer varieties being used in agriculture. This outcome, however, would be the result of improvements per se, whether through genetic alteration or conventional breeding methods— *regardless* of whether there was patent protection or not. Thus, on the question of morality, the EPO ruled that the exploitation of this patent could not be considered immoral or against public order. As a matter of fact, the invention could lead to new plants with better nutritive value and better management of food shortage in the world.

Fourth, on the nonpatentability of plant varieties and essentially biolog-ical processes, the EPO ruled as follows. The nonpatentability of plant vari-eties under the EPC was to prevent double protection for plants, which are also covered in most countries of Europe under UPOV (see "Patenting of Life Forms," above). Plant varieties under the protection of UPOV cannot be patented; but those not protected through UPOV do qualify for patentability. Moreover, the process patented is a technical process in plant molecular biology, which requires human intervention. Thus, it is not an essentially biological process.

Fifth, on the final point of contention (regarding novelty), the EPC did reject some of Lubrizol's initial claims. Documents from a conference showed that a vector such as Lubrizol claimed in its patent application was previously known. Thus, the novelty claim for the vector failed.

In conclusion, the EPO upheld the patent granted to Lubrizol, with mod-ifications based on the rejection of the novelty claims for the shuttle vector. For a summary of the objections and responses, see Table 3.2 (p.120).

Two aspects of the Lubrizol case deserve further comment. First, the EPO ruling on the Harvard onco-mouse (see "Animals," below) predated the rul-ing on the Lubrizol case by about two months. The EPO thus took into account the considerations of the ruling in the Harvard case on morality and the patenting of higher life forms. The EPO noted: "Although this guidance is not directly applicable to the patenting of plants, it nevertheless can be taken into consideration when it comes to the patenting of higher life forms such as plants" (EPO, 1992, p. 15). In the Harvard case, the EPO indicated that in decisions regarding higher life forms (specifically, the mouse), there must be a weighing of the merits and advantages of the invention on the one side against the risks and detrimental effects on the other side. Also there has to be a balance in favor of the interests of humankind, the protection of the environment, and the impact on the life form itself.

Second, the Lubrizol case was significant in its own right because it clar-ified and reiterated two points of European law. One was that plants and other life forms are patentable as long as they satisfy the three criteria of patent law. The other was that two forms of legal protection exist for plant innovations. If a plant breeder claims protection under one form for a new plant, he or she cannot claim simultaneous protection under the second form.

ANIMALS
In 1985 Philip Leder and Timothy Stewart, two scientists at Harvard Uni-versity, inserted a human cancer gene into the egg cells of a mouse. The result was mice that easily developed cancer: nearly half of all the female off-spring developed breast cancer within ten months of birth. This character-istic made the mouse a more valuable candidate than its nongenetically modified relatives in the search for a cure for cancer. An application for a patent was filed in both the United States and Europe.

Table 3.2 Summary of Arguments Against and For Patenting Plants

Objection	Reply
The claims on the bacteria lack sufficient disclosure because the term *bacteria* was too broad; there could be unknown strains that might not be appropriate.	It is sufficient to specify the appropriate strains, as was done in this case.
The claims—on the vector, the method for genetically altering the vector, and the resulting plant and its parts—lack the inventive step. Hence, they only constitute a discovery of what occurs freely in nature.	When a matter occurring in nature first has to be isolated and there is no previous knowledge of it existing in this purified form, then it is an invention. The matter being patented is an invention because it involves technical intervention in both method and results.
The subject matter goes against morals: plant genes as common heritage of humankind cannot be patented; patents do not recognize developing countries as sources of genetic materials; patenting leads to genetic erosion.	The genetic combination of the plant is the result of technical intervention and was previously unknown to the public; so it is not common heritage. Patents granted in Europe do not extend outside Europe; compensation for developing countries does not lie in the jurisdiction of patent law. Patents themselves do not cause genetic erosion. Since the invention could lead to nutritionally superior plants, it is not against morals.
The claim on the vector lacks novelty, as the vector was previously known. Argument was upheld.	The information appeared in the write-up of a conference. Patent was maintained with modification.

In 1988 the PTO in the United States granted a patent for the mouse, the first patent issued in the world for a mammal. "Public reaction to the announcement of the patent was relatively mild. Criticism came primarily from animal rights groups, some environmentalists and farmer associations" (Krimsky, 1991, p. 44).

In 1989 the Examining Division of the EPO rejected the application on two counts: first, because the EPC did not permit the patenting of animals per se and second, because there was insufficiency of disclosure (EPO, 1992). Harvard University appealed the case to the EPO Technical Board of Appeal, which, in 1991, requested the Examining Division to reconsider its decision. After studying the arguments of the Board of Appeal, the EPO Examining Division granted a patent in 1992. Antivivisection and animal-rights groups have since appealed that decision (EFB, 1993).

The Harvard application was for a nonhuman mammal, a rodent. The EPC uses three official languages, all of which are equally legally binding. In none of the three languages are animals as such excluded from patenting. According to the text of the EPC, no patents are allowed for an *animal variety, race animale,* or *Tierart.* Although the French term *race animale* (a subgroup of a species) and the German term *Tierart* (species) are clear, the English term *animal varieties* is not. *Animal variety* is not a recognized category in biological classification.

Clearly then, if the EPO was to interpret these terms in a narrow sense, then neither rodents nor mammals fell under the category of *Tierart* or *race animale*: a patent could be granted. The question was how the term *animal variety* should be interpreted. If mammals and rodents did not fall under the term *animal variety,* then there should have been no obstacle to issuing a patent.

The Examining Division was thus asked to reexamine the application in this light. It was also asked to weigh carefully "the suffering inflicted on the animals and the possible risks to the environment . . . against the invention's usefulness to humanity" (EPO, 1992, p. 588). Under the EPC, a patent may be withheld if the invention is deemed contrary to public order or morality. The harm posed to the animal itself and the environment could be sufficient moral ground for rejection. Now, the question was whether the potential good outweighed the possible harm.

In granting the patent in 1992, the Examining Division made a statement outlining its reasons for issuing a patent. It noted that though the term *animal varieties* is vague, it is clear that it is not a higher taxonomic classification than either *rodent* or *mammal.* This being true and there being no obstacle to patents on animals as such, a patent could be issued.

The Examining Division took into account the following factors. First, there is a basic human need to control or eradicate dread diseases. Cancer being a frequent cause of suffering and death, the contribution of the Harvard invention to developing new anticancer treatments and reducing human suffering could not be denied. Second, the use of animals with the onco-gene would lead to fewer animals being needed than the use of animals without the onco-gene. As such, the invention contributed to an overall decrease of animal suffering. Third, there is currently no reliable alternative to animal testing that is accepted by health authorities. Finally, the animals patented would be used in laboratories under controlled conditions and by qualified staff. One of the concerns that opponents raised was that these altered genes posed potential risks to the environment—because the mice might be released into the wild. The Examining Division decided, however, that the mice were destined for laboratory use and not for release. The risk of a release was limited to deliberate misuse or blatant ignorance. "The mere fact that such uncontrollable acts are conceivable cannot be a major determinant for deciding whether a patent should be granted or not" (EPO, 1992, pp. 592-593). The Examining Division thus concluded that in this particular case, the benefit to humans outweighed any other aspects. Within this framework the EPO finally decided to issue a patent in 1992 for the now famous Harvard onco-mouse.

The decision of the EPO was immediately appealed by various groups. A final decision on the EPO patent has yet to be made. Perhaps the most influential outcome is that a debate was sparked among the wider public in Europe on gene technology and specifically on patenting genetically modified life forms.

It is interesting to note in passing that the controversy around the onco-mouse patent was sparked in Europe rather than in the United States, where a patent was first granted. It is probable that differences in attitudes toward science, technology, the environment, and even public debate were key factors. It is also not unlikely that opposition groups in Europe had more time to rally their forces, since the EPO grant came more than a year after the U.S. patent.

A more significant footnote is that the arguments used in this case were vastly different from those in the Chakrabarty/General Electric application for the oil-eating bacterium. Opposition to the Chakrabarty invention focused their attention on the patentability of a living thing. In contrast, opposition to the Harvard mouse did not even argue whether life was patentable but focused on the harm and suffering caused in a higher life form. It seemed to be a given that patenting was allowed for living beings.

Yet another footnote is that the second reason for the initial EPO rejection of the application (namely, insufficient disclosure) was never an issue with opponents. The Examining Division originally argued that full disclosure of just one genetically engineered mammal was not a sufficient description to justify the broad patent claim by Harvard, which covered not just the onco-mouse but all nonhuman mammals with the gene. (The Board of Appeals deemed that the rejection was not justified and the Examining Division subsequently reversed its original judgment.) Far more interesting for us is that opposition groups did not focus on this line of argument but concentrated instead on an argument based on the welfare of animals in animal testing. Therefore, one may argue that the most important issue for opponents is animal suffering rather than patenting living beings. This finding would be consistent with the attitudes of animal rights groups who are among the primary opponents in the case. One could also possibly infer that there is a degree of emotional response in opposing the onco-mouse patent. For a summary of the objections and responses, see Table 3.3.

Table 3.3 Summary of Arguments Against and For Patenting Animals

Objection	Reply
The onco-gene causes physical harm to a higher life form. It is not only the risk that has to be considered but the harm done.	An animal with the onco-gene enables us to look for more effective cures against cancer, which causes suffering and death among humans—also a higher life form.
Animal testing constitutes cruelty to animals because it causes suffering. The application is thus contrary to public order and good morals.	There are currently no viable (reliable) alternatives to animal testing accepted by health authorities. With the onco-mouse, fewer animals are needed than in conventional animal tests. Thus, overall animal suffering is reduced.
It is conceivable that these genes may be released into the environment. The environment has to be protected from these unwanted genes.	The onco-mouse is intended for use in a controlled environment by trained personnel following strict guidelines. The release of these animals (that is, of these genes) into the wild is limited to a deliberate act or to an act of ignorance—neither of which as such is sufficient ground to withhold a patent.
The technology is potentially dangerous. No patents should be allowed.	Patents are granted for products or processes that are dangerous. Patent legislation is the wrong arena to control such technology. Other more effective means would be through other legislation enforced by qualified agencies.

HUMANS

The Human Genome Diversity Project (HGDP) consists of an international team of scientists whose mandate is to chart the diversity of human populations. Priority is given to the 722 minority ethnic groups around the world facing extinction. The aim of these scientists is to collect hair, blood, and tissue samples from these isolates of historic interest for a gene bank in the United States (Fischer, 1993; Keller, 1993).

As part of this international project, a team of Panamanian and American scientists were working together with the Guaymis of Panama. In the course of their work, the researchers came across a virus that occurs frequently in the Guaymi population and is similar to the human immunodeficiency virus (HIV). A case of special interest was a twenty-six-year-old Guaymi woman who survived a leukemia caused by the human T-lymphotropic virus type II (HTLV-II).

In her blood, Michael Lairmore and Jonathan Kaplan, two American scientists on the team, found a substance that gave her special resistance. If the scientists' hypothesis was correct, this substance could have been important in the search for a cure for AIDS. So they isolated T-cells from a blood sample from this woman and developed a culture from the cell line.

In 1990 the U.S. Department of Commerce applied for a patent in the United States with claims relating to the isolated T-cell line, the isolated cells, the virus, and methods for identifying anti-HTLV-II. In 1991 they also filed an application in Europe and in other countries (WIPO, 1992, WO 92/08784). The application to the PTO included claims for the cultured cell line, the isolated virus, a method for identifying anti-HTLV-II agents, and three tests for detecting and diagnosing HTLV infections.

The department did so without the knowledge or consent of the woman, the Guaymis, or the Panamanian researchers working on the HGDP project. In late 1993 the Guaymis, who found out about the patent through secondary sources, took their story to Europe to protest the actions of the United States and to demand a withdrawal of the patent (Fischer, 1993; Keller, 1993; Koechlin, 1993).

The Department of Commerce said that the goals that the patents would achieve justified the claims: namely, the development of substances and processes that might be of use in diagnosing for HIV, which is generally believed to cause AIDS. The Guaymis said that they would be happy to contribute an important medication to the world but free of charge. What the Guaymis were protesting was that the United States had taken without permission and claiming for itself an essential part of the Guaymi people, namely the cells of a Guaymi woman. For them, the action of the United States not only went against Guaymi traditions but was unthinkable in their view of the world (Koechlin, 1992).

The U.S. PTO granted a patent for the claim. By the end of 1993, the U.S. government had withdrawn its application from the EPO (Jensen, 1994), but the debate the case has sparked continues.

As a footnote, the U.S. Department of Commerce has also filed an international patent application for a cell line taken from citizens of Papua-New Guinea (see chapter 4) and the Solomon Islands. The cells contain a natural substance that fights off leukemia and is a potential drug for this disease. The government of the Solomon Islands has filed a protest against the U.S. government claiming that the United States has no right to a monopoly on the genes of citizens of the Solomon Islands, especially because the individuals concerned had not been told and had not given their consent. From the perspective of the Solomon Islands, this application was a violation of basic human rights (Däpp, 1994; Jensen, 1994).

These examples highlight a central issue behind patenting human genes: human rights, specifically the consent of the individual and the right to be informed. It is less a question of patenting and even less about gene technology. The underlying principle is that in a society that guarantees the freedom of choice, all individuals should have the right to exercise it. Hence, by not informing the persons involved and by not obtaining their consent to patent these genes, the United States violated this fundamental principle. Human-rights groups, in particular, maintain that the individuals in question were never told of the patents or even the intent to patent. As a representative of the Guaymi people argued, the action of the United States is one more example of the interests of the powerful North taking priority over those of the less powerful South (Koechlin, 1993).

In both the examples cited here, which show the complexity of the problems raised by patents of gene technology, the ethics of the U.S. actions have to remain separate from the ethical value of the patent system itself (see "Emotional Arguments Against Gene Technology Patents," below). For the Guaymis and the Solomon Islanders, the moral outrage is that the Americans have taken something that does not belong to them. Even without patenting, the moral wisdom and ethical behavior of the United States remain questionable—if not outright indefensible—in the eyes of human-rights groups, the Guaymis, and the government and citizens of the Solomon Islands. For them, the "theft" by the Americans is a continuation of the exploitation and colonialism that Western society has long perpetrated in the lands of native peoples (Fischer, 1993).

It would be easy to relegate these two examples to the realms of international politics and North-South ideological disputes. But, that still leaves unanswered a host of complex, questions directly related to human rights and gene technology:

Does a human being "own" the parts of his or her body? If human tissue with unusual (and valuable) characteristics is used for commercial purposes without the knowledge or permission of the person from whom the material was obtained, is this theft of that person's property? If a patent is granted for an invention involving the use of such tissue, is the person from whom the tissue was misappropriated entitled to an interest in the patent? These questions are fundamentally important for researchers working with human materials, and their commercial backers. If a person's property is misused or misappropriated, the wrongdoer(s) may have to compensate the owner and may be enjoined from further violation. (Byrne, 1993, p. 199)

A third example underscores the point that the issues are not merely ideological or political. It also comes from the United States but involves a U.S. national. Doctors treating a patient, John Moore, found unique characteristics in his spleen. They removed a tissue sample, cultured a cell line from it, patented the cell line, and licensed the patented cells to pharmaceutical companies, again, without the knowledge or consent of the patient. Moore sued his doctors for not obtaining his consent, breach of fiduciary duty, and theft of his body tissue. The question of theft begs another question: Does Moore own his spleen and the cell line cultivated from it? These are exactly the same questions and issues raised in the example of the Guaymis.

Moore's case finally went before the Supreme Court of California, which ruled against Moore on practical grounds and in principle. The reasoning was that if individuals could assert property rights over their own body, it would be a hindrance to biotechnological research and development. On being told of their commercially valuable body parts, certain individuals might simply seek the highest bid from medical institutes or go so far as to prohibit the use of the body part. The result would be a loss to society in general (Byrne, 1993).

Meanwhile, the debate continues. Both cases—the Guaymis and Moore—raise the same issues: breach of trust, theft, and ownership. In his conclusion, N. Byrne asks: "Is it fair, even if ethical, that the Mr. Moores of the world should be denied a share of the bounty derived from the commercial use of their body parts?" (Byrne, 1993, p. 202). But what happens if the person would prefer that there be no bounty at all (as in the Guaymi case)? How should the rights of the individual be balanced against the rights of society? What do we do when two worldviews or value systems clash?

Such questions are challenging enough in situations involving a country's own citizens. They become even more complex when different cultures, countries, or peoples are involved. Finally, it should be noted that, although the three examples cited here involved the United States, such conflicts occur in other countries as well (Däpp, 1994). For a summary of the arguments surrounding the patenting of human genes, see Table 3.4.

Table 3.4 Summary of Arguments Against and For Patenting Human Genes

Objection	Reply
The cell line that was cultured and the virus that was isolated were taken from a person without her knowledge of the end purpose and without her consent.	This is the first time the virus was isolated in a specific population. The cultured cell line and the substances developed from the culture were previously unknown (hence patentable) and the results are medically useful. Thus, the end justifies the means.
The Guaymis would contribute to the advancement of medicine but not for money and not in a way that is against Guaymi tradition.	The substances and the methods claimed could be useful for the detection and identification of HTLV infections.
The U.S. has claimed for itself an essential part of the Guaymi people. This action goes against the ways and culture of the Guaymis.	The U.S. action is justified by the benefits that result. The patented process and products will contribute to the identification of HTLV infections, including HIV.

GENE SEQUENCES

The more scientists learn about the genes of living beings, the more they will perceive genes and gene sequences as discrete entities. This perception will probably lead to an increasing number of applications to patent genes themselves, as distinct from the life form from which they came, a trend that will create legal and ethical challenges for society. The following case is a good example of the issues that will likely emerge.

In the late 1980s, Craig Venter, while working at the National Institutes of Health (NIH) in the United States, was trying to identify and sequence the complementary DNAs (cDNAs) from the human brain. Complementary DNAs are clones made from messenger RNAs and represent the coding regions of all the genes expressed in a tissue. Venter's approach was first to look for messenger RNAs and tag them using short stretches of genetic matter called expressed sequence tags (ESTs). The next step was to sequence those stretches with robots and then feed the data into a computer for analysis. From these sequences, investigators could re-create the tag using other techniques and pull out the entire cDNA clone from a clone collection (Marshall, 1994; Roberts, 1991). Using this new method, Venter and his team were able to identify up to about two thousand sequences a month, some of them representing genes never seen before. Once a cDNA is tagged and identified, however, Venter's method still does not indicate what the sequence does—unless the gene itself is known and its functions understood (Roberts, 1991).

In 1991 the NIH announced that it had filed patent applications for the first 350 unique gene sequences. "The claim covered each EST as well as the entire coding sequence for the longer clone, its protein product, and the method for obtaining and interpreting cDNAs" (Roberts, 1991, p. 185). The NIH further announced plans to file a second patent application for 1,500 additional cDNA sequences (Roberts, 1991). By late 1992, the agency had filed patent applications for about 2,700 human gene fragments with no known functions (Stout, 1992). As this case will illustrate, filing an application for a patent does *not* mean that a patent will be granted. It also depicts how the debate surrounding the question of patenting is often guided by emotions.

After the NIH announcement, the immediate fallout was an emotional debate in scientific circles—both in academia and in industry—about the action of the NIH and the implications for science. Critics feared that patenting these sequences without knowing their functions would discourage industry from investing in research and would undermine the efforts of researchers working on the Human Genome Project (Roberts, 1991). Other critics were more blunt, calling the NIH attempt an abuse of the patent system (Anderson, 1991b).

In his own defence, Venter said that the idea to patent these sequences came from Max Hensley, a patent lawyer at Genentech, a biotechnology firm in California. Venter said that Hensley had told the NIH that they would risk undercutting the U.S. biotechnology effort if they did not patent the sequences. Critics replied that no one would benefit from patenting these sequences. The real task was finding the function of the proteins that these sequences code for. If patents were already issued for these sequences and if they were so broad as to preclude subpatents, then industry would not be interested in developing inventions based on this work (Roberts, 1991).

Lawyers representing the NIH said the applications fulfilled basic patent requirements. First, the new genes were novel, since they had not been sequenced previously. The nonobviousness criterion was more difficult to prove: On the one hand, Venter applied known technology to sequence the segments. On the other hand, he was the first to see that large-scale cDNA sequencing and the search capability of DNA databases allowed for an unprecedented rate of generating human genes. Finally, as for the criterion of utility, the genes that Venter found expressed DNA whose function remained unknown. The NIH argued that while the genes might be "naked," researchers could use the sequence, for example, as a probe or to distinguish brain tissue from other tissue (Anderson, 1991a).

Late in 1992 the U.S. Patent and Trademark Office refused a patent on the grounds of a lack of utility (Kleiner, 1994; Marshall, 1994; Suiter and

Wax, 1994). The PTO further declared that the application also failed to meet the other two criteria for patenting, namely novelty and nonobviousness. The decisive factor for the rejection of the application, however, was the failure to meet the criterion of utility (Stout, 1992).

In early 1994 the new director of the NIH, Dr. Harold Varmus, announced that the NIH would not appeal the PTO ruling (Suiter and Wax, 1994). One outcome of the case was that it confirmed that threshold utility is the foremost criterion for the U.S. patent office (Suiter and Wax, 1994).

This summary of legal arguments reveals only part of the picture. At the heart of the debate was *not* whether gene sequences or even whole genes are patentable. Indeed, there appears to be a consensus in the scientific community that gene sequences per se should be patentable (Cookson, 1994; Moore, 1994). The conflict centered on what many people in science saw as unorthodox if not unethical behavior: the attempt to patent gene sequences *without knowing their function* amounts to creating a monopoly on scientific information and subverting an unspoken code of conduct requiring scientists to share material and knowledge.

Patenting naked genes would have undermined the work that many of Venter's colleagues had invested in gene research and especially in the collaborative work on the Human Genome Project (see "The Human Genome," chapter 2). Venter's method allowed him to sequence in a short time a large number of gene segments. If he had received a patent for each of these sequences, the work done in decoding the gene later on would have led only to products for which Venter would have had a patent.

For many of Venter's colleagues, the question is not *whether* gene sequences are patentable. Patent offices in the United States and Europe had already been granting patents for gene sequences and entire genes long before the NIH applications. Rather, the question is *when* gene sequences should be patented. Many scientists think that such patents should be granted only when there is a gene-based product (Cookson, 1994; Moore, 1994). For them, this rule would represent a win-win situation for all: science would gain in knowledge; industry would have a developable product; and society would gain an innovative product and help advance a useful technology. It is likely that the gene sequences would not have caused the furor that they did (at least in the scientific community), if Venter had been able show that the functions of these gene sequences were known.

There are two important footnotes to the NIH case. First, in 1992, the Medical Research Council (MRC) in the United Kingdom also filed an application for DNA sequences of unknown utility. It intended to pursue the case to establish the position of the European Patent Office on such cases. "However, the MRC . . . takes the position patents should not be granted on gene fragments with unknown uses" (Suiter and Wax, 1994, p. 20).

Second, in 1993, Craig Venter and some of his team left the NIH to join a private gene technology firm called Human Genome Sciences (HGS). HGS had a contract with SmithKline Beecham granting that Anglo-American pharmaceutical company exclusive access to HGS's data base of partial or complete DNA sequences. Because these sequences could not be patented, "HGS is keeping secret the sequences of the more than 45,000 genes it has found until their usefulness is known" (Bishop, 1994, p. B8).

Then, in 1994, in response to criticisms by and demands from outside researchers—both academic and industry—HGS and SmithKline Beecham announced that they would provide access to interested parties—for a price. The price would be that "outsiders surrender virtually all future rights for commercial uses of genes discovered with the help of HGS sequence data" (Bishop, 1994, p. B8). For HGS and SmithKline Beecham, it was a matter of protecting their investment in the data base. For others, it was a question of free exchange of scientific knowledge and collaboration (Marshall, 1994).

In the latest development, Merck, Sharpe and Dome, an American pharmaceutical manufacturer, announced plans to duplicate the HGS data bank and make it available to all interested researchers. The tactic was supposed to promote the free exchange of genomic data. But it would also undermine the effort of HGS and Merck's competitor, SmithKline Beecham. Although Merck's plans have yet to be finalized, they have already gained supporters from both the academic and industrial research community (Bishop, 1994; Cookson, 1994; Marshall, 1994).The arguments for and against patenting gene sequencing are summarized in Table 3.5.

PATENTS AND THE TECHNOLOGY OF LIFE: ARGUMENTS, SLOGANS, AND DEBATE

As noted in chapter 1, social acceptance of gene technology depends on both rational and emotional factors. The controversy surrounding patenting and gene technology amply illustrates this point. There are both rational and emotional arguments to be considered for and against patenting in gene technology. The emotional arguments are by far the more powerful and often take into account considerations outside the framework of patent law. These considerations deserve to be taken seriously in the appropriate context.

Unfortunately, in both the debate on patenting in gene technology and the wider debate on gene technology itself, slogans are often confused with arguments. Indeed, one sometimes has the distinct impression that "sloganeering" has become a substitute for debate. This section examines first the rational and then the emotional arguments that have been voiced in the patenting debate. The section also looks at the danger of mistaking sloganeering for debate.

RATIONAL CONSIDERATIONS

This section examines first the rational arguments against patents in gene technology and then the rational arguments for them.

**Table 3.5 Summary of Arguments Against and For Patenting
           Gene Sequences**

Objection	Reply
The application does not show novelty. After all, the sequences were derived from commercial brain-DNA clone collections.	The gene sequences are novel because this is the first time someone has sequenced them.
Both the concept of sequencing cDNA and the technology used to do it existed. In addition, some of the gene sequences contain smaller sequences that have already been published. Hence, the application is routine rather than unobvious.	The method used is nonobvious, as no one has been able to sequence genes in such large amounts at such speed before.
The application fails to demonstrate a practical use for the gene sequences. The sequences, although now disclosed, remain not useful.	Although the gene sequences have no current application, they could be used as intermediates in future application, notably for recovering entire genes.

Rational Arguments Against Gene Technology Patents

There are three rational arguments against the patenting of genetically modified life forms. First, living beings do not meet basic criteria for patents for three closely related biological reasons: life cannot be invented (Hug, 1993); life or living systems are by nature not patentable; and genetic mutations are mere discoveries. Second, patent laws are not suited for dealing with self-reproduction. Finally, the economic costs might outweigh the economic and social benefits.

Arguments on the Grounds of Not Meeting Basic Criteria for Patents—The first argument is based on the reasoning that no one can invent life. Scientists can discover ways to alter life forms or living processes, but they cannot create life itself. All living matter—cells, genes, plants, and animals—relate to a natural setting in their behavior, their outward forms, and even their ability to reproduce.

Today, gene technology allows scientists to take apart individual bits of an organism and put them back together in different combinations. Nevertheless, they cannot determine how the resulting life form will function, what its life span will be, or what impact the organism will have on the environment.

This unpredictability is what distinguishes life forms from nonliving matter and industrial inventions.

Closely related to this line of reasoning is the second line: life and living systems are by nature unpatentable. For something to be patentable, the inventor has to be able to describe the invention in detail. Because the patent is for a living thing, the characteristics described (and thus presumably patented) change with time (Reist, 1994). Thus, the subject of the patent is no longer what was described in the patent application; in other words, the genetically modified organism becomes something other than the thing for which a patent has been issued. This reasoning was put forward by Werner Arber, professor in molecular biology at Basle University and the winner of the 1978 Nobel Prize in medicine.

According to the third line of reasoning, genetically modified life forms fail to meet the criteria of inventiveness and novelty on fundamental biological principles. Arber argued from the following premise. No life form remains absolutely static. In any given population, there will always be mutations of one form or another. Such mutations are vital in ensuring ongoing evolution. Thus, even if a scientist has genetically determined a particular trait, the result is not an invention but rather a discovery. Strictly speaking then, the resulting life form has not been invented so much as it has been "stolen from Nature" (Reist, 1994, p. 2).

Arguments on the Grounds of Unsuitability for Self-Reproduction—The second argument against patenting focuses on a practical point: patent laws are not designed to deal with the ability of life forms to reproduce themselves (Krimsky, 1991). Normally, a patent is granted for an invention that can be replicated by mechanical means. Each mechanical replication results in the same product as the first time. By contrast, in biological reproduction, the progeny may develop in one of three ways. First, the offspring may be like the genetically modified parent or parents, expressing the desired physical traits (phenotype): this situation is a sure sign that the offspring also carries the desired genetic characteristics (genotype). Second, the offspring may not show the desired phenotype but may still be a carrier of the genotype. Third, the offspring may have neither the phenotype nor the genotype desired.

How then is a patent office to deal with life that gives rise to new life? Should a patent cover all three kinds of offspring? Is it fair to ask for a licence when an offspring does not show either the phenotype or genotype sought? What if the offspring shows only the genotype but not the phenotype? What happens to the patent if the characteristics patented naturally change over time or in subsequent generations? From this perspective, it becomes clear that patent law is not suited to deal with the ability—and instinct—of living beings to procreate. Nor does the law cover the variability of offspring.

Arguments on the Grounds of Economic Cost—Finally, from an economic perspective, patenting could lead to the abuse of exclusive rights and the concentration of economic wealth in a minority of society. This possibility would outweigh any economic or social benefit that society as a whole might otherwise enjoy. Patenting would encourage the type of research where the goal is securing the best patent protection available rather than serving the needs of society.

In the world of science, patenting can actually hinder the free exchange of knowledge. As the case with Craig Venter and Human Genome Sciences demonstrates, the promise of commercial returns offered by patent protection could become more important than the stimulation of scientific research. The current furor over the requirements of HGS is evidence that many in the scientific community find such practices not only unorthodox but also objectionable. However, that not everyone in the scientific community agrees is clearly underlined by the fact that thirty-five researchers from thirty institutes have already agreed to the terms that HGS has set (Bishop, 1994).

For the farming industry, patenting may represent both obvious and hidden costs, which may well outweigh any expected benefits to society. It is conceivable that one or two companies might hold a virtual monopoly on patents for farm animals. Such a situation would be similar to the one facing the world of science: farmers would either be forced to pay excessive licence fees or be denied access to these animals (and the desired genes) if they could not pay.

The hidden and more subtle costs come from the push towards genetic uniformity. If one company holds a patent for a superior breed of animal or a stronger variety of plant, market forces will lead to an increase and multiplication of the desired line. While the system rewards the inventiveness of the producer, it also increases the vulnerability of the farming industry, especially the risk of crop failure.

A diversified crop might consist of various strains of that particular plant. Naturally, some strains might have high nutritional content, others might have the ability to grow in relatively poor soil conditions, and yet others might be resistant to extreme temperatures. However, if one strain proves to be generally superior to, or more desirable than, most other ones available, most farmers will want to use the new strain. (Today, with commercial interest in crop strains and seed management, one must also consider the influence of marketing and sales in moving a product on to the market or defending its market position.)

The widespread use of one particular strain of a particular crop reduces the number of varieties in use, thus decreasing the resistance of the whole harvest to pests, fungi, or diseases. In human history, diseases have more than once wiped out large areas of uniform staple crops.

Genetic uniformity leads to crop vulnerability. The Irish potato farmers know what that means. In the 1840s, when their staple but uniform potato crop was wiped out by blight, more than one million people died of starvation. One and a half centuries later, the US maize (corn) farmers have also learnt the hard way. In 1970, 15 % of the US maize harvest was lost to the devastating effect of a little fungus-causing blight, with some states losing over half their harvest. (Hobbelink, 1991, p. 64)

Rational Arguments for Gene Technology Patents

The key objectives of patents, outlined earlier, are also the key rational arguments for patents in general. To reiterate, the goals of a patent system include the following:

- rewarding inventors, thus stimulating inventive activity
- encouraging the disclosure of the subject matter so that knowledge is in the public domain
- offering an incentive to produce the item

In the context of genetic engineering and its attendant problems, it would be wise to consider more specific arguments for patenting genetic products and processes. The first half of this section looks at some of these arguments, focusing on how patent law serves the public interest by guiding the development of gene technology. The second half looks at how the new technology, despite the challenges it presents, meets the requirements of patent law.

Arguments on the Grounds of Serving the Public Interest—Perhaps one of the most important considerations is the role of patents as providing public access to technological information. It is clear that gene technology holds tremendous potential. For many critics, this seemingly infinite potential for good could easily be misused. The patent system is one means for keeping that knowledge visible, thus giving society a say in whether an inventor's creation will further the general good.

The alternative to patenting would be conducting work in secrecy. In 1982 the Organization for Economic Cooperation and Development (OECD) sent a questionnaire on biotechnology and patent protection to its twenty-four member countries. In response to a question on alternatives to patenting in biotechnology, many of the nineteen countries participating "noted the existence of Plant Variety Rights, a form of protection distinct from patents and of possible use for new plants obtained by genetic engineering. The primary alternative to patents, which would be available to biotechnology inventions in general, was that of industrial secrecy (more commonly termed trade secrecy)" (Beier and Straus, 1985, p. 39). The authors of the report further wrote that compared to patenting, "in a rapidly moving technology, trade secrecy was more speedily utilisable and avoided the cost and effort of patenting"(p. 39).

First, given the debate on gene technology and the concern many people have expressed, it would be a mistake to allow scientists to carry on their work without the knowledge, input, or guidance of society. If this work were to disappear from view completely, the technology would remain a mystery and a source of fear. More significantly, unchecked, the technology might develop along paths that society would find undesirable and possibly uncontrollable. Second, given that industrial society has started down the road of gene technology and has reached a point where it is no longer feasible to turn back, it is probably wise to consider carefully the road ahead and decide on a carefully weighed course of action for the future.

It is critical, especially at this early stage, for society to guide this infant technology. Patenting, in encouraging disclosure of technical knowledge and placing it in the public domain, provides society with an opportunity to voice different and even conflicting views on these innovations. Thus, patenting allows society to determine the direction and speed of technological evolution.

Closely related to this argument is the fact that patenting makes publicly accessible information that might otherwise be hoarded (US OTA, 1989). In the case with Craig Venter and HGS, the absence of patents led to a situation where one group decided not to disclose certain information. Rather than the time-limited monopoly that patents would have granted, trade secrecy in this case created a complete and indefinite block on particular areas of scientific knowledge. The HGS was now in a position to refuse other researchers access to potentially useful information if they did not grant the company the right of first refusal on developments arising from the use of the HGS genetic data bank. If these researchers agreed, HGS and its allies would have access to scientific information before official publication, a practice that would go against the tradition of information sharing and peer review in the scientific community. This agreement would endanger a practice that has allowed science to build up knowledge based on previous discoveries (US OTA, 1989). Clearly, such a situation would not be in the public interest.

There is an incentive for private interests to keep such information secret: research and development, especially in gene technology, is costly. Patenting is one way to encourage the private sector to invest in R & D that is expensive but may eventually benefit many. For example, in Europe, the development of a new medication—from preliminary research to the end of the approval process for the final product (if there is one)—takes anywhere from ten to fourteen years (Canibol, 1994). An article in the *New Scientist* provides similar figures for the United States: "According to the US Pharmaceutical Manufacturers Association, it takes an average of 12 years and some $230 million to move just one new drug from the laboratory to the pharmacist's shelf" (Coghlan, 1993, p. 29).

During this period, obstacles could arise at any point during one of six key stages: synthesis, screening, chemical testing, preclinical trials, the three phases of clinical trials, and seeking governmental approval for the new product. In other words, a company could stand to lose the time and money it has invested in this effort. In arguing for patents in gene technology, proponents are partly saying that patents are an incentive for private investment in such risky undertakings. A patent protection of twenty years would thus allow the company approximately six years to reap the benefits of its investment. If the company succeeded, it would not be the only winner: the real beneficiaries would be victims of a disease, who would gain another option in their fight for survival or recovery.

At this stage, a blanket refusal to grant patents for innovations in gene technology would amount to a premature rejection of the technology without a balanced analysis of the inherent risks and benefits. Such a rejection would ignore the benefits of the patent system to the inventor, to society in general, and to individuals who want or need products that might otherwise not be available.

Finally, in arguing for patenting, proponents are not necessarily ignoring the ethical considerations surrounding gene technology. Although many of these concerns deserve thorough discussion in a public forum, patent law is not necessarily the most appropriate arena for such a discussion. As mentioned earlier, patent law in general fosters three goals: innovation in technology, encouragement of disclosure of technical knowledge, and an incentive to make the innovation publicly available. It is not equipped to deal with the attendant ethical challenges.

Arguments on the Grounds of Conforming to Patent Law—A patent office, consisting of technical and legal experts, cannot become a substitute for representative legislative institutions, such as parliaments and national assemblies whose prerogative is public debate and expression of citizens' opinions and concerns. If patent law includes a clause excluding patents on moral and ethical grounds, it is only as a provision for cases where the development of an invention will clearly be against public order or morality: "one has to consider whether it is probable that the public in general would regard the invention as so abhorrent that the grant of patent rights would be inconceivable" (EPO, 1992, p. 15). The EPO uses the case of a letter bomb as an example of an invention that might satisfy all three criteria for patentability but would not receive a patent on the grounds of morality.

Another factor that makes the patent office an unsuitable authority for rendering judgments on ethical controversies is the often lengthy period from the submission of a patent application to actual use of the patented matter. The patent office as society's moral court cannot foresee changes in social values and attitudes. For example, if a company were to apply for a patent for a new product today, that product might not be ready for public use for another ten years, during which time society might have developed a new opinion or understanding of the product.

For this reason, authorities decide whether a new medication is available for public use not during the initial patent application but at the stage of product registration. When the product is actually ready for public use, authorities are better able to decide whether society is ready to accept it. If the gap is narrower between the initial patent application and the actual availability of the product, then perhaps the patent office would be better able to reflect the ethical or moral judgment of society at large in morally controversial cases. That said, the decisions of a small of group of specialists cannot become a substitute for broad public debate on social issues.

A recent example in the field of medicine shows how patenting and social acceptance are two separate issues. In the mid-1980s, Roussel Uclaf of France (today merged into Hoechst Marion Roussel, a company in the Hoechst Group) produced a pill (called mifepristone or RU-486) that blocks gestation rather than conception. Because the medication works after conception (and is therefore not a contraceptive), it has also been referred to as the abortion pill. The pill was patented and in the late 1980s approved for distribution in France (Cherfas, 1989). By December 1990, the drug was available in China and was waiting for approval in various other countries including Sweden, the Netherlands, and the United Kingdom (Podolksy, 1990). In the United States, however, various groups launched protest actions against its introduction in that country. Indeed, due to the pressure from interest groups and members of Congress, the Food and Drug Administration (FDA) originally imposed an import ban on the pill. But under the first Clinton administration in 1993, the FDA asked Hoechst to make the pill available in the United States. Roussel Uclaf subsequently transferred all patent rights to RU 486 in the United States to the nonprofit organization The Population Control. In 1997 Hoechst transferred all patent rights for RU 486 in the rest of the world to Exelgyn, a company established by Dr. Edouard Sakiz, one of the original inventors.

This example underlines two key points. First, a patent does not guarantee approval from regulatory agencies or health authorities. The patent office has jurisdiction over questions of patentability only. Other regulatory bodies deal with such issues as health, safety, and the environment. Second, social acceptance of a new product or technology will vary according to countries and cultures, *regardless* of patent protection. As the case with RU-486 shows, the patent office cannot and does not determine social acceptance of a new technology; nor can it usurp the role of making ethical and moral decisions for society.

Nevertheless, the patent office is the appropriate forum for technical decisions on matters of patentability. On the OECD questionnaire, many countries said that "their present patent law was well suited to the requirements of biotechnology" (Beier and Straus, 1985, p. 38). In fact, some countries insisted on the necessity of "uniformity of treatment" (p. 39) of all technologies to ensure equal treatment for all fields of industry.

In the end, the patent system allows for a win-win situation for all concerned. The company or enterprise receives legal protection from theft for its inventions and a period of protection from competition for its products. Society obtains innovative solutions to its problems and at the same time is able to encourage private enterprise. Individuals obtain the products and utilize the options that they want or need but that may not be available without patent protection.

EMOTIONAL CONSIDERATIONS

This section reviews emotional arguments against patents in gene technology and the emotional arguments for them.

Emotional Arguments Against Gene Technology Patents

There are five emotional arguments against patenting in gene technology. First, patenting should not be used to encourage a technology with unknown long-term risks and side effects for the food supply, the environment, and even the economy. Second, cumbersome and ineffective in some areas, patenting in gene technology is inappropriate because the law was designed to encourage industries with engineering and chemistry bases. Third, humankind already has problems with the animals and plants in its care. There should be no encouragement for technology to produce new sorts until we learn to take better care of what we have. Fourth, patenting in gene technology encourages a narrow worldview that may even be contrary to the broader principles of the patent system. Fifth, society should stop and ask if it wants to encourage this technology without reflecting on the ethical and religious implications of allowing patenting in the technology of life.

Arguments on the Grounds of Risks—The basic principle behind patenting is the encouragement of technological development. Patents in gene technology are encouraging a technology of unknown potential for good and harm. It is really the second element that should be of concern: the unknown potential for harm. At this point, no one, not even scientists, really knows what the long-term effects of gene technology will be. It is unknown risks that cause uncertainty and fear. There is a need to address questions about the potential damage: Is it big or small? Can industry reverse the process to correct the damage? Does it affect one person or many?

Moreover, assessment needs to go beyond the technical risks: the chance of an accidental release, the number of clinical trials required, or the degree of safety containment necessary. A comprehensive assessment—especially of a new technology—must explore such nonscientific issues as the social consequences, the economic impact, the legal liabilities, and, of course, the ethical implications. These matters are not necessarily quantifiable, but that does not make them less important. For most people, the most immediate concern is how the technology will affect them personally—their jobs, their security, their family, and their health.

A study by H.-C. Röglin (1994) of the Institut für angewandte Sozialpsychologie identified three sources of fear regarding gene technology:

- First, the most often mentioned fear is that gene technology could become uncontrollable. Developments could be set in motion with irreversible and inestimable consequences.
- Second, there is the worry that the new knowledge of gene technology could lead to misuses for the purposes of manipulating human beings or for genetic selection in medicine.
- Third, the concern also exists that society with ever weakening values could never come to terms with the ethical implications of gene technology.

If these concerns are not (or cannot be) addressed, there should be no incentive to develop such a technology. Experience has shown that technological development frequently produces unforeseen harmful results that are at least as great as any alleged benefits. Obvious examples are cars, which are now a major contributor to air pollution; nuclear energy, which has more than once placed the world under threat of nuclear warfare and has resulted in catastrophic accidents such as Chernobyl; and electric power, which has led to the damming of rivers, resulting in the destruction of natural habitats and ecologically sensitive areas.

Clearly, if traditional technologies have produced such widespread and unforeseeable negative consequences, gene technology could unleash just as much harm. From this point of view, then, society would have no reason to allow patent protection in this field.

Gene technology poses a risk in three areas: the food supply, the environment, and the economy. Patenting would encourage the rise of fewer and fewer breeds of farm animals or strains of crop plants. The consequence for the food supply would be a narrowing of types in agriculture and, at the same time, an increased exposure or vulnerability to devastation by one particular sort of pest, virus, or bacteria. There could also be unforeseen side effects.

Two scientists, Dr. Richard Allison and Ann E. Green, from the biology and plant pathology department of Michigan State University, conducted research on plants genetically altered to be resistant to viral infection. Based on their research (sponsored jointly by the Department of Agriculture and Monsanto), they concluded that

> the inserted genes can recombine with natural plant viruses and produce wholly new viruses at a rate higher than had been theorised at the E.P.A. [Environmental Protection Agency] and the Department of Agriculture. The implication of the research, said Dr. Allison, was that engineering plants to be resistant to viruses might lead to entirely new types of viruses that could cause widespread damage to American harvests. (Schneider, 1994, p. A14)

There are also no data on the long-term effects of the consumption of genetically altered food products. In 1994 the U.S. Food and Drug Administration approved for market the first gene technologically produced food item, a tomato that would stay fresh longer and taste better at the same time. Despite the assurances of the FDA and the company to the contrary, some opponents of the tomato were concerned about the ability of the altered gene to counteract the effects of an oral antibiotic, thus possibly creating antibiotic resistance in humans who eat the tomato (Leary, 1994; McCabe, 1994).

Risks to the environment include the development of strong genetic hybrids arising from the release of such genes. These superior breeds will lead to the rise and dominance of fewer and fewer animal and plant genetic types, thus causing genetic erosion. So even if patenting itself does not directly lead to genetic erosion, it encourages practices that will lead to it.

There is also a risk to the economy—particularly in the farming sector. According to the study by Röglin, owners of small and middle-size farms are worried that the technology will place them at a competitive disadvantage and that it will accelerate the disappearance of farming as a way of life.

Arguments on the Grounds of Inappropriateness—Under plant-variety rights, breeders previously enjoyed the "breeder's privilege" or "research exemption," which gave them the freedom not only to use protected plant varieties in their breeding programs but also to commercialize the further varieties developed therefrom, without any royalty payment to the owner of the initial variety.

> Again, until the UPOV revision is taken up in national laws, farmers legitimately sowing seed of a protected variety are legally free to save part of the seed from the first crop of plants for sowing on their own farms to produce a second and subsequent crops (the "Farmer's privilege"). Recognising that the current scale of use of farm-saved seed thus deprives the breeder of significant royalty income, the strengthened right under the 1991 version of UPOV would now make this subject to the authorisation of the breeder. . . .
>
> In the case of transgenic farm animals intended as breeding stock, it would be less easy to enforce rights through successive generations and the animal breeders may well have to be innovative in devising commercially feasible methods of ensuring a return on their investment. (EFB, 1993, p. 3)

It is thus clear that patenting not only becomes problematic in the highly competitive farming sector but may actually place small-farm owners at a disadvantage. Licensing as a way of recuperating the costs of the original investment may also prove cumbersome for the breeder to enforce in the long term.

Thus, cumbersome or outright ineffective in the farming sector, patents should not be allowed on either farm animals or crops. More generally, it is argued that patenting may directly or indirectly promote methods and practices that may present a risk for the food supply, the environment, and even the economy. Thus, society really has no reasons to provide any incentive for the new technology through patenting.

Arguments on the Grounds of Arrogation of the Role of Nature—From another standpoint, it may be argued that gene technology has arrogated the role of nature. Genes have evolved into their current combinations over the millions of years since life first appeared on this planet. Science claims to be able to accelerate this process; yet scientists today can no better explain what life is than they could before. Thus, there is no essentially new knowledge, which means that no patents can be held on life. To obtain a patent, the inventor has to demonstrate an understanding of the essentials of the invention, that is, to explain how it works. If life is patentable (explainable), why has no one explained it yet?

To patent a better mouse trap, you must explain the mechanics of the mouse trap. So how can you patent a better mouse if you cannot explain the mechanics of the mouse? Life is more than just the genes, cells, tissues, organs, or even body of the organism. To use a cliché, life is more than the sum of all its parts. All gene technology has done is explain the parts without explaining the whole. One reason for its failure, of course, is that life is constantly in motion—changing, evolving, and adapting to its environment.

Furthermore, human beings already have problems existing in a mutually beneficial way with other animals and plants that they have had in their trust for millennia. Animals and plants are dying out around the world owing to human neglect, ignorance, or carelessness. Why should we encourage a technology to develop more exotic ones? We should be learning more about the ones we already have and protecting them while we still have them. If we can't cope with what we already have, how are we to deal with new forms of life?

It must also be said that while human beings have been domesticating useful animals and plants since earliest times, there are limits—however intangible and changeable these may be—to their efforts. What is clear is that human needs do not always outweigh animal interests. If they did, society would not have developed laws ensuring the humane treatment of animals (US OTA, 1989). No patents should be allowed for a technology where genetic crosses could result in serious and unpredictable—perhaps even disabling—side effects for the animal itself. No human need is great enough to justify the undue suffering of a fellow creature.

Arguments on the Grounds of a Narrow View of the World—From a social standpoint, one can also argue that the patent system implicitly promotes a narrow view of the world rather than a global perspective. The patent system is mainly the product of the nineteenth century, with its narrow concept of social justice. At the time, it was an unquestionable right of the colonial powers of Europe to take the riches of their colonies—minerals, plants, animals, or even human beings. The society of the day never even entertained questions of compensation. The idea of social justice would have been absurd.

This nineteenth-century worldview no longer sufficiently reflects the needs and conditions of the world today. At the end of the twentieth century, former colonies have become powers in their own right, and industrialized society is more aware of the need for diversity and respect for differences. Today, social justice requires respect for the rights of others—the freedom to choose, the right to equitable treatment, and entitlement to what is rightfully one's own. In that sense, the patent system lags behind society in its expectations and requirements.

For example, the issue of compensation for genetic contributions is closely linked to the question of social justice. From that perspective, the same theme binds three cases mentioned in this chapter: the patenting of plant genes and the contributions of industrializing countries (see "Plants"); the patenting of human genes and the individual's right to be informed (see "Humans"); the patenting of human genes and the North-South conflict of cultural values (see the same section). Society today requires that individuals, nations, or peoples who contribute, directly or indirectly, to the development of a new, useful, and industrially viable product or process be recognized for their share in the work and that they receive a proportionate amount of compensation for it. So far, the patent system has failed to recognize this need. The result is the ire and moral indignation of individuals such as John Moore or peoples such as the Guaymis. The emotional opposition to patenting developments in gene technology arises in no small part from perceptions of what is safe, what is right, and what is fair. If the patent system is incapable of dealing with these questions, then there should be no patents for developments in this technology.

Arguments on the Grounds of Overstepping a Fine Ethical Line—Finally, society may well have good reason to ask if we are not walking a fine ethical line or even if we have not overstepped it already. The patent system encourages innovation in areas where life—not simply nonliving matter—is at stake. As living beings, humans need to respect other life forms as well, apart from human uses for them. The resulting innovations may be contrary to the welfare and interests of humankind in the long run. It can also be argued that patenting in gene technology fosters double standards for the patent system—one set for gene technology and another for other technologies.

As one writer argues (Rehmann-Sutter, 1995), a person can take a television set and alter it for use as part of a computer system. The buyer or builder of the new set wants to draw on the economic benefit of the invention, as all future TV sets with these new constructions can be produced in mass quantities. However, if he or she were to try to claim sole and total patent rights for the invention without acknowledging the original inventor's work or rights, no patent office would ever grant a patent. The patent office would only grant a licence that corresponds to the contributions of the second inventor to the original work. In the case of gene technology, nature or the animal itself cannot claim original patent protection and hence prevent biotechnological companies from claiming sole and total patent ownership. In contrast to products of other technologies, there is a much higher proportion of "nonnew" material or construction in the "products" of gene technology.

From a religious perspective, by tinkering with life, are we not playing God? Life is sacred. More than mere ownership of animals for food or companionship, patenting of animals and even plants reduces life to material objects to be possessed or used at will. Patenting life is tantamount to a total denial of God. Where life is concerned, in claiming novelty and inventiveness as the domain of human beings, we may be placing ourselves on the same level as God the Creator.

Emotional Arguments for Gene Technology Patents

Emotional arguments in support of patenting gene technology include the fair reward for contributions, the well functioning of a system that has stood the test of time, the ethical need to encourage developments from which society benefits, the social obligation of industry to search for new solutions to society's needs, and the fact that patenting is not playing God.

Arguments on the Grounds of Fair Reward—Patents are ethically justifiable and fair because they reward hard work and innovation. Above all, patents offer protection for *intellectual* property, recognizing the inventor's intellectual contribution to society. Through patents, society acknowledges that contribution and allows the inventor to enjoy a share in the return on the investment of time, money, and energy. Just as a farmer retains a part of the harvest for personal use after investing the time, money, and energy required in sowing and cultivating a crop for the rest of the community, patents protect the inventor's right to a part of the harvest of his or her intellectual labors.

Patents in gene technology are no different from those in other technologies. What is new and intellectually creative is the combination of genes in the cell, tissue, microorganism, plant, or animal. The patent holder certainly has no privileges or rights of ownership over the animal or the plant itself other than what *other laws* of the land already allow. The patent holder as owner will have to respect these other laws, which protect the animals or other organisms against cruelty, mistreatment, or undue suffering. A patent does not absolve the patent holder (or the inventor) of his or her general legal and moral obligations.

Furthermore, patenting itself does no harm to life forms. In discussions on patenting in gene technology, critics often voice concerns about the ownership of organisms, the relationship of human beings with other species, the use of animals in laboratories, the welfare of animals, and the intrinsic worth of the organism. Nevertheless, it is also clear that these often legitimate concerns do not directly relate to patenting itself. In fact, many of these points were valid before the debate on patents in gene technology. As the OTA in the United States comments: "*It is unclear that patenting per se would substantially redirect the way society uses or relates to animals*" (US OTA, 1989, p. 137, italics in the original).

The patent holder must comply with the law in other areas relating to the public or commercial use of the invention. These other laws regulate such matters as the use of animals in lab tests, environmental safety, fair competition, health safety, and the disposal of biological matter—concerns outside the realm of patent law.

Arguments on the Grounds of a Well-Functioning System—The patent system works as well as any other systems humans have devised. Two elements attest to this fact: the concept has stood the test of time (evolving over three centuries since it was entrenched in legislation in England), and it has spread around the world in the last two centuries.

The patenting system contains corrective measures, including ways of preventing misuses (the lengthy and detailed examination of an application) and punishing abuses of the privilege of a limited monopoly. The second point deserves elaboration. The monopoly, as noted previously, is a privilege limited in time (that is, twenty years) and geography (there is still no worldwide patent). As a grant of privilege from state to individual, a patent implies a contract between two parties: the state offers protection from competition for a while, and the individual agrees to develop the invention within a reasonable period (usually three years from the grant of the patent or four years from the application for a patent).

> It is, therefore, not surprising that in most countries the patentee who fails to put his invention into practice in the state within a prescribed period may have his patent rights reduced or revoked. Failure to exploit the invention is regarded as an abuse of the monopoly rights, in most countries, and may lay the patent open to compulsory licensing, or to revocation or indeed may result in automatic lapsing of the patent. (Baxter, 1973, p. 146)

It must be emphasized, however, that the state will order a compulsory licence only if the patent holder fails to provide a legitimate reason for not working on the invention. The revocation of the patent is a last resort, when even compulsory licensing has failed. In addition to being a provision against failure, a compulsory licence is also available any time after a patent has been granted for substances used as food or medicine, for any process for producing food or medicine, and for any invention used as a surgical or curative device (Baxter, 1973).

The monopoly thus remains a privilege and not a right, although it is the right of the inventor to claim this privilege. When the privilege expires, the product is already on the market. At this point, the law of supply and demand comes into play. As a bonus, the knowledge that went into the invention is now in public hands. This is a win-win situation for all sectors of society.

It is obvious that the patent system works but, as with anything, *only* within the framework for which it was intended. The patent office acknowledges its own limits. In the decision in the Lubrizol case discussed earlier, the EPO included the following insight:

> Patent law is primarily an instrument for promoting research and technical advance associated therewith. It would be an overestimation of the potency of patent law if one considered it an appropriate instrument to suppress research which is dangerous or unacceptable for other reasons to certain groups of mankind. Human curiosity could not be hampered by the fact that patent protection [was] not available if such research promised an interesting result. . . .
>
> The development of new technologies is normally afflicted with new risks; this is an experience mankind has made many times in the past. This experience has also shown that these risks should not generally lead to a negative attitude vis-à-vis new technologies but rather to a careful balancing of the negative and the positive aspects and that the result of this consideration should be the determining factor in whether a new technology should be used or not. Only to a very limited extent can patent law play a role in this assessment (EPO, 1992, p. 13).

From this perspective, patenting is not inherently unethical.

Arguments on the Grounds of Benefit to Society—It is also arguable that the encouragement of innovation in gene technology would benefit a number of areas of society, especially medicine and farming.

In medicine, there is a need to seek out cures for diseases. This need, however, existed before gene technology appeared and will exist long after it is superseded by another technology. Chapter 2 has discussed the various applications of gene technology in medicine. At this point, medical science still has no cure for the common cold, let alone crippling or deadly diseases such as diabetes, hemophilia, leukemia, muscular dystrophy, cystic fibrosis, Alzheimer's, Huntington's, and Lou Gehrig's. Gene technology is but one more option in the search. Ethically, society has an obligation to explore all avenues in its search for treatments or cures.

In some cases, conventional methods of treatment or production of substances exist. In others, gene technology is either the only viable method or the best and safest method available. This is as true for the use of animals in laboratory tests as for their use in gene pharming, where genetically altered animals produce human proteins in their milk. Critics of patenting in gene technology who voice concern about animal welfare and the inherent worth of the animal must also remember that animal testing is the most reliable option in the production of a new medication and the only one currently accepted by health authorities (EPO, 1992). An article from the *Financial Times* reports:

> Recombinant DNA products already in use include hepatitis B vaccine, insulin and erythropoietin, which helps patients dependent on artificial kidneys. . . .
>
> The WHO pointed out that some of these products, such as erythropoietin, could not be made by conventional means while manufacture of insulin once required the slaughter of millions of pigs a year. Biotechnology can also help make drugs safer by avoiding infection risks.
>
> The UN agency sees some of the biggest benefits coming in developing countries where millions of people die each year from infectious diseases. The hope is that genetically engineered vaccines may overcome the limitations of existing vaccines. (Wiliams, 1994, p. 7)

Inasmuch as it is acceptable and indeed necessary to use animals in medical research, it follows that patenting should be an acceptable form of protection of animals that have been genetically developed specifically for research purposes and for the production of medical substances. Furthermore, beyond the considerations for the welfare of animals—where gene technology may actually make some positive contributions towards decreasing the number of animal slaughters—society must also consider the needs of human patients. If the lives of animals are just as valuable as the lives of human beings, then the quality of human lives deserves at least as much consideration. Often in hormone therapy and organ transplant, the only alternative to animal sources would be human donors.

As noted earlier, however, there is a serious shortage of human donors: although about four thousand organ transplants were carried out in Europe in 1993, an additional nine thousand were not carried out because of the lack of available organs (Eberhard-Metzger, 1995). As a result of this short-age, it is estimated that 20 percent of patients waiting for a heart transplant will die; as will 20 to 25 percent of those waiting for a lung; and 17 per cent of patients waiting for a new liver (Nieren aus dem Saustall, 1993).

In addition, the methods of gene technology can overcome some of the obstacles of obtaining sufficient hormone for treatment. For example, dwarfism is the result of a deficient supply of the human growth hormone. Before 1984, the only source of that hormone was extracts obtained from the pituitary glands of corpses. To obtain enough growth hormone for the treat-ment of one child for a year, pituitary glands had to be extracted and processed from about eighty cadavers (Micklos and Freyer, 1990). There was also a risk that certain diseases of the brain (specifically, Creutzfeldt Jakob disease and Gerstmann Sträußler syndrome) could be transferred from infected cadavers. Because these diseases do not manifest themselves for a long time, it was often not possible to identify potential carriers at the time of death. As a consequence, children receiving hormone treatment for dwarfism ran the risk of contracting these diseases as well. Through biotechnology, it is now possible to ensure a sufficient supply of the hormone in pure form and to prevent the transfer of infectious diseases.

Not only medicine but also animal husbandry and plant cultivation ben-efit from developments in gene technology. Innovations help a decreasing agricultural population satisfy the needs of a growing urban population. Such creative technological innovations deserve encouragement through the legal protection that society affords any other technology in such a situ-ation.

In the field of animal husbandry, one often overlooked contribution of gene technology is in the area of disease prevention. Veterinary medicine now includes vaccines produced by gene technology to immunize animals against viral and bacterial infections. Two examples are vaccines for rabies and cattle plague (Gen Suisse, 1994). The direct benefit is healthier animals, thus improving the welfare of the animals themselves. The indirect benefit is that the consumer is assured of a healthy source of meat, dairy products, and other animal by-products. For the farmers, there is the bonus of more choice when drawing from the healthiest animals in the herd or flock for breeding purposes. One benefit to society as a whole is animals that are more resistant to infectious diseases, which could potentially carry over to consumers.

In another example, gene technology can help to produce livestock that consume less feed and are leaner. Similar arguments can be made in plant cultivation. Losses from insect pests, microbial infection, and the elements account for a significant portion of overall crop loss each year (Schuchert and Meyer, 1992). Genetic alteration of seeds can produce plants that are more resistant to pests, diseases, and environmental factors; are resistant to pesticides and herbicides; use less nutrients and energy; stay fresh longer on the shelves; or have improved flavors and nutritional content. In the long term, the farmer uses less energy to produce a healthy harvest; the consumer enjoys more nutritious products and possibly lower costs.

All these benefits are important considerations in a society that is increasingly health conscious and demands responsible use of scarce resources. Gene technology offers innovative options or solutions for the problems in those areas. Thus, the beneficial results of gene technology are far-reaching. If society is to benefit from the creative genius of an inventor, then justice demands that the individual share in the rewards as well.

This argument does not detract from the valid arguments of animal-rights groups that the welfare of animals must always remain a priority. As this book repeatedly emphasizes, arguments for patent protection in gene technology do not exclude legitimate concerns in other areas. Arguments for animal welfare and respect for life are valid *regardless* of whether or not patents exist. The question of patents relates directly and exclusively to the encouragement of human ingenuity and the protection of intellectual property which benefits society.

Arguments on the Grounds of the Social Responsibility of Industry—In addition to social benefits, patent protection fosters openness and fair play in the economic arena. In business, what one company will not do, another one will. The corollary is that what one company can do successfully, others will compete for a share in. Such an attitude is in part a response to the natural forces of a competitive market and in part a response to market demands to satisfy human needs.

From another perspective, a company exists as a legal entity, for example, through instruments of incorporation. As such, it establishes a contract with society and becomes a corporate citizen, with all the attendant rights, privileges, and obligations. Implicit in its social contract is the obligation to pursue all options for efficiency and satisfaction of the needs of society in its area of business. For example, pharmaceutical companies are obliged to look for new or efficient ways to find cures or treatments for diseases—whether in humans, animals or plants. A company has a moral obligation to employees, shareholders, customers, and the state (as tax collector) to explore all possible venues in which it can satisfy the obligations of its contract within the limits of the law. It can be argued that companies in the pharmaceutical industry, biotechnology industry, and farming industry have an obligation to explore gene technology as alternative means of production. They also have a duty to comply with all the regulations governing safety, the environment, and production.

At the same time, these companies also have a right to expect appropriate legal protection for their products or processes. There are two legal ways to ensure such protection: trade secrets and patents. Trade secrecy enables a company to keep its production methods hidden from the public. Given the concerns surrounding gene technology, trade secrecy would be an even less desirable alternative than in other technologies. Patenting, the other alternative, has the advantage that companies will be obliged to reveal what they do. This disclosure not only ensures fair play but also allows society to see what companies do behind their walls. In that sense, patenting is also a form of social control because the government, the legislative assembly, and the patent office (which normally derives its powers from the legislative body or, in the last instance, the courts) can restrict or stop unacceptable practices (see "Options for Social Control" below).

Arguments on the Grounds That Patenting Life Forms Is Not Playing God— The last emotional argument for patenting is that patenting an innovation in gene technology is not playing God. In most monotheistic religions, God as Creator has an inherent and absolute right over all creation. A patent on a genetically altered plant or animal does not make the inventor God (or imply it) because a patent grants no rights over the plant or animal. The only thing it grants is recognition of the inventor's technological intervention. The only right it grants the *inventor*—not *creator*—is the right to claim the privilege of a monopoly within a specific time period and a geographical area. It allows the inventor to claim the right (or to assign it to someone else) to enjoy the rewards of his or her work.

THE DANGER OF SLOGANEERING AS DEBATE

Slogans are short phrases capturing single ideas. In military, advertising, or political campaigns, a slogan is a short and effective way of summarizing one side's stand or belief, and it can be a useful tool in swaying opinions. Slogans cannot deal with the breadth and depth of a complex issue.

In George Orwell's *Animal Farm*, the slogan of the animals' revolution was "all animals are equal." But, when a privileged minority (pigs) ascended to power, the slogan soon became "all animals are equal but some are more equal than others." Whenever the pigs' authority was challenged, they would remind their challenger of this absurd slogan, as if it were the answer to all problems. In other words, the slogan that started out promoting an ideal ended up preventing other views or voices from being heard.

That is the danger in slogans. As succinct summaries of one position (one slogan, one concept), they oversimplify a complex situation. Thus, in a situation where there are lots of gray areas, slogans force people to choose between black and white. Rather than discussing their differences and ways of resolving them, both sides become entrenched in their positions and exchange volleys of slogans, what is here termed "sloganeering."

Sloganeering is the danger facing the debate on gene technology. In reducing the challenges to one or two concepts, slogans are starting to cloud the issue, which remains unresolved. A slogan represents a fixed position: a change in your slogan means a change in your position—and vice versa. As long as slogans divide the gene technology debate into two opposing camps, there will be no room for middle ground, no room for consensus, no room for solutions.

THE REAL ISSUE IN THE DEBATE

In the discussions surrounding gene technology patents, patentability is really not the issue. Opponents do not dispute the value of the patent system, which has stood the test of time: if they did, they would be challenging all patents, not just those in gene technology. It is also obvious that the patent system works in favor of openness and critical review because it offers the public—special-interest groups, competitors, and concerned individuals—an opportunity to challenge patent applications and even patents already granted.

In terms of the technical requirements of patent law, many of the patent offices responding to the OECD questionnaire (see above, "Rational Arguments for Gene Technology Patents") said "that their present patent law was well suited to the requirements of biotechnology" and "that there should be no difference in the application of the patent law as between inventions in the field of living matter and those of the inanimate world" (Beier and Straus, 1985, p. 38). The question, then, is this: Why have the discussions on gene technology centered on patenting?

To raise public awareness and initiate public debate about a new technology, it is sufficient for opponents to stage a publicity event—a protest march, a blockade, a sit-in, or even a poster campaign. To voice one's opposition in an official setting, however, the patent office becomes the first forum in which to state one's case. Patenting is also the first time the new technology goes before a court of law and, more important, the court of public opinion. When a state grants a patent for a new technology, it is also implicitly giving sanction. Conversely, in denying a patent, the state is implicitly withholding its approval. The symbolic significance of a patent thus exceeds its mere commercial value.

In the key cases examined in this chapter, the importance lies not in the particulars of each case but in the principles behind the arguments and the judicial decisions. Each case represents the first application of the technology in that area, the first time that application went on trial, and the first time opposing arguments were brought forward. When the opposition's arguments fail, it must move to a new arena of legislation, for example, the safety of production facilities and proper labeling of products. In gene technology, this transition is already being made.

Hence, the debates around gene technology patents go deeper than just patents. The central issue is the lack of social acceptance. Opposition to such patents is a way of saying that there should be no economic incentive for this technology. For many critics, opposition is also a way of expressing their fear about its applications (Krimsky, 1991).

Thus, the proponents of the new technology need to define what social acceptance means and develop effective, appropriate measures of social control. They will have to take seriously the critics' fears and concerns. It is not simply a matter of "educating the masses" so that they will unquestioningly accept all applications of the new technology. Fear, as one analyst of risk communications (Röglin, 1994) writes, has a valuable function as a social indicator and can help society to recognize conflicts, prepare for risks, and take control of a potentially dangerous situation. Therefore, in addressing this fear of gene technology, it will be vital to consider measures of social control for its development.

OPTIONS FOR SOCIAL CONTROL

Patenting is one option for social control of new technology. This section briefly considers patenting and then proposes four alternative means of control: prohibition, restricted availability, product registration, and licensing outside the patent system. A short description of each option is provided, followed by a consideration of the pros and cons. All these options are legislative measures. The discussion deliberately ignores the alternative of refusing to grant patents, which amounts to premature rejection of the technology without a balanced analysis of its inherent risks *and* benefits.

PATENTS

It is important to remember that the disclosure requirement of patents serves not only the publication of new information but also provides a degree of social control, ensuring that a technology will not develop in unwanted directions and uncontrollable ways. Patents set the limits on availability and the conditions of use.

Social control occurs twice in the granting of a patent. The first time is during the initial lengthy examination process, which varies from several months to more than a year. Government officials, technical specialists, and legal experts examine the patent application to ensure that it conforms with the legal requirements of the state.

The second time is during an appeal period that follows the granting of the patent. This provision allows any interested person or group to inspect the patent and file an opposition. The appeal period varies according to the state (Baxter, 1973). As the cases discussed show, this important provision allows society to challenge the claims of an inventor and require him to justify the direction the invention is taking .

The debate on gene technology patents goes beyond whether patents should be allowed or not. As Krimsky says, "The issue of patenting living things has served as a social heuristic and provided a vehicle for discussions about the direction and control of technology" (1991, p. 57). Patents, however, like any social tool, must first of all serve the needs of society, adapting to new social conditions and requirements. As previously described, patenting has evolved from an instrument of privilege and monopoly in the fifteenth century to the present complex of economic, technological, and social incentives requiring the patent holder to exercise the patent or else face penalties.

Today, there is a variety of ways to exercise the rights received under a patent. The patent holder may grant an exclusive license, designating one party to do whatever a patent would otherwise exclude him from doing. The patent holder may grant a nonexclusive licence, allowing several parties to operate under patent protection. Further, if there is an agreement, the licensee may even sublicense those rights to third parties (Gregory et al., 1994).

When a tool no longer serves its original purpose, then the user must consider other existing instruments or else develop new ones.

PROHIBITION

The first alternative to the patent system as an option for social control is a prohibition, which is a legal ban by authorities. It would mean that no one would be allowed to use or develop gene technology. It would legally end all gene technology projects—in academia, industry, and government. The proscription could take the form of a moratorium (a ban of a limited period) or a general prohibition (a ban of an indefinite period). Prohibition would probably entail legislation by individual states, which would probably require the support of the majority of people and their representatives. The arguments for and against prohibition are given in Table 3.6.

It may be concluded that prohibition is not a realistic option. It is too extreme to be acceptable to most sectors of society. The sacrifice of the positive contributions of gene technology—especially in the medical sector—would be too high, especially for individuals who would benefit from the new products. In medicine, prohibition would probably cause more harm than good.

Prohibition in agriculture would perhaps be less drastic. Nevertheless, there would have to be careful reflection on viable alternatives to pesticides or herbicides, to better resource management and increased productivity, and to the contributions of gene technology to satisfying the needs of an urbanized society with declining agricultural resources.

Furthermore, prohibition is not an effective solution to the ethical and moral problems posed by gene technology. Nor does prohibition address other challenges that existed before gene technology: animal welfare in farm, industrial, and laboratory settings; human relationships to existing animals and plants; the use of the world's resources; genetic erosion arising from selective breeding; control of diseases; an ever declining agricultural population supporting an ever growing urban population; compensation for resources from developing nations to industrialized nations; the conflict

Table 3.6 Summary of Arguments For and Against Prohibition

For	Against
Society exerts its control, stopping a potentially dangerous technology before any real harm is done.	Prohibitions are generally difficult to enforce: they take much time and tend to encourage underground operations. Any person or group could produce products illegally.
A moratorium allows time to contemplate future courses of action. A general prohibition forces society to consider alternative means to fulfill its needs.	A moratorium or prohibition in one state may not lead to one in another state. If the technology stops in some and continues in others, then the prohibition has failed to achieve its goal.
Society takes a decisive position that rejects all known, unknown, and potential risks and hazards to human beings and the environment.	The same decision also rejects all known, unknown, and potential benefits and advantages to the individual, society, medicine, the economy, industry, or the environment. It is premature to reject a whole technology at the developmental stage before a weighing of the pros and cons, and without careful consideration of the full implications of such a ban.
The prohibition stops a technology with potential risk for both human society and the environment.	The action would be morally debatable because it amounts to the suppression of knowledge and the freedom of research and limits individual choice. All new technologies have inherent risks and benefits. Society has a moral obligation to weigh both potentials before resorting to extreme decisions.

between tradition and innovation; the rights and responsibilities of individuals and organizations in the face of common dilemmas.

No one would seriously claim that without gene technology, society would collapse. However, instead of totally rejecting it at the developmental stage, it is more prudent to weigh the long-term risks and benefits. To use an analogy, although knives can be used for killing, no one would seriously propose a prohibition on the steel industry. The question is how to exercise reasonable social control so that society can draw on the benefits and advantages of the technology while keeping the risks and hazards to a minimum.

RESTRICTED AVAILABILITY
Another option for social control is restricted availability, which limits the legal use of the technology or its results to specific conditions or sectors of society. Such limitation stops short of a moratorium or a general prohibition. Current examples include prescription medication, weapons control, and restrictions on the use of dangerous substances. It would be possible to restrict the availability of either processes, products, or both. Restricted availability is not synonymous with a restriction, which is a ban. In contrast, restricted availability only limits the degree to which a technology or its results may used or sold. This limit can be broad or narrow. The arguments for and against this option can be seen in Table 3.7.

One may conclude from these arguments that it will be necessary to define judiciously the parameters of the restriction. There are two challenges. The first is timing. At this early stage, gene technology offers potential for both good and harm; therefore, restricted availability is not the optimal choice at this point. The second is in deciding which areas of the technology merit encouragement and which ones do not. Too broad a restriction will be so ambiguous that it will create problems during the mature phases of the technology. Too narrow a restriction will stifle any development.

It is less easy to predict the effects of restricted availability than those of a prohibition. If availability is too broadly or narrowly restricted, then the measure will prove to be ineffective and will cause more problems than it would solve. If the measure is the result of a fair, well-managed, and evaluative process, then society will be able to regulate the speed and direction of the evolving technology in the light of a wide cross-section of interests.

Nevertheless, although restricted availability solves the problem of social control, it does not offer an innovative response to the challenges that modern society faces. It does not provide an answer to the problems that the new technology brought into focus but did not cause. Furthermore, it has no mechanism to encourage the disclosure of knowledge or to promote inventive interests; nor does it necessarily offer protection of intellectual property—some of the advantages offered by patenting.

Table 3.7 Summary of Arguments For and Against Restricted Availability

For	Against
Through restricted availability, society allows the technology to guide progress in acceptable directions.	At the early stages of a technology, restricted availability may prematurely limit choice and further development, resulting in a long-term negative impact on the economy, medicine, agriculture, and other areas.
A generous definition, leaning toward availability rather than restriction, would allow room for exploration while preventing progress in obviously undesirable directions.	As the technology develops, such a generous definition will likely lead toward lengthy court cases. The court room is not a satisfactory alternative to a broad, more democratic public debate.
If judicious and well managed, the option will strike a balance between prudence and technological progress.	It will be difficult to maintain a balance between prudence and technological progress. If the restriction is too narrow, it will be ineffective; if it is encompassing, it will be stifle the technology.

PRODUCT REGISTRATION

The third option for social control, product registration, is common in the pharmaceutical industry and the weapons industry, among others. Before a product could go on the market, it would have to satisfy all relevant legislation and the stringent requirements of a designated government body. Once approved, the product would be placed on an official government list. Only products on this list would be legal for commercial use. The arguments for and against product registration are given in Table 3.8 (p. 156).

It may be concluded that unlike weapons or pharmaceutical products, the applications of gene technology are not limited to one area of utility. They cover many different sectors: breeding, farming, and food production; human and veterinary medicine; and industrial and medical research. Where weapons or drugs would be registered with one or possibly two government bodies, products of gene technology might require registries in several departments or agencies.

In addition, in a number of countries, there are two or more levels of government with shared or independent responsibilities. For example, health

Table 3.8 Summary of Arguments For and Against Product Registration

For	Against
Society controls the technology by bureaucratic decisions about its results when the products are ready for use. At this time, such decisions reflect society's attitudes toward any inherent risks in the technology or the products.	Mismanaged registration becomes a gamble for producers, who could spend time and money on research and development only to find that the product failed to obtain approval. Society would face the dilemma of what to do with a genetically altered plant or animal that was not approved.
The products would receive approval only after government bodies have rigorously assessed them.	At this point, registration normally does not include mechanisms for public review. Reserved for specialists, the process would only isolate the technology even further from the average person.
Through the type and number of listed products, the registry would indicate the areas of growth and direction of development of the technology. Society could then determine whether such growth and direction were desirable.	It might become impractical to register every single genetically altered plant or animal, especially if used on farms for breeding. Because the registry might not include the progeny of the originally altered form, it might not provide as accurate a picture as desired.

care in Canada is shared between the Department of Health and Welfare at the federal level and the departments of medical services in the provinces. This division might require the maintenance of additional registries, making it a complex process to register some products. The visibility of the technology's growth and direction development would be obscured by the registration process itself. The alternative would be to create a separate department to regulate and register the new technology. But the overlap into existing areas of responsibilities would create such negative political ramifications that no government would seriously contemplate such a measure.

Thus, like prohibition and restricted availability, product registration offers only a partial answer to the broader questions raised in the debates on gene technology. If the current practice of using product registration as a complement to the patent system is extended to gene technology, then several issues are addressed: social control of the new technology (product registration), protection of intellectual property (patenting), disclosure (patenting), and public scrutiny of new technological innovations (patenting). It becomes obvious that product registration in itself does not offer any advantages over patenting.

LICENSING PARALLEL TO THE PATENT SYSTEM

The options for social control examined so far have failed to produce a satisfactory response to the needs of society today. What is needed is a new, global solution. Such a solution, the fourth option, would be a licensing system independent of patent licensing. Such a dual system exists already for pharmaceutical products, which must first receive the approval of patent authorities and then obtain a licence from regulatory bodies (for example, the U.S. Food and Drug Administration). Such a system could be specifically developed to meet the needs and challenges of gene technology. It must be remembered that patenting is not the only instrument to protect intellectual property and stimulate intellectual creation; there are also, for example, copyright and plant-variety protection. To be effective, the new system must take into consideration the nature of gene technology innovations (namely, that they are alive) and the human contributions to their existence. The system must also reflect the values of a more globally and environmentally conscious society.

In 1995 C. Rehmann-Sutter proposed a licensing system that would respond to most of these needs. It would consider gene technology as the middle ground between traditional breeding techniques and engineering methods. At the same time, it would take into account the interests of inventors, breeders, and the originating countries. Each case would be individually examined and would also be available for public scrutiny. The growth of the technology would be the result not of free market forces (that is, demand and supply) but of governmental policies, which would be open to appeal or contestation.

In Rehmann-Sutter's system, the granting of licenses would depend on the results of assessments of safety conditions, environmental impact, and social impact. The system would include a criterion protecting the worth and integrity of the life form. That is, officials would consider the existence of the animal as an independent living being and any suffering it would experience. Any assault on the animal's welfare would have to be unavoidable and justified only by the vital interests of humankind.

For Rehmann-Sutter, the patent system does not satisfactorily address all the problems that gene technology raises. A major problem is the complete reduction of life to an object, clearly violating the dignity of life. Equally problematic is the fact that genetically altered life forms depend much more than the products of other technologies on "non gene technology input." This fact is not recognized in the granting of patent rights to an applicant for gene technology mainly because the life form in question cannot claim prior patent rights in a court of law. (See also "Emotional Arguments Against Gene

Technology Patents" above.) The arguments for and against a parallel licensing system are summarized in Table 3.9.

In conclusion it may be noted that as the patent system was a response to the needs of nineteenth-century industrial society, the new license system proposed by Rehmann-Sutter might provide an innovative response to the complex needs of the late twentieth-century technological society, specifically, by guiding the development of gene technology.

Whether Rehmann-Sutter's system would work remains to be seen. The essential point is that it offers an alternative solution to a dilemma. Necessity is said to be the mother of invention. Thus, if existing options fail to provide a satisfactory answer to a new problem, then a solution must be tailored specifically to meet those needs.

Although the patent system adequately responds to the legal and technical challenges of gene technology, it does not address the attendant moral, ethical, and social problems. This is not to say that patenting is not the best option at the moment. Indeed, the patent system offers many advantages over other *existing* alternatives, including transparency of industrial research and development, the transfer of technical knowledge from the private to the public domain, and the encouragement of intellectual creativity. Nevertheless, finding a path through the labyrinth of ethical and social problems may require an ingenious solution. In the meantime, society must consider alternatives. There are two possibilities. One is to create a new and independent system, similar to the one proposed by Rehmann-Sutter. It is questionable, however, whether any single system could effectively deal with the two separate challenges it faces: the protection of industrial property and encouragement of technological innovation and the social control of a new technology.

The other possible alternative is to treat patentability and regulation separately by creating a new system as a complement to the existing patent system. To overcome the objection that gene technology, unlike technologies based on physics or chemistry, comes from and explicitly involves life, such a system would provide a mechanism for social control.

According to this two-pronged approach, the patent office would examine whether a product or process satisfies all the criteria for patentability: novelty, nonobviousness, and utility. If it did, the office would grant a patent, but it would not take effect immediately. Rather, when the patent holder was ready to bring the product to market, he or she would have to receive approval from another body, which would consider product safety (for individuals, society, and the environment) and other nonpatent questions. Only if the product satisfied all these criteria would the patent take effect and the product be allowed on the market. The decision of the second body would not affect the status of the patent. This process of conditional patentability is modeled on the drug registration process, where the drug is both patented and registered.

Table 3.9 Summary of Arguments For and Against a Parallel Licensing System

For	Against
Society would govern the speed and direction of development of the new technology. Market growth would be the result of governmental policies, which would reflect the interests of both industry and of society.	The system would lack acceptance in some countries, where government control would be in direct opposition to a nation's preferred approach. For example, in the United States, government intervention is less present (and less welcome) than in Canada and Switzerland.
The process would be open and participatory because each application would be subject to governmental review and public scrutiny.	Such an open and consultative process might end up delaying the launching of products. Opposition groups might use the process to veto or at least delay progress of any sort. There would have to be measures to prevent such veto or stalling tactics. Broad participation would have to be encouraged.
The system would incorporate a series of checks and balances. Input would come from government, industry, and the general public. Government decisions would be open to review by industry and public.	If every government policy in this process were open to questioning by industry and the public, few policies might actually be implemented. The process could be self-defeating if it became an opportunity for veto. Also a popularist government might abdicate its responsibilities to take the initiative in dealing with controversial matters.
The system would provide a flexible option, adjusting to changing conditions. This flexibility would give the system an advantage because there is an increasing need to find solutions quickly.	This flexibility might become a weakness if politicians and bureaucrats reacted to developments instead of actively providing firm guidance.
The system would provide an innovative response to a new, complex dilemma of industrialized society.	

RESPONSIBLE TECHNOLOGY

Gene technology presents society with a challenge because it enables human beings to intrude in the most basic processes of life in ways and degrees never before possible. It is a challenge because society has to accept the burden of responsibility that comes with that power.

Two themes have recurred throughout this chapter: the issue of social acceptance of gene technology that underlies controversies over its patentability and the need for social control that is the source of resistance to the technology. These themes have one point in common: the concept of responsibility.

Each of the five patent cases analyzed in this chapter was the first time that gene technology was applied in that particular area. It was also the first opportunity that critics had to challenge the technology and the new application within a legal framework. In effect, those creating, using, and overseeing the technology were being reminded of their responsibility to society. They were challenged to demonstrate that

- the technology would serve the needs of society
- the technology would bring the benefits promised
- the benefits would outweigh any risks or negative effects

It is worth noting that, in four of the five cases, the legal battles were fought on ethical grounds. The ethical aspect brought to light the conflict of values that gene technology has sparked.

This conflict should not be surprising. Gene technology brings together two powerful elements—life and high technology—that capture the imagination yet defy comprehension. It subjects genes, symbol of life, to technological manipulation, symbol of human ingenuity and achievement in the conquest of nature. Conflict arises between the proponents of gene technology, who tend to set a higher value on human achievement, and opponents, who set a higher value on life. They view life, as do most nonindustrial cultures, as veiled in an aura of sacred mystery and therefore reject a technology that seems to allow human beings a claim to have discovered its mystery.

To understand the battle over patents in gene technology, it is essential to recognize that it stems partly form the need for social control and partly from conflicting value systems. These two sources of the struggle will be discussed in chapter 4.

KEY POINTS

- To qualify for a patent, an invention must satisfy three criteria: novelty, nonobviousness, and utility.

- An invention is a form of intellectual property that industrialized society considers essential for economic and social progress. Through a patent, knowledge is placed in public hands.

- Although a patent grants an inventor the right to exclude others from making, selling, or using the invention, it does *not* grant that person the right to make, sell, or use the invention. The inventor must still satisfy laws controlling its use, sale, or production.

- Human invention is the criterion for patentability. This criterion was established through the *Diamond* vs. *Chakrabarty* case (microorganism patent), which set the precedent for the patenting of all genetically modified life forms in the United States.

- The patenting of higher life forms must weigh the interests of humankind against the protection of the environment and the impact on the life form itself. In Europe, this criterion was established through the ruling for the Lubrizol case (plant patent) and the Harvard onco-mouse case (animal patent).

- The central issue in the patenting of human genes is human rights. One of the underlying values in Western society is respect for the individual and free will. Therefore consent of the individual—freedom of decision—is essential to matters involving samples taken from human beings.

- The focus on genes has resulted in their being viewed as discrete entities in their own right. The legal dispute over the patent applications on gene sequences of unknown function underline this shift from organisms to genes themselves.

- There are both rational and emotional arguments for and against patenting in gene technology.

- The patent office, consisting of technicians and specialists, is equipped to deal with questions of patentability but not with ethical issues, which should be discussed in a legislative or other public arena.

- The patentability of products of gene technology is not the issue; social acceptance of the technology is. The patent office serves as the arena in which specific applications of the new technology come up for approval.

- In addressing the fear of gene technology, it is necessary to consider measures of social control. These measures may include prohibition, restricted availability, product registration, and licensing (parallel to the patenting system). Each has advantages and drawbacks.

- Gene technology brings together two powerful symbols: genes, the symbol of life, and high technology, the symbol of human accomplishment. Proponents of patents in gene technology value technology more highly; opponents to reject a technology that would allow society a claim to control the mystery of life.

- The struggle over gene technology stems from two sources: need for social control (safety and ethical concerns) and conflicting value systems.

REFERENCES

Adler, R. G. 1992. Genome Research: Fulfilling the Public's Expectations for Knowledge and Commercialization. *Science* 257: 908–914.

Anderson, C. 1991a. To Patent a Naked Gene. *Nature* 353: 485.

———. 1991b. US Patent Application Stirs Up Gene Hunter. *Nature* 353: 485–486.

Baxter, J. W. 1973. *World Patent Law and Practice*. 2d ed. London: Sweet and Maxwell.

Beier, F. K., and J. Straus, 1985. Patents in a Time of Rapid Scientific and Technological Change: Inventions in Biotechnology. In *Biotechnology and Patent Protection: An International Review,* edited by F. K. Beier, R. S. Crespic, and J. Straus, pp. 15–30. Paris: Organization for Economic Cooperation and Development.

Bishop, J. E. 1994. Merck's Plan for Public-Domain Gene Data Could Blow Lid Off Secret Genetic Research. *Wall Street Journal Europe*, 30 September, p. 4.

Browning, E. S. 1994. Drug Makers' Shares Surge in U.S. on Sign of Longer Lives for Patents. *Wall Street Journal Europe*, 21 December.

Byrne, N. 1993. Patents for Human Genes, Ownership of Biological Materials and Other Issues in Patent Law. *World Patent Information* 15 (4): 199–202.

Canibol, H.-P. 1994, Forscher gegen Bürokraten. *Focus*, May, pp. 220–222.

Cherfas, J. 1989. Stopping the Process of Pregnancy. *Science* 245: 1320.

Coghlan, A. 1993. Engineering the Therapies of Tomorrow. *New Scientist*, 24 April, pp. 26–31.

Cookson, C. 1994. The Ultimate Privatisation. *Financial Times*, 8 October, p. 8.

Däpp, H. 1994. Patentierung von Genen wirft viele Fragen auf. *Basler Zeitung*, 12 October, p. 7.

European Federation of Biotechnology. 1993. *Patenting Life* (briefing paper): Brussels: European Federation of Biotechnology, Task Group on Public Perceptions of Biotechnology.

European Patent Office. 1992a. Decisions of the Examining and Opposition Divisions: Grant of European Patent No. 0 169 672 (Onco-mouse/Harvard). *Official Journal EPO* 10: 588–593.

————. l992b. *Interlocutory Decision Against EP-B-0122791*: European Patent Office Opposition Division.

Fischer, M. 1993. Das Vampir-Projekt. *Die Woche Zeitung*, 2 December.

Gen Suisse. 1994. *Möglichkeiten und Grenzen der Gentechnik*. Bern: Gen Suisse.

Gregory, D. A., C. W. Saber, and J. D. Grossman. 1994. *Introduction to Intellectual Property*. Washington, D.C.: BNA Books.

Hobbelink, H. 1991. *Biotechnology and the Future of World Agriculture*. London: Zed Books Ltd.

Hug, P. 1993. Tiere sind keine Erfindungen der Menschen. *Der Tagensanzeiger*, 10 February.

Jensen, A. 1994. Wird der Mensch zur patentierbaren Erfindung? *Die Tageszeitung*, 7 January.

Keller, C. 1993. Eine Genbank für bedrohte Völker. *Die Wochenzeitung*, 15 October.

Kleiner, K. 1994. There's No Such Thing as a Free Gene. *New Scientist*, 15 October, p. 10.

Koechlin, F. 1992. Patente—ein Eigengoal. *Die WochenZeitung*, 11 September.

————. 1993. Wenn die Forscher zu Besuch kommen. *Die WochenZeitung*, 15 October.

Krimsky, S. 1991. *Biotechnics and Society: The Rise and Fall of Industrial Genetics*. New York: Praeger.

Leary, W. E. 1994. It's Red, Plump, Juicy, and Out of a Lab. *International Herald Tribune*, 20 May.

Marshall, E. 1994. A Showdown over Gene Fragments. *Science* 266: 208–210.

McCabe, R. 1994. Longer-Life Tomato Wins OK. *Sun-Sentinel*, 8 April, pp. D1-D2.

Micklos, D. A., and G. A. Freyer. 1990. *DNA Science: A First Course in DNA Technology*. Burlington, N.C.: Carolina Biological Supply Company.

Moore, S. D. 1994. Drug Makers Expect to See Brisk Trading in Human Gene Data. *Wall Street Journal Europe*, 22 September, pp. 1.

Nieren aus dem Saustall. 1993. *Der Spiegel*, 30 August, pp. 208–214.

Podolksy, D. 1990. Sorry, Not Sold in the U.S. (Birth Control Options). *US News and World Report*, 24 December, p. 65.

Rehmann-Sutter, C. 1995. Lizenzsystem statt patentrechtliche Regelung. *Neue Zürcher Zeitung*, 9 January, p. 15.

Reist, M. 1994. Ich finde es falsch, Lebewesen zu patentieren. *Bündner Zeitung*, 8 September, p. 2.

Roberts, L. 1991. Genome Patent Fight Erupts. *Science* 254: 184–186.

Röglin, H.-C. 1994. *Standortsicherung—auch eine Frage der Öffentlichkeitsarbeit und Informationspolitik*. Düsseldorf: Institut für Angewandte Sozialpsychologie.

Schneider, K. 1994. Go-Ahead Likely on Crop Tinkering, but Some Are Wary. *New York Times*, 25 May, p. A14.

Schuchert, W., and C. Meyer, eds. 1992. *Pflanzenproduktion und Biotechnologie*. Cologne: Max-Planck-Institut für Züchtungsforschung.

Stout, H. 1992. Patent Turned Down in U.S. for Human Gene Fragments. *Wall Street Journal Europe*, 24 September, pp. B1, B7.

Suiter, S. P., and B. K. Wax. 1994. The Patentability of DNA Fragments with Unknown Utility. *Patent World* 67: 16–23.

U.S. Office of Technology Assessment. 1989. *New Developments in Biotechnology: Patenting Life*, no.5: Washington, D.C.: U.S. Congress, Office of Technology Assessment.

Williams, F. 1994. Biotechnology Drugs Can Save "Millions of Lives." *Financial Times*, 9 November, p. 7.

World Intellectual Property Organization. 1992. Human T-Lymphotropic Virus Type 2 from Guaymi Indians in Panama (WO 92/08784). Geneva: World Intellectual Property Organization.

4 UNDERSTANDING THE LIVING WORLD

L ike many new technologies before it, gene technology presents a wide range of dilemmas for society. On the surface, these dilemmas can be reduced to a choice between unexplored opportunities and unknown risks. The degree to which a society accepts a new technology depends, in part, on how significant parts of society evaluate the potential risks and benefits.

For some people, the broad range of applications already available in gene technology (see chapter 2) hints at the potential for harnessing the biological processes of nature, just as previous technologies have used the physical powers of nature (heat, motion, and energy) and the chemical substances of nature (for food, medicine, and cosmetics). For others, the gaps in scientific knowledge and the lack of human experience with gene technology are both reasons for concern. This difference in outlook is one basis for the debates in society. Most people probably stand somewhere between the risk takers and the cautious. Most are probably trying to come to terms with the new technology, weighing its uses against its risks and struggling to understand how it will affect their lives.

This simple struggle in human nature—the willingness to take risks against the tendency for caution—does not fully explain the specific fears, concerns, and anxieties associated with the various applications of gene technology. Gene technology, as one area of biotechnology, is based on biology, the science of life. This technology will change not just any part of an organism but genes themselves—the substance that regulates living processes and systems, the molecules that determine physical features and the function they serve. This fact strikes a deep chord in many individuals. Controversy over gene technology arises, in part, from conflicting views of life, science, and technology in different parts of society.

One way to understand this controversy is to place it in the context of the human preoccupation with life and death—with living and surviving. This preoccupation can be taken literally or in more philosophical terms. In a literal sense, survival—the will to continue to exist—is a basic instinct of all living organisms, not just human beings: as such it guides the basic actions of feeding oneself, protecting oneself, and creating progeny. Throughout history, there have been many threats to human survival. It will be suggested in the first part of this chapter that many of the concerns relating to applications of gene technology can be traced to particular threats to human survival in the past.

In philosophical terms, two questions have probably preoccupied just about every human society: What is life? and Where does human existence fit into the scheme of the universe? To varying degrees, philosophy, religion, and science have tried to answer these two questions, but they have all produced more questions than answers. Indeed, recent developments in science and technology may have even challenged traditional assumptions about what life is—where the difference between life and nonliving matter lies. The rest of the chapter is devoted to exploring some of these questions in greater depth.

RELATING SPECIFIC CONCERNS TO LESSONS FROM THE PAST

Chapter 2 showed how specific applications of gene technology grew out of particular human needs. It also pointed out that the level of support for (or resistance to) gene technology depends on the area of application. Chapter 3 provided a number of cases that allowed a closer look at the many arguments for and against patenting innovations in each application of gene technology. It concluded that many of the arguments raised *against* patenting derived from concerns over the technology itself rather than patenting. At the same time, it noted that the nature of the objections varied according to the application.

The first half of the following section will continue to explore the differences between the concerns over gene technology applications. The second half will try to show how and why different applications raise very specific concerns, in particular, their link to key events and experiences in Western history that threatened human survival.

MICROORGANISMS
Projects involving genetically altered microorganisms raise general concerns about the environment and safety and more specific concerns about diseases.

Concerns Relating to Genetically Altered Microorganims
Many people fear that genetically altered microorganisms could unleash changes in the wild or cause an epidemic in the human population, both of which would be unpredictable and uncontrollable. The recent Swiss experience with a proposal to control rabies with a genetically altered vaccine shows the degree of anxiety sometimes expressed. Through bites, rabies can be transmitted from wild animals to domestic animals and then to humans. In early 1995, the Schweizerische Tollwutzentrale (Swiss Center for Rabies Control—SCRC) filed an application with the Bundesamt für Veterinärwesen (Federal Veterinary Services) to introduce a new rabies vaccine using cowpox viruses genetically altered to contain a key gene from the rabies virus. Since 1987, the new vaccine had already been used in Belgium, France, and the United States and was deemed more effective than the traditional vaccine, especially at temperatures over 21°C (70°F). Because of the length of the review process, the SCRC decided to continue with the traditional vaccine using attenuated rabies viruses but to use new, genetically altered variety—which was approved—in situations where the traditional vaccine would be less effective (Zanoni, Breitenmoser, and Peterhans, 1996).

The application was enough to spark protests from groups such as the Basler Appell gegen Gentechnologie, an anti-biotechnology group. Their greatest fear was that the genetically altered virus could somehow come in contact with a cowpox-related virus to produce a strain of super virus that would spread out of control, posing risks to wild animals and even human beings. Under laboratory conditions, two related species of viruses could be mixed to produce a new strain, but for that to happen spontaneously in real life both viruses would not only have to be in the same organism at the same time but also to occupy the same cell at the same time.

The SCRC argued that the harmlessness and effectiveness of the new vaccine have been well documented. Although the traditional vaccine (using live attenuated rabies viruses) very seldom caused rabies, it remained a possibility. With the new vaccine, this possibility was reduced even further: in laboratory tests, rabies affected only animals with weak immune systems. The possibility that human beings could come into contact with the genetically altered virus—contained in a capsule concealed in bait—was highly unlikely (Zanoni, Breitenmoser, and Peterhaus, 1996).

The same concerns—for wildlife and the environment following a deliberate release, as well as for human health after an accidental release—emerge in other situations involving genetically altered microorganisms. These fears overshadow projects ranging from the construction of laboratories to make genetically altered medical products to the disposal of genetically altered waste products.

Diseases in Agriculture, Animal Husbandry, and Human Medicine

Concerns about disease affecting plants, animals, and humans are genuine and understandable, especially against the backdrop of human experience with disease-bearing microbes. Infectious diseases have been among the oldest scourges of humankind, eliciting a sense of dread and helplessness. Diseases affect all parts of society, regardless of social status, age, or other qualities. Well into the twentieth century, infectious diseases such as polio, smallpox, and even influenza continued to claim the lives of many, especially children. Even today, in the age of vaccines and antibiotics, the word *epidemic* is enough to send ripples of anxiety and even panic throughout many parts of society. Examples of threatening disease can be found in three critical areas: agriculture, animal husbandry, and human health.

Agriculture—In the middle of the nineteenth century, blight, caused by the fungus *Photophthora infestans,* destroyed most of Ireland's potato crop. The ensuing famine aggravated an already strained social situation, leading to the starvation and death of a large part of the Irish population. Many Irish migrated to the United States, Canada, and Australia.

In the early 1970s, blight destroyed an estimated 15 percent of the U.S. maize harvest, with some states losing more than half of their crop. The extent of the devastation was due, in part, to the widespread use of one hybrid of maize, which proved to be vulnerable to this threat (Hobbelink, 1991).

Animal Husbandry—Well into the 1920s and 1930s, before the widespread use of vaccines for farm animals, an outbreak of foot-and-mouth disease was enough to destroy entire herds of cattle—and a quarantine was strictly observed. In many of his stories about his experience as a veterinarian during that time, James Herriot (see "Farming and Food Production Techniques," chapter 5) told of how a single outbreak of the disease would destroy entire herds of cattle and ruin the livelihood of small farmers.

In Australia, one of the biggest problems for many farmers was the rabbit population. Imported from Europe by settlers, rabbits were estimated to number 600 million in the 1950s. Without any natural predators on the continent, they spread uncontrollably, destroying plant life, causing soil erosion, and driving other herbivores to starvation. Attempts to control the rabbits failed. Then in the mid-1980s, scientists found a rabbit virus that might be the solution to the problem: *Rabbit calicivirus*, which kills rabbits within two days. To test the effectiveness of the virus, scientists set up an experimental station on an island off the coast of southern Australia. Despite security measures, however, the virus managed to escape from the island and spread across the continent. By the 1990s, the rabbit population dropped to 200 to 300 million. The runaway success of the virus was such that some people worried about what would happen to foxes or other animals that depended on rabbits for food. They feared that the foxes would now turn to indigenous and already threatened wildlife. People also feared that the virus might possibly be a threat to livestock as well.

Human Medicine—In the Middle Ages, the Black Death (a kind of plague) swept through Europe, killing more than half the population in many parts of the continent. Europe has never quite forgotten the devastation that this disease brought. To this day, the name Blackheath in London is a reminder of where the victims of the plague were buried in mass graves.

In the mid-1970s, the Ebola virus emerged in central Africa. It was identified for the first time in 1976 in Zaire (now Republic of Congo), where it killed more than 270 people, and in Sudan, and then a second time in Sudan in 1979. In the mid-1990s, the virus struck a third time, killing 245 of the 316 people affected in Zaire (WHO, 1996). This disease is highly dreaded because it is deadly and incurable. Of those infected, a great majority die. There is still no vaccine or other treatment for this virus, which may be transmitted through the air.

AIDS first came to public attention in the West sometime in the early 1980s, when a number of early cases broke out in North America. It is now known that the cause is the human immunodeficiency virus, first identified in 1981. According to the WHO (1996), about 20 million adults have been infected by HIV, and more than 4.5 million of them have developed AIDS since the pandemic started in the late 1970s. A lot of fear surrounds HIV and AIDS because there is still no vaccine against HIV and no cure for AIDS. Prevention is still the only protection.

As these instances—from the distant and recent past—show, microorganisms have on several occasions brought disease, destruction, and death to humans. It is thus little wonder that caution—if not outright suspicion—pervades public discussions about any attempts to change microorganisms. Although human beings admittedly need microorganisms—for making wine, cheese, bread, and medicine—the potential threats of microorganisms overshadow their benefits. There are two reasons

First, living in an urban, high-technological environment, many people are unaware of the necessity of microorganisms for human well-being because they are no longer in contact with many natural processes. As far as they are concerned, bread, cheese, wine, and soy sauce come from the supermarket. The role of microorganisms in creating these products is lost behind the packaging and distribution systems of the food industry. Indeed, most of people's needs seem to be met in sanitized, pasteurized, and vacuum-sealed packages.

In the West the transformation from agricultural society to high-technological society is virtually complete. However domesticated nature is on a farm, farm families are at least aware of the cycle of birth, growth, decay, and death in which microbial activities play an integral part. Life in high-technological society, by contrast, seems to be a constant reminder that microorganisms are harmful and to be excluded as much as possible. Personal experiences, such as a cold or some other infection, reinforce the idea that microbes are dangerous.

The second reason for the cautious approach to microorganisms is that a new technology changes not simply certain products and processes but everything in society. It requires new ways of thinking, doing, and even seeing the world. Such change can be a threat to established values and interests. Therefore, attempts to compare the new generation of biotechnology with traditional fermentation are simplistic, as discussed in chapter 2. Such comparisons ignore important differences in impact on society in a given time frame. Whereas fermentation techniques developed over centuries in different cultures, the transformations unleashed by gene technology—the paradigm shift (discussed in chapters 1 and 6)—in today's technological society are taking place in a relatively short time, causing much anxiety. For those unfamiliar with the history of gene technology, its power seems to have no precedence. Therefore, they are cautious. When the proponents of the new technology assert that microorganisms can be transformed, the blights and the epidemics of the past stand out as vivid reminders that microbes, though small, are also powerful and can be very dangerous.

These two reasons help explain why many people perceive the genetic alteration of microorganisms to be risky. Although 78 percent of those surveyed in the European Union in 1993 said they found the new technology acceptable (for example, for creating new products), 54 percent still thought it risky, as noted in chapter 2. Similarly, in Japan, 73 percent thought the procedure acceptable, but 59 percent thought it risky.

Humans may always have a tendency to associate microorganisms with diseases. To do so is neither irrational nor ignorant nor true only of lay people who do not understand biology. It should not be forgotten that when molecular biologists met at Asilomar after the first successful experiment in DNA recombination, the main discussion focused on two health considerations: containment (preventing the accidental release of genetically altered microorganisms) and safety (for laboratory staff). Although some of the laboratory safety measures introduced at that time have since been relaxed because they were unnecessarily stringent, the point is that it is human to react with caution when confronted with the unknown.

PLANTS

There is much concern about gene transfer to weeds and threats to biodiversity and about the potential negative effects on agriculture.

Concerns Relating to Genetically Altered Plants

Writing in the journal *Nature*, three researchers in Denmark (Mikkelsen, Andersen, and Jørgensen, 1996) reported that they had successfully transferred a novel gene from a genetically altered oilseed rape hybrid to a wild relative in order to obtain a hybrid. When the hybrid was crossed once again with the wild parent, *some* of the resulting plants carried traits from both parents. The gene in question codes for an enzyme that makes the oilseed rape plant resistant to the herbicide Basta. The Bund für Umwelt und Naturschutz (BUND), a German environmental group, used the report to argue that there is a risk that transgenic plants could result in pesticide-resistant weeds. The Danish researchers and German scientists replied that the environmentalists had deliberately misinterpreted the results. The findings of the report cannot be carried over to other transgenic crops. Maize and potatoes, for example, do not have any close weedy relatives.

Here it is important to point out that the media played an important role in creating a sensational and controversial story out of a half-page report in a scientific journal. *Die Zeit*, a German newspaper, retraced the evolution of the story (Sentker, 1996). The newswire service of *Nature* carried a news item on the report that was picked up by other news agencies. Ignoring an embargo on premature release, the Associated Press reported that the transferred gene had *spontaneously* crossed over to a wild relative: the word *superweed* was used. The German boulevard paper *Bild* picked up the story, reporting that the novel gene could jump to other related species (plural) in the wild and that herbicides would be ineffective against the resulting superweeds. In reaction, the BUND and the Green Party declared that there should be a stop to such dangerous and irresponsible experiments, comments that received extensive coverage in the German media. The *Frankfurter Rundschau* carried a statement from AgrEvo, a German company carrying out experiments involving transgenic rape and other plants. The company said the Danish results were not unexpected and that resulting hybrid weeds could be controlled using conventional methods.

This example highlights the fear of some people that pesticide-resistant genes could cross over into related weeds to create pesticide-resistant hybrids of weeds that would be difficult to control. Such critics are also concerned that some of the companies producing the new breeds of plants resistant to specific herbicides are also producing those very herbicides. They fear that as a consequence the herbicide-resistant crops would allow or even encourage farmers to use even higher concentrations of those herbicides.

There is also opposition from environmentalist groups to the use of gene technology for developing new breeds of crops. The following example illustrates the point. The bacterium *Bacillus thuringiensis* (Bt) produces a protein that kills certain types of insect larvae but not others (see "Resistance to Pests and Disease," chapter 2). This protein had been used as a pesticide for several decades. Then Ciba-Geigy (today Novartis), the Swiss manufacturer of biological and chemical products, developed a method for transferring the gene that codes for this protein directly into maize, enabling the plant to produce the substance directly as self-defense against these insect larvae.

Ciba subsequently licensed the technology free of charge to the Swiss Federal Institute of Technology (SFIT) in Zurich and the International Rice Research Institute (IRRI) in Manila for use in rice, an area where Ciba is not involved. The SFIT used the technology to develop a new variety of rice. After successful trials in Europe, the SFIT decided to send seed samples to the IRRI for further trials in greenhouses. On hearing of the decision, Greenpeace intercepted the package, arguing that it was irresponsible to send genetically altered organisms around the world without clear safety regulations. One concern was that the new strains of plants could spread and drive wild varieties of rice to extinction, narrowing the number of breeds available. Underlying this argument is a concern that the widespread use of uniform plant varieties would render entire crops vulnerable to yet unknown threats such as a virus or a fungus. Such an outcome would seriously affect not only the livelihood of the farmers in question but also the food supply for a large part of the population.

There is a common theme underlying both the concern with accidental gene transfer to weeds and the concern over biodiversity. That theme is fear that experiments in the agricultural area are gambling too heavily with modern technological society's food supply. The failure of essential crops such as cereals would mean a shortage for both humans and animals.

Agriculture—Times of Plenty, Times of Famine

Behind the fear of gambling with the food supplies lies the question whether modern technological society is able to feed itself. Regardless of scientific advances, food is still a fundamental human need. Agriculture has played a significant role in the development of human societies. Without a steady and continuous supply of food, early humans had to move from place to place with the changing seasons in search of more plants and animals. The development of agriculture meant they could give up a wandering life as hunters and gatherers and settle down in farming communities. The significance of this change cannot be underestimated: a steady food supply allowed human societies to turn their attention to other matters: art, religion, philosophy, and government. It is no coincidence that the words *culture* and *agriculture* are derived from the same Latin root, *cultus*, meaning "tilled."

Modern technological society is still as dependent on good harvests as were early human settlements. Indeed, the dependence may be even greater today, when the majority of the population live in cities and rely on an ever dwindling farming population to produce enough food to satisfy their needs. If farmers were to lose their crops to a drought, virus, or other disaster, most urban dwellers today would probably be the first to feel the effects. Furthermore, the ever increasing division of labor means that most city dwellers would probably be unfamiliar with the operations of a modern farm and thus unable to meet their own needs in an emergency.

In the past, the failure of a staple crop meant hardship and starvation for many people, especially the poor. At the end of the eighteenth century in France, a succession of poor harvests was the impetus for the peasants' uprising that led to the downfall of the French monarchy. It would be a gross exaggeration to say that lack of food caused the French Revolution, but it contributed to the people's hardship and underlined the need for fundamental social change. Similarly, in the middle of the nineteenth century, a large part of the Irish population starved to death because of the failure of the potato crop, which was the basic food of the poor. It seems unlikely that industrialized society would do much better in the face of a major agricultural disaster.

Another reason for resistance to agricultural applications of gene technology is the mixed results of the Green Revolution. In the 1960s and 1970s, it was hoped that the Green Revolution would help end hunger, undernourishment, and starvation in many parts of the world. It was based on special breeding programs that produced high-yielding, top-quality hybrids of cereals and other crops. However, the new strains needed very good growing conditions, which often required the use of chemicals—fertilizers, insecticides and pesticides. A number of technical and socioeconomic problems soon became evident.

On the technical side, the increase in chemical use had a number of negative side effects. For example, certain weeds and pests developed resistance to the chemicals that were supposed to keep them under control. In addition, some of the chemicals affected the health of farm workers who were exposed to them over a long period of time. Excessive use also led to chemical buildup in the soil—making it unsuitable for planting—and sometimes even to contamination of groundwater. Extensive irrigation to ensure a steady supply of water sometimes led to soil erosion.

On the socioeconomic side, the Green Revolution required large financial and technological investments. This requirement was a problem in certain industrializing areas where many farmers lacked the money for the new breeds or the chemicals. Nor did they have the money to install and maintain the technical infrastructure required. In some industrializing countries, the Green Revolution exacerbated inequalities between rich farmers, who could invest in the technology, and poor farmers, who could not afford to do so.

Furthermore, although the Green Revolution did produce crops high in yield and quality, the price for consistency in quality was uniformity in variety. As more farmers switched to the new hybrids, fewer and fewer varieties of crops were grown. If this trend continues, a single threat (such as a blight-causing fungus) would be enough to wipe out much or all of a harvest in a region.

Two more points about biodiversity in agriculture should be made. First, the shrinking gene pool on farms is not just a problem of the Green Revolution. The threat to biodiversity in agriculture lies not simply in gene technology or any other farming methods but in a combination of poor farming practices and market demands for consistent quality. The growth of factory farming and the demand for consistency have led to the use of only selected breeds and varieties that could guarantee high yields of grains, big tomatoes, large eggs, and lean ham.

Second, the need for biodiversity is not a recent concept: experience has taught that greater diversity reduces threats from a single source and enriches the habitat. For example, growing the same crop on one plot of land season after season drains the soil of essential nutrients, possibly leading to soil erosion and desertification; that is why crop rotation is an important part of farming practices.

As a result of these difficulties, by the 1980s, agricultural production had increased, especially in industrialized countries, but hunger and starvation were still problems in many places. By the1990s, the initial hope and confidence of many people in the Green Revolution had turned into disappointment and cynicism.

In raising a public debate over the potential risks of the agricultural applications of gene technology, critics remind society that despite advances in science and technology, simple human needs still have to be met. Two questions must be asked. First, if the agricultural industry's ability to provide food were threatened, what would the consequences be for a society of technology-dependent urban dwellers? Second, since the Green Revolution has taught that there are no universal solutions to all problems and that unforeseen technical and social consequences may arise from the use of any technology, would the world be able to cope with the implications of gene technology in agriculture?

ANIMALS

There is concern for the integrity of animals and their rights. The use of animals for food and companionship must also be considered.

Concerns Relating to Genetically Altered Animals

The word *xenotransplantation* comes from the unusual grafting of the Greek prefix ξενο- (meaning "strange" or "foreign") to the Latin word *transplantare* (meaning "to move to another place"). This unusual joining of two different languages in one word describes a unique procedure. Tissues or organs from an animal of one species are surgically grafted into the body of an animal of another species. In human medicine, where this procedure is still at the experimental stage, it means that the tissue or organ of an animal—for example, a pig or even a primate—can be used to replace a defective organ in the human body (see "Transgenic Organ Donors," chapter 2).

By the mid-1990s, a number of scientific and technological developments allowed medical scientists to take important steps towards xenotransplantation. As previously discussed, one of the main problems of organ transplants—even from human to human—is hyperacute rejection. One of the most important steps forward for organ transplantation was the development of immunosuppressive drugs that help prevent the human immune system from rejecting the new organ. These drugs raised the success rates of organ transplants, making them almost routine procedures. Despite this achievement, two trends, as noted earlier, have pushed the medical community to consider the use of animal organs—the decline of human donors and the rise in the number of patients waiting for organs.

At the same time, developments in gene technology enabled scientists to direct changes at the level of the genes. For xenotransplantation, the most important development was the creation of transgenic animals—that is, animals with new or foreign genes, as discussed in chapter 2. This achievement opened up new ways of getting around hyperacute rejection. One method is to integrate human DNA into the genome of such animals as pigs, whose organs are similar in size and shape to human ones, or into primates closely related to humans. Transgenic pigs would have porcine genes and certain human genes that produce proteins that would help the organ bypass the immune system's defenses.

By the mid-1990s, what had been the subject of scientific discussions shifted into the public and regulatory arena. Public attention focused on xenotransplantation, its potential and its many implications. One might choose the case of Jeff Getty as an arbitrary point at which the scientific debate was catapulted into the public arena.

In December 1995, Getty, a patient with AIDS, received a bone marrow transplant from a baboon. Because baboons seem to be immune to HIV, his doctors hoped that the baboon's bone marrow cells, which produce antibodies to fight infection, would boost Getty's body's own immune system in controlling the spread of HIV (Gorman, 1996). Baboons, however, can have other viruses or diseases that could threaten the health of the patient and possibly that of the population at large. Once such viruses cross the species barrier, they may spread rapidly, possibly causing an epidemic (Allan, 1996).

Although the Getty case did *not* involve gene technology, it had many implications for future xenotransplantation involving transgenic animals. Both advocates and critics of the procedure recognized that the Getty case involved unusual circumstances and that reasons of compassion allowed it to move as quickly as it did. They turned to debate on the merits of the procedure in general. At the center of the debate are two different sets of parallel but closely related issues. The first set is concerned with xenotransplantation itself. The second set focuses on the creation and use of transgenic animals, whether for xenotransplantation or other purposes.

Xenotransplantation—Critics of xenotransplantation base their opposition on two grounds—medical safety and ethical considerations. Xenotransplantation may pose a threat to the health of both the patient and the population at large. Under most circumstances, viruses and other disease-causing agents find it hard to penetrate the many barriers between species, including the skin, the digestive system, and, above all, the immune system. Xenotransplantation avoids this difficulty because the tissue or organ is grafted directly into the body, meaning that any viruses or other infectious agents in the foreign tissue could also be implanted directly. In addition, the use of immunosuppressants would reduce or temporarily disable the human immune system. Once lodged in one human body, the pathogen could spread quickly among the rest of the population before it was noticed. If it was a new disease, it could be virulent and incurable.

In the last three decades, some new diseases—including the Ebola virus and HIV—are suspected to have crossed from other primates to humans (Allan, 1996). Such crossing was one of the dangers in the Getty case. Baboons are closely related to human beings: if a virus can thrive in a baboon, it may also be able to survive the human immune system. For that reason, proponents argue, there is a need to use transgenic animals—specifically, pigs—in xenotransplantation. The animals can be selected, bred, and raised for xenotransplantation. They are already being raised in sterile and specific-pathogen-free (SPF) conditions for experimental purposes (Allan, 1996; Laing, 1996). Thus, practices already exist that can help reduce the risk of cross-species infections.

Several reasons favor the use of transgenic pigs. First, the fact that pigs are not as closely related to human beings as baboons and other primates reduces the risks of cross-species infections. Second, humans and pigs have coexisted for thousands of years—more than enough time for any parasites to cross the species barriers. Finally, pigs are already the source of medical products, including blood vessels, heart valves, and porcine insulin.

Evan Allan, a virologist who argues against the use of baboons as animal donors, points to the advantages of pigs as donors: "Pigs are more amenable to SPF colonies; they have a much shorter generation time; they have been bred in domesticity for thousands of years; and methods are being developed to genetically manipulate this species to deal with hyperacute rejection" (Allan, 1996, p. 20). Even with precautionary measures, however, it is not possible to rule out the risk that animal donors, even pigs, may harbor infectious agents for the organ recipient: "The most pressing concern with cross-species transplants is the inherent risk of transmitting animal viruses to humans" (Allan, 1996, p. 2). In its report for the Swiss pharmaceutical company Sandoz (merged with Ciba-Geigy and became Novartis in 1996), the investment company Salomon Brothers also devoted attention to the issue of infection risks in xenotransplantation (Laing, 1996).

Nevertheless, one cannot forget that tissue and organ transplantations, by definition, involve life-and-death situations where a relatively high degree of risk becomes acceptable. Often the patient would face certain death or decreasing quality of life without a new organ. Many patients die while waiting for a new organ. Even when the donor is a human being, there is always a risk that the organ may carry unidentified infections. The use of human-growth hormone in treating children with dwarfism (see "Emotional Arguments for Gene Technology Patents," chapter 3). certainly involved a risk that these children might contract Creutzfeld-Jakob disease. In the 1980s and early 1990s, a number of hemophiliacs contracted HIV and developed AIDS through the transfusion of infected blood and other tissues.

The pressing concern for opponents to xenotransplantation is not with the individual patient but with the possibility of an epidemic in the broader population. If a nonhuman virus took hold in a patient and if the patient survived the transplant, the patient might well become the entry into the human population for the virus. This is a risk that epidemiologists and other researchers are taking seriously (Allan, 1996; Gorman, 1996).

The danger is serious on two counts. First, there is no equivalent of an antibiotic against viruses. Most of the time, even with a cold virus, the only thing to do is to rely on the body's immune system. Second, a body must first be able to recognize the virus before it is able to fight it. One of the reasons for the success of HIV is that in most cases the virus is able to change constantly, staying ahead of the body's immune system.

Transgenic Animals—Even if the issues surrounding risks to human health were resolved, concerns with the ethical implications of both the creation of transgenic animals as such and their use for xenotransplantation are even more contentious.

Opponents argue that the creation of transgenic animals is unethical. They say that an animal has its own worth and dignity as a living being, independent of the value that humans assign to it. That view is the basis of laws in many countries that protect endangered species and their habitats—thus the worldwide ban on trade in new ivory. It would be shortsighted to see the natural world only in terms of the tangible benefits that humans can derive from it. Animals are not machines created to serve humanity. Just because an animal does not serve a human purpose does not mean that it does not have any intrinsic value: even the mere existence of these animals can teach us about the diversity of forms that life takes.

In addition, an animal should have the right to live according to its nature. It would be cruel to keep pigs, naturally social animals, in isolation, which would be necessary if they were raised for xenotransplantation. For animal activists, the fact that modern farming methods already isolate pigs in narrow individual stalls is hardly a justification.

Finally, respect for the highly intelligent pig should prevent us from treating it like a spare-parts factory for human organs. Respect for another creature that is capable of suffering should be grounds for stopping all research into xenotransplantation (Soldati, 1996).

Food and Companionship
Raising animals for human needs does not necessarily imply cruelty to animals or a lack of respect for them. For thousands of years, people have been raising different animals for a broad range of human needs, but we have not simply been seeing animals as factories on legs. Today, living in cities and surrounded by technological comfort, many of us can easily forget the complex relationships between human beings and animals. There are many reasons for domesticating animals:

- Food. Early human societies kept animals in or near the house in order to provide a steady supply of meat, regardless of changes in seasons and animal migration. Today animals raised under industrial conditions are still a major source of human food supply.
- Clothing. Furs, feathers, and skins of animals were early forms of clothing and have remained important items of apparel, even in the most technologically advanced cultures.
- Labor. Until the age of mechanization, domesticated animals were a major part of the workforce on the farm and even in the city (for example, cab horses). In many parts of Asia, water buffaloes have not yet been replaced by tractors.
- Protection. Some animals have always been a source of physical defense and security. Geese, for example, were effective burglar alarms because they are noisy when disturbed. Today, guard dogs and police dogs still fulfil a protective role.
- Companionship. Domesticated animals also provide psychological comfort and support. Some pets are treated almost like human companions.

The domestication of animals has at least two profound implications. First, domestication implies that even before gene technology, human beings have been creating new breeds of animals to obtain certain traits. By definition, the domestication of animals must go beyond the one-time act of taming a wild animal (a first step that already changes the relationship between human and animal). Selective breeding is necessary to retain or heighten certain traits that humans find useful or desirable, such as strength, size, watchfulness, or beauty. A dog is a domesticated wolf, yet there are important differences between a timber wolf and a poodle, which, after all, is the result of thousands of years of selective breeding.

Second, and perhaps more important, domestication establishes a bond between human being and animal. In the past, work animals were seen not only as beasts of burden but often also as work *companions*. The nuance is significant: human and beast worked together at tasks that neither could accomplish alone and there was a special relationship between them. As Antoine de Saint-Exupéry reminds readers in his novel *The Little Prince* (1944), the act of taming an animal establishes an emotional bond based on trust: at one point, the Little Prince learns that in taming the Fox, he has also been tamed by the Fox; and this bond cannot be undone.

Humans and Animals—Whether advocates and critics of gene technology are conscious of it or not, the bond between humans and animals lies at the heart of the controversy over xenotransplantation and, indeed, over transgenic animals. The importance of the debate goes beyond whether a gene should be added to or taken away from an animal's genome to obtain desired characteristics. This purpose, as supporters of gene technology argue, can be achieved through cross-breeding anyway, although with far less accuracy and speed. Rather the concern is over the consequences for the bonds or relationships, on the one hand, between human beings and animals and, on the other hand, between human beings. This concern explains why the debate is filled with concepts such as the dignity of animals, welfare of animals, or animal rights.

Hierarchical or Egalitarian View—But, critics ask, are animal rights not a "luxury" debate for a privileged few in a world where basic human rights are being wilfully violated (Bondolfi, 1994; Singer, 1993)[*]? A. Bondolfi points out that the answer depends on whether one takes a hierarchical or egalitarian view of the relationship between humans and animals.

On the hierarchical side, some people may say that plants and animals are things and, as lower on the hierarchy of being than humans, have no rights whatsoever. Others may recognize that nonhuman species have interests, but they are less important than even the nonvital interests of human beings. Still others may say that the vital interests of animals must outweigh the nonvital interests of human beings.

---

[*] An in-depth philosophical and ethical discussion of the relationship between humans and animals goes beyond the intent of this book. However, for those interested, A. Bondolfi, in Mensch und Tier: Ethische Dimensionen ihres Verhältnisses, provides a good overview of the ethical issues. This work includes excerpts from key thinkers (past and present) and an extensive bibliography. (p.16)

On the egalitarian side, some may say that if there is a conflict of interests between animals and humans, the interest of the being who is most capable of feeling pain outweighs the interests of the other. Thus, a human adult's interests outweigh those of an animal, but an animal's interests may outweigh those of a human being who is less able to feel pain—for example, a fetus or someone in a coma. Other egalitarians may hold that the question of species is irrelevant: the only question that matters is whether the vital interests of the individuals involved are threatened or not (Bondolfi, 1994).

Both Bondolfi and P. Singer take a utilitarian stance that reflects an egalitarian attitude. They argue that the principle that prevents us from denying other human beings their rights on the basis of appearance, sex, race, or abilities should also prevent us from denying animals their rights. Quoting the late-eighteenth-century British philosopher Jeremy Bentham, Singer points out that the ability to suffer is sufficient grounds for extending equal treatment to animals, equality being defined as equality of interests.

> If a being suffers, there can be no moral justification for refusing to take that suffering into consideration. . . . If a being is not capable of suffering, or of experiencing enjoyment or happiness, there is nothing to be taken into account. This is why the limit of sentience (using the term as a convenient, if not strictly accurate, shorthand for the capacity to suffer or experience enjoyment or happiness) is the only defensible boundary of concern for the interests of others. To mark this boundary by some other characteristic like intelligence or rationality would be to mark it in an arbitrary way. Why not choose some other characteristic, like skin colour? (Singer, 1993, pp. 57-58)

Ethical Conflicts—Bentham's position (and, ultimately, Singer's) highlights the complexities in the issues around the treatment of animals. In particular, it shows that there are many unresolved (perhaps even irresolvable) ethical conflicts in the values and attitudes underlying current human relationships with animals and with other human beings. To understand how these conflicts are relevant to the discussions over xenotransplantation one must first understand the extent of the impact of gene technology.

Gene technology has far-reaching consequences not just for a handful of industries but for society as a whole. It affects how people see themselves as human beings, how they view the world, and how they see the complex relationships between human beings and the living world. In short, a paradigm shift has occurred. As noted in chapter 1, a new technology challenges and eventually changes old concepts, traditional methods, and established conventions. This truth is essential to understanding the debate over transgenic animals and xenotransplantation.

In the Western world, the traditional view of the living world was dominated by Judeo-Christian teachings. According to this view, humankind (man) stands at the top and center of a world created by God. Each creature is different from the others: "And God made the beasts of the earth according to their kinds" (Genesis 1:25). In the nineteenth century, the concept of evolution challenged many traditional teachings on creation, but it reinforced the idea that species are clearly separated. The theory of evolution owes much to the field of taxonomy, which classifies organisms according to structural differences. When two individuals are so different in form that they cannot mate and reproduce, they are said to belong to different species. This is the concept of the species barrier: in a way, it is the scientific version of the biblical view of all life forms multiplying according to their kinds.

In the late twentieth century, gene technology introduced two concepts that reduced the significance of the species barriers. First, from a genetic point of view, all genes are made up of the same four nucleotides and share the same structure. So whether a gene comes from a bacterium or a whale, it is made up of the same material. Second, armed with this knowledge, scientists can transplant genetic material from one individual to another, *regardless* of species. Once in a functioning cell and activated, a gene will code for the same protein—regardless of the organism it is in. Thus, the species barrier can be overcome. Phrased differently: from the point of view of the sameness of the nature and function of genes, *all forms of life are equal*. These two concepts not only led to the creation of the biotechnology industry but also provided the impetus for progress in areas as different as health care, pharmaceutical production, agriculture, animal husbandry, and environmental protection.

A Paradigm Shift—A paradigm shift, caused by a new technology, is more than a change in the way things are done; it is also a change in the way people think and the way they understand the world (for example, Laënnec's stethoscope, mentioned in chapter 1). Part of the conflict between the critics and the advocates of genetic research comes from their respective rejection or acceptance of the new, genetic paradigm.

The old paradigm made two assertions: First, the genetic makeup of an organism is the unique result of either Divine Creation or evolution (that is, adaptation and natural selection). Second, the reproductive and other barriers between species serve to exclude certain combinations of genes (according to Divine Will or evolutionary principles). Thus, changing the genetic makeup of an organism is seen as tampering with the works of God or destroying the delicate balance that evolution has produced in nature. Either way, we risk triggering unpredictable and uncontrollable changes to the organism, human beings, and the environment.

The genetic paradigm rests on three propositions: First, a gene is composed of the same four nucleotides regardless of the kind of organism where it is located. Second, genes are the raw material for a new technology: they are powerhouses with unforeseen potential. Third, genetic resources can be safely developed within the framework of existing guidelines; decades of genetic research and centuries of cross-breeding provide a valuable knowledge base of the behavior of the organisms that scientists will be working with.

At one extreme, in rejecting transgenic organisms as monsters or abominations of nature, critics are taking the traditional view that the natural barriers between species should not be crossed. At the other extreme, advocates are favoring the genetic view that both traditional breeding methods and gene technology result in new combinations of genes, producing new organisms or even entirely new breeds of organisms. Examples of such conflicting views involve transgenic microorganisms, transgenic plants, and transgenic animals, as discussed in chapters 2 and 3.

In the old paradigm, some forms of life (in particular, human beings) were considered superior to others because of Divine Will (for example, the human soul) or because of evolutionary advantages (for example, the development of the cerebral cortex). In the new paradigm, all living organisms are the same from the point of view of the nature and function of their genes. However, the new paradigm exposes a fundamental weakness in the relationship between humankind and the rest of the animal world. If all forms of life are the same, why is there inequality in the way different life forms are treated?

Xenotransplantation, in this context, presents a Catch-22, that is, a dilemma with no solution. On the one hand, the transplant of organs from animals to human beings can be viewed as a symbolic statement of equality. It is an implicit acknowledgment that the fundamental differences between a human being and an animal are not that great. On the other hand, it is assumed that pigs (or other animals) are not entitled to the rights that human beings have. It is acceptable to kill a pig for its organs because we already kill pigs and other animals for their meat, skin, fur, or other parts. Thus, the premise for using animals for food, clothing, or scientific experiments is that animals have fewer rights than human beings—or no rights at all. But if a pig has fewer rights than a human being, is a person with a porcine organ any less human than one without? What is the difference that entitles a human being to rights that are withheld from the pig? If a pig has the same rights as a human being, should it be used for xenotransplantation (or food, for that matter)? If yes, then here is the slippery-slope question: if animals have the same rights as human beings and we still favor xenotransplantation, would it not be simpler to remove organs from another human being (for example, coma patients or convicts) for organ transplant without his or her consent?

Reduced to its simplest form, the debate over transgenic animals and xenotransplantation raises two fundamental questions that *must* be answered. First, why would it be more acceptable to create new hybrids of pigs by means of cross-breeding methods (including artificial insemination) than by altering the genetic combination of a pig ovum or embryo? Second, why would raising pigs for pork chops and pork liver be more acceptable than raising them for organ transplant?

HUMANS
Society is concerned about the possibility of genetic discrimination and about the rights of the individual as against the interests of the community.

Concerns Relating to Gene Technology and Humans
Although most applications of gene technology are controversial to some degree, those areas involving human beings are probably among the most hotly debated. There are a host of issues concerned with the human area. On the surface, many do not seem to have anything in common, yet, as the following three cases show, a closer look reveals common underlying themes.

Case 1—The first case centers on a U.S. anthropologist, Carol Jenkins, who was doing research on the Hagahai people in Papua New Guinea. In 1996 she was caught in a dispute between the governments of the United States and Papua New Guinea over a cell line isolated from tissue samples that she had collected. The U.S. Department of Health and Human Services filed for, and in 1995 obtained, a U.S. patent on a Human t-lymphotropic virus type I (HTLV-I) derived from the cell line. After a discussion with Jenkins, the secretary of Foreign Affairs and Trade of Papua New Guinea cleared her of wrongdoing. Although Jenkins, named as coinventor on the patent, was entitled to half the royalties from any resulting products, she assigned her share of the claim to the Hagahai people themselves (Dickson, 1996; Lehrman, 1996).

Case 2—The second case focuses on the implications of genetic testing for health and life insurance. Both the British Parliament and the U.S. Congress are looking at ways to legislate the use of genetic information in private health insurance and life insurance. The central question is whether insurance companies may use genetic information in considering applications.

On the one hand, insurance companies need as much information as they can obtain in order to calculate the potential risks that an applicant represents. Since insurance is based on spreading the costs of an estimated risk across the group, equitable contribution of payment is possible only if all relevant information is available from all parties involved: those who represent a higher risk to the group pay a higher premium (Masood, Lehrman, Shiermeier, Butler, and Nathan, 1996; Pokorski, 1994).

On the other hand, some people question whether insurance companies are equipped to deal with the complexities involved in interpreting genetic data.

It is worth emphasising here the distinction between predisposition and presymptomatic. If a genetic test identifies a predisposition to a disease, the disorder may or may not occur. By contrast, a genetic test that detects a presymptomatic disorder identifies a condition that is already present but whose symptoms have not yet developed. (Pokorski, 1996, p. 13)

More complexity arises when several genes or a combination of genetic and environmental factors are responsible. In addition, even monogenic diseases can be complicated. For example, 70 percent of sufferers carry a mutation in the gene associated with cystic fibrosis (CF), a monogenic disorder. Yet, a negative test for this mutation does not mean that the person will not develop the disease: more than five hundred other mutations on the *same gene* have been linked to CF (Abbott, 1996). How should an insurance company interpret this information in its calculation of risks?

Case 3—The third case revolves around the use of preimplantation diagnosis in combination with new developments in reproductive technology. As reported in *New Scientist* in 1995, a couple in northern England wanted to conceive a child, but they wanted to ensure that it would not suffer from the same cancer as the wife. The woman suffered from an inherited cancer that required the surgical removal of her lower bowel. Surgery left scar tissues that blocked her fallopian tubes, preventing conception. The way around that was in-vitro fertilization, which allows the ovum to be fertilized outside the body under laboratory conditions.

The woman, however, did not want her children to inherit the gene because they would have an 80 to 90 percent chance of developing the cancer by middle age. The use of preimplantation diagnosis to screen for the gene could prevent the gene from being passed on: only embryos that did not seem to carry the genes would be implanted in the woman's womb. Thus, embryos showing evidence of carrying the gene would be eliminated.

The ethics committee at Hammersmith Hospital in London and the government's Human Fertilisation and Embryology Authority approved the plan. The case raised a debate in the medical community, which can be summarized as follows: "Doctors can now screen embryos for genes that increase the risk of developing cancer in later life. The question is whether they should" (Vines, 1995, p. 14). Another question is: Where does society draw the line—at 50 percent risk of developing cancer, at 10 percent, or at 0?

One of the compelling factors in the case was the high risk (over 80 percent) of a child with the gene later developing cancer. But this risk in itself raised a number of difficult questions. If doctors are allowed to carry out preimplantation screening of embryos for high-risk cases, should they also be allowed to do it for cases where the risk is much lower? What if the test gives a false negative result and the fetus or child does have the genetic disorder? Is there a point at which society or doctors have a moral obligation to interfere with the reproductive decisions of a couple?

Differences—At first glance, the points of contention in the three cases above appear to be different. The first, involving an indigenous population from New Guinea, focuses on the rights of a group of individuals. Respect for the individual requires recognizing the person's rights and interests. In this case, the Hagahais have the right to decide if their donation could be used in a way other than originally agreed. In addition, they also had a legitimate interest in the outcome of the research to which they contributed. (As discussed later in this chapter the concept of a donation is an important point in this particular conflict.) Critics think the U.S. government violated the rights of the Hagahais by applying for (and, later, granting) a patent on the cell line *without their knowledge or informed consent.*

The second case, involving individuals applying for insurance, focuses on the potential for discrimination on the basis of genetic disorders or even predisposition and on the question of fairness. If existing medical information can affect the premium charged, then it would seem fair that the parties involved should have access to this information. Otherwise, if premiums are not sufficient to cover future claims, other parties will stand to lose: individuals may have to pay higher premiums, or the company may no longer be able to cover its losses (OECD, 1995).

A second aspect to be considered is why people should pay more for insurance or even be denied coverage simply because of the lot that fate has handed them. Such people are not responsible for their conditions (Masood et al., 1996). This position reflects the principle of solidarity between the sick and the healthy. It means that a sick person should have access to health care without personal financial loss: the expenses will be carried by society as a whole (von Wartburg, 1983).

For companies insuring life or health, the question is not fault or control but relative risk (Pokorski, 1996). Fairness for them is defined as distributive and proportional equality, meaning that those who present the same risk, pay the same amount of premium.

The third case, involving patients seeking medical options as part of family planning, focuses on whether preimplantation diagnosis and prenatal diagnosis should be an accepted part of clinical practice. The disposal of unwanted embryos after preimplantation diagnosis is likely to be a less emotionally charged option than the abortion of unwanted fetuses after a prenatal diagnosis has revealed genetic defects (Vines, 1995).

For the moment, the debate is taking place within the medical and scientific communities, where the distinction between the two kinds of diagnoses is clear. *When the debate reaches the public arena, it is highly probable that the two will be confused in the ensuing emotional cross-fire.* It is also likely that critics will not *want* to make a distinction between the two techniques, not because of the techniques themselves but because of the ethical implications and the social consequences. A serious concern is that both techniques might lead to the creation of a eugenic society based on "perfect" health or other socially desirable traits. Critics warn that the arguments of many governments in the 1930s, that the mentally disabled should not be allowed to pass on their defective genes, were used by the Nazi regime to bolster their racial agenda (see "Eugenics," chapter 2).

Today's concerns over eugenics do not stem from fears of governments trying to create a superior race. The impetus for eugenics is far more likely to come from the combination of money, available technology, and existing social pressures. There is a growing tendency to "medicalize" and "geneticize" conditions in life. The effort is not just to remove physical and mental disabilities: in an image-conscious society, there is tremendous interest in the genetic factors behind the aging process and intelligence. There are even suggestions (Begley, 1996; Toufexis, Mattos, and Silver, 1996) that genes may be partly responsible for someone's being a thrill seeker. What would stop parents from paying a doctor to eliminate genes associated with a mental or physical disorder, or some other socially undesirable condition, or even a thrill-seeking tendency? In the context of rising health-care costs and public health-care restraints, will parents literally pay (in higher private insurance premiums or even denied insurance) for their decision to carry to term a fetus with a genetic disorder?

Similarities—Despite the different concerns of these three cases, two threads provide common links: discrimination and equality.

The issue of genetic discrimination is often framed in terms of concerns about creating a two-tiered society: individuals with genetic disorders in one category and individuals without them in another. In the case of the couple from northern England, few would dispute the mother's anxiety to spare her children the suffering that she herself has endured. However, the issue goes beyond compassion for the individual to the implications of discrimination for society at large.

> Testing is ultimately a form of labelling, of distinguishing among individuals and placing them within specific categories based on biological criteria. While scientific knowledge provides a rational basis for classification, it also opens the way to discrimination, stigmatisation and vulnerability to control. Once a person is labelled as having a specific condition, or even a predisposition to one, others respond accordingly, attributing subsequent behaviour or physical manifestations to that condition. (Nelkin and Tancredi, 1989, p. 168)

In regard to insurance, the worry is that society will be divided between those who can obtain insurance and those who are denied it. There are already instances where individuals have been unable to buy insurance because of actual or potential genetic disorders (Nelkin and Tancredi, 1989). There are also concerns that genetic information might affect people's access to education, employment, or other opportunities, especially in places where access to public-health care is limited and employers pay part or all of the health-care insurance.

Closely related to the question of access is the need to balance the rights of the individual against the interests of society. The argument for equitable treatment rests on the equality of interests, as can be seen most clearly in the debate over genetic screening and insurance. The insurance company, representing all insured parties, must be able to see what kind of risks an applicant might present. "People will use genetic information to guide their insurance purchases. Life insurance companies will need access to the same information to classify the risks they are asked to accept in order to co-ordinate risk and premium" (Pokorski, 1996, p. 14). For that reason, insurers argue that all parties involved must have equal access to all available information, as has always been true with other types of medical information. Some worry that changing the rules now for genetic information would have serious consequences for the industry (Pokorski, 1996).

The potential for conflict is greatest if insurance firms require a genetic test before issuing a life insurance policy. The person may not want to know if he or she is predisposed to a particular disorder, especially if there is no treatment available. For this reason, some insurance companies will request the results of previous tests but will not require a genetic test (Masood et al., 1996). The danger is that this practice may prevent individuals from seeking genetic tests where something can be done (like a special diet) to prevent the condition. Some argue that this practice would "limit or nullify the anticipated benefits of genetic research" (Hudson, Bothenberg, Andrews, Kahn, and Collins, 1995, p. 391).

The question of equality was also a decisive factor in the Hagahai situation. Part of the conflict stemmed from the fact that the Hagahai community was not informed of the patent and therefore could not properly decide whether it was in their best interests. The conflict was resolved once the Hagahais were able to make an informed decision and were given a share in the rights to any benefits derived from the patented cell line.

Human Rights and Human Wrongs

It is perhaps not surprising that fear of genetic discrimination and respect for the rights of the individual are the two overriding concerns in the debate over the applications of gene technology in the human area. History, after all, is full of reminders that we may be our own worst enemies. Many conflicts arose from efforts to dominate, segregate, or eliminate those who were different—those that one group perceived as less intelligent, sophisticated, or advanced. For example, the Chinese built the Great Wall across their northern boundary to keep out the Mongol hordes. The Romans also tried to keep barbarians from the north out of their empire. European efforts to colonize other parts of the world were often marked by brutality toward indigenous peoples. In the United States, many states segregated whites and blacks well into the 1960s. The ethnic "cleansing" that took place during the civil war in the former Yugoslavia in the 1990s was only the latest reminder of the extremes that discrimination can reach.

In the context of gene technology, one particular memory stands out: the horror of the Holocaust, which the Nazis unleashed in Europe in the 1930s and 1940s. For the first time, science was used to justify a policy of racial hatred and to advance a program of genocide.

> Neither biomedical science in general nor genetics in particular were [sic] responsible for the rise of the Third Reich or the Holocaust, but some scientists and physicians used their skills and authority to create a "scientific" foundation for the racism that was pivotal in legitimating Nazism and bringing about the Holocaust. (Caplan, 199, p. 31)

More than fifty years later, the specter of the Holocaust still hovers over genetic research in the human area. It is one of the reasons why scientists have insisted that genomic research be accompanied by debate on the broad social and ethical consequences of this work.

Concerned that genetic information could be misused, scientists on the HGP in the United States set aside at least 3 percent of their budget to study the social, ethical, and legal implications of their work. The head of the National Center for Human Genome Research justified this decision by pointing to the Nazi program of genocide (Watson, 1990). Not surprisingly, social opposition to any effort in human genetic research has been strongest in Germany. It was not until 1995, almost six years after the official start of the HGP, that Germany decided to take part in the international human genome research program (Feder, 1995).

The eugenics movement, as discussed in chapter 2, started with an interest in ridding the population of "feeblemindedness" and "physical abnormalities." In the 1930s, enforced sterilization became legal in what are considered progressive countries: the United States (various states), Canada (several provinces), Germany, Denmark, Norway, Sweden, Finland, Estonia, and Iceland (Paul and Spencer, 1995). In Germany, such sterilization initially "ran independently of the regime's anti-Semitic policies" (Kevles, 1985, p. 117). In the name of the common good (in Germany, the purity of the German race), the rights of these "unfit" people were taken away and they were sterilized to prevent their defective genes from being passed on. As some authors (Kelves, 1985; Kelves, 1994; Paul and Spencer, 1995) point out, the program gained popularity when hard economic conditions made welfare costs a high concern for government and the public. This fact found a disturbing echo in the 1990s as the costs of health care and social programs were once again the focus fiscal restraint.

There are, however, important differences between the situation in the 1930s and the one today. The first is that progress in human genome research and diagnosis has increased the ability of doctors to detect the links between genetic disorders and many (but not all) diseases. As this work continues, it becomes clearer that most individuals are likely to have genes that predispose them to some genetic disorder (Berg and Singer, 1996; Kevles, 1994). Few, if any, will be in a privileged position to think that getting rid of those who are somehow genetically "unfit" will improve society.

A second difference is that on-going genetic studies of human diseases are giving greater insight into the causes of more of these diseases. This knowledge, no matter how slowly, is opening new ways to treatments and possibly even cures. Although not all human diseases have a genetic origin, genetic research may offer some surprises. A recent article suggested that bacteriophages, viruses that infect only bacteria, might be genetically altered to become important weapons in the fight against bacterial diseases, including cholera or tuberculosis (Bahnsen, 1996). As a number of bacteria are showing resistance to antibiotics, this discovery might be an important step in disease control.

A third difference between the 1930s and the 1990s is that earlier doctors and geneticists were among the champions or at least silent supporters of eugenic sterilization of the mentally and physically disabled. Today's geneticists are among the most conscious of the lessons of the past. In addition, their work is being constantly scrutinized by both internal and external parties: the ELSI task force of the HGP; the ethics committees of hospitals, universities, and government research institutes; groups representing those with mental and physical disabilities; religious organizations; the media; human-rights groups; and groups opposed to gene technology.

As the genetic basis of human diseases becomes clearer, the biggest challenge for society is overcoming discrimination. Discrimination is not a medical or scientific problem but a *human* problem. Probably it has always been a part of human society, not simply on the basis of race, nationality, religion, sex, or sexual orientation but also of illness and disease. In many premodern societies, lepers were social outcasts. They had to ring a bell wherever they went, shouting, "Unclean, unclean!" Another "solution" was to send them to leper colonies.

Although society is supposed to be more enlightened today, many illnesses are still the cause of prejudice and discrimination. Sometimes individuals face harassment or even assault because of a medical condition. Prejudice can be as simple as social silence about a disease: in many places, it is still taboo to talk openly about cancer, alcoholism, or psychological problems. Well into the twentieth century, the mentally disabled were simply locked away in institutions. In the 1990s the mentally and physically disabled still faced outright discrimination in terms of access to housing, education, employment, and other opportunities. Those with HIV or AIDS faced similar problems.

Discrimination and the loss of individual rights are two aspects of the same problem. Discrimination happens when one party refuses to recognize the legitimate needs and interests of another. Sterilization became legal in so many countries in the 1930s because governments assumed that certain groups of individuals no longer had the right to decide for themselves what was in their own best interests. Sometimes, as with enforced sterilization, discrimination has been disguised as being in the interests of society. Yet, as the Holocaust proved, when that reason is given for depriving some individuals of their rights, society itself has a lot more to lose.

As the three cases in the previous section show, maintaining a balance between the rights of the individual and the interests of society is a central issue in the debate over gene technology. Whether it is the Hagahais, insurance companies, or a couple wanting a healthy child, when the rights of the individual collide with the interests of society, how can this dilemma be resolved? What is the ethically justifiable choice?

GENE SEQUENCES

The subject of gene sequences brings up consideration of genes as natural resources and the history of our use of natural resources.

Genes as New and Renewable Resources

Some readers may be surprised to see gene sequences discussed alongside whole organisms such as plants and animals. But a discussion of gene technology must go beyond conventional ways of seeing the living world. As the technology matures, the focus of concern is shifting from individual organisms to individual *genes*. In a growing number of social and ethical debates, as well as legal and legislative disputes, genes themselves or gene sequences are treated as discrete entities, independent of the organism from which they are taken. This trend can be seen in moves by national governments to protect what is considered their countries' *genetic resources*.

Recent developments in India illustrate this point. In the mid-1990s, India started working on legislation that would allow the government more control over what genetic material leaves the country and how the results are used. The proposed law would "require foreign researchers using genetic material taken from India to ensure that any resulting technical advances—as well as a share in the profits from the eventual exploitation of this material—are transferred back to India" (Dickson, 1996, p. 13). Thus, the law intends to ensure that India also profits from its collaboration with scientists from abroad, especially those working for multinational companies. But the law is also a way of asserting India's sovereignty over its resources—in this case, its genetic resources (Dickson, 1996; Jayaraman, 1996; Jayaraman and Macilwain, 1996).

The conflict between Papua New Guinea and the United States presented earlier is another example of moves by some countries to protect their national genetic resources. There are two ways of interpreting the genetic concerns of India and Papua New Guinea. The first interpretation is that it is a battle between Goliath (the powerful, greedy, industrialized North) and David (the weak, helpless, industrializing South). Critics sometimes accuse the North of exploiting the South in a sort of genetic colonialism, especially if human genes are involved and if the Northern party intends to commercialize the genetic material taken (Fischer, 1993). This is how researchers from the Rural Advancement Foundation International (RAFI) saw the U.S. patent on the cell line derived from the Hagahai tissue sample. They argued that the patent was another example of a Western country trying to exploit people of another culture.

Part of the North-South conflict comes from the fact that a donation of blood or other human tissue has symbolic significance. In both preindustrial and industrial societies, such a donation is seen as a gift of life—or at least of life's essence (Dickson, 1996). Donations of organs and genes have very similar connotations. Attempts to make a profit from such donations are thus seen as violating the intentions of the donor. Moreover, from a legal perspective, if the donor is unaware of the intent to commercialize, then his or her right to consent and autonomy are compromised.

The issue goes far deeper, however, than the patenting of human genes and the commercialization of genes in general. If the issue was merely a case of sharing profits or other benefits, it could be resolved through trade agreements or economic forums. The second interpretation of the concerns of India and Papua New Guinea is that they represent the paradigm shift triggered by gene technology. This shift has at least two important consequences.

The first consequence is that genes themselves became the center of attention in scientific, medical, economic, and public discussions. Before the advent of gene technology, the focus was on the organism itself: the pain-reducing properties of certain willow trees, the nutritional value of fish, or the life-saving nature of a transfusion human blood. Since then the focus is on the properties of genes: people now talk of breast cancer genes, cystic fibrosis genes, or even "alcoholic" genes and "selfish" genes.

The second consequence of the paradigm shift is that it introduced the notion that living organisms and their genes are part of the genetic resources of a country. Before gene technology, genes were considered merely parts of an organism with no real economic significance. Gene technology changed that. The actions by India and Papua New Guinea are part of a trend that started almost a decade ago: more and more industrializing nations realize that their wealth of plant and animal life will be increasingly valuable as biotechnology matures, and they are taking measures to protect these resources. Where laws have not yet been passed, some scientists, as well as special-interest groups, are urging those governments to do so (Homewood, 1996; Jayaraman, 1996).

In his discussion on the impact of biotechnology on industrializing nations, R. Walgate presents a number of examples of the trend of increasing national control over genetic resources. In the 1980s, Ethiopia and Zimbabwe took steps similar to those of India. Ethiopia prohibited exports of germ plasm of important crops, including coffee, contained in its national gene bank. The move surprised Germany, which had helped fund the gene bank and had been hoping to receive duplicates of the Ethiopian barley collection in exchange.

Zimbabwe and Australia were trying to develop an animal vaccine against ticks, but Zimbabwe scientists were reluctant to share their genes with their Australian colleagues. They feared that the Australians would come up with a vaccine first and Zimbabwe would end up having no chance to benefit from their contribution to the research.

A number of cases show that the fear of exploitation is not unfounded. For example, a gene from a cowpea plant from Nigeria was discovered to produce a natural insecticide. The gene was isolated and commercialized in Britain. The cloned gene was then returned to Nigeria for free, "but it does not appear that any profits from the gene will be returned to Africa" (Walgate, 1990, p. 162).

To reiterate, cases such as these go beyond the commercial aspect into the area of ethics. If the genes of organisms are considered part of a country's natural resources, this view has tremendous ethical implications. Since all living organisms have genes, *any* living organism can be the source of economically valuable genes. In economic terms, genes can thus be seen as the raw material for established and new industries dependent on gene technology.

Such a perspective raises a number of troubling questions. Should organisms—possibly even human beings—be viewed merely in terms of what their genes can offer industry? Do the benefits to society outweigh the rights or other considerations of an individual organism? Does it make a difference if that organism is a fellow human being?

As these questions show, the paradigm shift has implications beyond the commercialization of genes and the fairness of profit sharing. It touches on the ethical values at the foundation of industrialized society. That is one reason why much of the battle over gene technology is fought over ethical issues. It is why RAFI objected to the patenting of the Hagahai cell line on moral grounds, making the *value judgment* that the U.S. government was morally wrong to seek, and later grant, a patent on human genes. In European patent law, no patent is granted if the invention is contrary to morality. This clause has been used by environmental groups and animal-rights groups in cases such as the Harvard onco-mouse, discussed in chapter 3. Also as noted in chapter 3, the issue is not patentability but social control. Whatever form it takes, social control is a set of rules and conventions that is founded on the values of a society. The ethical issues surrounding gene technology are not merely differences of opinion or clashes in philosophy but involve practical legal considerations. They are about the right to decide what happens to genes of scientific and commercial interest. They involve the rights of ownership and autonomy. They are about the equitable distribution of wealth. Finally, they are about the responsibility of stewardship—of humankind's duty to manage how we use the planet's resources.

Natural Resources—Abuses, Concerns, and Limits

The debate over the management of genetic resources is part of a wider debate over the management of natural resources. Two aspects of this broad debate also have significance for the debate over genes. The first is concerned with responsible stewardship—how to use the natural resources available. The second aspect involves the *right to decide* how natural resources are used and how the benefits should be distributed.

Responsible Stewardship—When European settlers arrived in North America, they introduced the novel concept of dividing land into private property. Indigenous peoples believed that no one owns the land, nor can they own it; the land is a gift for all to use and care for. The difference between the two views is important: Owners do as they please. Caretakers look after something that does not belong to them but that has been placed in their trust.

In much the same way, many people today are beginning to realize that natural resources are part of the common wealth. Human beings share this planet with other living beings, and future generations should also be able to enjoy it. It took time for industrialized society to come to this point of view. A number of factors were necessary. The first was the rise of the environmental movement. Another was the realization that plants and animals are dying out faster than science can classify them, let alone study them.

Once, most people thought that energy and other resources on this planet are limitless. Today, they are beginning to recognize that is not true. Deposits of coal, petroleum, iron, and copper are not limitless. Trees are not just a source of lumber and fuel but also help maintain the balance between oxygen and carbon dioxide on the planet. Forests can die—taking along with them countless animals and plants that live in them. Rivers and oceans can dry up, as did the Aral Sea. Soil can erode, and fertile lands can become deserts.

Entire species of plants and animals can become extinct. When Gerald Durrell founded the Jersey Wildlife Preservation Trust in the 1960s, he chose the dodo as its symbol as a reminder that countless species of plants and animals are becoming extinct every year as a result of human activities. As Durrell pointed out, the term *rare* in biology does not mean valuable but that an animal or plant is in danger of dying out.

The story of the dodo is the story of humankind's reckless behavior. In the nineteenth century, when sailors arrived on the island of Mauritius, they found a ready supply of meat in the form of the dodo. A large flightless bird of the same order as pigeons, it had evidently been in little contact with humans before. Instead of trying to escape, these birds just sat there while the sailors clubbed them. So the Portuguese sailors called them *doudo*, which means "fool" or "simpleton." But in killing these birds, the sailors also ended up depriving themselves of meat. Within a century, the dodo had been wiped out.

The moral of the story is not that entire species of animals can die out in a short period of time. We know that can happen naturally: dinosaurs became extinct without any help from human beings. Rather, the story of the dodo teaches a lesson about the impact of human activities—human "progress"—on other organisms living on this planet. Human activities since the Industrial Revolution have speeded up the pace of extinction.

The increasing sophistication of technology contributes to the serious decline in wildlife. The gravity of the problem could be seen in the standoff between Canada and Spain during the mid-1990s over depleting fish stock in the North Atlantic. Fishing today involves more than the net and boat of ancient times. Fishermen use sonar equipment to detect where fish are feeding and then move in with nets, which may be several kilometers (miles) long and go down 10 meters (yards) or deeper. The fish—and any other marine life forms—caught in those nets are then mechanically hauled on board, where they are processed immediately and stored in deep freeze. As this procedure happens over and over again, technology starts to outpace what nature can replace (as will be discussed more fully in chapter 5).

> We really "came into our own" with the dawn of the industrial age early in the 1800s. As we harnessed nature and worked with the natural laws of science, we learned to destroy forests and pollute the air, water and soil very efficiently; and this efficiency has, over the last two centuries, increased exponentially. (Caldicott, 1992, p. 97)

The Right to Decide—One of the main problems in managing resources is the growth of the human population. More and more resources are needed to support the increasing number of people on earth. Resources, however, are not endless, nor are most of them distributed evenly around the globe. Thus, the question of "ownership" is of strategic importance. *A crucial fac-*

tor for the future is who decides how resources are used. This question is one of the driving forces behind the moves by India, Papua New Guinea, Ethiopia, and Zimbabwe. The North may well have the technology of the future, but the South has the raw material—the genetic resources—necessary for this technology.

In the past, some nations or ethnic groups have had little say in how resources on their land were developed, and the people themselves profited little from the benefits that these resources, especially minerals, generated. An example is the conflict between Shell and the Ogoni people of Nigeria over petroleum exploration in the region. In Canada, as another example, one of the critical areas in settling land claims of indigenous peoples involves rights to (or compensation for) minerals and other resources found in them.

Despite the importance of minerals, if economic forecasts are accurate (Ernst and Young, 1996), the future lies not in mineral or energy resources but in biological resources (especially if they are genetically interesting). This is one of the reasons many countries rich in genetic resources are moving quickly to make sure that they will have a say in what happens to those resources and the benefits derived from them.

The image of colonialism used by RAFI and others has more than just rhetorical value: countries such as India, Papua New Guinea, and even Canada were once colonies with little say over how resources were developed and what happened to the benefits. In the nineteenth century, railways and telegraph lines improved the efficiency of export routes for diamonds, spices, fur, and lumber. In the twentieth century, highways, telephone lines, airplanes, and satellite links have further increased that efficiency.

In the twenty-first century, the two key technologies are likely to involve information and genes. Many industrializing nations may have to import the material and knowledge needed for information technology. But they have the greatest abundance of genetic material, needed for biotechnology. Clearly they have to start protecting their long-term interests.

WHAT IS LIFE?

As the preceding discussions show, human experience affects human concerns over gene technology. Objections to many of its applications suggest a fear that they will unleash deadly consequences on the human population: epidemic-causing microbes, crop-destroying superweeds, or eugenic plans to eliminate certain groups of society. Much of this fear is based on past threats to large segments of humanity.

These past threats offer only a partial explanation for the level of anxiety expressed. As was said in the introduction, such anxiety is part of humankind's preoccupation with life in this world and the meaning of human existence. The following sections will try to illuminate this preoccupation.

THE NATURE OF LIFE

What is life? Humans have asked this question probably since the beginning of their existence. Possibly no other technology has provoked as much thought and discussion on this question as gene technology, for a number of reasons. First, gene technology is based on the the scientific study of life in all its forms. Second, unlike most previous technologies, gene technology harnesses the basic substances and processes of cellular life. Third, and perhaps most important, the development of gene technology coincides with concerns about the quality of life on this planet, specifically, the environmental movement. In the 1960s, ordinary citizens started to worry that pesticides and herbicides were killing wildlife. Evidence was mounting that harmful chemical residues were building up in soil, water, plant and animal tissues, and even mothers' milk.

The early 1970s was a defining period in the story of gene technology. The first successful experiment in recombinant DNA took place about 1973. Only two years before that, in 1971, Greenpeace was founded to protest against the American testing of nuclear weapons and, eventually, to raise public awareness of environmental problems.

In the 1990s, those fears and concerns have not disappeared. Environmental pollution, health risks, and endangered species are still important social and political issues. The scientific community is still debating about the effects of certain chemicals on sperm count in human beings and other animals (Baumann, 1996). People are worrying about how we are treating life on this planet.

Western society's attitudes toward other forms of life on Earth have been influenced by Greco-Roman philosophy, Judeo-Christian beliefs, and scientific rationality. These three streams of thought shaped the values of Western culture and, consequently, those of modern technological society. Some of the conflicts over gene technology can be traced to contradictions inherent in these three traditions. It is also important to remember that no society exists in isolation. Contacts with other cultures have often proved to be powerful catalysts for change.

By the mid-1960s, many people in the industrialized West had started to challenge the basic values of Western society. The 1970s were marked not only by rising concerns over the environment and life on Earth but by the turning of many people, especially the young, toward the East for answers to their angst. In the process, they discovered philosophies and religions that reconcile the needs and interests of humankind with those of other living beings who share this world with us. They encountered cultures that approach life in its entirety rather than in its dissected and isolated parts. They discovered beliefs that people may be reborn as animals in their next life. Such new ideas caused people to question Western attitudes toward one another, nature, and life itself.

The following sections will focus on the question What is life? in the Western tradition. There are two pragmatic reasons for this narrow focus. First, gene technology developed in the West, and many of the concerns about it come from the West or countries influenced by Western thinking. Second, neither time nor space allows an in-depth examination of all philosophical thought on this question, which would require several volumes.

The Classical View

Since early times, people have made a distinction between what is alive and what is not—between life and matter. For the Greeks and Romans, the special quality that distinguishes life is the soul or spirit. The idea of a soul or spirit moving living things is so important that its traces can still be found in our vocabulary today. In English, the words *animal* and *animate* come from the Latin *anima*, meaning "breath," "life," or "soul." The English word *spirit* (Latin *spiritus*) also means "breath" or "soul."

The idea of the soul being the "breath of life" is not unique to the Greco-Roman world. Other ancient cultures shared this view (Margulis and Sagan, 1995; Schriefers, 1982). For example, in the Judaic tradition, God formed man out of the soil "and breathed into his face the breath of life, and man became a living soul" (Genesis 2:7). In Chinese, the word *ch'i kung*, meaning "life force," derives from *ch'i*, meaning "breath" (Margulis and Sagan, 1995).

For the ancient Greco-Roman world, spirit and matter are two aspects of reality. Matter is infused with a spiritual force or soul. This animistic concept is expressed in the Greco-Roman belief in Poseidon, god of the sea; Demeter, goddess of the grain; and a host of minor spirits who inhabited springs, streams, rivers, trees, and forests. Aristotle believed that even plants have that part of the soul which enables living beings to take in nourishment. In his view, the ability to seek nourishment is the most basic faculty in any living being (Bondolfi, 1994). Plants can be said to be alive because they take in nourishment, they grow, and they breathe.

The Judeo-Christian View

In contrast to the animism of the Greeks and Romans and most other ancient peoples, Judaism holds that there is only one true God, who created everything that has ever existed. This monotheistic view was continued in Christianity and gradually superseded animism when Christianity was legalized in the Roman Empire. In the monotheistic Judeo-Christian view, spirits and gods do not inhabit the material world; only humans have a spirit or soul, which is the link between God and humankind.

A value judgment comes into play here. In Christian thought the emphasis on the unique nature of the human soul does not simply separate humans from the rest of creation. Borrowing from Plato, Christianity taught that the spirit triumphs over matter: the immortal soul is more important than the material body. For example, the New Testament teaches that even though the material body is mortal, the spiritual soul itself cannot be destroyed.

Far more important, humankind is different from the rest of creation because only humans have a *rational* soul: "The spiritual soul is the principle of the spiritual mental life and, at the same time, the principle of the corporeal (vegetative and sensitive) life" (Ott, 1960, p. 97). Man stands in the center of creation *only* because he is created in the image of God (that is, he has a soul). This view was to have an impact on thinkers in the Western world, especially Descartes.

The Cartesian View
Perhaps like no other before him, the seventeenth-century French philosopher and mathematician René Descartes laid the groundwork for modern scientific thought. He proposed a dualistic view of reality based on the division between the self-conscious mind and the nonconscious world. For Descartes, only human beings are conscious, because we alone have a rational soul. This view is closer to the Judeo-Christian view of a world in which humans stand at the center; it is certainly far from the animistic tradition that all things are inhabited by spirits.

In a way, the Cartesian view can be seen as a logical product of the attempt to reconcile two divergent perspectives—the monotheistic Judeo-Christian tradition and the animistic beliefs of the Greco-Roman world. In Judaism, there is only one true God: there is no room for the gods and spirits that inhabit the world of the Greeks and Romans; being created in God's image, only humans have spirits or souls. More important, in the Jewish and Christian tradition, nature or creation is sacred; any attempt to discover the secrets of nature is seen as a challenge to God. The Greeks and Romans, in contrast, saw nature as a teacher: Aristotle, for example, was not only a philosopher but also a keen student of nature.

Descartes, as a Christian, wanted to reconcile the monotheistic and anthropocentric teachings of the Judeo-Christian faith with the animistic, nature-oriented perspectives of the Greco-Roman world. The Cartesian solution is an anthropocentric view combined with a justification to explore nature that does not question God's creation: humankind stands at the top and center of a mechanistic world that we can explore without been seen as challenging the work of God. As will be shown later, this compromise is important for both Descartes and the development of Western science.

TWO VIEWS OF THE WORLD
Although animistic Classical thinkers and monotheistic medieval Christian thinkers distinguished between the spiritual and the material, they believed the one was somehow connected to the other—the world was a whole. The importance of the Cartesian compromise was that it allowed Western thought to go a step further by making a clear separation between what is

alive and rational on the one hand and everything else on the other. In adopting the Cartesian compromise, science accepted a mechanistic view of the world. There was no conflict—as long as this view was restricted to physics or even to chemistry. When applied to biology, however, conflicts arose. This section will discuss animism and mechanism in their early forms and their later development.

The Animistic View

According to the animistic, or vitalistic, view of existence, the universe is a living entity. Spirits provide the life force of all existing things. The wind, rivers, mountains, and trees have a life of their own that is explained by the inner spirit that moves them. From this idea developed pantheism, the belief that God and the universe are identical.

Animism was the popular belief of the Greeks and Romans and most other ancient peoples, as previously discussed. One of the Greek divinities associated with natural phenomena was Gaia, the mother goddess Earth, who brought forth the sky, mountains, and seas. Similarly Tellus was the Roman goddess of earth and fields, referred to in Latin as *terra mater*, "mother earth."

Long submerged by the mechanistic Cartesian view, animism began to reappear in a new form in the late twentieth century. Throughout the 1950s and 1960s, there was a growing awareness of the harmful effects of pollution not only on plants and animals but also on the planet itself. Then, in the 1960s, interest in space exploration, ironically, sparked an interest in life itself. The search for life in space presented scientists with a challenge: how were astronauts to detect life in space if scientists have not yet understood what life is?

These and other factors contributed to the realization that the Earth consists of more than just air, soil, and water supporting a variety of microorganisms, plants, and animals. According to this view, the Earth is a living system. James Lovelock and Lynn Margulis, both scientists, first used the name *Gaia* to describe this living system when they put forward the Gaia hypothesis in the early 1970s:

> Specifically, the Gaia hypothesis said that the temperature, oxidation state, acidity, and certain aspects of the rocks and waters are at any time kept constant, and that this homeostasis is maintained by active feedback processes operated automatically and unconsciously by the biota. The conditions are only constant in the short term and evolve in synchrony with the changing needs of the biota as it evolves. Life and its environment are so closely coupled that evolution concerns Gaia, not the organisms or the environment taken separately. (Lovelock, 1991, p. 10)

Is the Earth a living system? By definition, living systems are capable of self-reproduction, self-construction, self-organization, and self-regulation (Schriefers, 1982). Lovelock and Margulis argue that the Earth fits into the definition of living systems. The Earth is in constant change: it renews itself, and new forms of life arise. This process of self-renewal—or autopoiesis (literally, self-making)—occurs in all living systems, whether at the molecular level or at a much higher level:

> An autopoietic being metabolises continuously; it perpetuates itself through chemical activity, the movement of molecules. Autopoiesis entails energy expenditure and the making of messes. Autopoiesis, indeed, is detectable by that incessant life chemistry and energy flow which is metabolism. Only cells, organisms made of cells, and biospheres made of organisms are autopoietic and can metabolise. (Margulis and Sagan, 1995, p. 23)

The Gaia theory stops short of adopting an animistic view, but it tries to give new insight into traditional scientific studies of living organisms and life. Margulis rejects the vitalization of matter, just as she rejects the mechanization of life. The Gaia theory, though initially not accepted in scientific circles, has slowly gained the interests of other scientists: there is evidence, for example, suggesting that plankton have an effect on the Earth's climates. Therefore, in contrast to Cartesian thinking, Lovelock and Margulis are saying that the world is more than the sum of all its mountains and lakes. They reject the idea that living things can be considered in isolation from their environment or the planet to which they belong.

For the purpose of the current discussion, the Gaia hypothesis is intended to illustrate a number of points. First, the basic idea of animism—that the world is alive, just as an animal is alive—is perhaps not as absurd as it might sound to someone raised in a science-oriented society. Second, and more important, the way conventional science looks at life is neither unbiased nor the only way of understanding life. Lovelock and Margulis, in proposing the Gaia hypothesis, have challenged science to reexamine its own assumptions.

The Mechanistic View

For the most part, science operates on the assumption that humans can gain a better understanding of the world by dissecting it into smaller parts and studying them. Science deals with tangible, objective, quantifiable phenomena—what can be detected, measured, dissected, and analyzed. This way of thinking, as discussed earlier, can be traced back to Descartes.

Descartes uses the terms *res cogitans*, "thinking matter," and *res extensa*, "extended matter." According to his view, the conscious mind can be experienced through internal, subjective knowledge; the nonconscious world can be described through external, objective experience. Based on this dualistic proposition, Descartes was able to conceive of the world in mechanistic terms. He saw the world as a machine that could be taken apart, measured, and analyzed without reprisal—either by the church or by God.

The audacity of Descartes's view can best be seen against the backdrop of his time. In seventeenth-century Europe, the Catholic Church was trying to reaffirm and reconsolidate its position in the aftermath of the Protestant Reformation in the previous century. Asserting its authority, it condemned works that departed from traditional church teachings, including Galileo's support of a Copernican universe with the sun at its center. In response, Descartes had to reconcile his view of the world with the church's teachings:

> To this day the Cartesian permit rallies scientists to study a universe that is wide open for investigation, but in the "fine print" is found the exception: the conscious human soul—which, in Descartes's time, was unquestionably made in God's image. Moreover, the Cartesian permit still contains in the fine print this assumption: the universe is mechanical and set up according to immutable laws. Neither the exception nor the assumption is science. At the heart of the Cartesian philosophy are thus metaphysical presuppositions, springing from the culture that gave rise to science. (Margulis and Sagan, 1995, pp. 38-39)

In the Cartesian view, with the exception of the human mind and the human soul, everything else in this world, even animals, is a machine to be taken apart for study. One result of this focus on the parts rather than the whole is that science became specialized, and scientific knowledge was divided into various disciplines: biology, chemistry, physics, geology, and so on. Science left the intangible, the subjective, and the qualitative to other fields. The traditional division of academic disciplines into the faculty of arts and the faculty of science reflects this Cartesian tendency to separate the mind from the body and spirit from matter.

The Cartesian distinction allowed science to progress without entering into conflict with church teachings. As long as science confined its activities to areas that did not question the existence of the human soul, science was left to pursue its theories and principles. Newton was able to define planetary motion in mathematical terms. Physics replaced magic. Chemistry replaced alchemy. Biology replaced metaphysics. Rivers, the wind, and the seasons ceased to be governed by the will of invisible spirits: fixed, universal scientific principles now provided *the* explanation for their movement.

It was not long, however, before even the exception in the fine print—the prohibition on the study of the human soul—was ignored, forgotten, and, finally, abandoned. This development led to conflicts between religion and science, conflicts that Descartes had hoped to avoid with his compromise. In the nineteenth century Charles Darwin, for example, ran into trouble with the church but not for proposing that plants and animals evolved through natural selection. As a matter of fact, long before Darwin, others had suggested that species of plants and animals arose through a process of natural selection: Georges Louis Buffon, and Jean-Baptiste Lamarck in the eighteenth century and Erasmus Darwin, Charles's grandfather. But, Darwin was among the first to suggest that humans descended from apes:

> Darwin documented, without any explicit anti-Christian statement, that neither humans nor ancestral apes were created by God. . . . No longer, Darwin insinuated, was man excluded from connection with nature. Even the perceiving mind, describing itself, evolved from mechanical laws of random variation and natural selection. (Margulis and Sagan, 1995, p 39)

Darwin's proposition created an outrage for two reasons. First, it rejected the idea that man was created at all, let alone created in God's image: humans are just as much a part of the animal kingdom as apes or, indeed, guinea pigs. Second, it meant that the Cartesian premise was false: human beings, *as* animals, are made of unfeeling matter; we do not have souls and we, too, are valid subjects of scientific investigation.

For Darwin, the human body and even the human mind were material objects that science could—or had to—explore, examine, and explain. The movements of the limbs could be explained in mechanical terms—leverage, flexion, and extension. The activities of the human body, like those of animals, could be understood in terms of the functions of organs and various bodily systems. The mind could be described in terms of electrical neural stimulation and chemical activities. Physical traits and living processes were explained by the functions of genes.

THE RISE OF SCIENCE AND TECHNOLOGY AS AN INSTITUTION

By the sixteenth century, the Renaissance and its humanistic philosophy that man, not God, was the measure of all things, was establishing itself throughout Europe. The discovery of works from Classical antiquity and the introduction of works by Muslim philosophers led to new ideas. In Poland, Copernicus put forward the thesis that the sun was at the center of the universe, and in Italy, the Flemish scholar Vesalius laid the foundation for modern anatomical studies.

At the same time, in Germany, Martin Luther argued that salvation comes not through the intercession of the church but through individual faith in God. In challenging the authority and structure of the church, he opened the door to individual inquiry and weakened the church as an institution of authority. Finally, the invention of the printing press allowed the wide dissemination of views other than those advocated by the church. Knowledge was no longer limited to the Word of God transmitted through the Catholic priesthood. The time was ripe for a society based on secular learning.

The seventeenth century marked an important turning point in Europe. It was the beginning of the age of the Enlightenment, the age of Reason. It was the age in which four men provided the foundations for a new, materialistic outlook of the world and so shaped the development of modern scientific principles.

Francis Bacon proposed that nature can be understood through direct observation. Galileo Galilei saw the universe as something to be explained in mathematical terms. Isaac Newton showed that the same gravitational forces regulated the movements of heavenly and earthly bodies. René Descartes, as previously described, proposed a mechanistic model of the world: mindless, soulless, and emotionless. These men saw the universe as following an order and a logic that, once understood, is predictable. Observation, theory, and experimentation became the cornerstones of science.

For a long time, science remained the intellectual pursuit of individuals interested in how nature works. It was still a concept or ideal reflecting a certain philosophical outlook: Descartes himself was more a mathematician and philosopher than a scientist. A basic premise of science was to improve the human condition through a better understanding of nature and natural phenomena. The results of that knowledge should be put to use to improve society.

In the late eighteenth century, science took on growing economic and, consequently, social importance. Scientific research moved out of the backrooms and cellars of individuals into the laboratories of universities and industry as it became a recognized profession. Throughout the nineteenth century in Europe and North America, the process of industrialization, itself a product of science, helped established science as an institution of society. Towns grew up not around churches and castles but around mills and factories. This transition marked the beginnings of the rise of science and technology as an institution of industrial society and, later, of postindustrial, or modern technological, society.

SCIENCE AND TECHNOLOGY AS A SOCIAL INSTITUTION

Are science and technology really an institution of society? L. Sklair argues that they are. According to a model that he uses, a social institution has six essential features: a charter, norms, material apparatus, activities, and function. The charter defines the institution's system of values. Those working in the institution are organized according to authority and functions as well as duties and privileges. Certain skills and legal standards are recognized and accepted by those working in the institution. An institution has assets in the forms of equipment and financial means. The functions of the institution are the sum results of its organized activities (Sklair, 1973). Table 4.1 provides a summary of the key features of the institution of science and technology.

An in-depth structural analysis of science and technology as an institution is not necessary in the context of the current discussion. The important point is that science and technology can and should be viewed as an institution. Even more important, they are an institution that has replaced the church and the secular state as a source of authority and a point of reference in society (see "From Institutional Authority to Individual Autonomy," chapter 5).

In a religiously oriented society, priests and theologians set guidelines for everyone: they set the standard for what is and what is not acceptable. For example, medieval European society turned to the Bible and the teachings of churchmen for guidance. In later secular society, legislators and civil servants establish guidelines and standards, through laws, policies, and regulations: the highest court and the constitution remain the highest instance of appeal in many secular nation-states.

In industrial and modern technological society, science and technology are an important source of authority. Scientific and technical experts play an increasingly important role in implementing legislation and regulation. In the areas of risk assessment, for example, these experts help lawmakers define what levels of pollution are acceptable; they help decide what amount of a substance should be considered safe and under which conditions; and they help establish what safety measures need to be considered for a new technology. Scientists, doctors, and technical experts are called as expert witnesses in courts of law: the data, however complicated, can be crucial to the jury's decision.

The point is not that science and technology have taken over people's lives or that there is a technocratic conspiracy but that they are an essential element in the structure of modern technological society. They affect the choices that people make as individuals and the options that are available to society as a whole.

> Though the social institution of science and technology may seem a rather abstract and remote thing, it is really about how certain people (for example, scientists, bureaucrats) act in certain social situations (scientific research, laboratory management), and how these actions affect other people (for example, industrial workers, politicians, generals, the hungry) in other social situations (for example, threatened redundancy, economic crisis, war, famine). (Sklair, 1973, p. 72)

Science and technology are an institution of modern technological society insofar as decisions and actions taken in this area often have political and social implications for the rest of society. The introduction of a new tech-

Table 4.1 A Functional Comparison of Science and Technology as a Social Institution

Features of a Social Institution	Science	Technology
Charter: system of values that attracts people to the institution	• Science exists for its own sake: the pursuit of knowledge for the sake of knowledge. *or* • Science exists to serve the interests of humanity. *or* • Science is mainly a way of earning a living.	• Technology exists for its own sake: solving a problem because the problem exists. *or* • Technology exists to serve the interests of humanity. *or* • Technology is mainly a way of earning a living.
Personnel: people working in the institution and adhering to its rules and norms	• They tend to be found in universities and other academic settings. • They tend to hold at least a first degree and often a postgraduate degree. • They have a reward system where prestige and status tend to be based on published scholarly articles that are well received by peers.	• They tend to be found in industry. • They tend to hold diplomas or certificates rather than degrees. • They have a reward system where prestige and status tend to be based on administrative and managerial success.
Norms: rules and standards of the institution	• The way individual workers behave or operate tends to reflect the rules of an academic setting.	• The way individual workers behave or operate tends to reflect the rules of an industrial setting.
Resources: funding and equipment	• They are on a smaller scale than in technology (less funds for research).	• They are on a bigger scale than in science (more funds for R&D).
Activities: what the people do	• Scientists focus on basic research, some applied research. • They often teach as well.	• Technologists focus on applied research and product development. • They often have administrative and managerial responsibilities as well.

Table 4.1 A Functional Comparison of Science and Technology as a Social Institution—continued

Features of a Social Institution	Science	Technology
Function: integral results of organized activities	• Science functions to increase economic and military capacities of society.	• Technology functions to increase economic and military capacities of society.

nology, for example, has economic, legal, environmental, political, and social consequences. As an institution, science and technology embody certain values and principles—a charter and norms—that will inevitably run into conflict with the values and principles of other institutions or even individuals.

Because science is concerned with tangible, objective, quantifiable phenomena, complex problems in society are often reduced to technically and logistically definable dimensions: those working with science and technology tend to assume that these problems have material, technical, and quantifiable solutions. Thus, world hunger is defined as a problem of selling or transferring more technical aids—machinery and chemicals—to increase farming production: world hunger is not seen as a result of inequitable access to resources. Illiteracy is seen as a problem that can be solved by providing more books and other learning aids rather than as a complex social problem involving individual rights and fairness in distributing income and allocating resources. Disease and poor health conditions are linked simply to medical needs—medication and medical equipment—rather than to wider problems such as poverty, overpopulation, and the role of women in a given culture.

This materialistic, quantitative model of problem solving has come under fire from critics, especially in the arts and humanities. One target of criticism is the model's limited scope, which restricts its ability to take into consideration other, equally important, nonquantifiable factors. Thus, exclusive reliance on the model often prevents scientists from seeing the broader implications of their work.

The quantitative and materialistic model works for physics and even chemistry, where activities can be measured and predicted. In the area of biology, however, prediction becomes difficult if not impossible. The environment, the interaction of organism and environment, and even the will of the organism must all be taken into consideration. The mechanistic model of molecular biology suggests that better understanding of the *molecular* activities of genes will lead to better understanding of how organisms function and might even help us understand what life is. Critics challenge this assumption and, in so doing, the norms of science as an institution.

THE VALUES OF SCIENCE AND TECHNOLOGY

Science and technology, as has been pointed out, are not neutral. Like any social institution, they have a charter and norms that define their values, principles, and outlook. Those working as part of an institution may have their own values and principles as individuals, but *as members of the institution*, they have to accept the institution's charter in order to help the institution serve its function. Dissenters who depart from or challenge the collective wisdom of the institution are not tolerated (Sangalli, 1996).

Science and technology, adopting the Cartesian premise, assume that the world is made of lifeless matter that follows certain fixed mathematical principles and is detectable, measurable, and predictable. This assumption is one reason why research results are not accepted as factual until they have been reproduced by other peer groups using the same methods.

Part of the resistance to gene technology stems from a rejection of the values of science and technology as an institution. For example, those opposed to gene technology also frequently oppose the use of other new or complex technologies. This is an essential point to grasp in the resistance to new technologies: "Science meant safety for its adherents, but danger for its opponents. It was the scientific origin of the technologies themselves, their remoteness from everyday experience, which became an element of high risk in the eyes of many critics" (Radkau, 1995, p. 337).

This remoteness is relevant to the debates over gene technology. The world of the geneticist seems remote to most people. Scientists seem to be isolated in their ivory towers, protected by the walls of jargon and technical formalities. In addition, the Cartesian materialistic outlook, inherent in the institution of science, has become a source of conflict in the development of gene technology. A closer look at the arguments reveals a conflict in the values and perspectives of the advocates and opponents of gene technology.

For many supporters, better understanding of genes and their functions will open up new knowledge about life. If humans can learn how genes regulate the functions of living organisms, that knowledge can be used to satisfy the health, agricultural, or environmental needs of society. This is an example of the charter value (see Table 4.1) that science exists to serve the interests of humanity. This concept derives from the Baconian proposition that "scientific and technological discoveries are historic achievements in the long quest to dominate nature" (Smith, 1996, p. 65).

For many opponents, the substance of life is intangible: it belongs outside the realm of Cartesian science. Their protest against gene technology is, in a literal sense, a rejection of the narrow view that life is nothing more than sticky strings of chemical substances. They reject the idea that better genetic knowledge will lead to a better understanding of what life is. They reject altogether the Cartesian premise that living things are soulless, let alone soulless machines. In opposing patent claims on animals or other organisms as discussed earlier, these opponents make the counter-claim that these organisms are not soulless machines and have an existence beyond serving humankind's needs. They reject the Baconian assumption that, through science, it is possible to gain dominion over nature for the benefit of humankind.

Many of these opponents see the world—especially the living world—as a connected whole, as animists do. That is why environmentalists are concerned about the long-term and indirect effects of the release of genetically altered organisms on the environment. Plants and animals are not merely a collection of atoms whose behavior can be predicted with certainty. Because they are living beings, animals, plants, and even microorganisms are more complex than all their genes put together. The whole-system view is also partly why some religious leaders warn against treating animals and plants simply as renewable (or disposable) genetic resources. They are concerned that if we see plants and animals as mere commodities, we may treat human beings that way as well: this possibility is the essence of the concerns over the patenting of human cell lines (see "Humans," chapter 3, and "Concerns Relating to Gene Technology and Humans" earlier in this chapter).

A good example of the conflict in perspectives can be found in the battle over the medical applications of gene technology. For many medical researchers and the supporters of gene technology, human genome research and transgenic lab animals will provide medical science with important insights into origins and development of many human diseases. Some of that research may enable better diagnosis of a disease or even an estimatation a patient's predisposition to certain hereditary diseases. Better understanding of the role of genes may lead to new treatments such as gene therapy. Other areas of research may produce new medication that could help ease patients' lives.

In contrast, many critics and opponents are worried about the single-minded focus on genes. Genes have been said to be responsible not only for a growing number of human diseases but also for various types of human behavior and characteristics. "Recent biomedical discoveries have redefined a broad spectrum of diseases and behaviors as biologically determined, diagnosable and predictable" (Nelkin and Tancredi, 1989, p. 159).

Gene technology, in particular, allows doctors and medical researchers to diagnose and predict predisposition to a genetic disorder, the stage of a disease, available treatment, and even the life expectancy of the patient. The desire to prevent or treat a disease does not pose a problem in itself, but the sole focus on a person's genes seems to reduce or even eliminate the role of lifestyle, the social milieu, or the environment in human diseases. It implies that the genetic code decrees a sort of inevitable destiny.

Conflicts arise because critics argue that living organisms are not predictable: in the world of living things, one factor can trigger a complex sequence of events. Lifestyle and the environment probably play an important role in human health and human behavior. Although critics do not disagree that genes are a factor in complex human traits, they worry that the single-minded focus on genes will increase social prejudice: individuals will be viewed more and more through the filter of their genetic predisposition.

At the same time, critics object to the implicit image of the human being as a soulless machine, genetically programmed to behave in a certain way or to develop a particular state of health. In the case of the woman who wants to free her child from disease, discussed above, no one is disputing her concern as a mother. The objection is that society will come to a point where future generations can be genetically programmed by the deletion of an "undesirable" gene or the insertion of a "more desirable" one. That means that society today will have determined the lives of these future individuals. They will have lost not only their freedom of choice but the recognition of their free will as human individuals.

This is an area where genetic science is seen as violating the fine print— the assumption and the exception—of the Cartesian permit. As long as genetic research focuses on lifeless and soulless DNA in isolation, it is working within the acceptable boundaries of the Cartesian permit. On the assumption that humans are superior to other life forms (in the Judeo-Christian tradition), there is little resistance to the genetic alteration of microorganisms or even plants. Even somatic-cell gene therapy (as noted in chapter 2) does not encounter great resistance because it only involves the alteration of human cells and tissues—soulless matter.

Gene technology is forbidden to touch the essence (or the soul) of the individual: the germ line (see "Germ-Line Gene Therapy," chapter 2), or genetic factors linked to intelligence, personality, or the way a person thinks or acts. The fear is that science some day will cross into a zone that should remain off limits. Science, critics say, should not try to discover the soul of life. Life is more than the living functions of an organism. DNA provides the molecular basis of life, but DNA is not Life itself (with a capital L).

It is ironic that despite ideological differences, both advocates and opponents of gene technology have something in common: a fascination with life. In their own ways, the genetic scientist and the environmentalist are both trying to understand what life is.

SCIENCE, TECHNOLOGY, AND LIFE

The paradigm shift is a recurring theme in this book. New technologies trigger change and challenge the way people look at the world. Perhaps more than any other technology, gene technology has challenged individuals and institutions to reexamine the values underlying their attitudes towards this planet, the environment, living things, and life itself. It has brought into sharp focus conflicts of values that, until now, were easy to forget, ignore, or dismiss. Other new technologies in the twentieth century—concerned with information and reproduction—have also made us reconsider our theories about life and what it means to be alive.

Western science, as described earlier, divides the world into the tangible and the intangible, the quantitative and the qualitative, the objective and the subjective. The realm of science deals with the former. Modern technological society, itself a product of Western science, assumes that it is possible to consider one side of the apparent dichotomy of mind and body, spirit and matter, organisms and machines, people and technology in isolation from the other.

This dualistic view has allowed human beings to harness the forces of nature and make use of the natural world. It has led to great scientific discoveries and monumental technological achievements that made possible the development of industrial society in the nineteenth century and high-technological society in the twentieth century. So it is ironic that new technologies should be the reason for questioning the very foundation of technological society. Perhaps this process of questioning and challenging is necessary: it forces public debate about the fundamental values of a society and helps set priorities that will affect choices in the future.

SCIENCE: THE TREE OF THE KNOWLEDGE OF GOOD AND EVIL

Few would dispute that science and technology have improved our understanding of the world and, perhaps, even of ourselves. Medical science has helped improve the standard of living in many parts of the world. The majority of people today lead longer lives than even their grandparents. Space exploration has provided insight into our planet and on how unique life is.

At the same time, each new discovery seems to underline how little science understands about what life is. It is a paradox of gene technology that on the one hand, genetic science and other areas of biology have increased scientific knowledge about living organisms, yet on the other hand, each new piece of knowledge also shows the depth of our ignorance about what life is. Never before have we known so much about how little we know.

Nevertheless, having gained that knowledge, we cannot go back. This impossibility is perhaps the lesson of some of the world's oldest myths. After the Titan Prometheus had given human beings the knowledge of fire, not even Zeus, the king of the gods, could take that knowledge back. After Adam and Eve had eaten the fruit of the tree of the knowledge of good and evil, they could not give back what they had learned.

When Descartes proposed the rule of reason as the guiding principle for society, he assumed that humans, created in God's image, have a rational mind that separates us from nonthinking matter. Rational skepticism became the standard by which scientific enterprise is measured. Objective knowledge was defined as the result of scientific thinking and scientific methodology and was deemed more important than subjective experience. Scientific thought replaced religious belief as society shifted from a religious foundation to a secular one. The myths and religious stories of the past no longer provided the explanation for the universe. People no longer believed the myths of many cultures that Earth is the mother goddess who gave birth to the gods, the stars, the mountains, and the rivers. Instead they looked to science to provide the answers to old human questions about how things work and why things are. Astronomy tells us that Earth is just a planet among many spinning in the void of space. Physics tells us that matter does not have a soul, just energy. Chemistry teaches us to look at the world in terms of elements and compounds. Biology explains that living things are made of complex systems and functions.

Today, however, surrounded as we are by the products of science and technology, there is a growing realization that the Cartesian dualities of mind and matter are arbitrary and that they reflect two aspects of the same reality. We are aware that human beings have both a mind and a body, neither of which can exist independently of the other. The spiritual side of the person needs something that science cannot offer. This is *not* to say that people reject science: on the contrary, as noted earlier, most people approve of continuing support for research activities in many areas of gene technology, which suggests that they find value in science. But they do reject the scientific idea that reality is made only of matter, which is detectable and quantifiable. Ironically in this high-technological age, a growing number of individuals are looking beyond science for answers to fundamental questions.

This recognition of the limitation of science is one reason for the growing interest in the healing nature of spirituality: where their parents may have asked a doctor for a prescription, many people today are exploring nonscientific therapies such as meditation, acupuncture, and chiropractic. Even scientists are intrigued by the potential correlation between faith and healing. They are recognizing that science can provide only a partial answer to the question: What is life? That is as much a philosophical question as it is a scientific one.

TECHNOLOGY: SHIFTING PARADIGMS AND CHANGING PERCEPTIONS

In 1946 two scientists at the University of Pennsylvania built the world's first computer, the electronic numerical integrator and computer (ENIAC). It was considered a monument to modern technology: it could calculate a ten-digit number within 1/350 second. But that achievement still pales in comparison to the abilities of the human brain. The brain receives thousands of signals at the same time from our five senses; it processes these signals, translating them into information and storing it in the memory.

At the dawn of the computer age, it had seemed that Descartes was right: the thinking, reasoning human mind separates humans from the rest of the soulless, unthinking material world. But fifty years later, the use of silicon chips has speeded up developments in all areas of microelectronics, notably in the computer, automation, and robotic industries. Today's computers are capable not only of mindless, repetitive tasks but also of analyzing complicated data and making complex decisions.

In 1996 the Russian Garry Kasparov, world chess champion, entered a chess competition against Deep Blue, an IBM computer designed to play chess. Kasparov won—by a narrow margin. The Kasparov-Deep Blue showdown opened debates about what the mind is. For Descartes, almost four hundred years ago, the mind was evidence that human beings were created in God's image, set apart from animals and the rest of unthinking matter and had the capacity to exercise free will. When a computer loses a chess game by a *narrow* margin to a world champion (indeed, Deep Blue won in a rematch in 1997), it raises questions about the differences between the human brain and a computer. Can machines think? It seems so: computers *communicate* with one another; security systems *recognize* codes or even fingerprints. It is even possible to speak of *artificial intelligence* and *intelligent machines*.

New technologies, including information technology, seem to be blurring the dividing line between life and matter. If people in technological society are describing computers with the terminology usually applied to living things, they are also increasingly describing the processes of life in the vocabulary of information technology.

> The sheer semantic spread the term [information revolution] has achieved owes much to the discovery of DNA. . . . Indeed, John Maynard Smith explains how the concept of information applies in modern molecular biology not as metaphor, but as a literal account of the operations of the genetic code. August Weismann discovered a century ago that heredity is about "the transmission, not of matter or energy, but of information". The technical terms include messenger, code, transcription, translation, proofreading. (Smith, 1996, p. 67)

As this chapter has discussed, the Western world has always made a clear distinction between life or spirit and matter, as indeed have most cultures. In the West, though, the two drifted apart and finally split with the rise of scientific thought, which studied matter and left the world of spirit to religion and philosophy. This split offers an insight into the furor over gene technology, which is testing the strength and the validity of the dividing line between life and matter. As chapter 3 points out, the real issue in the patenting of gene technology innovations is not the patent system but the values that gene technology as a branch of science embodies. It is revealing that opponents—often from environmental groups or religious organizations— say that they cannot accept the idea of patents on *life*—not just living organisms (see "Microorganims," chapter 3). It is also striking that, in Europe, where there is a morality clause in patent law, the objection is often based on the argument that the subject matter or even the patent claim itself goes against the morals of society.

These two lines of argument suggest that the opposition rejects a simplistic worldview that cannot go beyond the material aspect of living beings. This reductionist model suggests that by understanding the parts—right down to the atoms and molecules—it is possible to understand the whole world. Likewise, by studying genes we can understand life. For the opponents of gene technology, animals, plants, and even microorganisms are not simply products of matter but have an essence that goes beyond their genes and cells. Life is a quality that is not definable either by scientific principles or by a court of law. A new combination of genes resulting in a new form of life is not just a composition of *matter*, as patent law says, nor is it the *result* of that form.

This battle over the patenting of living organisms and processes is symbolic of a larger conflict between two opposing sets of values or worldviews. If claims to patent living things are upheld, it is a triumph of science, that is, of the mechanistic, materialistic conception of life. It is vindication of the view that humans can understand nature and use it to improve the human condition, according to the charter and function of science as an institution. That is why utility is the most important criterion in patent claims, as discussed in chapter 3.

If claims to patent living things are rejected, it is a blow to science. Society is rejecting the scientific view as too shallow. It is saying that living beings cannot be treated like clockwork to be taken apart on a whim. Life has a soul, which lies outside the realm of science. These are the stakes in the battle.

It should be clear by now that the social acceptance of gene technology goes beyond the mere acceptance or rejection of different applications and the weighing of inherent risks and benefits. Indeed it represents fundamental changes for society. Technology theorists agree and also agree that technology imposes a filter on our perception. Whether this filter has a positive or negative effect on society depends on one's perspective. On this point, there are three schools of thought: technological humanism, technological nihilism, and technological realism (Kroker, 1984).

Technological humanists (for example, Marshall McLuhan) propose that, in balance, the effects of technology are positive. Technology allows human beings to extend our natural abilities and consequently our personal freedom. Technological humanists see gene technology as a tool that improves our ability to meet our health, agricultural, and environmental needs.

In contrast to this optimistic view are technological nihilists, such as George Grant, who argue that technology is a trap because we become dependent on it. When that happens, we lose a part of our free will and our soul (that is, our humanity). Technological nihilists fear that gene technology is a Faustian bargain, that is, in making material gains in the short run, we lose our soul in the long run. Indeed, technological nihilists fear that we may have already sacrificed the essence of our humanity to technology in such matters as human reproduction.

Finally technological realists, such as Harold Innis, take a pragmatic approach to technology. The question is not whether technology is good or bad; it is, above all, about power. A new technology alters established power structures and the control of resources and triggers economic, political, social, psychological, and legislative changes. Technological realists argue that the debate on gene technology should focus less on whether an application like preimplantation diagnosis is good or bad and more on how it affects the distribution of power and resources in society.

The first two of these positions take a more philosophical view, whereas the third takes a pragmatic approach. Despite their differences, all three perspectives offer an important lesson. The power of a new technology lies not in the technology itself but in how it transforms society.

This transformation is what people have to understand about new technologies. How does gene technology change our perception of the living world? How will it affect the distribution of existing or new resources? As noted earlier, fundamental changes have already taken place: seeing living organisms as genetic resources, industrializing nations moving to protect their genetic resources, and conflicting worldviews in the legal battles over the patenting of gene technology innovations.

GENES: CHEMICALS OR LIFE?

Advances in genetic science have increased human knowledge about the processes of life. At one point, it was possible to think that genes would solve to the mystery of life. With each new discovery in genetic science, however, the realization has dawned—first among scientists and increasingly among lay people—that genes are not the substance of life.

Although we certainly know more about *how* living organisms function, at the same time we have lost the comfort of being able to think that DNA holds the secret of life. Genetic science offers *some* answers: Life is made of matter. Living things are made of cells. The biological functions of living things depend, to some extent, on the information coded in nucleic acids. The paradox is that life is all of these things and none of them. For all we know about genes as the chemical essential to cellular life on Earth, we are no closer than previous generations to understanding what life is and why it exists. Like Adam and Eve and like people of Prometheus' time, we cannot return the knowledge we have gained. With knowledge comes responsibility. Once Adam and Eve gained the knowledge of good and evil, they had to leave the comfort and security of Eden and make hard moral choices for themselves. Once human beings had fire, they had to decide how to use that fire, wisely for warmth and security, carelessly for destruction.

These myths hold a lesson for people in high-technological society. We have to pay a price for genetic knowledge. The price has two aspects. First, we have to recognize and accept the limits of scientific knowledge and technological ability—not just regarding genes and life but also technological risks, social control, the use of the planet's resources, and the distribution of society's resources. Second, we must be willing to accept the responsibility attached to the technology—for its use and for the consequences.

Like Adam and Eve, we must leave the Eden of previous paradigms and struggle with the challenges of the new paradigm. However desirable it may seem, it is not an option to go back to an age where gene technology does not exist. The only real option today is how to use that technology. In every decision, there is the cost of opportunities lost; for every path taken, a countless number of other paths were ignored.

Nor do we have the option of choosing only the benefits of the technology without accepting the costs. That choice does not exist. As one technology theorist notes: "It is inevitable that every culture must negotiate with technology, whether it does so intelligently or not" (Postman, 1993). In this negotiation process, society tries to maximize the benefits while minimizing the costs. The difficulty is that with an emerging technology, both the long-term benefits and the long-term costs remain largely *unknown*: this is why the word *potential* often appears in discussions surrounding gene technology.

In the face of the unknown, experience with other technologies will affect the choices that people take. That experience will probably not, however, provide an accurate model for decision making. A new paradigm means that there are no previous models to follow. Nonetheless, human experience may provide some insight into the mistakes of the past and perhaps into ways of not repeating them.

In the face of the unknown, the best choice may be one that reflects the values and interests of society as a whole. Of course, that is not easy: the values and interests of different segments of society will inevitably conflict. Slinging around slogans, making overblown promises, and predicting doomsday will hinder rather than help society to take decisions. What is needed are mechanisms that will allow conflicting concerns to be represented. All segments of society should have a voice in a process that will affect their lives.

Western society today has started this process, through public debates, discussions, and even confrontations. It is equally important for society as a *whole* to establish its priorities because choices taken today will affect not only different segments but also future generations. Once decisions have been taken, they cannot be undone. That is why the participation of a wide cross-section of society will be critical in the decision-making process called social acceptance.

Perhaps the greatest contribution of the gene technology paradigm to postindustrial society, so far, is that it has prompted a debate of fundamental issues. First, this debate has led people to question the values of the institutions of society. For example, regarding plants and animals as genetic resources has forced us to think about the inequitable distribution of resources between industrialized and industrializing nations. Second, the debate has forced us to reflect on how we think about and use the world's resources. The case of xenotransplantation discussed earlier provides a good example.

Finally, the debate has focused attention on the dialectic between animistic and mechanistic views of matter. To some degree, this ancient philosophical debate between worldviews has been recast in terms of genes. DNA is the chemical substance, with a tangible structure, found in all living matter on Earth. Without it, life on Earth would not exist, certainly not as we know it. But it is doubtful whether DNA can be called the substance of life, which is itself intangible. An organism is greater than the sum of all its genes because a gene, though essential for life, is itself not alive. A gene cannot ensure its own existence. The power of the gene has captured the imagination of scientists and ethicists alike. Genes have been the subjects of academic symposiums and scientific conferences; reports in the print and broadcast media; novels, plays, and movies; public lectures; and parliamentary assemblies. Such wide interest shows that the gulf between philosophy and science—or between life and matter, society and technology—may not be as deep as Western society since Descartes has assumed.

KEY POINTS

- Some of the fears and concerns associated with specific applications of gene technology can be linked to specific historic threats to human survival, for example, disease, famine, human conflict. Despite technical advances, certain basic human needs have to be met.

- Because gene technology is based on biology, the science of life, it raises questions about the living world and life itself, challenging traditional assumptions about the essential difference between life and matter.

- The emergence of gene technology has shifted attention from whole organisms to genes. Genetic resources are considered part of a nation's natural resources and an industrial commodity.

- A paradigm shift involves not only a change in technology but also a shift in values. This shift is why much of the conflict over gene technology is taking place on ethical grounds. Whatever form it takes, societal control is a set of rules and conventions that is founded on the values and principles of a society.

- Gene technology, being based on the science of life, raises the age-old question, What is life? This is a question that has preoccupied human societies since ancient times. The Chinese, Greeks, Romans, and Jews started with a distinction between life and matter.

- In the West, the two concepts of life and matter drifted further apart until Descartes, in the seventeenth century, declared that everything in this world is lifeless matter except for the human mind, the seat of the human soul. This is a materialistic view. Descartes claimed the world of matter for science.

- Descartes—like his contemporaries Bacon, Galileo, and Newton—thought that the universe, even living organisms, functioned according to fixed mathematical principles and mechanical forces. This is a *mechanistic* conception of life.

- This materialistic and mechanistic outlook was the foundation of science as it gained economic and social importance in the eighteenth and nineteenth centuries. Science eventually replaced religion and, to a certain extent, the state as a source of authority. As a social institution, science has a system of values, follows a set of norms, and favors a particular view of the world, reducing it to tangible, objective, and quantifiable phenomena.

- Part of the resistance to gene technology stems from a rejection of the values of science. Critics see it as an attempt to define life in a materialistic and mechanical fashion.

- The conflicts over gene technology are, in part, conflicts of values. Supporters of gene technology argue that a better understanding of genes will benefit humankind. Critics reject the idea that genetic knowledge will improve human life because the lives of organisms—whether bacterium, human, or whale—are not determined solely by genes.

- New technologies trigger change, forcing a public debate about fundamental values that helps set priorities on society's needs and resources that will affect choices in the future.

- The power of any technology lies in the way it transforms society and filters human perception.

- Genetic knowledge forces society to recognize the limits of science and technology and it requires society to accept responsibility for its use and for the consequences.

- Because society's acceptance of a new technology requires choices that will affect all segments of society and future generations, the participation of a wide cross-section of society is critical.

- The greatest contribution of the gene technology paradigm to society is that it has prompted a debate on fundamental issues, forcing people to question the values of their society and reflect on how they use the world's resources.

- DNA is essential to cellular life on Earth, yet it is neither alive nor life itself. This paradoxical link between life and matter has raised again the age-old question that philosophy, religion, and science have all tried to answer: What is life?

REFERENCES

Abbott, A. 1996. Complexity Limits the Power of Prediction. *Nature* 379: 390.

Allan, J. S. 1996. Xenotransplantation at a Crossroads: Prevention Versus Progress. *Nature Medicine* 2 (1): 18-21.

Bahnsen, U. 1996. Lizenz zum Töten. *Facts*, 6 June, p. 97.

Baumann, N. 1996. Panic over Falling Sperm Counts May Be Premature. *New Scientist*, 11 May, p. 10.

Begley, S. 1996. Holes in Those Genes. *Newsweek*, 15 January, p. 41.

Berg, P., and M. F. Singer. 1996. Genetic Testing and Insurance. *Nature* 380: 385–386.

Bondolfi, A., ed. 1994. *Mensch und Tier: ethische Dimensionen ihres Verhältnisses*. Freiburg, Switzerland: Universitätsverlag Freiburg Schweiz.

Caldicott, H. 1992. *If You Love This Planet: A Plan to Heal the Earth*. New York: W. W. Norton and Co.

Caplan, A. L. 1991. Handle with Care: Race, Class and Genetics. In *Justice and the Human Genome Project*, edited by T. F. Murphy and M. A. Lappé. Berkeley: University of California Press.

Dickson, D. 1996. Whose Genes Are They Anyway? *Nature* 381: 11–14.

Ernst and Young. 1996. *European Biotech 96: Volatility and Value* (industry annual report). London: Ernst and Young International.

Feder, T. 1995. Germany to Launch New Gene Programme. . . . *Nature* 375: 175.

Fischer, M. 1993. Das Vampir-Projekt. *Die Woche Zeitung*, 2 Decmber.

Gorman, C. 1996. Are Animal Organs Safe for People. *Time*, 15 January, p. 40–41.

Hobbelink, H. 1991. *Biotechnology and the Future of World Agriculture— The Fourth Resource*. London: Zed Books Ltd.

Homewood, B. 1996. "Piracy" Law Leaves Brazil Open to Exploitation. *New Scientist*, 1 June, p. 7.

Hudson, K. L., K. H. Bothenberg, L. B. Andrews, M. J. E. Kahn, and F. S. Collins. 1995. Genetic Discrimination and Health Insurance: An Urgent Need for Reform. *Science* 270: 391–393.

Jayaraman, K. S. 1996. Indian Researchers Press for Stricter Rules to Regulate "Gene Hunting." *Nature* 379: 381–382.

Jayaraman, K. S., and C. Macilwain. 1996. Scientists Challenged over "Unauthorized" Export of Data. *Nature* 379: 381.

Kevles, D. J. 1994. Eugenics and the Human Genome Project: Is the Past Prologue? In *Justice and the Human Genome Project,* edited by T. F. Murphy and M. A. Lappé, pp. 14–29. Berkeley: University of California Press.

———. 1985. *In the Name of Eugenics: Genetics and the Uses of Human Heredity*. Berkeley: University of California Press.

Kroker, A. 1984. *Technology and the Canadian Mind*. Montreal: New World Perspectives.

Laing, P. 1996. *Sandoz: The Unrecognised Potential of Xenotransplantation*. London: Salomon Brothers.

Lehrman, S. 1996. Anthropologist Cleared in Patent Dispute. *Nature* 380: 374.

Lovelock, J. 1991. Mother Earth: Myth or Science? In *From Gaia to Selfish Genes: Selected Writings in the Life Sciences,* edited by C. Barlow, pp. 3–24. Cambridge, Mass.: MIT Press.

Margulis, L., and D. Sagan. 1995. *What Is Life?* London: Weidenfeld and Nicolson Ltd.

Masood, E., S. Lehrman, Q. Shiermeier, D. Butler, and R. Nathan. 1996. Gene Tests: Who Benefits from Risk? *Nature* 379: 389–392.

Mikkelsen, T. R., B. Andersen, and R. B. Jørgensen. 1996. The Risk of Crop Transgene Spread. *Nature* 380: 31.

Nelkin, D., and L. Tancredi. 1989. *Dangerous Diagnostics—The Social Power of Biological Information*. New York: Basic Books.

Organization for Economic Cooperation and Development. 1995. *The Global Human Genome Programme*. Paris: Organization for Economic Cooperation and Development.

Ott, L. 1960. *Fundamentals of Catholic Dogma*. Translated by Patrick Lynch. 4th ed. Rockford, Ill.: Tan Books and Publishers.

Paul, D. B., and H. G. Spencer. 1995. The Hidden Science of Genetics. *Nature* 374: 302–304.

Pokorski, R. J. 1996. Genetic Information and Life Insurance. *Nature* 376: 13–14.

———. 1994. Use of Genetic Information by Private Insurers. In *Justice and the Human Genome Project,* edited by T. F. Murphy and M. A. Lappé, pp. 91-109. Berkeley: University of California Press.

Postman, N. 1993. *Technopoly: The Surrender of Culture to Technology*. New York: Vintage Books.

Radkau, J. 1995. Learning from Chernobyl for the Fight Against Genetics? Stages and Stimuli of German Protest Movements—a Comparative Synopsis. In *Resistance to New Technology: Nuclear Power, Information Technology, and Biotechnology*, edited by M. Bauer, pp. 335–355. Cambridge: Cambridge University Press.

Sangalli, A. 1996. They Burn Heretics, Don't They? *New Scientist*, 6 April, p. 47.

Schriefers, H. 1982. *Was ist Leben?* Stuttgart: F. K. Schattauer Verlag.

Sentker, A. 1996. Die neue Mär vom Superunkraut. *Die Zeit*, 22 March, p. 38.

Singer, P. 1993. *Practical Ethics*. 2d ed. Cambridge: Cambridge University Press.

Sklair, L. 1973. *Organized Knowledge*. London: Hart-Davis, MacGibbon Ltd.

Smith, A. 1996. *Software for the Self: Technology and Culture*. London: Faber and Faber Ltd.

Soldati, V. 1996. Das Schwein—ein besonderes Haustier. In *Herz vom Schwein?* by Basler Appell gegen Gentechnologie, pp. 2–11. Basle: Basler Appell gegen Gentechnologie.

Toufexis, A., J. Mattos, and E. Silver. 1996. What Makes Them Do It. *Time*, 15 January, p. 42.

Vines, G. 1995. Every Child a Perfect Child? *New Scientist*, 28 October, pp. 14–15.

von Wartburg, W. P. 1983. *Gleichheit und Gerechtigkeit im Gesundheitswesen*. Basel: Helbling und Lichtenbahn.

Walgate, R. 1990. *Miracle or Menace? Biotechnology and the Third World*. Budapest: Panos Institute.

Watson, J. D. 1990. The Human Genome Project: Past, Present, and Future. *Science* 248: 44–49.

World Health Organization. 1996. *The World Health Report 1996: Fighting disease, fostering development (Report of the Director-General)*. Geneva: World Health Organization.

Zanoni, R., U. Breitenmoser, and E. Peterhans. 1996. Mit Gentechnologie gegen die Tollwut. *Neue Zürcher Zeitung*, 16 April.

5 TECHNOLOGY IN THE CONTEXT OF SOCIETY

The arrival of a new technology, as noted in chapter 1, marks the beginning of a process of change and adaptation for individuals and society. People cannot be separated from technology. After all, they create it, and it affects their lives. How society confronts a new technology must be seen in the context of its experience with previous technologies. This chapter first explores the role of technology as a driving force of change in modern, high-technological (postindustrial) society. It then looks at the influence of several key technologies on that society. Finally it analyzes the issues surrounding gene technology in the context of a growing malaise with technology itself and in the even broader context of society's on-going search for direction. Such an exercise may shed new light on the public debate over gene technology and offer some ideas about directions society might take.

TECHNOLOGY AS THE DRIVING FORCE OF CHANGE IN POSTINDUSTRIAL SOCIETY

Throughout history, technology has provided society with many useful tools and added significantly to human knowledge. At the end of the twentieth century, more sophisticated, or high, technology has become a dominant presence in so-called postindustrial society. Most people are surrounded by its products: television, cars, computers, telephones, and microwave ovens are among the most visible and common. Through these and other products, many people enjoy a higher standard of living than was possible in past centuries or even decades.

These benefits derive from the essence of technology, which is speed: the reduction of time, distance, and effort.

Technology shrinks time. Replacing telegraphs and telexes, the fax machine has speeded up communication despite great geographical distances. Advances and innovations in information technology have increased this speed even more dramatically. It now takes a couple of seconds for a message on electronic mail (E-mail) to travel from one continent to another. Using conventional postal service, the same message would need a few days at the very least.

Technology shrinks distance. Satellite television has enabled people to follow "news as it happens" halfway around the world—whether it is the wedding of the Prince of Wales or war in the Persian Gulf. At the individual level, jet airplanes, high-speed trains, and transcontinental highways offer more personal mobility than ever before. At the beginning of the twentieth century, going from one continent to another was a matter of long-term planning, and the journey often lasted several weeks or even months. At the end of the century, the same distance is often easily crossed in a matter of hours.

Technology shrinks effort. Much of technology has been aimed at reducing the human effort required to complete a task. There is perhaps no more dramatic example than the mechanization of the farm. Up to the early part of the twentieth century, the harvest required the effort of entire families and even communities—from the oldest to the youngest. (One legacy of this practice in many countries of Europe and North America is ending school holidays in autumn, when farm children used to have to help with the harvest.) Today, the same amount of land can be harvested by a handful of individuals on tractors and harvesters.

EFFECTS OF TECHNOLOGY ON INDIVIDUALS AND SOCIETY

Nevertheless, it would be limited to view technology only in terms of its resulting processes or products and the higher standard of living they offer. One of its major achievements is an increase in average life expectancy as a result of better medical knowledge of the cause and prevention of diseases, mass availability of medication through improved chemical synthesis, and improvements in water supply and waste treatment.

Technology has not simply raised the minimum standards of health. It also offers better hygiene and greater convenience. For example, refrigeration not only allows food to keep cool and stay fresh longer, but it also slows down microbial growth, reducing the dangers and costs of spoilage—thus safeguarding health, offering convenience, and cutting costs for both producers and consumers. Refrigeration, pasteurization, vacuum packing, and other modern food-processing techniques have been key in the exporting of exotic or delicate food items. In the past, items such as fresh seafood or tropical fruit were not available to or affordable for the average household. Refrigeration and fast modes of transportation have made such items more accessible and often available all year round.

Perhaps more than anything else, technology offers the individual the power of choice. In reducing time, distance, and effort, technology has given people the opportunity to pursue needs and wants beyond the basic necessities of food, clothing, and shelter. The automobile not only provides transportation between home and work but also allows the individual to take a job outside the immediate geographical area. The telephone not only allows communication between vast distances but also offers relief from isolation for people such as the sick, the elderly, or those living in remote areas.

Malaise and Disillusionment
At the same time that technology has provided individuals with both material goods and intangible benefits, it has caused a social malaise or at least ambivalence about it. It is not obvious whether this malaise, disillusionment, or frustration is widespread or is felt only by a minority. It is probably fair to say that it has grown increasingly important as a theme of private conversations and public discussions, books, and media reports since the 1960s and especially since the 1980s.

Some people think that technology is not only a help but also an intrusion. For example, the telephone provides a useful link to the outside world, but it has also become a disruptive nuisance: a cellular phone rings in the middle of a movie in a cinema or in the middle of dinner in a restaurant. Another example is E-mail, which allows people to communicate quickly and simply but also makes possible bombardment by messages that are of little relevance to the majority of recipients.

In addition, people have the increasing impression that technology is not only a tool but also a crutch. This sense of technological dependency comes to the fore when failures in technology result in paralysis of the entire social system or significant parts of it. Jet airplanes allow business people from Frankfurt to sign deals in Melbourne, but an overload of air traffic at one international airport sends ripples to other airports around the world. A power failure in New York, Berlin, or Tokyo can bring the entire city to a standstill.

A further source of malaise and frustration with technology is information overload. People feel helpless and angry because they cannot deal with the large amounts of information they receive and the speed with which they receive it. In the past, a search for information might require journeys to libraries or lengthy correspondence by letter. News took days, weeks, or even months to travel across a continent or sea. Today, computers process and transmit vast amounts of data with great rapidity. News is sent halfway around the globe in seconds. E-mail sends messages quickly. But human beings still have their limits. A person can handle only so much information and needs time to react to it. Political leaders, business people, news reporters, and ordinary people often find they do not know where to begin sorting out relevant data or do not have the data they need to make an informed response. They then rely on an "expert" to provide the interpretation. By the time they reach a decision, new developments require attention.

Yet another contributing factor to people's disillusionment with technology is the widening gap between the haves and the have-nots. Although technology itself is not necessarily the cause of this gap, it seems to widen it. At the very least, the speed and concentration of technological developments highlight the difference. This gap exists not only between the rich countries of the mainly industrialized North and the poorer countries of the mostly industrializing South. There is also a growing gulf within modern technological society between those who have the wealth and access to technology and those who do not. Nothing dramatizes this gulf more than the situation in U.S. schools where some have ready access to the latest equipment, while others struggle with outdated tools and machines. The speed of technological development further aggravates this imbalance as each innovation pushes existing technologies further toward obsolescence.

Speed, Scale, and Complexity

Society's sense of helplessness and frustration in the face of modern technology derives from technology's three characteristics: high speed, large scale, and great complexity. Before analyzing these characteristics, it may be useful to consider some of the most influential technological changes that have taken place in the twenty-four years between the birth of gene technology in the 1970s and its emergence as a social issue. They include the maturation of jet travel, advances in space technology (resulting in "routine" space flights and satellite communication links), the use of silicon chips in microelectronics technology, the integration of information technology, and the introduction of fiber optics in communication technology. Of these developments, one of the most powerful is perhaps microelectronics, which makes possible microwave ovens, microcomputers (desktops and later laptops), and cellular telephones (replacing or, in some cases, displacing the pager).

Other developments include vacuum packing and refrigeration, which have transformed the market for fruits and vegetables and encouraged the growth of supermarkets; photocopiers and fax machines, which with desktop computers have transformed the office; videos and video recorders, which have changed the cinema industry; and the transition from records and tapes to compact discs (CDs), which has changed the music industry.

Three examples highlight the rapid pace of technological evolution in the last twenty-odd years. First, in the 1970s, commercial satellite transmissions were still novelties. By the mid-1990s, space technology had evolved to such a point that limits had to be set on the number of satellites orbiting the planet because of their sheer clutter. Second, in the early 1980s, computers were still beyond the reach of the average person; by the early 1990s, they were installed in many households; and by the mid-1990s, words such as *cyberspace* and *information highway* had become part of popular vocabulary. Third, desktop publishing (DTP), still a new concept in the 1980s, by the early 1990s, had become a common feature of small communications firms and communications departments in larger companies. By the mid-1990s, it looked as if DTP was gradually being replaced by the technology behind multimedia, CD-ROMs, or even more recent developments.

Along with the speed of technological development is a dramatic increase in the scale of technology. The term *technology* conjures up images of something big. Although the physical size of many products has actually shrunk (for example, the evolution from giant mainframe computers to the portable laptop), the scale of technology is ever growing in the sense that it takes increasingly more technology to support new technology. Aviation provides a clear example. The modern jet airplane depends less on the pilot for staying airborne than on state-of-the-art instruments: radar monitors, microprocessors in the engines, automatic sensory controls, flight-to-ground communication equipment, and computerized flight programs. The flight crew's main contribution lies in technical expertise, especially in monitoring the proper functioning of the instruments. In other words, aviation technology depends on computer, satellite, and communication technologies.

As the scale of technology is constantly growing, so is its complexity. The newer technologies depend on groups of experts with different specialized knowledge and skills. Although there may be some cooperation among them, more often they all work in their own compartmentalized little worlds and have limited understanding of other areas of specialization. For example, the genome researcher is likely to be helpless if the computer or electron microscope malfunctions. This phenomenon of compartmentalization is not specific to any particular field but to recent technology in general. In a way, a new technology in the 1990s no longer deals with one particular field or several related fields of applied science but with a complicated web of many different areas of knowledge and skills.

These three aspects of recent technologies—speed, scale, and complexity—contribute to society's perception that technology is massive and unmanageable. Indeed, many individuals probably do not understand the technologies they use on a day-to-day basis. Even those who frequently use or benefit directly from specific technologies have at best a minimal grasp of what is involved. Most passengers in an airplane probably know little about the science of flight or aviation technology. Most drivers behind the steering wheel of a car know as little about mechanical engineering and petro-chemical compounds as about quantum physics. The last thing on people's minds when they start their cars, open the refrigerator, or turn on the tele-vision is the technology behind these products. It is a paradox of modern technology that most of the people who benefit from it still consider it remote, unfamiliar, and somewhat frightening because they associate it with experts, specialized knowledge, and complex processes that seem to have little to do with their daily existence.

The Assumption That Change Means Progress

As has been stated, much of the change in postindustrial society is *techno-logically driven*. This expression has two levels of meaning. On the surface, it simply means that technology causes change. On a deeper level, it means that change is almost invariably synonymous with progress, which is gen-erally understood as *technological* progress. For example, one of the dis-tinctions between *developed* nations and *developing* ones is the level of industrialization or technological development. Despite rich cultural tradi-tions or a complex system of values, a nation is not considered "developed" if it does not have a strong technological infrastructure.

Because it is assumed that technological change always leads to some-thing better, technology is often described by such words as *progress*, *advancement*, *development*, and *improvement*. Those words apply not only to technological areas but also to social conditions. It is assumed that tech-nological progress will make everything else in society better, too. "Progress means that scientific and technological achievements trigger welfare, free-dom and happiness" (Touraine, 1995, p. 45). This belief can be traced back to Descartes and philosophers of the Enlightenment, who argue that reason can be used to advance all areas of life, thus initiating the domination of sci-ence in Western thought and culture.

Today, a society is often measured in terms of science and technology. A "good" hospital has the latest in medical equipment. A "top" school or uni-versity has the newest computers and laboratory equipment. A "developed" country has a solid technological infrastructure and industrialized economy. (For example, South Africa under apartheid was considered one of the most modern, highly developed countries among all African states.) Admittedly, other factors play a role in determining the quality of an institution, service, or country. For instance, the reputation of a good university is also based on the quality of teaching, the level of academic research by professors, and the success of its students in later life. The point is that the technological aspect may outweigh other considerations. At the same time, the displace-ment of other values in favor of scientific and technological progress has led to a reexamination of the values and assumptions of modern technological society. Technologically driven changes are reconsidered from the aspect of their effect on the environment and society.

To say that changes in society are technologically driven does not simply mean that they are the result of technology. It also implies that human beings are not the only drivers of change. Technological progress seems to have its own momentum. Development in one field spawns innovations not only in the same area but also in nonrelated areas, such as developments in micro-electronics that increased the capacity of products in information and communication technologies. In turn, the improvements in these technologies allowed rapid advances to be made in genetic research. The inventors of the silicon chip or the microprocessor were not likely to have foreseen the role of their invention in the location of, for example, the gene responsible for Huntington's disease.

As noted earlier, as one technological innovation leads to others, it becomes increasingly difficult for people to keep informed of all aspects of technological progress, let alone manage technological change. The pace and range of such change have literally outstripped the capability of individuals and organizations to respond. Already in the mid-1960s, one technology analyst, Marshall McLuhan, predicted the long-term effects and broader social impact of technological change. Referring to the effects of faster communication technology, he wrote as follows:

> All means of interchange and of human interassociation tend to improve by acceleration. Speed, in turn, accentuates problems of form and structure. The older arrangements had not been made with a view to such speeds, and people begin to sense a draining-away of life values as they try to make the old forms adjust to the new and speedier movements. (McLuhan, 1964, p. 95)

The legislative chaos left in the wake of the explosion in communication and information technologies offers an excellent example of how technology is stretching the capability of individuals and organizations to cope with change and how institutions are trying to make old arrangements adjust to new technologies. In most countries, copyright law is the product of a print society, when the retrievable record of ideas, thoughts, and creative genius was in print format (here, broadly defined to include both text and images). In the early 1990s, the challenge was to include multimedia works and works on CD-ROMs under existing copyright legislation. Because these media include sound and motion (each of which can be copyrighted separately), this effort raised particular difficulty in defining authorship and assigning copyright. It is not easy to determine who should get the royalty for a sequence from a film showing particular dance steps: the film director, the writer of the screenplay, the choreographer of the dance steps, the composer of the dance music, or any combination of these people. Before that legislative issue was resolved, the mid-1990s saw legislatures and courts being asked to apply some control to the unauthorized dissemination of copyrighted works on the Internet, a service that is unregulated and virtually impossible to patrol.

Focuses of Malaise and Frustration

Much of the malaise, frustration, and anger evoked by modern technology is directed at the very institutions that promised a better life through reason, science, and technology: business and industry, academia, and government. Business and industry, in particular, become the target of resentment because they are seen as the main beneficiaries of technology. The computer and information-network industry depends mainly on computer science and electroengineering. The aviation industry is based primarily on aeronautics, mechanical engineering, and electroengineering. The pharmaceutical and chemical industries have long made use of organic chemistry, biochemistry, and biotechnology. The gene technology industry is founded on genetics, biochemistry, cellular biology, and molecular biology.

Universities are under attack because science, owing to its contributions to industrial development, seems to have gained importance over other areas of learning. It should not be forgotten that science was originally one branch of knowledge among others of equal importance. Before the Enlightenment, respected men of learning such as Galileo, Leonardo da Vinci, and François Rabelais —all examples of the many-sided Renaissance man— were as much artists, writers, statesmen, or philosophers as they were doctors, scientists, astronomers, or students of nature. Science as the basis for economic prosperity and industrial development is a later concept. Nowhere is the rise and dominance of science more clearly marked than in the history of the university. Universities were created in the Middle Ages in Europe as places where scholars in several areas of higher learning came together to teach. Although many students attended university to train for a particular profession such as theology or medicine, some studied in several disciplines or at several universities to acquire a well-rounded education. Later, *gymnasia* in Europe and colleges in the United States sought to provide students with a broad general understanding of the world, whether or not they went on to university for professional training.

Today many colleges and universities seem to serve less as independent centers of knowledge than as producers of human resources for business, industry, and government. In North America, campus recruitment is a popular method for soliciting new employees. At the end of the academic year, representatives from corporations or government departments advertise positions that are open and conduct interviews on campus with graduating students who apply. In Japan, entry in one of the prestigious universities is almost a guarantee of a job in public administration or in management in the corporate world. *Les grandes écoles* in France serve a similar purpose. To a lesser or greater degree (depending on the institution), the modern student is still encouraged to acquire a broad education; but in the end, all students are required to specialize in one or perhaps two disciplines (a *major* at English-speaking colleges or a *Schwerpunkt* at German-speaking universities). Industrialization, which increased the division of labor and the specialization of knowledge, has meant the death of the ideal of the well-rounded individual, the Renaissance man.

Along with the trend toward specialized areas of studies, universities (especially in North America) have placed growing emphasis on the natural sciences and the applied sciences to the detriment of the liberal arts and social sciences. This trend may result in part from the increasing demand for scientific professionals in a technology-driven society. Another reason may be that with cutbacks in government funding, universities in North America are turning more and more to private and corporate sources. This need has led to the rise of various forms of partnerships between universities and industry on scientific research projects. It is no longer unusual for companies to fund specific projects of basic research in selected scientific disciplines. The motives are mixed. Sometimes this funding comes as part of corporate sponsorship. Other times, it is strictly part of a business agreement: the company funds a certain project in exchange for at least the right to first refusal, if not also the right to develop or commercialize the outcome.

Another noteworthy trend at universities, especially in North America, is the rise of the professor-consultant. More and more, professors in business management and the applied sciences act as consultants or expert advisers to companies on various problems.

Individually, these trends in universities may appear interesting but not significant in the context of the current discussion. Together, however, they point to close and often formal links between the academic and corporate worlds, links that, according to critics, undermine the role of universities as independent centers of knowledge. These trends also suggest that business and industry are the key beneficiaries of science and the main driving forces behind technology. Indeed business and industry have been the chief advocates of technology. In the late twentieth century, corporations have used advertising campaigns and lobbying efforts to ensure that the sciences form an important part of the core educational curriculum and that technology remains a high priority in public policy. In addition, business, industry, and government have all been actively promoting the sciences in schools and universities, arguing that technology is a necessary element for social and economic well-being.

By placing too much emphasis on the economic argument, corporations (and, to a lesser degree, government) risk giving the impression that economics is all that matters. Business and industry are already seen as one of the driving forces behind technology. They would arouse even more animosity if they were also perceived as saying that it is up to people to adapt to technological progress rather than adapting technology to human progress.

Corporate Social Responsibility

The concept of corporate social responsibility is a recent development in the history of industrialization. It holds that all organizations have a responsibility to society for their decisions and actions and can be held accountable for them. That is, organizations have a responsibility to meet the needs and interests of society. The concept was born of the consumer movement, which started in the United States in the mid-1930s. Independent organizations tested different products and advised consumers on a wide range of concerns, including product safety and performance. The movement took on new meaning and a new form in the 1970s when the consumer activist Ralph Nader successfully raised public (and government) awareness of serious safety problems with a line of cars produced by General Motors. GM eventually acknowledged the problem and withdrew the model. When companies realized that activists such as Nader could rally the public and government to action, they took seriously the concept of social responsibility. They acknowledged the need to "manage with an eye on the effects of their decision on society as well as on the organisation" (Grunig, 1992, p. 240).

Sometimes, though, it appears that human considerations still fall by the wayside. Social issues—such as justice, equity, rights of the individual, rights of society, values, and ethics—are often seen as separate from technological issues. An example in this book is the fact that the patent office has technical expertise but no ethical competence over the acceptability of a technology or its results (see "Rational Arguments for Gene Technology Patents," chapter 3). The situation is not the fault of any particular organization. Rather it stems from a reductionist point of view that is prevalent in technologically driven society and that leans towards specialized knowledge rather than overall competence. The result is that humans seem to have to keep pace with technological change rather than technology meeting human needs.

It is sometimes tempting for critics to point the finger of blame for this situation at big institutions. In the past, the place of nonscientific and nonbusiness issues has been low on the agenda of R&D policies, especially in the private sector. Frequently, industry and government hesitated too long in responding to the ethical and social implications of many technologies. This slow reaction fueled negative public sentiments toward technological change. Those segments of society who felt that their interests were not being met become suspicious that technology mainly serves corporate interests rather than the public good. Suspicion was especially strong among those groups that traditionally have been marginalized—women, cultural minorities, the physically disabled, and the peoples of industrializing countries. When the objectives of big institutions collided with the tide of public opinion, the result was an open confrontation, which often brought to light other problems and issues.

Examples of Conflict Between Institutions and Public Opinion

The mid-1990s provided a number of examples of such collisions between institutional agenda and public opinion. These conflicts involved not only different types of institutions but also different technologies. The first example concerned the confrontation between Royal Dutch/Shell and Greenpeace over the disposal of the Brent Spar (a decommissioned offshore oil-storage platform). Although it was essentially an environmental issue (using the sea for industrial waste disposal), an important aspect was the lack of credibility—of industry in general and of a multinational corporation in particular. (Ironically, Greenpeace was later to issue an apology to Shell for publishing inaccurate information about the platform and for exaggerating the negative impact of sinking it.) The case also highlighted Shell's distance from its shareholders and its ignorance of the emotional strength of public sentiment, a strength that Greenpeace used to its advantage.

The second example concerned the French government's decision to proceed with nuclear testing underneath the Mururoa atoll in the South Pacific. The decision came in the face of objections from different national governments (especially those in the region), criticism from various international bodies, and protests by people around the world. The main issue was the long-term effects of nuclear radiation over the region. Other issues also emerged as the conflict escalated: the wealthy North imposing its will on the poorer South, the indifference of the French government toward the interests of nations in the South Pacific, and breaking the spirit (although not the letter) of an agreement among nuclear powers to stop testing by 1996.

The third example concerned an American company's patent of a pesticide derived from a medicinal tree native to India. W. R. Grace and Co. invented a process to extend the shelflife of an extract made from the seed of the neem tree. Although the patent did not affect Indian farmers or cover the traditional products of this plant, the company faced the outrage of Indian members of parliament and a court challenge from a coalition of opponents. The central issue was the equitable distribution of wealth created from the world's natural resources.

Another issue was the need for fair compensation. Many industrializing countries are rich in natural substances, which their farmers already use in traditional ways. But companies in many industrialized countries usually have developed the technology to refine or expand the use of these substances. Some say that these companies should be able to protect and enjoy the benefits of their investments. Others argue that farmers from industrializing countries are not fairly compensated for their contributions.

A third issue in this example was the need to manage the world's biodiversity, that is, to make use of natural and genetic resources in a sustainable way. Although genetic resources were at the center of this controversy, the conflict over the neem tree did not involve gene technology at all. The issue was the incapability of current international trade and legal instruments to deal comprehensively with the issues that new technologies have raised in the area of biological substances.

These three cases show that many people in modern technological society are tired of paternalistic attitudes, which often still pervade larger, long-established institutions. In the past, these institutions—both big companies and governments—seemed to suggest that they had a monopoly on understanding risks or that their answers were the best or indeed the only ones. To justify their decisions, they called on *their* team of experts, analysts, and engineers, who had all the hard scientific and technical data to support their argument. They seem to say "We know best . . . and we also have the experts to prove it!"

On average, people today are more educated, more critical, and less trusting than in the past. They have their own sources of information. They can propose equally viable solutions. And they want to have their say—in front of the media, in a court of law, or in the court of public opinion. This situation makes it increasingly difficult for institutions to ignore public views or tell just *their* side of the story. In the past, it was easier to withhold information that was not in an organization's financial or competitive interest. Today, the speed and scope of information technology is such that no organization can keep a secret for long. In addition, interest groups like Greenpeace want to tell their side of the story. So do the employee, the neighbor, the labor union, or the community whose interests are also at stake. Furthermore, the media act less and less as interested observers and more as public watchdogs. Rather than simply *reporting the facts*, they often raise questions of human interest and show the emotions of people.

From this discussion it is evident that there has been a change in society. In the past, authority and decision-making power were vested in institutions rather than individuals. Today, an educated, critical, and media-conscious public no longer passively accepts decisions from industry or government without public scrutiny. History has shown that industry can be wrong and governments make mistakes. Concerned citizens will mobilize their friends, their neighbors, and their community and even link with other unrelated groups to form a special-interest coalition. For example, Jeremy Rifkin, an antibiotechnology activist in the United States, successfully formed a coalition of different religious groups, including Christians, Jews, Muslims, and Hindus. The power and credibility of this coalition rested on one fact: if an issue could move such diverse (and often divisive) world beliefs to join forces, then it must be important. This coalition's views commanded public attention.

More than ever, concerned citizens' groups, special-interest coalitions, and entire communities are willing to take corporations or even governments to court to settle their differences. Even outside the courtroom, ordinary people realize that they can make their opinions heard. More consumers are linking their purchasing power to a company's environmental responsibility and, to a lesser extent, its social responsibility. The Brent

Spar controversy led to boycotts of Shell's products and services, resulting in a decrease of 20 percent in sales (Dickey, 1995). Consumers have also found that they can express their dissatisfaction with a foreign government's decisions and actions by boycotting products from—or tourism in—that country. For years, the nations of the Commonwealth not only imposed trade sanctions on apartheid South Africa but also led an international boycott against South African products, services, and other activities.

Seen in isolation, these public actions—protests, boycotts, confrontations, and legal proceedings—may seem sporadic and unrelated. Taken together, they seem to form an important trend. Many individuals are no longer content to let change be technologically driven or institutional interests override the interests of individuals and communities. Such people want a part in shaping change, even if it means challenging the very institutions that promise a better life through technology. This observation offers a partial explanation for the intensity of the public debate over gene technology.

RELEVANCE OF TECHNOLOGY TO SOCIAL PERCEPTIONS OF GENE TECHNOLOGY

This overview of technology as a driving force in modern society has touched on three critical points—speed, complexity, and conflicting values—that may provide some insight into industrialized society's response to technology in general and gene technology in particular.

The high speed of modern technological change is a challenge for many people trying keep up with developments and the way they affect their lives. Some people try to cope with speed and sensory overload by escaping it. They yearn for what seem like simpler times (that is, when there was less technology), go back to nature (for example, camping in the wilds), or call for a return to traditional values.

Part of the resistance to gene technology comes from this struggle to cope with a multitude of new, fast developments. Gene technology is speedy because of its ability to make genetic changes directly at the molecular level, bypassing the lengthy processes of traditional breeding. Some people are concerned that gene technology is developing too fast for individuals and society to cope. This concern has been expressed in many ways. They try to limit or prohibit the use of this technology through public protests, court action, or the proposal of restrictive legislation.

Gene technology, like other technologies, is enormously complex, requiring a huge technological infrastructure. It depends extensively on developments in information technology and microelectronics technology (for example, the refinement of the electron microscope through smaller, more powerful integrated circuits). Many of the discoveries and innovations in genome research programs rely on progress in robotics technology and information technology. The acceleration in gene sequencing and gene mapping depends on improvements in automation and robotics. In turn, the rapid analysis, processing, storage, and retrieval of so much information depend on major advances in information and data-processing systems. Much of the work in genetic research is the result of collaborative efforts of teams of researchers in different parts of a country or the world, requiring data bases and electronic links between individuals and institutions.

The established institutions of technological society—business, industry, government, and academia—have been key advocates and beneficiaries of technological change, but they have often been slow in responding to non-scientific and nonbusiness issues. In that respect, gene technology marks a radical departure from the route of past technologies because it has taken the initiative in drawing attention to ethical and social issues. Most programs in genome research set aside a portion of the budget for dealing with non-scientific issues (see "Eugenics," chapter 2).

More often, however, business, industry, and government have been quick to focus on the economic contributions of new technologies, which they promote as the main (if not the only) element of industrial competitiveness, economic prosperity, and even social progress. The United States, Japan, Switzerland, the EU, and a number of other countries have all argued that they need gene technology to be internationally competitive.

Their argument is not necessarily untrue, but it is an *old* argument, whose power to persuade has decreased with overuse. It is an argument that government and industry have put forward for almost every new technology: nuclear energy, superfast trains, supersonic aircraft, space flights, superconductors, and, most recently, gene technology. Such an argument ultimately ignores the facts that economic prosperity does not depend exclusively on any single technology, and social progress does not consist solely of prosperity but is also a matter of ethics and justice. When the broad needs of society and the narrower objectives of institutions come into conflict, the result is social distrust and suspicion leading to public resistance to the new technology. The resulting open confrontation brings to light other problems.

KEY TECHNOLOGIES OF THE TWENTIETH CENTURY

Just as it would be naive to separate people from technology, it would also be foolish to look at the public reaction to a new technology in isolation from other technologies past and present. If it is true that personal or collective experiences often provide a framework to guide us as in unfamiliar situations, as argued in chapter 1, then the technologies—familiar and new—that surround us today will shape our attitudes toward technology in general and toward emerging new technologies.

Modern, high tech society had its origins in the Industrial Revolution, which included the first large-scale production of energy—coal power, water power, and steam power—and the mass production and mass transportation that energy made possible. The resulting industrial society was characterized by intensive urbanization, increased specialization, and the channeling of natural, human, and financial resources toward mass production and mass consumption.

This section will take up the story about the end of the nineteenth century with an overview of selected technologies dating from that time that may provide a background for current attitudes toward newer technologies. The section will consider the public perception of the technology, the reputation of the industry behind it, the risks and benefits, and its impact on the public perception of recent technologies. The section also looks at technologies developed in the late twentieth century.

TELECOMMUNICATIONS

Telecommunications is the first and perhaps the most important technology in modern society. The invention of the telephone in the late nineteenth century marked the beginning of the information age. The telephone, telegraph, radio, television, answering machine, mobile pager, fax machine, and cellular telephone radically changed the way people conducted business, exchanged information, and lived. Telecommunications made possible the development of the information society, where the resources needed for the socioeconomic structure are no longer just land, labor, and capital but also information. Telecommunications remolded the very organization of communities.

Telecommunications technology is in high public regard. In the 1993 Eurobarometer study, about 83 percent of the people surveyed thought that telecommunications would "improve our way of life in the next 20 years" (Marlier, 1993). This was the highest level of optimism expressed toward seven key technologies. One possible reason is that the reputation of the industry is generally positive. Another possibility is that many of the larger companies in the telecommunications industry (especially those providing telephone, radio, and television services) are government owned and run in many countries. Thus, the telecommunications industry—like government bodies that provide hospital services or highways—is seen as the provider of a common good. In North America and slowly in Europe, deregulation and the end of monopolies have allowed the introduction of private providers, which may lead to a change in the public's favorable perception.

A more likely explanation for the public's high regard for telecommunications is that there are comparably few risks for the many benefits it offers. Not until the mid-1980s did serious concerns emerge over the pervasiveness and intrusiveness of the technology. For example, portable telephones were so common in the early 1990s that various U.S. school boards banned them from the classroom. There were other issues surrounding the protection of personal privacy. **Calling line identification** is an optional feature on telephones in North America that allows users to identify the telephone numbers of callers before answering the ring. Such a service, however, may put battered women at risk, especially when they have to reach men they had to leave. To prevent this risk, telephone manufacturers issued telephones with **call block**, a standard feature that blocks calling line identification. Thus, someone with calling line identification would simply read "private number" instead of the caller's number. The wiretapping of telephone conversations and fax transmissions was also a threat to privacy.

These concerns came to the fore partly in response to technical advances that changed the range and complexity of the consumer products and services at a tremendous speed. They arose in 1984 partly because the date was the title of George Orwell's novel (1949) which paints a nightmarish vision of a totalitarian state in the year 1984 using communication technology (electronic visual devices) to spread propaganda and control its citizens in all areas of their lives and at all times. Although portable telephones and calling line identification were introduced in the early 1990s (thus, several years after the apocalyptic date), the concerns with the technology itself were still fresh in people's minds.

Nevertheless, these concerns did not outweigh the well-established position of the technology. Life in modern society would be unimaginable without the telephone and other telecommunications devices. More important, the technology provides more benefits than risks for the majority of people. The risks that do exist apply to a small part of the population and can be easily reduced. The disruptions of phone calls in class were ended with a ban. Call block is now a standard phone feature that prevents calling line identification. The benefits themselves are tangible, immediate, and personal. Just about every one can think of a long list of uses for the telephone— staying in touch with family and friends, ordering products and services, reaching services in an emergency, and reaching suppliers or customers. Radio and television provide news and entertainment. In a growing number of countries, **distance learning** uses television to broadcast school and university correspondence courses. Concepts such as the Open University in the United Kingdom have proven very popular with those who cannot attend regularly scheduled courses but wish to pursue their education: for example, individuals living in remote areas or those working full time.

Both these factors—limited risks to and direct benefits for individuals and society—help form a positive image of telecommunications technology. Familiarity also makes changes in the technology appear less threatening. Indeed, one might argue, because the overall effects of the technology have been positive in the past, changes are likely to be expected to be good. In general, telecommunications technology has little in common with gene technology and does not affect public reaction to gene technology.

ROADS

Another technology that has influenced modern society is the building of roads and the motor vehicles that use them. This discussion does not look at waterways and railways because air travel (to be discussed later) and automobile travel have caused both to decline. Like telecommunications, road technology has been an inseparable component of modern technological society. Unlike telecommunications, however, the road industry has no significant influence on public perception of the technology. Also unlike telecommunications, road technology is accepted *although* the public perceives it as generally involving high risk (DeLuca, Stolwijk, and Horowitz, 1986; Slovic, 1987). According to P. Slovic, motor vehicles ranked among the five most risky of thirty activities or technologies in risk-perception studies. At the same time, motorized transport is seen as offering great benefits that outweigh the risks.

One explanation for this ambivalence could be that most of the risks are known, controllable, and voluntary. The risks are generally limited to the users of automobiles and their immediate social circles without major social impact. Two examples involve speed and responsibility (among the chief causes of automobile accidents). Both risks can be attributed directly to the driver rather than to the technology itself. In addition, both risks can be reduced through a combination of legal, technical, and social measures. There are speed limits on all roads with reminders clearly displayed at regular intervals. In addition, seat belts and, increasingly, airbags are now standard safety features. Responsibility is encouraged by proper driver training, testing, and permits—legal measures that are stringently enforced in most countries. Drinking and driving, another aspect of driver responsibility, is not only a criminal offense but also a socially unacceptable combination reinforced by advertising campaigns and social pressure. Finally, automobile insurance is an economic incentive for safety and an economic deterrent for irresponsible behavior.

Two other risks of road technology deserve comment, both involving the environment: pollution and land use. Here, the impact is no longer strictly voluntary, and experience already points to negative long-term effects. Exhaust emissions, petroleum fuel, tar for roads, and heavy oil for machine parts all contribute to the contamination of air, soil, and water. Liquid spills from accidents and normal oil residue on the road are washed untreated into sewers (and eventually rivers) or into the ground alongside the road, polluting water and soil. The effects of these pollutants can be limited, but pollution cannot be eliminated. With research data pointing to a thinning ozone layer, there is greater awareness of the contributions of various technologies—including automobiles—to the problem. Moreover, pollution affects not simply the environment but also human health. Smog is such a problem in large metropolitan centers—such as Los Angeles, Mexico City, and Athens—that smog warnings or restrictions on automobile traffic are necessary.

Concerted efforts have been made to reduce the effects of automobile pollution. Solutions have involved a combination of regulations and technological devices, as well as action on the part of individuals: maximum exhaust emission standards, recycling of automotive parts (mandatory in Germany), stricter regulations on petrochemical compositions, and awareness and action campaigns promoting mass transit (to reduce the number of vehicles on the road). In combination with an interest in a healthier lifestyle, some people are relying more on alternative means of transport such as bicycles or in-line skating.

In addition to polluting the environment, road technology requires vast tracts of valuable land for roads and highways. This problem is especially acute in countries that have limited arable land or that need to house a growing population. Highways often do not lead *to* nature but *around* it. In the air-conditioned insulation of their soundproof cars, city dwellers can drive along a highway cut through a forest, into a tunnel under a mountain, and onto a bridge over a river. Paved roads increase the speed, comfort, and efficiency of automobile travel. But they also mean the destruction of trees and other plants, which, as important sources of oxygen, play an important role in slowing down ozone depletion. Questions of environmental impact are also raised when highways are built near a community's water supply or an ecologically sensitive habitat. Accidents or even high traffic volume could place these resources at risk.

The risks of both pollution and excessive land use no longer affect a small number of individuals but are global, involuntary, and difficult to control. Yet they have not led to a rejection of road technology. One possible reason is that the risks are hard to translate into immediate and personal terms for most people, especially those living in the concrete urban jungle. Also, people feel they can make a personal effort to reduce negative effects by using car pools or mass transit.

At the same time, as in telecommunications, the benefits are tangible, personal, and immediate. Most individuals in modern society rely on some form of automobile technology (cars, buses, or motorcycles) for transportation on a regular basis. Automobile technology enhances personal mobility for professional or recreational purposes. Even when individuals do not personally use a car or even a bus, the goods or services they use—food, clothing, mail, and other items—all need transportation at some point. In fact, at the societal level, the transportation of goods or people has become an indispensable part of the economic infrastructure.

Although road technology has more benefits than risks, it has made people aware of the risks of technology in general. Part of the reason may be that during the century that road technology has existed scientists have had ample opportunity to study its various effects—short and long term, immediate and secondary, individual and societal, economic, technological, and environmental. It is also possible that road technology, more so than others, has made individuals more aware of *their* roles and *their* contributions to the global problem of pollution. Every user of a car, motorcycle, or other motor vehicle is tacitly aware that he or she enjoys concrete benefits but also adds to the bigger problem.

AVIATION

Aviation has also had a strong impact on life in modern technological society. Along with telecommunications and road transportation, aviation has helped redefine our perception of the pace of life, our concept of time and space, and our impressions of technology. If attitudes toward road technology are ambivalent, opinions of aviation technology are even more divided. Some perceive fairly great risks with commercial aviation; others perceive relatively low risks (DeLuca et al., 1986). Undoubtedly much of perception has to do directly with the safety aspect—namely, air accidents and catastrophes.

In the 1990s, many people around the world probably associated Lockerbie, Scotland, with Pan American Airlines. In December 1988, a Pan Am aircraft exploded in midair and crashed into the Scottish village, killing all 259 people on board and a dozen on the ground. The result of terrorist action, this disaster was an example of the risks of commercial flights. Yet it did not lead to a public debate over the inherent safety of aviation technology, except in the area of airport security. One reason is that people felt that those in charge of the technology were victims of circumstance, as much as the passengers and their families were. The explosion was also seen as an exception rather than the rule.

In general, however, the risks of technical or mechanical failures leading to a disaster are well known. It is generally assumed that passengers have at least tacitly accepted such risks. Also, the impact of any accident or failure is controllable for the most part through mandatory pilot training and equipment inspection and is limited to the passengers and their families. As in road technology, the aviation industry plays a small role in influencing public perception of the technology as such, probably because of the diversity of the companies: aircraft manufacturers are distinct from airline companies, which are independent from air traffic control. Mechanical failures tend to focus attention on the manufacturers (responsible for faulty parts) and airline companies (responsible for maintenance of equipment), while errors in human judgment tend to focus attention on the airline company or air traffic control (providers of service).

Important issues surrounding aviation technology, like those involving road technology, focus on pollution and land use. Since these issues have already been analyzed, the present discussion will focus on examples. Growing awareness of the importance of marshlands as ecological habitats has led to increased protests against or at least debates over airport expansions. Concerns focus on the effects of air traffic on animals and on the physical changes to the land itself. For example, the sound of airplane engines destroys the shells of eggs and scares away animals, destroying the ecological balance of the habitat. Draining marshland and paving over meadows and arable land damage the land. Airplanes also cause air and noise pollution.

The benefits of aviation, like those of road technology, outweigh the costs, even though most people are aware of the technical and environmental risks. Similarly, aviation is such an integrated part of the social and economic infrastructure that the costs of eliminating it would be higher than maintaining it—at least until the emergence of a new technology that will offer greater benefits and fewer costs. If road technology helps city dwellers go around nature, air travel helps them bypass it altogether: the insulation of the car is exchanged for the isolation of the aircraft. Thus, aviation technology echoes and amplifies the message of road technology: technological solutions create further problems.

SPACE

Space exploration emerged largely in the context of the cold war. From the very beginning, the development of space exploration was largely driven by the ideological, technological, and military rivalry between the United States and the Soviet Union. The first Soviet cosmonaut (1961) was followed closely by the first U.S. astronaut (1962). The space race—with its dreams of human colonies on the moon or nearby planets—soon became part of the arms race. Rockets had been used in combat as early as World War II. Advances in space technology greatly increased the sophistication of rocket-driven weapons; long-range nuclear weapons traveled through space. But this technology also allowed human beings to achieve the dream of reaching the moon and the planets.

In 1969 the first man landed on the moon. In the euphoria that followed in the early 1970s, airline companies received calls and letters from people wanting to make reservations for the first commercial flight to the moon. This eagerness was perhaps due in part to associations with aviation technology. The concept of passenger space flights was easy to compare with jet travel. In addition, there was tremendous public interest in supersonic aviation as France and Britain developed the *Concorde*. Members of the U.S. Congress debated funding for an American supersonic aircraft. Throughout the rest of the 1970s and into the 1980s, the reality of supersonic aviation proved too costly and the dream of passenger space flights overoptimistic.

In the 1980s space exploration began to decline in public esteem. In 1986 the U.S. space shuttle *Challenger* exploded, killing all seven crew members on board, including Sharon McAuliffe, the first nontechnical observer on a space mission. The mission, televised around the world, was highly publicized because McAuliffe, a secondary school teacher, was supposed to conduct two lessons from space. The disaster raised questions about the necessity and benefits of space flights and space exploration. For many people, this area was one that brought little obvious benefit. In the 1993 Eurobarometer survey, many people did not think that space exploration would improve our way of life over the next twenty years (Marlier, 1993).

Although one result of the interest in space exploration was the development of satellite TV and other telecommunications links, their impact on the lives of most people was not immediately evident. Furthermore, space technology was still linked with war and defense, not least because of the U.S. Strategic Defense Initiative in 1983, which proposed the use of space as a means of defense against nuclear attack. For many critics, this proposal had the potential to lead to an escalation in nuclear weapons as one side placed barriers in space and the other tried to penetrate them.

The decline of interest in space technology must also be viewed in the context of the time. The mid-1980s saw the start of a general recession, the growth in unemployment in many industrialized countries, hunger and starvation in many parts of the world, and the continuation of the cold war. In view of these problems, many people saw space exploration as a wrong priority. Space technology was (and continues to be) seen as a high tech pursuit, requiring scientific expertise, a high degree of technical precision, and heavy investment in research and development. The disillusionment with it added to the general frustration with technology and called into question the meaning of progress in modern technology society.

CHEMICALS

Chemical technologies—for there are several—have had a strong but not always visible impact on modern technological society. They include the analysis, production, and application of a broad variety of chemicals, ranging from antibiotics to vitamins (pharmaceuticals), from fertilizers to pesticides (agrochemicals), and from household detergents to industrial solvents (industrial chemicals). The public assessment of these technologies is clearly divided. On the one hand, pharmaceuticals (antibiotics, vaccines, and other prescription medication) and health-care products (such as vitamins or over-the-counter remedies) are seen as overwhelmingly positive. They allow people to remain healthy and they prevent the spread of disease. Agrochemical products keep pests and plant diseases under control, ensuring a continuous food supply. Industrial chemicals provide synthetic dyes and fabrics. On the other hand, agrochemicals and industrial chemicals are also seen as largely harmful (DeLuca et al., 1986; Slovic, 1987).

> Non-medical sources of exposure to chemicals (e.g., pesticides, food additives, alcohol, cigarettes) are seen as [having] very low benefit and high risk; medical chemicals (e.g., prescription drugs, antibiotics, vaccines, vitamins) are generally seen as [having] high benefit and low risk, despite the fact that they can be very toxic substances and human exposure to them is quite great. (Slovic, 1987, p. 127)

There may be several reasons for this polarized view. First, as mentioned elsewhere (see "Traditional Uses of Microorganisms," chapter 2), the discovery of penicillin marked the modern era of medicine. To a large degree, antibiotics and vaccines remain symbols of modern medicine because they have saved so many lives and eliminated the threat of many life-threatening childhood diseases (for example, measles, polio, and smallpox). This fact alone outweighs the inherent risks of medication. The costs of diseases to individuals (the suffering of patients and their families) and society (the loss of lives) are high enough to justify the attendant risks.

Where agrochemicals and industrial chemicals are concerned, this assessment changes, due to three situations. DDT (dichloro-diphenyl-trichlorothene), Love Canal, and Bhopal have come to represent the negative aspects of nonmedical chemicals.

DDT provided a critical first lesson on the dangers of chemicals and of technology as a whole in the 1960s. A fat-soluble chemical used since the early 1940s as an insecticide, DDT was indiscriminately sprayed over large areas to control flies, fleas, and mosquitoes. Initially, it was extremely effective. However, these insects quickly developed resistance to DDT. Also it indiscriminately killed other insects that would have helped keep the pest population under control. In addition, DDT also accumulated in fatty tissues of animals that ate plants or insects sprayed with it and of humans who ate crops sprayed it. Moreover, the chemical persisted in soil and was carried by rainwater and waste-water systems into rivers and lakes. In the process, trees and other plants started dying, animals in the food chain were killed, and human beings (especially children) became seriously ill.

Rachel Carson, in her book *Silent Spring* (1962), was one of the first to raise public awareness of the dangers of DDT and other chemical pesticides. She argued that there were links between these chemicals, the increase of diseased trees, the death of animal wildlife, and the higher incidence of cancerous diseases in human beings. She also pointed to the effects of long exposure to, and accumulation of, pesticides and other chemicals in different organisms: damage to chromosomes, genetic mutations, and other changes in the genes. Her work eventually led to the ban on DDT in the United States and some other countries.

About fifteen years later, Love Canal in New York State drew attention to the long-term negative effects of chemicals, this time in the form of disposal of toxic chemical waste. For about a decade, chemical waste from nearby industrial sites had been dumped into the canal. The site was filled in and a real estate development grew up over it. Then in the late 1970s, toxic sludge began to surface at a school playground and in houses. Love Canal became a national issue across the United States, raising concerns about the potential health effects and prompting the EPA to investigate and clean up other chemical disposal sites. Since then, Love Canal has become synonymous with toxic wastes, in particular industrial chemicals.

Then in December 1984 an explosion at a Union Carbide plant in Bhopal, India, killed two thousand people, disabled at least another one thousand, and injured more than eight thousand. At the time, the plant was producing a chemical destined to be a component of a pesticide. Later studies found that the substance in question was possibly a cause of cancer and could also cause genetic damage (Lappé, 1991).

These three events, which took place within a twenty-five-year period, helped define public opinion of chemical technologies. DDT became a symbol of the unfavorable ecological impact of chemical technologies. Love Canal became a synonym for the pollution of the environment from toxic waste. Bhopal underlined the danger of chemical technologies. More important, these three events raised public awareness of the links between technology in general and its negative effects on health and the environment. In addition, they underscored the influence of technology on the innermost functions of living beings—whether at the level of the body, the organs, the cells, or the genes. This fact is an important point in the gene technology debate: the more science understands about how life functions at the most basic levels, the more we realize how deeply the results of technology affect all living organisms.

The lessons of DDT, Love Canal, and Bhopal have contributed to a growing realization that continuous and unlimited use of agrochemicals and industrial chemicals could lead to the buildup of toxic substances in the body and the environment at harmful levels. "The image of most chemical technologies is so negative that when we asked college students and members of the public to tell us what comes to mind when they hear the word 'chemicals,' by far the most frequent response was 'dangerous' or some closely related terms" (Slovic, 1992). Even with pharmaceutical products, there is an awareness that the body develops resistance to a medication over a period of time, or that some strains of bacteria have started to show signs of resistance to antibiotics and other medication. This fact has led a small but growing number of individuals to seek nonconventional medical treatment, for example, from ancient healing methods such as acupuncture to more recent developments such as homeopathy. In agricultural products, there is a market demand for crops that have not been sprayed with chemicals.

Of the technologies discussed up to this point, chemical technologies perhaps have one of the most important influences on the public perception of gene technology. The promises of better health, improved crops, and a healthier environment all have haunting echoes in the arguments for gene technology. At the same time, it is not lost on people that the institutions that made such promises often did not consider the long-term and indirect costs. In the debate over gene technology, the same concerns are being raised.

FARMING AND FOOD PRODUCTION

At first, it may seem unusual to consider farming and food production to be technological. Yet, beginning in the 1930s, farming in many countries has been transformed into a sophisticated technology. In the United Kingdom, the start of this transformation and its impact on farming communities are vividly described in *All Creatures Great and Small* and other books by James Herriot, which were the basis of a BBC television series.

The first step in the change was the mechanization of the farm—the introduction of tractors and automatic harvesters—which meant the disappearance of the work horse. Later veterinary medicine gradually became a standard feature of farming practice. Later still, in the 1950s, the introduction of chemical fertilizers and insecticides transformed the farm even further. Along with the use of specially bred varieties of crops, this change came to be known as the Green Revolution. Today, the modern farmer probably has a degree from an agricultural college and training in a number of scientific disciplines.

Food processing was originally an inseparable part of farming. The harvest period was the peak in the manufacture of food, as fruit, grain, meat, and milk were prepared and stored for the coming winter. After World War II, this activity became a separate industry and took on the features of a sophisticated technology. It is easy to forget that the supermarket is a relatively recent addition to food production.

Because the farming sector consists of a large number of small players and a small number of big players it is hard to develop a quick snapshot of its technological concerns. But some recent trends highlight some of these concerns. Such trends include the continuing disappearance of the small family farm, the consolidation of small farms under one management, and the increase of factory farming. Factory farming has a production-line approach in which efficiency is a priority. Often animals are confined in rows of narrow pens until they are ready for slaughter (Anderson, 1987).

The disappearance of the small farm can be linked with more competitive economic situations, the continued migration of younger people to cities in search of employment, and changes in climactic conditions, which can result in severe crop loss and bankruptcy for farmers. To remain competitive, farmers have to invest more and more in technology: effective but environmentally friendly chemical products, more efficient machinery, and sturdier breeds of animals or varieties of plants. If they overuse the land—from continuous planting of only one type of crop or from excessive chemical buildup—they run the risk of depleting nutrients in the soil and eventually causing soil erosion.

These changes on the farm are often not visible to people living in cities, for whom a farm still conjures up images of a pastoral idyll. Indeed, for many city dwellers, a farm represents all that is wholesome and natural. This image is often shaken by issues that erupt on the media. Animal-rights groups have been key in bringing certain farming and food production issues to public attention: the crowding of animals in confined spaces, the mishandling of animals in long-distance transport, the suffering of animals in the slaughtering process. Such issues have an impact on issues surrounding gene technology applied to farm animals.

Another key issue in farming and food production that affects gene technology discussions is overproduction. In industrialized countries—including France, Germany, Switzerland, the United States, and Canada—supply sometimes outstrips demand in grain, fruit, meat, and dairy production. Then producers, supermarkets, or other suppliers end up dumping loads of farm produce into the sea or municipal dumps. Sometimes the problem is linked with government subsidies and price controls. Other times, surplus is linked to the very success of farming and food production technologies. Regardless of the reason, many people see the dumping of surplus food simply as waste, which is especially reprehensible in the context of hunger in both industrializing *and* industrialized countries.

In 1974 the World Food Conference in Rome closed with the *Declaration on the Eradication of Hunger and Malnutrition*. The resolution aimed to end world hunger within a decade, with the help of the Green Revolution. In the mid-1980s TV images of starvation in Ethiopia and elsewhere were a forceful reminder that hunger was still a major world problem. In many industrialized countries, including the United States, economic recession and unemployment broke the ability of some households even to buy food. This situation led to the development of **food banks**, community locations where food donations are received and distributed to those who are unable to buy food. Clearly, not all problems have a technological cause or a technological solution, but technology does appear to aggravate existing inequalities between those experiencing overproduction and those suffering from hunger.

These issues led to a discomfort among segments of the population with the impact of technology on food. As some people turned to alternatives to conventional medicine, some sought natural food items, or **biofood** products: eggs from free-range hens, meat from animals that have not received antibiotic or hormone injections or that have been slaughtered before transport, fruit and vegetables that have not been sprayed with insecticides or pesticides. Many city dwellers feel alienated from nature on the one hand and long for a return to nature on the other.

Road, aviation, space, chemical, and farming technology offer the following lessons for those living in modern technological society:

- Technology inevitably leads to change.
- Technology in general is not benign.
- Technology comes at a price—negative effects on the environment or human health.
- Technological solutions often lead to other problems.

NUCLEAR POWER

The lessons of telecommunications, roads, aviation, space, and farming technologies have been reinforced by the more recent technology of nuclear power. The public still associates nuclear technology with war. Part of the reason is that nuclear research was originally aimed at weapons development. In August 1945 the Americans dropped the world's first atomic bombs in Japan. Since then Hiroshima and Nagasaki have been reminders of the destructive power of nuclear technology. It was not until the 1950s that the first nuclear power stations were built, giving nuclear technology a civilian as well as a military aspect.

Nuclear energy was seen as a revolutionary new source of energy because it was nonpolluting. It was also less costly than petroleum and was an alternative to nonrenewable supplies of coal and oil. During the oil crisis of the 1970s, an important economic argument in the United States was that nuclear energy reduced dependency on other countries for energy. These advantages were offset by fears of accidents at civilian nuclear power plants. These fears were reinforced by accidents such as those at Three Mile Island in the United States in 1979 and Chernobyl in the Ukraine in 1986, and by radioactive leaks at the nuclear processing facilities at Windscale/Sellafield in the United Kingdom in 1986. Moreover, in the public mind, nuclear technology never lost its destructive military connotations. Until the end of the 1980s, the cold war and the nuclear arms race between the United States and the Soviet Union kept the danger of nuclear war firmly before the public. In 1995 France, despite international protests, insisted on carrying out military nuclear tests in the South Pacific.

The industry behind nuclear technology for civilian use, namely, the electricity supply industry, and the regulatory agencies responsible for nuclear power have generally tended to lack credibility. One reason is that some government bodies, such as the Atomic Energy Commission in the United States, were simultaneously promoters and regulators of nuclear energy, a situation that aroused suspicions of a conflict of interests (Edwards and Winterfeldt, 1986). Another reason is that the arrogance of government regulatory bodies and proponents of nuclear energy set a pattern of distrust early on:

> Scientists in various countries [in the 1970s] raised doubts about nuclear power and collected signatures to express their dissent. This, of course, provoked governments and the pro-nuclear lobby to engage in a counter-campaign in which, for the most part, *the challengers' arguments were not taken seriously.* (Rucht, 1995, p. 280, italics added)

From the beginning, the use of nuclear energy has been filled with examples of institutional dismissiveness and paternalism. Sometimes "nuclear power programmes were implemented in the face of significant opposition"

(Rucht, 1995, p. 277). Often decisions were taken without informing or consulting the population affected. One example is the siting of a facility for the disposal of toxic waste at a small community in Ontario in 1974:

> Analysis of this early activity shows that there had been little in the way of public information activities and no public consultation prior to starting the work. There had been no mention of the activity in the local news media. Information to the local population came from casual conversations with some of the geologists about their activities in the area. (Greber, Frech, and Hillier, 1994, p. 25)

Perhaps more than with previous technologies, the experience with nuclear technology set a new framework for disputatious encounters among industry, government, critics, and the public. Resistance to new technologies is nothing new. The term *Luddites*, referring to those who fight against technological change, had its origins in the early days of the Industrial Revolution in Great Britain. What is new in the experience with nuclear technology is both a sense of urgency and a sense that the issues affect just about all sections of society. For the first time resistance to a new technology was coordinated and supported across national, religious, and professional boundaries.

This sense of international urgency is due to the potential risks. Once released, radioactivity is difficult to contain, and its impact is global. "Radiation fallout from accidents like Chernobyl poses *risks without limits*; the event had consequences in Northern Scandinavia within days" (Bauer, 1995, p. 9, original italics). The victims of the atomic bombs dropped in Hiroshima and Nagasaki were living proofs of the effects of radiation. Perhaps the most frightening aspect is that the five senses of the human body cannot detect the effects of long-term exposure to low radiation levels. This inability leaves people feeling vulnerable and helpless, especially knowing that radiation may also affect the lives of future generations.

These powerful fears about nuclear technology have left an indelible impression on many people. Nuclear technology became a paradigm for other revolutionary technologies, but as with all paradigms, it is a good decision-making model only so long as *all* the conditions remain the same. It will be argued here that it is not appropriate for social decisions about gene technology, even though *some* fears, such as the unknown effects of radiation and gene mutation, appear similar.

The differences between the two technologies outweigh the similarities. Where nuclear technology emerged in the context of war, gene technology developed out of a medical need—the search for cures to diseases that conventional medicine had been unable to treat. Nuclear technology has a narrow civilian application, energy production. Moreover, there are alternative forms of nonpolluting energy such as water, wind, solar power, alcohol, and natural gas. In contrast, gene technology has a variety of applications—medical, pharmaceutical, and agricultural. In many of these diverse applications (see chapter 2), there are no alternative solutions. For example, there exist few effective methods for cleaning up environmental contaminants. Chemical pesticides or herbicides are not always target specific. There is still no viricide in agriculture, veterinary care, or human medicine. Genetic diagnosis and gene therapy are the direct results of a long search for cures or treatment of genetic disorders and other life-threatening diseases. The question of necessity helps explain why the public tends to accept genetically altered medication and rejects genetically altered food items.

There is another crucial difference between the two technologies. The products of nuclear technology (electricity and nuclear waste) are *life threatening*. The products of gene technology (food and medicine) are *life sustaining*; indeed they are primarily destined for consumption—in the form of food or medication. These significant differences between nuclear and gene technology create a **paradigm shift**, which heightens public anxiety.

INFORMATION

Like other technologies previously discussed, information technology, based on the microchip, was also heralded as a technological revolution. Yet, unlike other revolutions, it met with little resistance or even criticism. There are a number of possible reasons.

First, the public generally does not associate computers and information technology with war. As M. Bauer rightly points out, computers were an integral part of the development of missile technology during the cold war, but they quickly entered the domain of private enterprise. Unlike nuclear technology, information technology was quickly adopted in a number of different nonmilitary settings. By the mid-1950s, mainframe computers were used in many respected institutions—for example, banks, hospitals, universities, and large companies—for storing and processing large amounts of information. By the mid-1970s, the first home computers appeared. The gradual introduction of automated teller machines (ATMs) in North America during the mid-1980s also increased public familiarity with the technology.

Second, information technology is associated with telecommunications technology. The public's long experience with the telephone and television, in particular, provided a familiar point of reference. The computer monitor (screen) found a ready parallel in the television screen. Modem connections found similarities with cable television and telephone cables. The Minitel in France or Videotext in Switzerland further blurred distinctions between telecommunications technology and information technology. Subscribers to this European information service operated by French and Swiss telephone companies can call up on a screen attached to their telephones a wide range of consumer information—from offers in stores to rail and flight timetables to weather forecasts. The service can be considered a forerunner of the Internet in the United States.

Like telecommunications, information technology has become a model for comparison with other technologies, such as gene technology. Whereas in the past, textbooks described genes as chemical building blocks and cells as chemical factories, more recent works present nucleotides as letters of an alphabet, genes as words, chromosomes as chapters, and the genome as the book of life. One speaks of encoding or decoding DNA or RNA and the transmission of information bits. A genetic disorder is the result of false information signals. Like telecommunications, information technology has the ability to change our view of the world, often without our realization, and has met with little resistance.

Nonetheless, people had concerns about information technology. Some people objected that because of ATMs bank tellers would lose their jobs. Others feared that customers would lose the familiar personal service they enjoyed at banks. Robberies and holdups at ATMs (often late at night) created serious problems, as did the vulnerability of access cards with personal identification numbers (PINs). These concerns were addressed by the installation of video cameras at ATM locations, reminders to card users to keep PINs confidential, and various incentives for using ATMs. More important, customers had the choice of using a teller or an ATM during banking hours. ATMs also gained popularity once people realized they could carry out transactions outside banking hours and at almost any location with an ATM. A network of ATMs across North America provided ready access to cash even outside of the traveler's town or country of residence—replacing traveler's checks.

The use of ATMs shows that even with a technology that gained relatively quick acceptance, there were several stumbling blocks to acceptance. But in general, few of the concerns over information technology were controversial. In the mid-1990s in the United States there were some proposals about legislative control over some areas of this technology. Those proposals focused mainly on **cybersex** (pornography on the Internet) and **computer hacking** (trespassing in restricted areas or breaching security measures to retrieve information).

The three principal issues in information technology revolve around security, privacy, and confidentiality. Information technology involves more than just computers. It uses an electronic network that links individual computers, data bases, news groups, E-mail systems, and electronic bulletin boards. Signals are transmitted via a modem (which encodes and decodes electronic signals) connected to existing telecommunications infrastructures. Unlike telecommunications services, however, the boundary between private and public access is not very clear. A message on a news group can elicit responses either directly from the news group (open to public view) or through a private E-mail message.

The first issue, information security, is mainly technical. Because information passes through an open network, an experienced user can intercept restricted material. The banking industry, for example, was shaken in 1995 when a young Russian in St. Petersburg transferred about $10 million from different accounts at Citibank, one of the major U.S. banks (Mason, 1995). Although the case was unusual, it highlighted the fact that security is a weak point in information networks. Breaches of security undermine the trust people place in the institutions—financial, medical, or other—that have access to personal information.

The second issue, privacy of information, means that an individual has the right to decide who should have access to certain personal facts. Privacy is closely linked to the right of the individual to autonomy, including freedom of decision and freedom of movement. For example, employees providing comments to their superiors may have a valid interest in not revealing their identity. Remaining anonymous on the E-mail system becomes a challenge, as all E-mail messages show the sender's address.

The third issue, information confidentiality, means that the information user or holder has access to this information in trust. Due care must be taken in protecting the information; third parties should not have access without the consent of the person involved. Such access could become a problem, for example, when several parties have access to various information on the same data base. At the heart of the discussion is the question of trust: individuals will divulge information only if they can assume that it will not be given to a third party and will used as tacitly or expressly agreed.

As more information is processed, stored, and exchanged on electronic information systems, the issues of security, confidentiality, and privacy will become more urgent. The results of a genetic test or other medical information, for example, would be of interest not only to the individual in question but also to potential employers, health insurers, or even spouses. Would health-care providers be able to protect this information when it is stored or as it is sent? Although information technology is not the cause of the problem, its speed, its accessibility, and its vulnerability add another level of complexity to existing concerns.

REPRODUCTION

New reproductive technology is generally not familiar to the general public. Infertility clinics are even less known. However, where this technology has entered public discussions, perceptions have been ambivalent. On the one hand, it is viewed as beneficial because it assists infertile individuals to conceive a child. Part of this favorable perception may be due to associations with conventional medicine such as gynecology or obstetrics. Part may result from the fact that research in this area is giving medical science understanding of human reproduction and prenatal and early childhood diseases.

On the other hand, new reproductive technology raises a range of ethical and legal concerns. Some stem from the fact that the industry is highly commercialized but little regulated. The techniques used are expensive, are often not covered by health insurance, and have no guarantee of success. Indeed, some clinics have already been accused of raising false hopes through false advertising or making false claims about success rates. There are also concerns about the impact on the couple's physical health and psychological well-being. One or both partners may be required to receive hormone injections or surgical treatments (if there is a blocked passage). These procedures could be physically draining and psychologically exhausting. Despite all this effort, a couple might never be able to conceive.

More generally, the issues raised by reproductive technology are part of the larger debate on the intervention of medical technologies in human life. In the past, the debate has ranged from abortion and contraception to euthanasia and technologically prolonging life. Regarding reproduction technology, debate centers on ethical questions surrounding the practice of uniting sperm and egg in a laboratory setting, the use of embryos in research, the disposal of unused embryos following a successful pregnancy, the use of paid surrogate mothers, and the system of anonymous sperm donors. There is also a debate about whether parents will expect more of the "miracle" child because of the high price they paid for it.

This debate raises two fundamental questions. First, to what extent should human beings be using technology to intervene in the creation and preservation of life? Are we not playing God? Second, is technological society reducing human life to a mere commodity? Is life another "consumer good" to be bought, sold, and customized according to human whims?

Reproductive technology and gene technology share much in common. On a technical level, there are overlaps of research and development, for example, embryo research and research aimed at the diagnosis or treatment of diseases at the embryonic and fetal stages. At the ethical level, both are raising similar concerns that human beings are directly and increasingly intervening in essential life processes and that human life is being devalued. Both have unleashed a debate over the reductionist attitude of modern technological society built on a paradigm of specialization and compartmentalization. Both have provoked a debate over the complex relationships among life, technology, and human values.

CONSEQUENCES OF EXPERIENCE WITH PREVIOUS TECHNOLOGIES

Over the course of the twentieth century, each new technology—space technology, information technology, nuclear technology, reproduction technology, and, most recently, gene technology—has raised hopes and expectations and also doubts and warnings. All promised a technological revolution. As Bauer points out, new technologies "gave rise to sociological imaginings of the 'coming new era,' sometimes optimistic and enthusiastic in terms of revolution, pessimistic in the light of doom, but often ambiguous" (1995, p. 5).

The hopes and promises of all these technologies—and the results—have shaped public opinion of technology. Some delivered what they promised.

Others fell short of all expectations. Still others proved to have huge costs. When disappointments became more frequent, people became cynical and suspicious. The arrogance of institutions and their paternalism, dismissiveness, and unwillingness to listen to concerns alienated the public, setting unnecessary barriers to future relationships with neighbors, communities, prospective employees or clients, and special-interest groups.

In a society dominated by technology, conflicts over technology cannot be isolated from other social problems. People's attitudes toward a new technology are shaped by previous conflicts, current social dilemmas, and concerns about the future. Of the three, current problems in society probably have the greatest influence. At the end of the twentieth century, the increasing burden of technological costs has produced two trends: concern for the environment and concern for health.

The Environmental Movement

From a fringe movement in the late 1950s and early 1960s, care for the environment has become a reality of doing business in the 1990s. Many companies have factored environmental considerations into their decision-making process. Environmental-impact studies have become almost standard components of project proposals. More and more, companies are liable for emissions and waste disposal during the production phase. At the end of operations, they are often held responsible for cleaning up the site. Where companies have failed to take the initiative, government bodies such as the Environmental Protection Agency in the United States have provided regulations and, when needed, enforced compliance.

The environmental movement has become a power to reckon with: it has strength to challenge big business and win. An example is Greenpeace. Founded in the early 1970s by a few opponents to nuclear power, Greenpeace has become a worldwide environmental organization. One reason for the success of the environmental movement is that those who were once on the environmental fringe in the 1960s have become managers, political leaders, and decision makers in the 1990s. Another reason is greater awareness of technological burdens from the past.

A third reason is that in contrast to many government and business organizations, environmental groups understand how people at the grass-roots level think, and they are able to speak in terms the average person can grasp. This ability came out clearly in an exchange between Peter Duncan, the head of Shell in Germany, and Jochen Lorfelder, a Greenpeace activist in Germany, during the conflict over the sinking of the Brent Spar:

> Peter Duncan . . . explained that dumping was the best option scientifically. Mr. Lorfelder shot back, "But Joe Six-Pack won't understand your technical details. All he knows is that if he dumps his

car into a lake, he gets fined. So he can't understand how Shell can do this." (Bahree, Pope, Rohwedder, and Sullivan, 1995, p. 4)

A fourth reason is that in addition to the ability to speak in understandable terms, environmental groups also have a high credibility among large segments of the public. In the past, they were among the first to warn the public of environmental pollution. Activists such as Rachel Carson, as noted, listened to the concerns of ordinary people and took those concerns seriously, even when many experts felt there was insufficient scientific evidence. Furthermore, environmental organizations are seen as *doing* something about environmental problems. More important, many people feel that they themselves can make a difference, by joining in protest demonstrations, signing petitions, or supporting other actions initiated by environmental groups. Where government and industry are too often slowed by size and administrative bureaucracies, many environmental groups are accessible and visibly active, especially at the local level. Through these groups, many individuals have found a voice and feel empowered to make changes.

Concern for Health

Concerns over the impact of technology on human health can be roughly divided into three, somewhat overlapping areas. The first is worker safety. Early in the Industrial Revolution, the effects of technologies on the health of workers seldom bothered either employers or consumers because neither group was directly exposed to occupational hazards. As industrial society dissolved the boundaries between social classes and as social attitudes slowly changed, measures were taken to protect workers from harm. The concern still exists that some workers may face greater risks than the average population because of long-term exposure to harmful substances.

The second area of concern deals with consumer safety. For example, the introduction of steamboats in the mid-nineteenth century met with considerable opposition because of fears that they would endanger people's lives. Another example is chemical substances whose long-term consumption, either intentional (for example, oral contraceptives) or unintentional (for example, pesticide residues on fresh produce) could have negative effects on the body.

The third area of concern focuses on long-term, often invisible effects of technology such as low-level radiation leaks from nuclear reactors and electromagnetic fields from high-tension power lines. These risks are usually little understood in the scientific community but have received broad attention in the mass media. Whereas previous worries were on behalf of specific groups, that is, workers or users, today this area of concern is wider in scope including the worry that future generations may end up paying for the consequences of the current technologies.

Aggravation of the Gap Between Rich and Poor

Along with the awareness of the costs of past technologies, there is growing attention to the role of technology in widening the gap between the rich and the poor. On the one hand, sophisticated technology has created a situation where non-Western or non-Northern societies are increasingly dependent on the West or North and thus relegated to the margins of modern technological society. This process of marginalization began in the days of colonial exploitation and is continuing today through modern technology, which is controlled by the West and the North. Richer countries fret about the Internet and electronic privacy, while poorer countries still struggle to meet basic needs for food, medicine, education, and telephone lines. The gap between them is further widened by the rapid pace of technological development, requiring ever more capital and skills, and by the complexity of one technology depending on many others, as discussed earlier, leading to a cycle of technological dependency.

On the other hand, technology has also helped to widen the gap between rich and poor within industrialized nations. Some may argue that a discrepancy between rich and poor has always existed in society—in both ancient and modern times, in the East and in the West. The new element in this situation is modern technology and access to it. Unequal access to technology has contributed to unequal access to health care and education and to job opportunities. Those who do not have access to new technologies find themselves at a disadvantage.

This double marginalization of the poor and disadvantaged—between nations and within nations—has led to the rise of special-interest groups that champion their needs. This trend in the arena of society runs parallel to the rise of activism concerning the environment. Representing three thousand nongovernmental organizations, the United Nations Fourth World Conference on Women in Beijing in September 1995 showed the number and strength of some of these groups. Perhaps paradoxically, it should also be noted that technology has enabled some members of traditionally marginalized groups—including women, ethnic minorities, and the physically disabled—to take their place as equals in society.

More and more, debates focus on the impact of these new technologies on different groups in society. The testing of nuclear missiles in the South Pacific raised accusations of colonial paternalism. Use of new reproductive technologies raised important questions about the rights of women as human beings. Issues concerning the remuneration of farmers in the South for their contribution to genetic diversity remain unresolved. Questions of equity and discrimination in employment and health insurance are still key issues of gene technology.

The technological and economic impact of the technology is emphasized as much as the ethical and societal consequences. Perhaps for this reason, the nonscientific evaluation of technological risks goes beyond the number of injuries and fatalities. Some consequences are not quantifiable or fore-seeable, for example, stress, cancer, or infertility. Nor are all qualitative effects negative: new opportunities, improved standards of health, and more choices for the individual. An important lesson for modern technological society is the following: "Unforeseen consequences stand in the way of all those who think they see clearly the direction in which a new technology will take us. Not even those who invent a technology can be assumed to be reliable prophets, as Thamus warned" (Postman, 1992, p. 15). Thus, to understand the anxiety and the intensity of the gene technology debate, it has to be seen in the broader framework of society's concerns with technol-ogy in general.

GENE TECHNOLOGY IN THE CONTEXT OF THE MODERN TECHNOLOGICAL AGE

Viewed against the background of society's experience with other technolo-gies, the concerns surrounding gene technology appear to fall into two cat-egories. Some relate specifically to gene technology itself—its novelty and its unknown potential. Others involve fundamental problems with technol-ogy as a whole.

ISSUES RELATED TO GENE TECHNOLOGY

Concerns for the impact of gene technology center on areas of basic human needs—food, health, and safety. Experience of crop failure, cancer, and acci-dents has shown how vulnerable these areas can be. A big fear is that, in trying to direct genetic changes in different life forms, we may end up dam-aging or destroying the very elements that support all life. There are four areas of concern (related to the central controversies identified in chapter 4).

The first is the integrity of the natural state, expressed by controversies over the genetic alteration of organisms, especially human beings and ani-mals. The life forms that we know today are the result of divine creation or natural evolution. Each form has a place in the order of existence, even if it is not clear to human beings now. By intruding on that order, human beings risk creating monsters that have no place in this order.

The second, closely linked area is environmental integrity or ecological balance. The environment is seen as a whole system that can tolerate vari-ations and slow changes but may not be able to absorb sudden or radical change. Therefore, there is a furor over both deliberate and accidental release of genetically altered microorganisms or plants. By introducing new life forms, there is a risk of upsetting the existing balance in the ecosystem.

The third area of concern is the well-being of the human individual, as expressed in debates over food derived from genetically altered plants or animals and, to a lesser degree, over pharmaceutical products or medical procedures. Food, medication, and gene therapy all enter the body directly and thus directly affect its inner workings. Because scientists are still learning about gene technology and its long-term effects are unknown, the anxiety is understandable.

The fourth area has to do with the impact of gene technology on social balance. At the global level, debates focus on working out an equitable distribution of wealth between industrializing and already industrialized nations. The former are often rich in natural and biological resources, many of which have been used in traditional medicine or agriculture. The latter are often strong in technological knowledge and have developed new uses from these resources. At the rational level, within industrialized countries, various groups—genetics researchers, government officials, ethicists, and even private companies—are struggling with questions of social equity such as the prevention of discrimination on the basis of genetic information in employment, insurance, or health care.

These four areas of concern have led to calls for greater social and personal control over gene technology in order to limit the risks to human beings and the environment. One example is proposals for legislation or prohibition of deliberate release or field trials. Another example is the increasing use of public consultation in the selection, planning, and building of laboratories or test sites.

There is also a need for greater individual control over personal exposure to the risks of gene technology. Representative of this need is the discussion on the labeling of food products derived from genetically altered plants and animals. In 1998, for example, the European Parliament passed a law requiring the labeling of food and food ingredients derived from genetically altered organisms. But the issue goes beyond what a label on a package says. People want a guarantee of their right to choose. Although they may accept genetically altered pharmaceutical products out of necessity, they want to decide for themselves about food.

People also want autonomy, the right of the individual to make a choice without undue scrutiny or pressure from outside groups. This desire emerges most clearly in the call for governments to regulate mandatory screening for employment or private insurance. If genetic information is used to restrict access to jobs or medical coverage, many individuals will be seriously hampered in their ability to choose for themselves. As it is, their purchasing decisions are already known to credit card companies; the government knows their employment history; and their insurers can probably tell them how many times they have visited a doctor in the last ten years.

All these concerns over the impact of gene technology on basic areas of life and the calls for more control arise partly from the fact that gene technology it is still new with yet unknown potential. But they also reveal a deeper level of anxiety involving technology in general.

ISSUES RELATED TO TECHNOLOGY IN GENERAL

Gene technology, perhaps more than other new technologies, provides a focal point for much of society's malaise—disappointment, resentment, anxiety—about technology as a dominant force in industrialized society. All technologies affect the way people live and think. One reason why gene technology has become the center of attention is its enormous power to make changes at the most basic physical level in all living organisms. It has the power to alter genes, the very substance regulating the functions of life.

The Problem with Technology

In Western culture, there is a long-standing desire to change the environment to suit human needs (a theme explored in chapters 1 and 4). For centuries, people dreamed of regaining paradise lost: perfect crops, perfect animals, and even perfect human beings. Gene technology, by showing how much of life is regulated by four small chemical compounds, appears to offer the potential to make many changes that were not possible in the past. For the first time, perfect living organisms appear to be within reach. The question becomes: Do we need perfection? More important, Do we really want it? There is, paradoxically, the fear of a dream turning into a real nightmare.

In many ways, gene technology has become a symbol for technology itself, with all its drawbacks (as discussed earlier in "Roads"). This fact may be one reason why it has drawn such criticism. The potential of gene technology to make long-term (perhaps even irreversible) changes comes close to people's deepest fears about technology. They worry that the path of gene technology leads deeper and deeper into the technological labyrinth where there may lurk a monster of our own creation. They fear not only a one-way street leading to a dead end but that there will be no return on technological progress. This fear is often expressed in the slippery-slope argument: "If we start with this, where do we stop?" This is the nightmare of technological dependence.

A second reason why gene technology drew the fire of criticism is that from the beginning, its advocates promoted it as the greatest technological revolution. The label *technological revolution* carries strong connotative associations. For one, a revolution is an uprising, usually of a group against the dominant class. The parallel here is that the struggle over gene technology is a form of rejection of the technological elite and the dominant institutions of modern technological society. For another, a revolution promises drastic changes that will lead to a better future, but it often involves suffering and loss for those in the present, especially those who have the least say in decisions about change. If gene technology is a revolution that will change the future, someone must pay the price in the present. Certain groups seem to feel that they may bear too much of the burden: those who fear genetic discrimination, those afraid they will be unduly exposed to the risks, those concerned about damage to the environment. By calling the technological and social changes that gene technology unleashes a revolution, advocates have drawn attention to the very source of people's anxiety about technology. Gene technology as a revolution has become a symbol of the intrusive nature of all technology.

A third reason why gene technology attracted so much attention is that it provides a summary of all the risks and benefits of past technologies. It makes all the hopes and fears of technological society a real possibility, but at the same time people are afraid that it would lead to similar problems and disappointments. The realism of Michael Crichton's *Jurassic Park* (1990) is the late twentieth century's answer to Francis Bacon's dream in *The New Atlantis* (1677) and Aldous Huxley's nightmare in *Brave New World* (1932). For the first time, the boundaries between imagination and reality blurred. In May 1995, five years after the publication of Crichton's book, two researchers in California reported that they had retrieved and successfully cultured bacteria from the gut of an insect trapped in amber for at least 25 million years (Cano and Borucki, 1995; Fischman, 1995).

With gene technology, technology has crossed invisible social limits as well. Advocates say that gene technology will help us pass medical boundaries. Opponents say that researchers and their sponsors have crossed ethical boundaries. Both sides argue that gene technology allows human beings to go beyond the limits of nature—which, depending on the speaker's perspective, can be either positive or negative. Even in the most neutral sense, gene technology (like all new technologies) has challenged the limits of existing laws and legal definitions.

A fourth reason why gene technology has attracted criticism is that it blurred the line between academic research and commercial application, between the university and business, between knowledge and property. Gene technology emerged as a science, but it quickly became a technology when industry became interested. In the 1980s there was some resentment toward the commercialization of knowledge, especially in the life sciences. There was a steep growth in new biotechnology enterprises as more and more academic scientists started to found their own firms—while retaining their teaching positions at, and access to, university facilities (Krimsky, 1991). In the 1990s, universities continued to form more links with industry on scientific research. The commercial development of gene technology came to represent all that is wrong with a market economy led by big business and built on the technology developed by big industry. Some have perceived a serious conflict of interests in this trend towards the industrialization of genetic knowledge. Advocates have promoted gene technology as the hope of medical science, but not all genetic research is aimed at fighting diseases. In fact, some of its applications may possibly add to existing problems, for example, overproduction of certain farm products in industrialized countries.

There is also some resentment of the attitude that knowledge is valuable only when it is applicable, when it can be quantified in terms of money. Quite often, advocates of gene technology, particularly representatives from industry, point to the commercial usefulness of genetic science. Even opponents are guilty of this attitude when they ask, "But what use is that?" Perhaps with the exception of genome research, little attention is given to knowledge for its own sake. Some people feel uncomfortable with the materialistic world view that everything becomes a commodity, that even knowledge and life itself must have a utility and often a commercial value. This view is a departure from the origins of science, a word derived from the Latin *scientia*, meaning "knowledge." "Science is no longer a small community of distinguished minds: it is part of the economic and of the political systems, and decisions about science are not entirely scientific" (Touraine, 1995, p. 49).

A fifth reason why gene technology became the target of criticism is the deep fear that human beings may lose control over technology. This fear goes beyond the question of technical risks to a deeper discomfort with the long-term social, cultural, and psychological implications of high technology's effect on society. Accepting gene technology implicitly means that progress in human society will now be more closely linked with technological progress than ever before. The connection has always been true, especially in the minds of technocrats, but this time, there will be no turning back. Through germ-line gene therapy, human beings from conception could be shaped to suit the needs of parents or even institutions. If the imagination could give us the vision of *Brave New World* and science the means to realize it, one day some individual will want to bring the vision and means together.

Another aspect of fear of loss of control of technology is fear of human dependency on it, a theme already presented in this chapter. The word *dependency* suggests something more than *dependence*, which simply means being linked to or supported by something or someone else. Dependency suggests a degree of helplessness if that support no longer exists. Earlier it was said that there is fear that without technology, society cannot function any longer, or at least, only with great difficulty. This sense of helplessness comes to the fore when a storm or other natural disaster disrupts the technological infrastructure of an area: there is no communication and no transportation; food and water are in short supply.

Thus people fear that technology is taking over human society. There is a sense of inevitability: the technological juggernaut rolls forward. Then what happens to human beings? What becomes of their humanity? This fear lies behind the worst-case arguments ("What could human beings possibly do if something went wrong with this technology?") or the slippery-slope argument ("If we start here, where do we stop?"). This fear emerges clearly in discussions on ethics.

The Orientation of Modern Technological Society

The public debate over gene technology leads to deeper questions about the orientation of modern technological society. If gene technology represents technology in general, then the acceptance of gene technology means accepting all that is good and bad about technology.

Such acceptance leads to the question of how to cope with change (discussed earlier). Do people adapt to technological progress or does technology adapt to human progress? Because people have to keep up with technology all the time, some of them may find technological change to be a mixed blessing. They may feel helpless in the face of change, overwhelmed by the pace and volume of technological innovations. As an example, the transformation of the workplace by telecommunications and information technologies is not a one-time event but a constant process as new products, new systems, new methods appear. These changes require new skills, which provide an opportunity for those with the ability to learn and adapt. But for many people, the requirement can also be a threat to job security. They may have invested years in perfecting their skills in one area, only to find that those skills are no longer needed or that they must learn to do their job differently. There may also be pressure from employers and peers to learn a new technology.

It should be recognized that there is a limit to the ability of individuals to keep changing and adapting. Already technological change has pushed the limit of institutions (made up of large numbers of individuals) to cope. Challenged by changes in other aspects of their lives, individuals may feel pushed to their limit. They need time to cope with or absorb changes. But the pace, volume, and complexity of technological progress do not seem to allow the luxury of time.

Acceptance of technology also can lead to the sense that the human individual is lost in technological considerations. Developments are so fast that no single individual or even group has an overview anymore. Knowledge resides primarily in technical experts, who have no more knowledge outside their own fields than the nontechnical public. This fragmentation of knowledge and experience continues a trend that started in the nineteenth century as part of the process of industrialization. Specialization by both workers and students makes for a highly efficient production system, but it has also led to the growth of bureaucracy.

More and more people feel that too much decision-making power resides in large, and inflexible institutions. Although their functions differ, they all present a face of anonymity and monolithic bureaucracy to the individual that approaches them. There are many examples: a patient entering a hospital, a plaintiff appearing in court, a student registering at university, or an employee joining a large company. In such stressful situations many people would welcome individual attention and human understanding, but a bureaucratic system strives above all else for efficiency. That goal can lead to inflexibility—from the standpoint of the individual both as service provider and as service consumer. Small wonder if some people feel they have become part of a nameless mass.

The emphasis on science and efficiency means that discussions of ethical values, such as civil and economic justice, are relegated to the background. Such discussions are often led by nonscientific experts who have little influence on decisions of public policy and technological development.

Along with the impression that institutions are monolithic goes a sense that decision makers are remote from the lives that their decisions affect. Decisions taken at administrative headquarters are often reached without consulting those whose lives might be influenced or whose choices might make a difference. More than ever before, people think that decision makers do not always represent the public interest. This perception is reinforced by perceived or actual examples of decision makers who demonstrated a lack of personal accountability. An example is the so-called tainted-blood scandals in France, the United States, and elsewhere. Despite information pointing to the risks, senior health officials failed to intervene in the distribution of untreated blood products, some of which were contaminated by HIV.

In many large organizations, an attitude of self-preservation prevails over other considerations. An example from the university world is the attitude of publish or perish. Often, tenure and advancement appear to be linked to the number of publications by a professor rather than the quality of his or her teaching. Another example, from the world of business, is the principle that the bottom line (the financial results) should be the deciding factor in any situation.

Efforts have been made to hold senior officials and managers personally accountable for their decisions. This effort is underscored by environmental laws in various states of the United States that hold senior managers personally liable for environmental pollution. In some countries, managers have stood trial for the role their actions or inaction played in industrial accidents. In France and other countries, health officials involved with the tainted-blood scandal have been sued by hemophiliac societies and the families of victims for not acting on the information they had.

Such measures suggest that people are questioning the values of high-technological society. They want to reexamine the underlying values of decisions taken in institutions. They are looking at the role of technology in changing society and asking, Is technology a help or is it just a nuisance?

The paradox is that technology is both a help and a nuisance. For example we search for security in what is familiar and traditional, yet we rely on technology to support that search. At the individual level, people seek the comfort of home and friends, **cocooning**, as it is called, partly out of desire to escape the frantic pace of technological society caused by faxes, cars, telephones, television, and other modern conveniences. The paradox, of course, is that people rely on technology—stereo systems, home entertainment systems, calling line identification, and other gadgets—to ensure their escape. Technology is what people are running from, but it is also what they are running to. They are trying to find or reestablish human contact in a world that is increasingly technology oriented, but they rely on technology to provide contact with close friends and to screen out strangers.

At the societal level, the same phenomenon of cocooning can be seen in the search for the security of traditions and fundamental values: moral conservatism serves as a counter movement to technological innovation. Yet at the same time, people readily embrace the goods of technology. For example, the fundamentalist preacher uses television to preach against the sins seen on television.

This longing for a return to old morals and conduct can be seen as a search for guidance from past paradigms to help cope with changes in the present. Looking at past decisions and working models may be useful, but there is one danger. As society evolves, old paradigms may no longer be adequate. Old norms and frameworks may no longer respond to new needs. If there is a paradigm shift, turning to the past may in fact increase people's sense of loss and helplessness.

Another aspect of the technological paradox is a movement toward a return to nature. Many people, especially those living in urban centers, feel alienated from nature. Their urge to rediscover nature in its splendor and untouched state has led to the development of new markets. There is a demand for natural fabrics—wool, linen, cotton. Travel agencies offer trips to the wilderness of the Canadian Far North and the Australian Outback. There is interest in back-to-nature weekend trips. Advertisements skillfully tap into this desire for nature by presenting images of sunsets on a calm lake, families picnicking in green meadows, or a lone fisherman in a clear river. In reality, however, nature is very different from such gentle images in the minds of urban dwellers. The paradox is that often people return to nature equipped with the latest in technology: large snowmobiles in the Far North, all-terrain vehicles in the Outback, helicopters for heliskiing on the pristine slopes of the Alps. Without communications, without transportation technologies, nature for them would remain distant and unfamiliar.

It is in the context of such apparent conflicts—human progress versus technological advancement, individual choice rather than bureaucratic decisions, conservatism versus innovation, escape from technology versus escape through technology, natural creation versus technological production—that gene technology has emerged and become the focal point of debate. That debate has raised four important and related issues: control over decisions, maintaining ecological balance, conflicting perceptions of life, and the equitable distribution of wealth.

Control—Many segments of society believe that technology must above all serve human needs, that is, it must be controlled. Human beings—especially the individual—must be the focus of consideration in any technological enterprise. The emphasis should be on the rights of the individual. The average citizen is an intelligent person with the ability to form personal opinions and make decisions. He or she has the right to be asked. No institution can take away the right to choice. Partly in recognition of this assumption, government and industry have made increasing use of public consultations in the planning and development of large projects. In the cases of John Moore and the Guaymi natives (see chapter 3), a key issue was the right of the individual to be informed.

Individuals also have the right to question. In a society where freedom of opinion is implicitly or explicitly guaranteed, individuals have the right to choose their own sources of information. More and more individuals in modern technological society are exercising this right. At the personal level, this trend can be seen in changes in doctor-patient relationships. Patients are no longer willing to accept what their doctors are telling them. Increasingly, if a patient is dissatisfied with the opinion of a doctor, he or she will not hesitate to obtain a second medical opinion. At the community level, public or industry officials must be willing to defend their data and conclusions. As in the Shell Brent Spar debate, a nonscientific public will turn to alternate sources for information (in this case, Greenpeace). Not all sources are equal. Greenpeace was originally seen as having more reliable data and conclusions, although it later turned out that both were incorrect.

If individuals have the right to be asked and to question, it follows that they also have the right to reject a decision. If an institution's decision affects them, they have the right to be consulted and to make decisions in their own best interests including the rejection of a proposal that does not serve them. If institutions fail to consult, they risk being viewed as arrogant or paternalistic, accusations that have often been heard. The public asserted its right to have a say in decisions that affect its interests in many of the situations cited throughout this book: court cases over patents in gene technology, protests against nuclear testing, and boycotts of products from one company or country.

Control also means that those who enjoy the benefits of technology have a responsibility to think in advance about its consequences for others and for the environment. In taking part in the decision-making process, challenging the proposals of organizations, and recognizing opposition groups, the public is sending a clear message that those responsible for technologies have to assume their liability.

In the past, the burden of technological pollution and cleanup was ignored until it was impossible to do so any longer. Often the industry that created the problems paid no attention until it was forced. To be fair, consumers who enjoyed the products of technology also preferred to think of the problems as someone else's. Today, we are recognizing that everyone contributes to pollution and has a responsibility to help prevent, control, reduce, or eliminating it. Lakes dying, arable lands becoming deserts, soil eroding from clear cutting, depleting of the ozone layer—all should have taught us to avoid such high costs in the future. After Love Canal, the *Exxon Valdez*, Bhopal, and Chernobyl, there is no excuse to say, "We didn't know this could happen."

Ecological Balance—The second issue concerns the growing realization that all life forms, including human beings, depend on a healthy environment, which means keeping the ecosystem in balance. The relationships among human beings, technology, and the environment are complex and fragile. In the past, people exploited and exhausted what nature had to offer, producing soil erosion, acid rain, a thinning ozone layer, and dead water systems. Today, people are beginning to see nature as a rich but limited well of resources. Its fragility is revealed by the extermination of species and the destruction of natural habitats through human activities. As we come to recognize that human existence is intrinsically linked to the sound management of natural resources, we redefine *natural resources* to include not only land, air, and water but also energy, life forms, and entire ecosystems.

After a century of living with high technology, we have learned that all technologies exert a toll on nature, from which they derive their power. The more powerful the technology, the stronger its impact on all life and the greater its costs. If gene technology is indeed as powerful as some advocates claim, then its toll on nature can be exorbitantly high.

Conflicting Perceptions of Life—The third issue raises fundamental questions about the way people in modern technological society view life. What is life? How does it differ from inanimate matter?

In the Judeo-Christian tradition (as discussed in chapter 4) life is sacred. Human life was created by God in his image and set apart from the rest of creation. To take away human life—that of another or one's own—was and remains a major sin in the teachings of the church. Medieval society saw the universe and its rhythms of the seasons and of life and death as part of a divine order centered on God. To intervene in this order was to commit sacrilege, an act against God himself; the consequences would be felt throughout nature. In Shakespeare's *Macbeth*, for example, the murder of the king was heralded by unusual storms and other disturbances in nature.

Science and technology slowly changed this view. Nature and its rhythms were explained in terms of geological, physical, chemical, or biological bodies and functions: observable, definable, reducible to the constituent elements. An organism is made up of organs, composed of tissues, consisting of cells, containing chromosomes, made of DNA. The functions of life are guided by DNA, which controls the production of proteins. By making different combinations of DNA, it is possible to alter the forms and processes of living organisms. Such change is not considered an act against God but an act made possible by advances in science.

Some people disagree with the scientific view, arguing that life is more than the sum of all its genes. Reducing living organisms to their genetic composition is too simplistic, perhaps even a violation of creation. They oppose making transgenic animals as breaking the reproductive barriers between different species set by God. For such people, experience with science and technology has shown that human beings disturb the order of things at their own risk.

Proponents of the scientific view hold that studying nature in all its parts will give human beings a better understanding of natural phenomena and the processes of life, an understanding necessary for confronting the problems we face. Proponents of the view that nature should be treated as an inviolable whole compare human interventions into the functions of life with a child taking apart an exquisite and complicated clock without understanding how the parts fit together. The debate over gene technology reflects these two views.

It is important to recognize that gene technology did not spark the debate, which started long ago, when medicine became a science. That turning point might arbitrarily be set at the first publicly acknowledged dissection of the human body in the fourteenth century. (Previously dissection was forbidden as a sacrilegeous act.) The twentieth century provided a new dimension to the debate over the value of life as doctors for the first time were able to prolong life, for example, through the artificial respirator. Doctors and lay persons must deal with a range of gray ethical areas involving medical technology: patient consent to undergo a life-saving medical procedure such as a blood transfusion; the rights of parents and offspring in abortion, artificial insemination, and surrogate motherhood; patent rights in termination of life support and doctor-assisted suicide.

The definition of life, once a purely philosophical question, now is also a scientific one. Gene technology is not likely to provide the answer, but it has certainly turned new light on the question.

Social Equity—The fourth issue addresses the matter of how the wealth and other tangible benefits created by technology should be distributed. Past technologies have helped widen the gap between powerful, high tech nations in the industrialized North and those with natural resources but little high technology in the industrializing South. Greater environmental awareness and the disappearance of more and more rain forests have made people in the North more conscious of the precious resources and wealth of biodivirsity in the South. Gene technology in particular has made them aware of the untapped resources in living organisms. The economies of some countries depend mainly on exports of a small number of crops. The fear is that genetically altered substitutes for these crops from industrialized countries will drive such economies to total collapse. There is also concern about the contributions of farmers in industrializing nations to the breeding of certain crop plants and farm animals over the next hundreds or even thousands of years. If Northern countries are to benefit from these plants and animals, some critics think that the nations of origin should also share in the benefits. Otherwise gene technology will further polarize the North and the South.

The same concerns about polarization apply to the rich and poor within industrialized nations. In the past, especially since the Industrial Revolution, the benefits and risks of technology were not equally distributed. Wealth was concentrated in the hands of a small number of people who controlled technology. The technological elite—factory owners, government regulators, and even technical experts—dictated their wishes to workers or communities affected. They often placed mines and factories and waste-disposal sites near small or remote communities, as they still do. It was rare for people to influence the decisions that affected their lives. The fear is that the key players and investors in gene technology, companies that have been around for a long time, may continue this institutional paternalism, as expressed by the uproar over field testing in rural areas. The public's negative image of many institutions in technological society may turn out to be the biggest challenge to those institutions in the future.

From Institutional Authority to Individual Autonomy
In Western society there has been a slow, gradual shift from the authority of institutions directing society to individuals making choices for themselves. This process resulted partly from wars and revolutions, which redrew political boundaries and redistributed power among classes, and partly from technology. Before exploring the theme of individual autonomy, it is important to look at the changes in Western society that made it possible. Western society has always been a complex of religious, political, and economic (technological) influences, but at different periods different influences had the upper hand.

Society Dominated by Religion—The collapse of the western part of the Roman Empire in the fifth century left a power gap that was gradually filled by the church about the ninth or tenth century. Throughout the Middle Ages, the church acted as a stabilizing and centralizing force as secular lords fought one another for power. Medieval Europe was above all a religious society, with church teachings providing the ultimate guideline for everyone. The church was not only a moral authority but also a point of reference. Its teachings influenced secular laws and decisions. Power and authority rested in ecclesiastical institutions: bishops had political influence, churches were centers of worship, hospitals and alms houses provided welfare, and monastic and cathedral schools were places of learning. The church taught that all knowledge comes from God through the church to society. Knowledge, in fact, allowed the church to be a force of stability. Libraries in monasteries preserved not only the teachings of the Church Fathers but also the works of Greek and Roman writers. Priests and nobles came to the church for education. The first universities in Europe, such as the Sorbonne in Paris, were originally established as theological colleges.

The first move toward the greater autonomy of the individual was the gradual separation of church and state. Ironically, the success of the church as a temporal power led to the secularization of society. Power struggles between kings and bishops and within the church weakened its authority. Technology also played an important role in this process, as Europe began to manufacture paper in the fourteenth century, gradually replacing expensive parchment, and in the fifteenth century developed printing with movable type, which made possible speedy and accurate reproductions of text. These technological innovations ended the monopoly of the church on knowledge. City guilds could now compete with (and indeed outpace) Europe's monasteries in the production of new publications.

Society Dominated by Politics—By the eighteenth century, most of the modern states of Europe had taken on the forms that they were to retain more or less intact into the twentieth century. The state took the place of the church in many instances, acting as social authority and point of reference. In England, Parliament asserted its supremacy over the crown. In France, the king established the absolute authority of the crown and declared: "L'état, c'est moi!" For the next three hundred years, government legislation set moral guidelines (for example, pornography laws) and determined social policies (for example, welfare contributions and pension funds). In many countries, power rested in one of three branches of the state: the executive, the legislative, or the judiciary. State institutions gradually took over from the church such social responsibilities as education, welfare and health care.

Many European countries had already established colonies in the Americas and the East, which provided new sources of raw material. Throughout the seventeenth and eighteenth centuries, France and England developed vigorous policies to encourage colonization and trade in their new territories. The merchant class, or bourgeoisie, gained new prominence not only in Europe but also in the colonies.

By the end of the eighteenth century, the need for change was again sweeping across the countries of Europe and their colonies. The new merchant class saw itself excluded by the old social structure, which dated from feudal times: the king presided over an assembly of lords temporal and spiritual. The merchant class had the money but not the political power to shape decisions in society.

In North America, the French had lost most of their colonies to Great Britain. With the constant threat of war with France removed, the merchants and plantation owners in some of the British colonies felt that the French defeat was their opportunity for greater autonomy. Britain paid them no heed and lost its southern colonies in the resultant revolution. In France, excesses at the royal court and a series of poor harvests leading to famine brought about a peasants' revolt. The bourgeoisie joined in the call for a revolution, which gave them a much larger place in society. In Great Britain, technology was starting the Industrial Revolution, which led to an increase in the autonomy of the individual.

Society Dominated by Industry and Technology—The Industrial Revolution introduced new concepts and new methods. Mechanization and factory production replaced production by hand. The ideas of Descartes and other philosophers in the seventeenth century had given primacy to science, which throughout the next two centuries provided industry with new ideas, new processes, and new products. Western society became an industrial society, guided chiefly by scientific and economic principles in place of church teachings or national politics. For example, the patent office decided if a product or process qualified as an invention that would advance society's knowledge and serve its needs. Increasingly, scientists took on the role of expert advisers in such social decisions as regulating the impact of technology on human health and the environment. The doctor became the expert on the patient's health: sickness and disease were reduced to a set of emotionless physical symptoms. Power was vested in industrial institutions, rivaling or superseding religious or state institutions. Corporations became partners with the state and individuals in contributing to unemployment insurance and old-age security plans.

By the middle of the twentieth century, industrial society was facing another need for change in the aftermath of World War II. During the war, women worked in factories and ran businesses, supporting themselves and contributing to society. After the war, they wanted to retain their rights as individuals capable of determining their own future. Many women rejected the old structure that deprived most of them of autonomy and called for recognition as individuals. In the United States, blacks, also seeking recognition, started the civil-rights movement. In many other countries, political refugees and those seeking economic improvement, aided by aviation technology, increased immigration and other population shifts, making recognition of the rights of all individuals whatever their culture all the more urgent.

The introduction of high technology further shifted the balance of power from men. A forklift or a robotic arm eliminates the need for gender-based jobs; with such tools anyone can lift a couple of hundred pounds of goods. Washing machines and microwave ovens allow women to work outside the home. With a computer and a printer, a single person can produce a book that, in the past, would have required a whole team of typesetters, designers, and printers, who were traditionally men.

Society Dominated by the Individual—Today's high tech society seems to be leading toward a society dominated by the individual instead of by religion, government, or scientific principles, as in various periods in the past. Where institutions once had sole authority to make vital decisions, the choices of individuals, according to their values and needs, have become the new guidelines for social decisions. Individuals are aware that they can make a small difference and that together they can make a large difference. "The first principle of the New Age movement is the doctrine of individual responsibility. . . . each individual is responsible for everything he or she does" (Naisbitt and Aburdene, 1990, pp. 298–299).

In a society dominated by the individual, the power to make decisions resides in individuals who have the ability to unite as a local organization or community or special-interest group to make their wishes known. For example, people can use their purchasing power as individuals to bring about change. If enough consumers decide not to buy French wine because they disapprove of the policy of the French government or not to buy fuel from Shell because they think Shell should not have sunk the Brent Spar, that government or corporation might be forced to change its policy.

Another expression of the shift toward individual choice is the concept of letting market forces decide. By "market forces" managers and economists mean individual consumers making choices. Two closely allied trends are the empowerment of employees and the decentralization of institutions. Transnational companies such as Asea Brown Boveri (ABB) realize that employees know best what the problem is in their work area and how to solve it. Similarly, managers living in a country or region understand local customs and expectations better than a manager sent out from the head office. Banks, health-care providers, insurance companies, and other organizations are realizing that no single solution will solve all problems. Many such institutions, recognizing that people want real choices, now offer flexible options that can be tailored to suit the needs of the individual customer or employee.

The shift in the control of information from institutions to individuals is probably the most important contributor to the rise of a society based on choice. Possessing information means controlling power. This fact is probably what Postman is referring to when he writes, "Luther understood, as Gutenberg did not, that the mass-produced book, by placing the Word of God on every kitchen table, makes each Christian his own theologian—one might say his own priest or, even better, from Luther's point of view, his own pope" (1992, p. 15). Postman's point is that having the Bible meant that people could decide for themselves what the Bible means; it gave them direct access to the Word of God, access that was once the monopoly of the church. In a way, the laity now had the same authority as priests. The relation of information to decisions is relevant to the gene technology debate where people want information that will allow them as individuals to make the choices that suit their needs.

> He [Paul Sites] placed power in a realistic perspective by attributing effective power, not to authorities but to individuals and groups of individuals pursuing their ontological needs. These individuals would use all means at their disposal to pursue certain human needs, subject only to constraints they imposed on themselves in their need to maintain valued relationships. (Burton, 1987, pp. 15–16)

In the information age, decision-making authority rests in the hands of individuals because they possess information. There is no longer a center of information. Anyone can become a sender of information, as well as a receiver and keeper. Faxes, cordless telephones, portable computers, hand-held video cameras, E-mail, and the Internet allow information to be distributed through individual channels of communications quickly and inexpensively. McLuhan saw this trend long before most other people did. He foresaw that society in the age of electronic communications would be all center and no margin (McLuhan, 1964). New telecommunications technology and information technology have contributed to the rise of interest groups by making them the source of information. Greenpeace provides a good example:

> Then there's the Greenpeace armada . . . and state-of-the-art communications equipment, from cellular phones to a digital "squisher" that enables them to make satellite transmissions high-speed bursts. Greenpeace cameramen captured last week's commando raid [on Brent Spar] on tape, and a video clip of it was even put up on the Internet. (Dickey, 1995)

Thanks to these innovations in communication, information is no longer simply what an institution says. This change can be understood in two ways. On the one hand, special-interest groups are now authoritative sources of information. In the debate over the Brent Spar, most media agencies gave at least as much weight to data from Greenpeace as to data from Shell. On the other hand, the nature of information has changed—notably it is more visually oriented. Words must be matched by action. In twenty seconds or less, a television news report can show how an individual or an organization reacts. In using water cannons to deter Greenpeace activists from storming the Brent Spar, Shell did more to hurt its own credibility than anything

Greenpeace could have said. The images were captured on television for viewers around the world and were also available on the Internet, a medium used by students and other potential consumers.

The power of visual information lies in its immediacy. Images appeal directly to emotions. In a twenty-second news clip, viewers can hear the report and respond to the images—joy, fear, happiness, anger, or sadness. Numbers are transformed into images of living beings or tangible objects. In that sense, the intellectual and emotional elements of social acceptance and decision making (see chapter 1) come together as one. Some of the most memorable technological catastrophes of the twentieth century were captured on camera: the crash of the *Hindenburg*, the oil slick of the *Exxon Valdez*, and the victims of Bhopal and Chernobyl. People could literally see for themselves that institutions are made up of people who are human. Government officials can be wrong. Technical experts can make mistakes. Independent analysts are capable of errors. Managers in industry do not always make the right decisions.

The introduction of electronic networks—E-mail and the Internet—has further transformed the communication of information. Views and opinions can be exchanged between interested parties (customers, potential customers, potential employees, and critics) without the intervention of any institution or traditional news filters. The novelty of the Internet is that there are service providers but no one who owns the Internet. That means that users can form their own opinions. For that reason Greenpeace put an excerpt of the water cannon fiasco on the Internet so that it would spark a discussion. The images spoke for themselves. There were no spokesmen, no public relations officers, no journalists, and no experts to shape opinions. The users of the Internet were the experts. Drawing on the Internet, stakeholders (those with the potential to affect the outcome of a situation in which their values or interests are at stake) can select any information from anyone of their choice. If the information they have is not sufficient, they can rely on the experience of others to fill in the gaps. No one has greater credibility than someone who has gone through the experience. All these developments have changed the nature and distribution of information and where decision-making authority lies.

KEY POINTS

- Technology offers people a higher standard of living, along with greater personal choice. At the same time, technological change has resulted in a certain malaise or ambivalence about it.

- The essence of technology is speed: the reduction of time, space, and energy. Yet speed has also narrowed the gap between action and reaction, leading to information overload.

- In the twenty years since the birth of gene technology, the speed, scale, and complexity of technology have increased dramatically, adding to the impression that technology is something massive and unmanageable and causing frustration and malaise.

- In modern technological society, progress is often defined as *technological* progress, a view that displaces other values in favor of scientific judgment and technological development.

- Much of the frustration with technological change is directed at the large institutions that seem to benefit most from it and often appear to be its chief advocates: business, industry, government, and academia.

- There is a marked change in society: authority and decision-making power are shifting away from the institution to the individual. Many people are not as tolerant as previous generations of the paternalistic attitudes of large institutions because people today tend to be more educated and more critical and have their own sources of information. They want a part in shaping changes in society and are mobilizing friends, neighbors, and others to do so.

- People's reaction to a new technology is shaped, in part, by their experience with other technologies: their impact on public perception, the reputation of the industry behind the technology, and the risks and benefits of the technology. When new technologies raise hopes that too often are disappointed, people become cynical about the promises of new technological revolutions.

- At the end of the twentieth century, the burden of technological costs from the past has resulted in growth in environmental activism, growth in the power of environmental groups, and greater awareness of the impact of technology on human health. All of them shape social discussions of new technologies.

- The concerns over gene technology fall into two broad categories: concerns specific to this particular technology and concerns relating to technology in general. Specific concerns include the integrity of nature, ecological balance, the well-being of the individual, and equitable distribution of wealth. General concerns include the fact that technology can have negative consequences for society and its future direction.

- Modern technology has taught four hard lessons: it is not benign, it comes at a price, it causes change, and a technological solution is likely to lead to other problems.

- The acceptance of gene technology implies the acceptance of all that is good and bad about technology in general.

- Technology has played a part in the shift from a society dominated by institutions to a society dominated by the individual, communities, and local organizations.

- The social acceptance of a new technology goes beyond accepting risks and benefits to making choices about future directions.

REFERENCES

Anderson, W. T. 1987. *To Govern Evolution: Further Adventures of the Political Animal.* Boston: Harcourt Brace Jovanovich.

Bahree, B., K. Pope, C. Rohwedder, and A. Sullivan. 1995. Giant Outsmarted: How Greepeace Sank Shell's Plan to Dump Big Oil Rig in Atlantic. *Wall Street Journal Europe,* 7 July, pp. 1, 4.

Bauer, M. 1995. Resistance to New Technology and Its Effects on Nuclear Power, Information Technology and Biotechnology. In *Resistance to New Technology: Nuclear Power, Information Technology, and Biotechnology,* edited by M. Bauer, pp. 1–41. Cambridge: Cambridge University Press.

Burton, J. W. 1987. *Resolving Deep-Rooted Conflict.* Lanham, Md.: University Press of America.

Cano, R., and M. K. Borucki. 1995. Revival and Identification of Bacterial Spores in 25- to 40-Million-Year-Old Dominican Amber. *Science* 268: 1060–1064.

Carson, R. 1962. *Silent Spring.* Boston: Houghton Mifflin Co.

DeLuca, D. A., J. A. J. Stolwijk, and W. Horowitz. 1986. Public Perceptions of Technological Risks: A Methodoligal Study. In *Risk Evaluation and Management,* edited by V. T. Covello, J. Menkes, and J. Mumpower, pp. 25–67. New York: Plenum Press.

Dickey, C. 1995. The Green Machine. *Newsweek,* 24 July, pp. 46–47.

Edwards, W., and D. v. Winterfeldt. 1986. Public Disputes About Risky Technologies: Stakeholders and Arenas. In *Risk Evaluation and Management,* edited by V. T. Covello, J. Menkes, and J. Mumpower, pp. 69–92. New York: Plenum Press.

Fischman, J. 1995. Have 25-Million-Year-Old Bacteria Returned to Life? *Science* 268: 977.

Greber, M. A., E. R. Frech, and J. A. Hillier. 1994. *The Disposal of Canada's Nuclear Fuel Waste: Public Involvement and Social Aspects,* AECL-10712, COG-93-2: Atomic Energy of Canada Ltd.

Grunig, J. E. 1992. What Is Excellence in Management? In *Excellence in Public Relations and Communication Management*, edited by J. E. Grunig, pp. 219–250. Hillsdale, N.J.: Lawrence Erlbaum Associates.

Krimsky, S. 1991. *Biotechnics and Society: The Rise of Industrial Genetics.* New York: Praeger.

Lappé, M. 1991. *Chemical Deception.* San Francisco: Sierra Club Books.

Marlier, E. 1993. *Biotechnology and Genetic Engineering: What Europeans Think About It in 1993,* Opinion Survey Eurobarometer 39.1: Brussels: The European Commission.

Mason, J. 1995. Banks' Security Chains Rattled. *Financial Times*, 20 September, p. 12.

McLuhan, M. 1964. *Understanding Media: The Extensions of Man.* New York: McGraw-Hill.

Naisbitt, J., and P. Aburdene. 1990. *Megatrends 2000: Ten New Directions for the 1990s.* New York: William Morrow and Co.

Postman, N. 1992. *Technopoly: The Surrender of Culture to Technology.* New York: Vintage Books.

Rucht, D. 1995. The Impact of Anti-nuclear Power in International Comparison. In *Resistance to New Technology: Nuclear Power, Information Technology and Biotechnology*, edited by M. Bauer, pp. 277–291. Cambridge: Cambridge University Press.

Slovic, P. 1987. Perception of Risk. *Science* 236: 280–285.

———. 1992. Perception of Risk: Reflections on the Psychometric Paradigm. In *Social Theories of Risk*, edited by S. Krimsky and D. Golding, pp. 117–152. Westport Ct.: Praeger.

Touraine, A. 1995. The Crisis of "Progress." In *Resistance to New Technology: Nuclear Power, Information Technology and Biotechnology*, edited by M. Bauer, Cambridge: Cambridge University Press.

6 COMING TO SOCIAL DECISIONS IN A FAST-CHANGING ENVIRONMENT

At the end of the twentieth century, individuals and organizations are faced with rapid change, continual conflict, and increasing uncertainty, in other words, a turbulent social environment. The winds of change have been sweeping through the familiar world of the generations living after World War II. Since the 1980s, the changes in politics, economics, the physical environment, and society itself have been more dramatic.

In world politics some of the most memorable events included the fall of the Berlin Wall as a symbol of the cold war, the collapse of communism in eastern Europe, war in the Balkans, the end of apartheid in South Africa, and tentative moves towards peace in Northern Ireland and the Middle East. At the same time, Tiananmen Square remained a symbol of the need for improved human rights in China and elsewhere. Among notable trends in the realm of economics were the rise of Japan as a world power, the prolonged recession in North America and Western Europe, the formation of regional trading blocs, and the emergence of new markets in Asia and Eastern Europe. This period also saw the development of microelectronics, telecommunications, and biotechnology in Japan, the United States, and Europe.

Environmental concerns included awareness and fund-raising campaigns to save the tropical rain forests; a major chemical spill into the Rhine River; the oil spill from the *Exxon Valdez*, which covered a sensitive area of the Alaskan coastline; the depletion of the ozone layer; and global warming. The United Nations Conference on Environment and Development in Rio de Janeiro led to the signing of the Montreal Protocol by more than a hundred states.

An important social change was the economic recession in industrialized countries, which marked the end of expectations of lifelong careers. A job for life with one company, once the norm in many countries, was no longer a certainty. The recession also meant that many governments had to cut back on spending in areas where it had been a matter of course: education (especially at the postsecondary level), old age security, unemployment insurance, and health care. Individuals had to pay more for these social benefits or faced cuts in services.

Technology played a special role in all this turbulence. It speeded up the pace of change, and new technologies created new pressures, adding to problems already facing modern technologically driven society.

These different forces of change—political, social, economic, and technological—combined to challenge existing structures and systems and underlying values and assumptions.

> New expectations of the role of business in society, changing demographics, critical social problems such as spiralling health care costs, educational reform and child care, and environmental degradation are posing serious challenges to business organisations and society as a whole. (Austrom and Lad, 1989, p. 22)

The conditions of rapid change, uncertainty in task and environments, and highly interdependent and complex relationships (Austrom and Lad, 1989; Cammillus and Datta, 1991) have put increasing pressure on different segments of society—individuals as well as organizations—pushing the limits of their ability to respond. As they strive to satisfy their values and interests, they compete for attention, priority, and resources. Thus it becomes almost inevitable that some of these segments will collide.

This stressful situation has tremendous implications for the public controversies surrounding gene technology. Some understanding of the competing values and interests may help create a foundation on which individuals can make choices.

Technology adds to the turbulence of modern life in at least two ways. First, there is the stress of change itself. For individuals and organizations, getting used to a new technology means adapting to new ideas, new methods, new structures, and new forces of competition. Problems arising from the application and interpretation of existing legislation often highlight some of the social challenges that new technologies pose. The introduction of multimedia works, CD-ROMs, and other new techniques of communication raised a number of difficult questions about copyright law. The introduction of gene technology is raising similar questions in the area of patent law.

Significantly, both of these areas of law protect intellectual property: part of the struggle over intellectual property comes from the value—both social and economic—given to knowledge in the present information society. This value is a radical shift from the older industrial society, which emphasized machines and factories.

The second way technology contributes to the turbulence of life is by the anxiety that comes from changes in paradigm (see chapter 1). As Postman points out, a new technology does not simply add something to society (or take something away): it changes everything. In this instance it is the transformation from a society dominated by machines and factories to one dominated by information. P. F. Drucker calls this change the shift from a society of manual workers to one of knowledge workers. The paradigm shift to a society requiring information as well as land, labor, and capital may be seen in the changing role of writers. Writing has always been a respected profession. Scribes played an important part in the courts of the Egyptian pharaohs and Chinese emperors. What has changed is the number of writers and the value given to writing as a means of recording and transmitting ideas and information.

In the past, relatively few people knew how to write (even in the 1890s there were only a few professional authors and journalists), and those who did were servants of royalty and other leaders. In the 1990s opportunities for writers exist in many fields, including journalism, advertising, marketing, and public relations. Good writing skills are essential for many managerial and research positions. Moreover, because more social and economic value is attached to ideas and information, people who write, who communicate, are themselves leaders—of businesses, nonprofit organizations, and governments. This new value given to intellectual property is especially important in the context of innovations arising from information technology and gene technology.

The controversy over gene technology must be placed in the broader context of changes in traditional values and the impact of those changes on different segments of society as they struggle to protect their interests. Gene technology has revised traditional understanding of the living world, providing new concepts and techniques in health care, food production, and environmental management. It has altered patent laws and provided new forces of economic competition in the rise of the biotechnology industry. More important, gene technology has led to a redefinition of the concept of natural resources (traditionally minerals, forestry, and natural sources of energy) to include genetic resources. This expanded definition changes the way human beings relate to the living world.

This change of perspective is more than just a question of evolving definitions. Since genetic matter is the raw material for gene technology, its use calls into question economic assumptions about the potential assets of different countries or regions of the world. As already noted, many countries in the Northern Hemisphere tend to be rich in technology, while many in the South tend to be rich in genetic resources. Gene technology might influence the distribution of wealth between industrialized and industrializing countries and thus shift the balance of power.

A paradigm shift involves more than economic changes. Access to genetic information may change the balance of power between institutions and individuals, for example, between employer and potential employee, or between insurance company and potential insurance holder. The genetic point of view that all organisms are made up of the same four chemical molecules is a radical change from the traditional taxonomic view, which classified living organisms into a hierarchy, with human beings at the top of the evolutionary tree.

A paradigm shift invariably is, at the same time, a potential threat to the values or interests of some part of society and a potential opportunity to satisfy the interests of other parts of society. Developments that hinder any group from satisfying its interests are called issues throughout this book. Some of these issues touch on gene technology specifically (see "Issues Related to Gene Technology," chapter 5). Others involve technology in general (see "Issues Related to Technology in General," chapter 5). When values are threatened or interests collide, the result is conflict.

A satisfactory resolution of a conflict depends on the ability of the parties involved to reconcile their interests. Often these interests are obscured by the inflammatory slogans and rhetoric of entrenched positions. In the case of gene technology, this conflict is framed in terms of its acceptance by society. Such acceptance—at least as understood in this book—is the result of an informed decision of different segments of society. To win acceptance, the legitimate interests of these different segments must be acknowledged, understood, and addressed.

This chapter address two questions. First, how do the various applications of gene technology affect some of the basic values and interests of different segments of society? Second, how can the parties involved enable individuals to come to informed decisions over the diverse applications of gene technology?

CONVENTIONAL APPROACHES TO RESOLVING CLASHES OF VALUES AND INTERESTS

There are three conventional ways to deal with the debate on gene technology. First, the clashes in the debate are technological. A technology involves risks and benefits, or more precisely, how they are perceived by different groups in society. Any social decision on the acceptability of different applications must carefully balance these risks and benefits. Assessment of a technology attempts to anticipate its immediate and secondary effects on different areas of society: technological, environmental, economic, social, legislative, and political. Technology assessment, carried out by a government, is an important tool in developing public policies.

Second, the debate involves the interests of different segments of society and the issues that arise when their interests are blocked. These segments see facts (a political announcement, a social or technological change, a disaster) affecting their interests differently, and so they react differently. Issue management tries to understand the underlying interests and reconcile them in a public setting.

Finally, the debate is a broad and complex conflict. Conflicts have three components: attitudes, behaviors, and a situation. To resolve conflicts, one of these three components must be changed. Often the legitimate values and interests of the different parties may not be incompatible, but they may become hidden behind inflexible positions, especially as conflicts become prolonged. The difficulty is in separating the fundamental values and interests (which are not negotiable) from the demands and tactics (which can be changed) used protect and achieve them. Conflict management tries to guide the course of conflict so that the values and interests of the parties involved can be respected and the beneficial consequences can be maximized.

Both issue management and conflict management seek to reconcile legitimate interests and bring about an outcome that will allow the different parties to pursue them. More important, both offer a new perspective to the debate over gene technology.

Technology Assessment

Although governments in the past may have encouraged public debate over new technologies or developed policies on certain technological developments, there was no systematic approach. For the purposes of this discussion, the term *technology assessment* will be understood in a narrower sense, as a **systematic process** by which a government analyzes and anticipates the impact of a new technology on different areas of society in order to develop appropriate public policies.

Thus technology assessment often takes the form of scientific studies that try to predict or at least anticipate the various effects of technology in a region or country. Such assessments may include analysis of technical risk and studies of environmental, economic, and social impact.

> Technology assessment became a defined endeavour—some would even call it a movement—in the late 1960s. Its ambitious purpose is to assess the primary, secondary and derivative consequences of emerging or expanding technologies, including their tangible and intangible effects, over the intermediate to long term, on health, employment, communication or other aspects of life. It can involve a variety of methods: trend projection, polling of expert opinions, cost-benefit analysis. (Lowrance, 1985, p. 134)

A discussion of technology assessment should perhaps begin with a discussion of risk assessment, which is an inherent aspect. The implicit question is usually, How can a government or other public institution maximize the benefits of a technology while minimizing its risks and costs? Traditional risk assessment relied almost exclusively on mathematical models, in particular statistics and probabilities. These models tended to focus on the quantitative aspects of risks, for example, the value of property damage or the number of fatalities or injuries expected. The underlying assumption was that technical risks can be calculated. There was little room for the qualitative features of risks, for example, the degree of impact, the magnitude of loss, and the nature of loss, death, or injury (Freudenberg, 1992; Lowrance, 1985; Nelkin, 1985; Otway, 1992; Otway and Haastrup, 1989; Otway and Wynne, 1989; Slovic, 1987; Slovic, 1992).

Although technical experts saw risks in quantitative terms, the lay public saw them in qualitative terms. Experts, stressing their formal education and professional training, tended to dismiss the public's evaluation of risks as emotional or irrational because it did not always rely on calculable factors. In scholarly works this bias is often reflected in the contrast of *expert assessment* of risks (a term suggesting objective facts) and *public perception* of risks (a term suggesting subjective values). "Such experts are wont to contrast real risk with perceived risk, using real risk as a code phrase for expert (quantitative) risk assessment. The former is implicitly correct while the latter is incorrect. (Leiss and Chociolko, 1994, p. 31)." The result is often surprise and lack of comprehension on the part of experts and the institutions that hire them when confronted with an angry public resisting a project proposal or the introduction of a new technology that the experts deemed to carry low risks.

There are two parts to the problem of assessing risks. One part stems from the fact that in the past there were few means of integrating the values of nonscientists and the interests of communities into the process. Attempts to communicate risk through public inquiries, community meetings, or fact-finding panels often appeared to divide rather than bring together scientific and governmental specialists on one hand and the public on the other hand. The responsibility for this division did not rest on one side only:

> Charges of media bias or sensationalism, of distorted or selective use of information by advocates, of hidden agendas or irrational standpoints, and of the inability or unwillingness of regulatory agencies to communicate vital information in a language the public can understand are common. Such charges are traded frequently at public hearings, judicial proceedings and conferences, expressing the general and pervasive sense of mistrust felt by many participants towards others. (Leiss and Chociolko, 1994, p. 36)

The other part of the problem probably lies in the way organizers (often public officials) perceived and still perceive such efforts to communicate. There are three elements to consider: content, structure, and timing. The following discussion has been shaped as a contrast between what is frequently true and what should be true, that is, between a stereotype and an ideal. In addition, perhaps some of what is said about communication of risk applies to other aspects of technology assessment as well.

Content is the way the process of risk communication can be defined. If it is defined as a scientific or technical process, the content of a community meeting will be limited to technical problems and "hard" (quantitative) data. If that is less than what the community wants or expects, the "communications" exercise may do more harm than good by pitting different groups against one another. In contrast, if the process is defined as a social or communications process, a community meeting will be used as an opportunity for the public to raise their concerns and have them affect the final decision. The meeting will be a chance for different opinions to be heard and a wide range of options to be presented.

Structure is the way the process of risk communication is organized. If a public meeting is structured as a one-way exercise in imparting information, even if it is supposed to be a forum for discussion, it will be a question-and-answer session in which scientific experts give out information and answer technical questions. The public may ask questions and make comments, but their input will have little impact on the broader decision-making process. If, by contrast, a public meeting is structured as a two-way communications effort, there will be an opportunity for those concerned to make a contribution and for options to be considered. More important, there will be later opportunities for participants to follow up on the discussion and for organizers to show how input from participants has or has not been used. Follow-up is an essential part of the communications process: it establishes a pattern of behavior that demonstrates commitment to openness and willingness to listen and is thus a critical element of building credibility and trust.

Timing is when the public process of communication becomes official. It is as important as content and structure. Communications can be **reactive**, coming in at a later stage of risk assessment, as a response to pressure for greater openness and public input. Part of the mistrust mentioned by W. Leiss and C. Chociolko may stem from the fact that the official communication efforts were frequently left until long after the discussion in public and perhaps even in the media had taken place. Or, communications can be **proactive**, coming in at an earlier stage of risk assessment, as an initiative to maintain on-going public consultation and public involvement. Such early communications with nonscientific groups can allow different options to be considered, perhaps tried, and then integrated or rejected before a final decision is made.

Official public meetings are sometimes the *result* of mounting unofficial but public exchanges between officials and members of the community (Greber, Frech, and Hillier, 1994). In such situations, those affected may understandably become suspicious that decisions have already been taken without their input and perhaps even regard for their concerns. By the time a public meeting is called, participants have probably formed special-interest coalitions. Such a meeting also means that intangible interests have already been translated into tangible positions. The public meeting becomes an outlet for venting anger and frustration. Not unexpectedly, government officials, industrial representatives, or technical experts are likely to be accused of arrogance. Some participants may be concerned that the community's fears and anxieties will not be taken seriously. This perception is reinforced by attempts of officials and technical specialists to stay with "rational" (scientific) or "factual" (quantitative) data that the "experts" have prepared in advance.

A number of risk analysts, many of whom had some background or interest in the social sciences, came to realize that a purely technical assessment of risk was not enough. S. Lichtenstein, H. Otway, O. Penn, P. Slovic, D. von Winterfeldt, and B. Wynne, to name a few, recognized the need for better integration of both the technical and social assessments of technology. They slowly arrived at a fuller, multidimensional picture of risk that took into consideration factors that had previously been ignored. Still, however, the focus was on risk.

At least two factors led to a growth in the systematic assessment of the impact of technology in a broad social context in the second half of the twentieth century. One factor was calls for more public accountability on the part of business, industry, government, and other institutions. Another factor was the increased awareness that technology is not neutral, that it can have both positive and negative effects on people and the environment. Some of the practices of conflict management (see below) were also applied to technology assessment.

In the late 1980s, Denmark developed a special form of public meeting as part of technology assessment. A **consensus conference** involves "ordinary citizens with their different backgrounds in the assessment of technology" (Hansen and Grundahl, undated, p. 3). In a consensus conference, which lasts three days, a group of lay individuals tries to reach a consensus about political or social issues in a particular technological area. Members have the opportunity to raise key questions with a panel of technical, political, or ethical experts whom the group selects and agrees on. On the third day of the conference, the consensus of the lay group is formally presented to the public but as agreement of the lay group, rather than of Danish society as a whole (Hansen and Grundahl, undated; Joss and Durant, 1994). The goal of such conferences is to spark public debate on technical issues that have not yet been resolved. Since 1987, Denmark has had about half-a-dozen consensus conferences on gene technology in such areas as agriculture and industry, irradiation of food products, and the future of infertility (Hansen and Grundahl, undated). One conference led to a full debate in Parliament. In 1993 the Netherlands adopted the Danish innovation, although with some modifications in the intent and timing. In 1994 the United Kingdom held a consensus conference (Joss and Durant, 1994). In 1998 France held a consensus conference on gene technology, more specifically on its applications in food and agriculture. The results were integrated into a two-part parliamentary report presented to the government.

Issue Management

Issue management, which draws on experience in organizational communications and public affairs, looks at changes in society from the point of view of an organization, especially if these changes might affect its ability to satisfy its interests. Issue management, like conflict management (see below), focuses on resolving the underlying clash of values and interests (Bigelow, Fahey, and Mahon, 1993), but it tends to see the players involved in relation to one another as members of society.

Usually as an issue grows, so does the likelihood that the media and the government will become involved. If an issue is not resolved at an early stage, resolutions are likely to involve a public institution (Ansoff, 1980; Austrom and Lad, 1989; Bigelow et al., 1993; Cammillus and Datta, 1991; Ewing, 1980; Grunig and Repper, 1992; Mahon and Waddock, 1992). The public institutions involved could be legislatures, government departments, regulatory agencies, or the courts.

While there are many ways of defining issues (Bigelow et al., 1993; Chase, 1984; Ewing, 1980; Grunig and Repper, 1992; Mahon and Waddock, 1992), the definition given by B. Bigelow et al. is perhaps one of the most comprehensive:

> In general, issues are defined as developments that will have an impact on an organisation's performance and ability to meet its objectives . . . , and that are important in terms of resources required or precedents set. . . . Public issues are ones that involve multiple stakeholders with competing interests and involve some form of collective action. . . . While this collective action is often defined in terms of the public policy process, it may occur in arenas other than governmental ones such as bargaining with local communities or intersectoral collaborations. (Bigelow et al., 1993, p. 19)

Issues arise when there is a gap between the actual performance of an organization and the public perception of what that performance should be (Bigelow et al., 1993; Grunig and Repper, 1992). This discrepancy is the first of four possible stages in how an issue may evolve (Bigelow et al., 1993; Post,

1978). Again, Bigelow et al. provide one of the most comprehensive descriptions of the possible evolution of an issue. Instead of a linear development, they see a life cycle.

In the earliest stage, **emergence**, there is a gap between what is and what other segments of society think should be. Issues begin with facts that are signals of changes. "Facts are as diverse as changing demographics, economic or political trends, technological breakthroughs, crises, events (such as the election of new political leaders) or statements by public officials" (Bigelow et al., 1993, p. 21).

In the next stage, **interpretation**, those affected try to define what the issue is and what the implications for them might be. Some individuals or groups in society may believe that their values or interests are being ignored, shaken, or threatened. In other words, something important is at stake: a **stakeholder** is someone who can affect the outcome of a situation in which his or her values and interests are at stake. "Facts, in and of themselves are neutral. However the meanings different stakeholders ascribe to them are not" (Bigelow et al., 1993, p. 21).

In the third stage, **positioning**, the different stakeholders frame their interests in terms of positions. Different groups may be drawn into the issue and advocate a particular stance. Stakeholders may form coalitions. All sides try to sway public opinion in their favor.

Finally, in the fourth stage, **resolution**, the issue is debated and attempts are made to resolve it in a public arena. The outcome may take the form of new public policy, legislation, or regulation. Resolution may also, however, take place outside a governmental setting, if stakeholders agree on a settlement.

As Bigelow et al. point out, not all issues follow this cycle: they may be stopped or interrupted at any stage or may skip certain stages (especially in the context of a crisis). Other issues may affect the cycle. Different stakeholders may enter or leave the debate at different stages, affecting the evolution. In other words, some issues may follow a normal course of evolution toward resolution; others may become cyclical or enduring.

Although this book does not represent the point of view of any organization, it considers issue management particularly helpful in providing a better understanding of the relevance of gene technology to the interests of different segments of society. First this approach allows the identification of key players who have the potential to influence or to be influenced by the applications of gene technology. Second, this approach allows for the identification of the interests of these players, the way the current discussion affects them, and the way they can affect the outcome of the public discussion. Finally, together with conflict management, issue management it may offer alternative scenarios for allowing society to come to a decision over gene technology.

CONFLICT MANAGEMENT

Conflict management draws much from experience in international relations and industrial relations. Although the public debate over gene technology may not appear to have much in common with warring nations or labor disputes, the conflict management approach helps focus on some of the essential characteristics of all conflict.

Sources of conflict include limited resources, different values, incompatible objectives, and change itself, themes that surface time and again throughout this book as it explores the issues beneath the public controversy over gene technology. But what is conflict? Some use the term to refer to differences in attitudes: "For us *conflict* means *perceived divergence of interests, or a belief that the parties' current aspirations cannot be achieved simultaneously*" (Puitt and Rubin, 1986, p. 4, italics added). For others, the term is more comprehensive, describing "inconsistencies as well as the process of trying to solve them; [conflict] has physical and moral implications; [conflict] embraces opinions as well as situations and a wide range of behaviour" (Bercovitch, 1984, p. 3).

According to J. Bercovitch, drawing on the work of Galtung, conflict h as three components: situation, attitude, and behavior. Seen from this angle, one could thus describe the controversy surrounding gene technology as conflict.

A **conflict situation** is a position where the goals or values of different parties collide. Gene technology, like many new technologies, has brought about significant changes that have challenged old concepts, traditional methods, and established frameworks. As a result, the values and interests of different segments of society collide. (Some of these interests will be examined more closely later in this chapter.)

A **conflict attitude** is a conscious or subconscious mental process resulting in or arising from such a situation. As was discussed earlier in chapters 1 and 5, part of the controversy over gene technology comes from a conflict in attitude toward taking risks, toward life and nature, and toward the estimation of risk and benefits.

A **conflict behavior** is an action taken by one party to harm, hinder, or eliminate the other. In the gene technology controversy both sides have engaged in conflict behavior: when protest groups stage a demonstration or block access to fields where trials are carried out, when companies call in the police to remove the protesters, when environmental groups take companies to court over patents or over proposals to do field tests, or even when both sides launch publicity campaigns challenging the other side's positions or defending their own positions.

To enable individuals to come to informed decisions over gene technology, these three aspects of conflict must be managed. Managing conflict means "increasing . . . beneficial consequences and decreasing costs and harmful consequences" (Bercovitch, 1984, p. 7). As D. G. Puitt and J. G.

Rubin phrase it: "Conflict is the seedbed that nourishes social change" (1986, p. 6). In the long run, beneficial consequences of the conflict over gene technology may include, at the very least, a focus on the underlying values and interests of the parties involved, an opportunity to rethink and reassess technological society's relationship to nature and to life, a discussion on the values of technological society, a discussion on the controls necessary for gene technology, an opportunity to review a wide range of options for managing the costs and benefits of gene technology, and perhaps a clearer vision about future directions for society.

One potential cost of the conflict may be the stifling of technological innovation and social growth. The opposite—unlimited technological change—would be equally undesirable. Growth in society depends on vision, innovation, and taking risks but not at all costs and not without prudence. Other potential costs may include on-going or growing confrontations between different segments of society, the rise of the view that technological innovation and social progress are mutually exclusive, inability to balance the needs and goals of different segments of society, or simply polarization and entrenchment of differing views and positions.

Benefits can be increased and costs reduced by changing one of the three components of conflicts: attitudes, behaviors, or situation. Like issue management, conflict management focuses on reconciling the underlying clashes of values and interests. The process may make use of such tools as bargaining, mediation, negotiation, or some other form of third-party intervention to help achieve a desirable outcome for the parties involved (Burton, 1987). Third-party interventions may not be possible or desirable in resolving the conflicts over gene technology. However, the process of analyzing and highlighting fundamental values and interests is likely to be useful.

Although conflict management helps resolve conflict, it frequently looks at the problem in the narrow context of the conflict situation, in contrast to issue management, which tends to see the players involved as members of society. In the conflict over gene technology, one should not forget the broader picture.

IDENTIFYING THE INTERESTS AT STAKE
Whether it is called a social conflict or a public issue, an open controversy will have different meaning for different segments of the population. How the conflict evolves and how or if it is resolved will have different implications for different individuals or groups. Affected parties can and probably will try to influence the outcome of the conflict in favor of their own interests. Identifying who these parties are and where their interests lie can help provide these parties and observers with a better understanding of the various interests at stake—or at least what they perceive to be their interests. This understanding may help identify otherwise unforeseen obstacles and determine viable options.

Technology assessment, conflict management, and issue management can all provide much insight, but they have their limitations. Traditional technology assessment, as noted, has a tendency to favor quantitative data over qualitative information. One reason for this preference is the need for objective information that policy makers can use to make policy decisions to anticipate the impact of a new technology. However, as pointed out in chapter 5, technology is never divorced from human activities: it *is* a human activity. Thus, objectivity is difficult, if not impossible, to achieve. More recent forms of technology assessment include qualitative, or sociological, information as well. Nonetheless, even using consensus conferences, technology assessment is not sufficient to manage some of the more complex social dilemmas that new technologies pose. At best, it is only one way to help policy makers come to a decision about the impact of new technologies.

Both issue management and conflict management are limited in that they generally assume that the impact of an issue is concentrated in a particular political or geographical area and that there is, therefore, some degree of cohesion or framework in which to look for solutions. But even if that were true, the great differences in attitudes toward gene technology that exist in any given population seem to transcend all borders—political, social, or otherwise.

Furthermore, both issue management and conflict management assume that there are representatives that voice the concerns of those affected. In conflict management, it is clear that the resolution process will probably require representatives to negotiate on behalf of those affected. Often calls for third-party intervention is needed. But in complex conflicts over gene technology, which touch on so many aspects of modern life, it is difficult to find a third party who can be expected to remain neutral.

In issue management, it is understood that the boundaries between social groups tend to be fluid: individuals play different roles at different times. For example, a teacher can also be a concerned parent, a political conservative, and an active environmentalist. It is also assumed that individuals will often support a group that shares their main concerns and interests on a particular issue. In the gene technology debate, however, many of the organizations involved in public-awareness campaigns tend to present a completely positive or a completely negative image of gene technology. The media also tend to emphasize reports of either potential success or feared risks. Yet, if public opinion surveys are any indication (see "Differences in Social Acceptance of Gene Technology," chapter 2), many of those surveyed tend to hold complex, subtly distinct views of the various applications of gene technology.

In issue management, with its organizational orientation, the population is divided into passive stakeholders and active stakeholders called publics (Grunig and Repper, 1992; Lawless, Jones, and Jones, 1986).

> People are stakeholders because they are in a category affected by decisions of an organisation or if their decisions affect the organisation. Many people in a category of stakeholders—such as employees or residents of a community—are passive. The stakeholders who are or become more aware and active can be described as publics. (Grunig and Repper, 1992, p. 125)

Thus, passive stakeholders and active publics are defined in context of an issue but first of all and *always* in relation to the organization affected. There may be consumers protesting against genetically altered tomatoes that stay fresh longer, but if their action does not affect a company producing genetically altered enzymes for making cheese, that company would not be likely to consider these protesters as stakeholders or publics. In other words, the organization stands in the center of the issue. The media are usually seen as passive stakeholders because of their indirect influence on the public perception of the organization. Likewise, politicians can be either stakeholders or publics, depending on their ability to shape the issue in relation to the interests of the organization. This conventional approach may be useful for organizations trying to resolve specific issues, but it may not be the most appropriate for the complex, paradigmatic issue of gene technology. Neither is it appropriate for solving conflicts that require a different perspective and perhaps even vocabulary.

Despite the shortcomings of these conventional approaches, they offer many useful insights. The next section draws essential concepts from all three, especially issue management and conflict management. Both approaches assume that conflicts arise when legitimate values and interests are at stake. Both assume that resolution will have a short-term and long-term impact on the relationships between the parties in conflict. Both propose that the path to resolution starts by finding interests in common or at least that can be mutually satisfied.

This chapter also uses some of the tools of technology assessment, recognizing the need not only for better communications but also for meaningful ways for citizens to participate in the process of making public policy. Thus the chapter synthesizes the approaches of conflict management, issue management, and technology assessment. At the same time, it tries to provide an alternative approach to the debate.

A DIFFERENT APPROACH TO MANAGING CONFLICTING INTERESTS

As stated in chapter 5, the social acceptance of a new technology is a process in which individuals make informed choices about future directions that will affect them, their families, and society as a whole. In this context, individuals and groups will fight to make their interests known and make sure they are taken into consideration.

Thus, the challenge is to understand what interests are at stake for different groups. Drawing from the concepts of issue management and conflict management, the following discussion will try to identify

- who the main players are
- what their interests are
- how the gene technology debate can affect those interests
- how these players can affect the outcome of the debate

As pointed out earlier, neither approach is broad enough to solve the complexities of the gene technology debate. Such a solution requires a way of describing different segments of the population in relation to the impact of gene technology on their values and interests. The following terms are used in such an analysis.

Stakeholders are those who have a vital stake, or interest, in the outcome of the conflict. Examples are people who have genetic diseases, farmers contemplating adopting new varieties of crops or farm animals, and companies using products and processes of gene technology. Their success or failure in defending their interests will make a difference in their future, perhaps in their ability to survive.

Value advocates are those who have no direct interests at stake but whose values are threatened if the conflict goes against them. Examples include environmental groups and animal-welfare activists. They defend specific causes not necessarily because the changes affect their interests but because these changes are in conflict with their worldview. They are the people who, in the long run, launch important social changes.

Problem interpreters include the media in particular and, to a lesser extent, lobbying groups and advertising and publicity agencies. Their interests are staying competitive, reaching a wide audience, and making a profit. As a group, they have the power to shape the way others perceive a problem or conflict. By focusing on particular trends, events, or situations—whether it is the need for tougher pollution control or new treatments for cancer—the media magnify these issues for many segments of the population. At the same time, the comments of journalists, the angle they choose to highlight, and the editorial stance all influence public perception of issues. Lobbyists in certain countries such as the United States and publicity agencies also amplify and interpret issues, by drawing public and legislative attention to them.

Policy integrators are legislators and civil servants. In democratic systems, legislators are elected to put forward the interests of the voters. Their own interest is to do so in order that they may be reelected. Civil servants (advisers, regulators, or administrators) are supposed to provide legislators with the necessary support to carry out this mandate. Their interests are indirect because they are not elected. In legislatures, representatives of different values, interests, and perspectives of society come together in debate. Resolution of conflicts may come in the form of legislation and regulation or a change in government policy. Political realities often differ from this ideal, for example, differences in access to legislators, the influence of lobbyists on legislators and regulators, and the requirement to vote according to party line rather than conscience. Nonetheless, this book sees existing democratic processes and institutions as a means for integrating the values and interests of different segments of society.

A model for analyzing the effects of a paradigm change on different segments of society may be seen in figure 6.1. These segments are grouped according to the roles they play in shaping the outcome of the controversy. In the middle, closest to the change, are *stakeholders*. Surrounding and overlapping this central group are *value advocates*, *problem amplifiers*, and *policy integrators*. As this diagram shows, the paradigm change does not affect all players to the same degree. In addition, the players influence one another and also the external sociopolitical environment. Finally, other forces of change also have an impact on the outcome of the paradigm change, on the decisions of the different players, and on the whole sociopolitical environment.

Fig. 6.1 Effects of Paradigm Change on Different Segments of Society

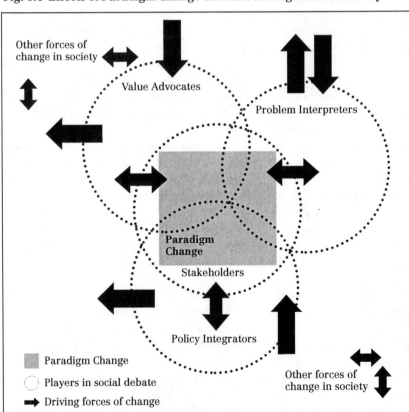

STAKEHOLDERS

A social conflict develops when one or more segments of society perceive certain changes in society as a threat to their values and interests, which give meaning and direction to their lives. As the conflict progresses, these values and interests, some of which may be intangible, become hidden behind the demands, slogans, and rhetoric of entrenched positions. Those most likely to be affected by the way the conflict is resolved will probably try the hardest to protect what they have at stake. Paul Sites, a behavioral scientist,

> placed power in a realistic perspective by attributing effective power, not to authorities but to individuals and groups of individuals pursuing their ontological needs. These individuals would use all means at their disposal to pursue certain human needs, subject only to constraints they imposed on themselves in their need to maintain valued relationships. (Burton, 1987, pp. 15-16)

Perhaps not surprisingly, this concept of linking power to the needs of existence recalls A. H. Maslow's theory that human beings are motivated by a hierarchy of needs. When basic needs have been met, another level of needs will develop. "And when these in turn are satisfied, again new (and still higher) needs emerge, and so on" (Maslow, 1970, p. 17). According to Maslow's hierarchy, there are five levels of basic needs (in ascending order): physiological needs, safety needs, belonging and love needs, esteem needs, and self-actualization needs.

Of particular interest to the current discussion are the first two levels. Physiological needs include nourishment, health, sexual satisfaction, and sleep. Safety needs include stability and security, freedom from fear and anxiety, and structure and order (Maslow, 1970). Many needs in these first two levels coincide with areas in which gene technology plays a role: health care and pharmaceutical production, agriculture and food production, environmental care. Some people may perceive these applications of gene technology as a threat to their ability to satisfy their basic needs, and they therefore bring powerful emotions to the conflict.

Because of these emotions and because of the wide range of applications of gene technology, it is difficult to identify all stakeholders. For example, individuals include patients hoping for treatment of a genetic disorder, a disease carrier contemplating starting a family with another carrier, those buying food, and those seeking environmentally friendly products. Therefore, the following sections will focus on some of the major groups of stakeholders.

Scientific Community

The scientific community is made up of different subgroups. Some work in academic institutions doing primary research or teaching; some work in industrial laboratories concentrating on viable products. Others work in government agencies, testing products or helping determine health or safety limits. Still others work in nongovernmental organizations such as the UN or in other nonprofit organizations. The interests identified in this discussion will not have the same urgency for these different subgroups.

Nevertheless, some interests are common to all scientists. The first is probably the need for clear guidelines on the minimum standards expected and the maximum freedom allowed. Sometimes, scientists establish their own standards and impose restrictions on their own research. For example, in 1975, not long after the first successful experiment in recombinant DNA, scientists in molecular genetics came together to discuss the implications of their work for public health. They proposed policy guidelines that were later adopted by the National Institutes of Health in the United States and by other research bodies around the world. Greater knowledge and experience in genetics research since that time have led many government regulatory bodies to soften or eliminate some of the stringent guidelines initially adopted (Berg and Singer, 1995; Cantley, 1995).

In general, scientists and researchers prefer to work in an environment of political and legislative stability. Given limited public or private funding and academic or industrial competitiveness, it becomes a question of priority what areas of research should receive attention. Clear guidelines in the form of policies or legislation provide direction. Guidelines can be seen as a form of social mandate to pursue research in certain areas while limiting or prohibiting work in other areas.

For scientists, especially in public institutions, a shifting political and legislative landscape makes it difficult to know what is expected or required and what is off limits. For example, in Germany differences in federal and state regulation make getting permits for projects an exercise in frustration for both academic and industrial researchers (Shlaes, 1995). Scientists everywhere need laws and regulations that reflect the current state of knowledge about their fields.

At the same time, scientists must be able to understand the needs of stakeholders outside the scientific community. Communicating with the nonscientific public requires skills different from writing scientific papers or addressing a scientific congress. But there are times when scientists have to enter into dialogue with groups from the larger community, either to talk about their own work or to discuss the community's concerns.

A second interest of the scientific community is having the freedom to do research without unnecessary interference, delays, or hindrance. Such freedom does not, of course, mean that scientists are free to do what they want. They are always subject to government legislation, organizational policies (especially of funding bodies), ethical review boards (which look at research proposals), and peer review of research methods and findings.

A third interest, especially of scientists in an academic or governmental setting, is in obtaining the on-going support of government funding agencies. At a time when governments in many industrialized countries are reducing the budgets in many areas of public service, research projects must compete with other programs, for example, in education, health care, and unemployment insurance. In addition, different areas of a discipline compete for the resources set aside for scientific projects—particle research with other areas of physics, genome research with other areas of biology, research on infectious diseases with other areas of medicine.

The gene technology debate has a profound impact on scientists doing work in genetics in two ways. The first is that the on-going uncertainty over social acceptance is a stumbling block for research efforts. Without definitive guidelines from society, or even a consensus on what such guidelines might be, research suffers delays in project approvals, interruptions during experiments, and even legal challenges in later stages of projects. Even if there were agreement on appropriate guidelines, it would not necessarily eliminate opposition. Dissension is a healthy and, indeed, necessary part of a pluralistic society based on choice. But guidelines would at least focus research and set priorities.

The second way debate on gene technology affects the scientific community is the selectivity of its decisions. An indiscriminate response would treat all applications of gene technology in the same way, regardless of their benefits and costs. Thus research in all areas would face the same future. A discriminating response would weigh each application for its merits and weaknesses, giving funding and priority to different areas. For example, the introduction of rigid controls for some applications would tend to discourage research in those areas; more flexible measures would probably have the opposite effect.

At the same time, members of the scientific community can have an impact on the outcome of the public debate. Scientists, particularly those at academic institutions, have a reputation of trust. In a disaster public officials, the media, and private citizens often turn to a scientist for answers—an analysis, a prediction, or perhaps an explanation. One likely reason for this trust is that scientists are seen as neutral figures who work with facts, without any obvious vested interests. Another reason is that academic scientists are not linked to industry. In public opinion surveys, scientists who work in industry are often deemed less trustworthy than their academic colleagues but are still considered more credible than managers from that industry.

The public should recognize, however, that scientists have a vested interest in the gene technology debate because it will affect the funding and priority of research. Moreover, some academic scientists are directly linked with industry. In addition, there seem to be important differences between the views of many scientists and the views of concerned individuals, which create differences in the risks perceived and the anxiety felt. Some scientists may find it difficult to discuss those risks or to take such anxiety seriously.

Despite their lack of neutrality, scientists can still help set the tone in public discussions. They can bring greater clarity to the debate by underlining the areas of agreement—between people with a background in biological sciences, genetics, and ecology—and acknowledging areas of uncertainty. Scientists can also take nonscientific considerations into account in their research and especially in their efforts to communicate it.

Disease Awareness and Research Associations

Another category of stakeholders are groups that organize public-awareness and fund-raising campaigns to encourage the prevention of, or research on, specific diseases or disorders, such as heart and stroke, cancer, cerebral palsy, muscular dystrophy, cystic fibrosis, and AIDS. Specific examples include the American Lung Association, the Imperial Cancer Research Fund in the United Kingdom, the Heart and Stroke Foundation in Canada, the Hereditary Disease Foundation (focusing on Huntington's disease) in the United States, and the Association française contre les myopathies (AFM—a muscular dystrophy association) in France.

Most of these disease awareness and research associations (DARAs) are set up as nonprofit organizations or charities. While the legal definitions of these terms vary from one jurisdiction to another, DARAs are usually organizations that are legally bound to direct most of the funds they raise toward a stated activity that benefits the community. Because most DARAs depend on donations from individuals and organizations, one of their chief interests is fund-raising, on which they often have to invest a lot of time and energy. Fund-raising is often an integral part of wider public-awareness campaigns, which highlight, for example, the number of people affected by a disease or its impact on individuals and society. They also point out the need for funding research for treatments or cures and underline the need for hope. Besides public-awareness campaigns, DARAs sometimes lobby legislators or government officials for more funding in public research programs or for speeding up regulatory review processes.

In their awareness campaigns DARAs often appeal for greater understanding and acceptance of individuals with disorders or diseases that carry a social stigma such as mental or physical disabilities and HIV or AIDS.

Another interest of most, if not all, DARAs is obtaining better public understanding of the needs of those affected. Still another interest is improving the scientific knowledge of the disease in question—how it occurs, how it develops and how it can be prevented or treated. The underlying concern is improving the quality of care available to those affected.

Since the rise of gene technology, medical projects such as human genome research and clinical experiments using gene therapy have attracted a lot of publicity and raised high hopes of potential cures for a wide range of diseases. Not all DARAs, however, think that medical technology is the best or only answer to the social problems surrounding disease and suffering. There is, as noted in earlier chapters, a wide range of opinions about the ethical questions surrounding genetic research, diagnosis, and therapy.

The AFM, representing one group in the range of DARAs, underscores the hope they place in the medical applications of gene technology. In 1991 it joined the Centre d'études du polymorphisme humain to create Généthon, the research facility that established one of the first complete physical maps of the human genome (see "The Human Genome," chapter 2). Another example of this group is the Hereditary Disease Foundation, set up by the husband of a woman with Huntington's disease (Miller, 1993).

The Swiss Association of Disabled People (Schweizerischer Invalidenverband, 1991), represents groups that take a different position from that of the AFM. They think that developments in human genetics have created a serious social dilemma that needs urgent discussion: the prevention of disabilities and the integration of disabled individuals. One of their biggest concerns is that the quest for genetic cures could increase the stigma associated with certain disorders, especially those leading to physical or mental disabilities. For example, prenatal diagnosis might lead to increased social pressure on expectant couples to abort fetuses predisposed to genetic disorders.

> People with hereditary diseases and disabilities fear that increasing access to genetic information through prenatal screening, together with the increasing acceptability of selective abortion of "defective" foetuses, will devalue them and their experiences, leading to increased discrimination against those who are physically different. (Nelkin and Lindee, 1995, p. 174)

Such pressure could come from public institutions, medical advisers, health insurance companies, or even family and friends. Where is the boundary between disorder and variation? What is *normal* in human terms? In the 1930s, those with mental disabilities were the first to be sterilized under eugenic laws (see "Eugenics," chapter 2).

These groups are concerned that genetic diagnosis has focused public attention on the eradication of genetic disorders rather than on the acceptance of individuals with disabilities (Schweizerischer Invalidenverband, 1991). They believe that after all, health and disease are both part of the human condition. There should be more focus on people as individuals, the diversity of human nature, and the dignity of the human person. For them, the biggest problem is the social problem of *discrimination* against people with disabilities, not the medical problem of disability itself.

Public opinion is critical to all DARAs. On one hand, a blanket rejection of gene technology would set back a lot of medical advances in the understanding of such genetic disorders as sickle-cell anemia, Huntington's disease, and cystic fibrosis. On the other hand, surveys in Europe and elsewhere, as noted in chapter 2, show considerable public support for applications of gene technology in both medication and direct genetic alteration of human tissues. Indeed, the determined efforts of DARAs in the search for treatments for cancer or AIDS would probably not have gone as far as they have without the financial support and goodwill of private donors.

Although DARAs are being affected by public debate, they also have an important voice in it. As stakeholders, they are likely to enjoy a high level of public credibility. People will probably give careful consideration to what they say and believe their commitment. There are at least two ways in which DARAs play an active role in the debate. First, they can show how the public debate has a direct impact on the lives of individuals, thus revealing the human face of the debate, which is often obscured. The plight of the individual cancer patient, for example, is a powerful appeal to instincts and emotions. The danger is that such appeals to the heart can easily be misused or misinterpreted as a sort of emotional blackmail. There is also a risk that the problems of one individual can become generalized to the whole group or even to other groups, which the individual does not necessarily represent. Thus, the fine line between emotional appeals and emotional blackmail must be scrupulously respected. Otherwise DARAs will lose their credibility in the public mind.

The second way DARAs influence the debate is by helping to highlight the complexity of the dilemmas that gene technology raises, especially in discussions on ethical issues. Their wide range of attitudes toward gene technology is good and perhaps even needed: decisions over gene technology are not simple binary choices—to have it or not to have it. Rather they involve a host of complex questions with benefits to some, costs to others, and dilemmas for many.

Health-Care Industry

At the end of the twentieth century, one of the biggest challenges of industrialized countries is meeting the health-care needs of an ageing and increasing population. In such countries as the United States, France, the United Kingdom, Switzerland, and Germany, health-care professionals face the additional challenge of continuing to provide the best care possible while governments restrict health-care budgets or limit access to the health-care system. At the same time, health-care professionals are expected to keep up with the latest developments in diagnosis, treatment, or cures. In the United States, for example, "litigation has established the physician's obligation to warn patients of potential problems if it is possible to gather such information through diagnostic technologies" (Nelkin and Tancredi, 1989, p. 56).

Because health matters affect everyone, the medical issues surrounding gene technology are likely to attract a lot of attention from the media, legislators, and regulators, as well as other segments of society. The medical applications of gene technology will affect the tools and quality of health care that professionals can provide. The outcome of the debate will affect both medical science (which involves theories and research) and clinical practice (which deals with the well-being of individuals).

In the area of medical science, decisions on human genome research may help scientists understand better how genes relate to the various processes of life. Likewise, decisions on the use of transgenic animals can have some bearing on further research on the origins of diseases and on their treatments. Decisions on the use of genetically altered microorganisms in pharmaceutical production may have an impact on many segments of the population. Decisions on gene-based medical procedures (for example, genetic diagnosis, gene therapy, or transgenic animal donors) may affect some people more directly than others.

In the area of clinical practice, the safety aspect of clinical trials will influence public decisions about different applications of gene technology, whether new drugs or new therapies. These decisions (support or resistance) in turn will determine whether such trials continue.

As it is influenced by public debate, the health-care industry in turn has an impact on that debate. Health-care professionals, especially those in medicine, enjoy a reputation for care and integrity. Moreover, they have no obvious financial or other interests at stake in the outcome. In addition, most have not yet taken a stance and are consequently perceived to be neutral. For all these reasons, their voices are credible, and the opinions carry weight.

Health-care professionals influence the debate in a number of ways. First, many people see the technological benefits to the health-care industry as benefits for individual patients and for society as a whole. As discussed in chapter 2, there appears to be a high level of public acceptance of gene technology applications that will solve serious medical problems, for example, cancer or infectious diseases. If it is true that health care remains a prime concern for many people, then health-care professionals are likely to play an important part in the public debate over gene technology.

Second, research in, and applications of, gene technology have produced new knowledge, tools, and methods that are concrete advantages to individuals and society. Thus, if the health-care industry benefits from this technology, that translates into benefits for society as well. Conversely, if the health-care professionals reject certain medical applications of gene technology, that is also likely to send a strong signal to the nonmedical public.

Finally, health-care professionals are influential because they already enjoy a degree of familiarity with large segments of the population. They serve an important "cross-border" function: on one hand, their formal education and training place them in the same category as other professionals in science and technology; on the other hand, their work means they have more frequent—indeed, daily—contacts with nonscientists.

Pharmaceutical and Biotechnology Industries

Two points need to be made here. First, there are overlaps between the health-care and pharmaceutical industries and between the health-care and biotechnology industries. Some see health care as the umbrella term covering all areas that deal with the health needs of society. Others prefer a more structural view, in that health care in many countries was once the domain of government bodies (one referred to the health-care *sector* rather than the health-care *industry*); pharmaceutical production was the domain of private enterprises. Health-care providers were concerned primarily with services, while pharmaceutical companies dealt with the production of drugs. Today, however, the distinction between the health-care and pharmaceutical industries is blurring. In an effort to cope with rising costs and diminishing public resources, many governments are moving toward privatizing government-run health-care services, for example, turning state-run hospitals over to private citizens or shifting health-care costs to private health insurance companies.

The second point is that there are also significant overlaps between the pharmaceutical and biotechnology industries. For the most part, though, these two industries differ in their history, structure, and business focus. Many pharmaceutical companies tend to be relatively old; many are multinational corporations—often with research, production, and distribution facilities in different countries. Most if not all were originally based on chemical analysis, synthetic chemistry, and biochemistry. They may have used microorganisms for fermentation as part of production, but biotechnology was not (and often still is not) their main business focus. Many of these companies have added gene technology to their research, development, and production efforts.

In comparison, biotechnology firms tend to be younger: the earliest were founded in the mid-1970s in the United States. Most came into existence after 1980. The majority are small firms: according to a survey, 75 percent of the biotechnology firms in the United States and 81 percent of those in Europe have fewer than fifty employees (Ernst and Young, 1995). The most important difference from the pharmaceutical industry is that the new biotechnology firms are based primarily on the science, tools, and techniques of biology, in particular molecular biology. Their business activities focus on biological systems, processes, and products for use in one or more of the following areas:

- health care—diagnostics, prevention, and therapeutics
- farming—new breeds of plants and animals and protection of plant and animal health
- industrial products or services—such as enzymes and proteins
- environmental care—including pollution diagnostics, prevention, and cleanup

As with health care and pharmaceuticals, the distinction between the pharmaceutical and biotechnology industries is also blurring. For one thing, biotechnology and gene technology will provide both with important tools for research, development, and production—not just in human medicine but also in veterinary care, plant protection, and environmental management.

In the public debate on gene technology, many interests of the pharmaceutical and biotechnology industries are similar, if not the same. Both need new ideas for research, development, and production. For both the constant search for innovation is driven by one or more of the following factors: unsolved problems; problems requiring more effective solutions; competition for market shares through products that are more effective, are less costly, or have fewer undesirable side effects. Sometimes the drive for new products comes from changing consumer expectations or new government regulations, for example the trend toward environmentally friendly products, such as biodegradable enzymes in washing powder.

Both the pharmaceutical and biotechnology industries are heavily regulated in such areas as worker safety, health effects of products, environmental impact of products and processes, hazardous waste disposal, pollution control, and even product pricing. These industries, then, need a stable legislative and societal environment in which to achieve their missions. This need also reflects their basis in science, which requires experiments, fixed rules, standard procedures, and control factors for comparison.

Both the pharmaceutical and biotechnology industries, like any other industry, have to meet their business, ethical, legal, and environmental obligations. They have to apply gene technology in a responsible way, obeying rules and guidelines and respecting both the letter and the spirit of the law. Exclusivity rights, for example, should not be misused. They also have to deal with the social and ethical issues that gene technology raises.

Like other industries, the pharmaceutical and biotechnology industries must protect their investments and property. The current patent system is a challenge for them because the difference between the twenty years of patent protection and the ten to fourteen years it takes to develop and approve a product is only six to ten years (Canibol, 1994). That is not a long time in which to sell a new product under patent protection. These figures have several implications for these industries. Investments in R&D require both long-range planning and a long-term commitment; they cannot be turned on or off at will. Moreover, there must be enough time to enjoy the return on the R&D investment.

The ability to make and carry out long-term plans is important to industry, especially where new technology is concerned. Investment in a new technology is costly in itself and means less capital for other needs. Industry requires a firm legislative and regulatory framework in which to make investment choices and determine costs and timing. When it decides to invest, industry has to acquire the new technology. The installation of new equipment requires capital investment and long-term commitment. Personnel must be trained to use it. From concept to reality, it could take ten years or more for such technology to become fully operational.

The public debate over gene technology is very much a sociopolitical debate with serious implications for both the pharmaceutical and the biotechnology industries. On one hand, government policies, legislation, and regulation shape the legal-political environment that determines the ability of these industries to meet their needs—the degree of freedom to make decisions. On the other hand, social acceptance will have an impact on their research and investment priorities. Their success and perhaps even survival depend on public support. Without it, these industries will find it more costly to achieve their goals and will face an uncertain political environment that is unfavorable to long-term investment plans.

These industries thus have an interest in fostering the public understanding and support that will create the stable environment they need. That environment does not happen by itself. It is built on trust and mutual respect. Trust has to be earned. As discussed in chapter 1, it requires openness, truthfulness, and the willingness to share knowledge and experience. The attitudes and behavior of the pharmaceutical and biotechnology industries will determine their ability to earn trust. Earning trust requires that they be willing to listen to, and able to respond to, the concerns of different groups in society. Obviously, such listening and response should not be simply short-lived outreach exercises during times of crisis but on-going efforts at dialogue and cooperation. The pharmaceutical and biotechnology industries should also be able to show shared interests with other segments of society. Finally, they should demonstrate goodwill toward, and faith in, these segments.

Farming and Food Production Industries
In some ways, the basic interests of the farming community have not changed much throughout history. The primary challenge is to assure a bountiful harvest within the constraints of seasons, terrain, pests, diseases, and inconsistencies of nature. Modern farmers also face new struggles such as satisfying the needs of a growing urban population with declining human resources. To cope, they must often rely on technology while respecting the constraints of health and environmental safety regulations. In countries such as the United States, small farmers feel that they are at a disadvantage when competing with the large factory-farms that can afford new technologies, equipment, or breeds of plants and animals.

The food production industry is a specialized extension of the farming industry. With the increasing specialization that comes with industrialization—the food-processing activities of the traditional farm have grown into a food production industry, which is part of the chain that serves urban consumers. Because the majority of supermarket chains manufacture many of the products they sell, they also are part of the food production industry.

In many industrialized countries, there are a number of large food-pro-cessing companies and some smaller ones, resulting in a lot of competition. The larger producers have the advantage of economies of scale. The smaller producers can better meet the needs of local customers in specific market niches. For the larger companies in particular, the most serious challenge is the growing number of health-conscious consumers, many of whom want to know the origins of the food they buy—where it is from, how it is produced, and how it is handled or packaged. Because many consumers today expect taste, quality, and value for their money, they are willing to pay more for produce from small local farms or for bio-food items (produced without chemical fertilizers or pesticides).

The interests of farmers and food producers coincide to some degree. Their main interests lie in anticipating or responding to consumer needs and expectations along a long distribution chain including middlemen (wholesalers and marketing boards), industrial customers (food-processing companies or supermarkets), and individual customers. Thus it is in their interest to ensure the quality of the products that reach the market: meat and milk from healthy, undiseased animals, or fresh fruit and vegetables undamaged by pests. Likewise, the sound management of existing farm land and other natural resources is important because they contribute to these products.

With or without gene technology, farmers and food manufacturers will still have to meet market demands. The main impact of the gene technol-ogy debate on farmers is that it will determine the options available to them in meeting those demands—options in fighting pests and diseases, develop-ing sturdier or more nutritious crops, maintaining animal health, and improving animals breeds.

At the same time, farmers must decide which applications of gene tech-nology will best serve their interests. Several factors will influence their deci-sions. An important factor is government programs, such as farm subsidies, and whether they are managed in a way that is fair to smaller and larger farms. Market pressure from middlemen and consumers is equally impor-tant in shaping farmers' decisions. Finally, other pressures, such as the abil-ity of farmers to compete in domestic or export markets, will influence farmers' decisions. If investing in gene technology will push costs (and the selling price) too high, they will be less receptive to it.

Farmers could affect the outcome of the debate over gene technology either way. Many small U.S. farmers have already joined the opponents of gene technology because they feel it poses a threat to their livelihood. In their eyes it gives an unfair advantage to the factory-farms, which can afford the new technology. The role of the factory-farm operations and of food processors is still uncertain. Because their large size makes them seem more like traditional industries in public perception, they will probably face some of the same problems of trust that traditional industries do.

Food producers will, in turn, be affected by the public debate. For example, in the preparation of food, high heat is sometimes needed to kill microbial activities, ensuring quality and safety but often destroying taste, color, and sometimes essential nutrients. To correct this loss, processors may use coloring, flavoring, or other additives, which may change the look or taste of the final product. Some food producers are looking at genetically altered produce that would keep its original flavor and nutritional value in the manufacturing process.

Despite such advantages of gene technology, producers will be affected by consumer opinion and market pressure in deciding whether to accept it. In opinion polls, gene technology in the area of food receives low support. In addition, many consumers who oppose gene technology have great flexibility in that they do not always have to buy processed foods, such as frozen dinners or canned soups. For other items, such as cheese, they can buy from producers who do not use gene technology.

Financial and Investment Community
The goal for investment portfolio managers, private investors, and financial advisers is maximizing returns on investment while minimizing losses. Investors are an important source of capital for companies. One of their main interests is obtaining a profit on their investments, while their advisers want to help them find secure places to invest. For new enterprises, outside investors can mean the difference between success and failure because they provide an important source of funds for research and development.

Uncertainty and lack of clear direction make investment a risk venture. If a given situation (economic, political, or social) is not stable, a company is likely spend a lot of time, money, and energy just managing controversies. Such a company will be rather unattractive to investors, who rely on stability for security. In the public debate on gene technology a decision will help clarify the current ambiguity and send a signal to the financial and investment community about future directions.

Given the current atmosphere in the United States and much of Europe, the financial and investment community will probably have more impact on some areas of gene technology than others. Applications in pharmaceutical and health care are more likely to attract investment for several reasons. First, the majority of the public can see clear, concrete benefits for both individuals and society. Second, investments from large pharmaceutical companies provide a degree of stability in research and development agendas and also a lead for smaller or private investors. Third, academic institutions and government health agencies, which are also involved in genetic research in the field of health care, are still trusted. In Europe, schools and universities consistently rank high on the list of organizations "most likely to tell the truth" (Marlier, 1993, p. 83; European Commission, 1996, pp. 69–70).

In contrast, the farming sector is less likely to attract investments. First, although a few large factory-farms may have investors, the many small farms are family-owned operations. Second, government intervention in the form of marketing boards or subsidies lessens the need for investment. Finally, many small-farm owners, especially in the United States, already fear that genetically altered crops and animals will give the bigger farm operations an advantage over them and so threaten their livelihood. Many have joined Jeremy Rifkin in a protest against the use of gene technology in farming and food production.

As these two examples show, the impact of the financial and investment community on the public debate is likely to vary from industry to industry. Industries that have broad ranges of potential products or methods are more likely to attract investors, and more investment means more capital for development for present and future projects.

Nevertheless, the investment community is unlikely to have a *direct* impact on the debate because the issues are technological and social rather than financial. Also investors focus their attention and money on specific companies, rather than on any particular technology. In addition, a certain amount of research, especially in medicine, is developed in academic, government, or even nonprofit programs, where investors have little or no direct influence.

Health and Life Insurance Industry

The business of insurance is, by nature, concerned with risks and chance. The insurance industry takes on risks that individuals, organizations, or governments cannot or will not assume. Not all individuals, however, are subject to the same degree of risk, nor can everyone afford to bear the costs incurred. The insurance industry fulfills an important social function by spreading the costs of such risks over a wider population base.

The insurance industry must provide coverage at reasonable premium rates to insured parties while minimizing losses through poor risk assessment. It prefers applicants with low health risks and either excludes, or charges a higher premium to, those with higher risks (Nelkin and Tancredi, 1989). "Insurance works on the principle that a policy-holder pays according to the degree of risk he or she brings to the insurance fund. So high-risk individuals pay more, low risks pay less" (Masood, Lehrman, Shiermeier, Butler, and Nathan, 1996, p. 389).

The accuracy of premium calculations thus rests on the ability to predict the likelihood of a risk in a large population: the greater the likelihood, the higher the premium. This is a relevant point in the gene technology discussion. Health and life insurers need to obtain as detailed and accurate a background as possible of the persons to be insured, including previous illnesses, family medical history, and lifestyle. Genetic information and diagnosis can help make the profile of an applicant much clearer, including *likelihood* or *probability* of his or her predisposition to a genetic disorder. With this greater knowledge comes the responsibility of the industry to inform its potential clients about the interpretation of genetic information and how it affects insurance policies.

The health insurance industry has two overriding interests. The first is to improve its ability to make accurate assessments of applicants' potential health risks so that they can be classified according to the level of risk assumed (Nelkin and Tancredi, 1989). The second is to prevent abuse of the insurance system through false claims or invalid information. Fairness means that both the insurance company and the client have access to information that would affect the nature of the risks assumed. Otherwise, there may be a risk of "adverse selection or anti-selection," that is, those more likely to be at risk will want to obtain insurance, while those in lower risk categories will want to avoid or delay buying it (Masood et al., 1996). Genetic diagnosis raises the stakes for both insurers and applicants. For many people, the use of genetic diagnosis already has the appeal of an infallible oracle. However, the novelty of this procedure means an element of uncertainty that both applicants and the industry must weigh. Tests indicate only probability, not certainty.

The gene technology debate will affect the insurance industry in several ways. Advances in various areas of genetic research will affect the definition of health risks. On the one hand, discoveries in the human genome are likely to provide more information about the role of genes in how diseases develop. Gene therapy will redefine health risks and health-care options as diseases once considered incurable become curable. More treatment options may possibly change the health risks that insurers are willing to underwrite. On the other hand, the fear of discrimination based on genetic information may prevent people from taking genetic tests. If insurers force applicants to do so, this action may be considered an abuse of individual rights and may lead governments make laws to prevent such abuses. In the United States, where health insurance is often not publicly funded, a number of states have enacted laws that "prohibit insurers from denying coverage on the basis of genetic test results, and prohibit the use of this information to establish premiums, charge differential rates, or limit benefits" (Hudson, Rothenberg, Andrews, Kahn, and Collins, 1995, p. 392; Masood et al., 1996). Similar concerns can be found in other countries: France and the Netherlands have imposed moratoria on genetic testing for insurance purposes; the British Parliament has asked the insurance industry to define its position on this issue or face regulation (Dickson, 1995). Meanwhile, Belgium, Austria, and Norway have imposed an indefinite ban on the insurance industry either to ask for a test or to obtain information from previous tests (Masood et al., 1996).

The health insurance industry will affect the public debate according to the role of private health insurers in particular countries. The ability or willingness of health insurers to establish an industry-wide policy on the use of genetic information will affect the public view of genetic diagnosis and genetic counseling. Health insurers will have to address policy issues surrounding the appropriate use and limits of genetic information such as compulsory DNA testing, confidentiality, invasion of privacy, and responsibility in storing or transmitting genetic information. Health insurers are unlikely to have much of an influence on the acceptance of other applications of gene technology.

VALUE ADVOCATES

Value Advocates are a broad category of groups, which can be classified roughly by four main areas of focus: the environment, biotechnology, consumer advocacy, and developmental aid. Other groups include human-rights organizations and religious bodies. Some depend partially on government grants; others rely primarily on private donations. Yet others are affiliated with a major organization. These different groups may have different causes and goals, but often they also have shared visions and interests.

Most of them face the challenge of alerting the public and government to existing problems or injustices in society. The formation of such advocacy groups is often the first sign of change in the social climate. Although they may start as small collectives trying to bring problems to the attention of established institutions, they can grow rapidly and gain broader support. If need be, they will use protests and public demonstrations to draw attention to a particular situation and thus galvanize the wider community into response.

Often these groups do not reflect the mainstream thinking or belong to established institutions. Because they address the concerns of a small group of people they are called special-interest groups. These special interests, however, can become the interests of a wide cross-section of society if more and more people feel that they are also affected. Because of their initial small size and local origin, many of these groups remain relatively small and decentralized. Thus they can stay close to those who are affected, and all members can play a part in initiating change.

Greenpeace provides a good example of such groups. In 1971 a dozen Canadians in Vancouver formed a group to protest the testing of nuclear weapons in Alaska by the United States. Since then, Greenpeace has become a world presence with its headquarters in Amsterdam. It has the ability to challenge some of the world's largest business corporations—and win. Despite its size and power, Greenpeace has retained the image of being anti-establishment. It has also remained highly decentralized, with local sections retaining much control over local matters. Individual members thus have an opportunity to participate in local decisions, which gives them a sense of empowerment that is important in the context of the helplessness that some feel in the face of technological growth. Here lies part of the success of locally based value-advocate groups. Rather than waiting for industry, university, or government to move, individuals themselves take action as members or supporters of these groups.

Whatever cause they work for, value advocates generally represent the rights and interests of those who might otherwise not be heard: disenfranchised people, opponents of gene technology, animals as living entities, the Earth and the environment. Many of these organizations advocate an alternative, whole-system view of the world rather than the reductionist perspective often associated with industrialized societies. This worldview extends from relationships within human society to other living things and the environment.

For example, many developmental-aid groups are concerned not only with the growing gap between technologically developed countries and countries rich in natural or biological resources, but also with the gap in modern technological society between those who have access to new technology and those who do not. Likewise, many environmental groups emphasize the integral bonds between human society, technology, and the environment. They argue that the environment sustains all life on earth; we tamper with it at our own peril.

This integral approach is one reason for discussing all value advocates together rather than looking at them as specific subgroups, as was done with stakeholders. Another reason is that value advocates readily form coalitions on specific questions. For example, environmental groups, animal-rights activists, and opponents of gene technology have joined to protest patents on a wide range of innovations in gene technology.

Understanding the integral view or holistic approach is key to understanding many of the points of confrontation in gene technology. The differences between the holistic approach of value advocates and the specialist focus of certain stakeholders underline important differences in values and interests that lie at the heart of the social conflict. It is perhaps useful to consider some of these differences in greater depth at this point.

As stated in chapter 5, modern technological society and its institutions, universities and industry, in particular, are based on the specialization of knowledge, skills, and activities, and on the streamlining of processes and products for mass production and mass consumption. Specialization is required because it would be difficult for any individual or organization to master all technical knowledge and industrial activities. Nor is there room for exceptions, things that do not belong to one of the predefined and streamlined categories.

Value advocates are the by-products of modern technological societies. By definition, they represent those whose interests are not satisfied by a mass-production approach or a mass-consumer society. To reconcile these differences, value advocates champion a whole-system worldview that would accommodate the interests of all groups in society.

Many of the issues raised in the debate over gene technology exist independently of gene technology and affect most of the value advocates: the equitable distribution of wealth between industrialized and industrializing nations, the value of local people's knowledge and use of indigenous natural resources, the use of animals as food and in research, the prevention of environmental pollution, and the need to preserve biodiversity. Many value advocates that have been actively working with such issues can claim some degree of expertise, which gives them a high degree of credibility in the eyes of the public.

The conflicts over these issues in the context of gene technology have various origins. One is the concern that this new technology will aggravate existing imbalances and problems. Another is the desire to prevent the advocates of this new technology from adopting attitudes and decisions similar to those that led to existing problems. A third is distrust on both sides probably based on past contacts as adversaries.

For some of these value advocates, the debate may have provided an opportunity to raise other concerns, even if not all participants agree on their importance. An example is concerns raised by some animal-welfare groups over transgenic farm animals used in gene pharming (see "Gene Pharming," chapter 2). They oppose such experiments on the grounds that they are cruel to animals or violate the dignity of the animal. Proponents of gene pharming disagree, arguing that the animal is not injured. They point out that the high costs of such experiments are incentives to make sure that these animals are kept in good health.

In some areas, both sides of the debate will agree that a discussion is beneficial. Many animal-welfare activists and environmentalists are concerned that animals in modern technological society are seen more as marketable commodities than sentient beings. Others disagree, pointing out that animals have been used as food and traded as commodities from earliest times. Whether the different sides reach a consensus or not, such discussions may provide a useful forum for talking about how people in modern technological society relate to the living world around them. As a result, all parties gain a better understanding of the values underlying that society.

In the 1993 and 1996 Eurobarometer surveys, most people chose environmental and consumer organizations as the most reliable sources of information (Marlier, 1993; European Commission, 1996). For example, in the controversy over the Brent Spar in 1995, most people chose to believe the data that Greenpeace provided, even though it later turned out to be wrong. Greenpeace apologized to Shell for exaggerating the potential damage and survived with its reputation intact (Rohwedder, Nelson, Kamm, and Pope, 1995). A large part of that credibility comes from the fact that as these groups operate at the local level, they are in tune with what people at the grassroots are saying and can speak the same "language." Their messages make sense to people because they reflect popular concerns. Also, most of them do not stand to make any direct financial gains in winning their causes. Most have earned a reputation for being trustworthy and have been proven right in the concerns they raised. In the debate over gene technology, these value advocates have the ability to rally public opinion to their support.

The power of these groups lies in their ability to form coalitions to mobilize quickly and efficiently different forces in society and the necessary resources. They can galvanize alert but passive segments of the public into action if needed. In 1995 Rifkin formed a coalition of religious organizations—Christian, Jewish, Muslim, and Hindu—called In the Name of God to oppose patenting in gene technology.

Their credibility and their ability to mobilize other interested parties make value advocates key players in the gene technology debate. But it is not certain how the different groups, holding different views, will influence one another. Some groups see gene technology as an opportunity to find new solutions to existing problems. Other groups stand clearly opposed to the technology because the potential risks and hazards are still unknown. Yet others find themselves somewhere between these two poles, recognizing the potential for benefits but also taking into account the need for an ethical and legal framework to minimize risks.

PROBLEM INTERPRETERS

The media serve as interpreters in the gene technology debate. They play an important role in the information society. Newswire services play a vital part in the gathering and distribution of news. They provide links between local and international news bureaus. They are an important source of news for many other news agencies, especially those with a limited number of offices.

The media can be classified according to the interests of the media agencies. The general media have broad interests. Specialized media focus on specific areas, such as finance or a particular industry. The media can also be classified according to format, which affects their needs. The print media—newspapers, magazines, and journals—use the printed word. They rely on colorful quotes, sometimes supplemented by photographs or graphics. The electronic media—radio and television—use air waves to carry sound and, for television, visual images. They can go on the air quickly, offering live, up-to-the-minute reports. In that sense, they offer the biggest competition for daily newspapers, which were once the source of the latest news. Today, stories tend to appear in newspapers the day after they have been broadcast on radio or television. The spread and speed of such broadcasts have resulted in fundamental changes for newspapers. Rather than just reporting on events, they now provide in-depth analysis of "yesterday's news." Televised news provides no depth—an average news item is about twenty seconds long. Current affairs programs such as *60 Minutes* in the United States or *Spiegel TV* in Germany may provide longer, more detailed reports but usually cannot fully explore complex problems.

Despite their differences, all media have many interests in common. The first is to get the story quickly and accurately. This may not be easy, for journalists and editors face a number of obstacles. Journalists have to meet deadlines. The newspaper has to go to press on schedule; the program has to go on air on time. But the journalist is dependent on reliable sources—a witness, an insider, an expert—who may not be available or willing to provide information. Expected to give fair coverage in a controversy, journalists must present both sides of the story. Complex issues may have several sides with many factors to consider, but the pressure of time or space may not allow an opportunity to deal with such complexities. When sources themselves have a stake in the controversy, the job of the journalist becomes even more difficult.

At the same time, journalists may also face a conflict between telling a story "right" or telling it the way the bosses want it. Although journalists may cover a story, editors often decide which items appear on the news and which do not. They also decide what is said in an article and what is left unsaid. This selectivity is important, because information, or the lack of it, shapes people's perceptions and choices. For example, if a majority of news reports focus exclusively on the potential hazards of a technology, or even the containment measures in place to prevent accidents, then people will probably suspect that this technology is dangerous.

The political leanings of a newspaper or its owner may also shape the content of news. This influence is probably more true in Europe, where newspapers are often associated with certain political views. For example, in the Britain, the *Daily Telegraph* tends to be conservative, whereas the *Guardian* leans more toward the left. In Germany, the *Frankfurter Allgemeine Zeitung* tends to be on the right, while the *Frankfurter Rundschau* favors the left. In the United States, newspapers are supposed to be neutral observers. This objectivity is changing, however, as the media have increasingly become watchdogs of society. According to D. Nelkin, journalistic objectivity is an American concept, partly because of the growing influence of science in the nineteenth-century United States.

> Central to this attitude was the belief that facts, standing above the distorting influence of interests and pressures, can and should be distinguished from values. The press in effect adopted the ideals of science at a time when science was coming broadly accepted as an apolitical basis of public policy, a model for rationality in public affairs. (1993, p. 92)

Far more than political leanings, economics has a powerful influence on the news. One of the biggest pressures on editors is meeting the bottom line. Plain economics determines the size of the news staff and other resources available. The size of the staff affects what news is covered and what is not, and the depth of the coverage. In larger news agencies or newspapers there may be reporters or even editorial departments responsible for specific "beats"—finance and economics, law, politics, science and technology, medicine, or arts and culture. The reporters and editors in these beats usually have an educational background or working experience in the field they cover. In many of the smaller and even some mid-size newsrooms, however, the lack of staff means that the same journalist must cover political, community, scientific, medical, and legislative events. Without special training in a particular field, a journalist may not be equipped to deal with the complexities of a stories in this area. This is an important point for news reports on gene technology.

Economic pressures also stem from the need to maintain a steady revenue base. State-owned radio or television stations can rely on state financing or on license fees. For privately owned newspapers, however, advertising is usually the biggest source of revenue. It accounts for about 65 percent of a newspaper in the United States. This fact has made editors and publishers, especially in smaller operations, careful not to offend their bigger advertisers.

In many countries, there has also been a trend toward the consolidation of media ownership. Although most owners are content to leave the day-to-day running of the newsroom to their editors and journalists, the owners' preferences do influence the choices of their employees as to what stories appear and how they are covered. The concentration of media ownership means that a smaller number of people have the power to influence what the majority of consumers read, hear, or watch.

The first interest of the media is to stay competitive, not only as a news leader but also as a business. Being a news leader means being the first to report an event and being able to do it accurately. Their reputation depends on a consistent record of bringing valid and accurate information to consumers. Their second interest is to reach a wide audience. In reporting specialized events, such as in law, economics, or science, the journalist must often explain complicated matters to an audience that does not have a specialized knowledge. Reaching a wide audience is also a business objective because it is critical for attracting advertisers, who want to reach a broad consumer market. Finally, the media have an interest in profitability. As already noted, most privately owned media derive most of their revenue from advertising.

Issues that involve wide cross-sections of society, like those surrounding gene technology, tend to have a long life in the media, lasting several months or even years. During this time, the media will shape the news and information that most people receive and use as the basis for forming opinions and making decisions.

The outcome of the gene technology debate will have limited impact on the media industry itself. For the most part, the debate is just one more topic to cover. But the debate process may have some effect on the needs of the industry. For example, as the debate becomes more heated, there may be a greater need for journalists and editors with a background in the life sciences. It will probably be an advantage for reporters to have more knowledge in this area. A better understanding of scientific principles can help them probe deeper into claims or question basic assumptions beyond the slogans and rhetoric of different positions. The financial media will need more reporters who understand not only finance but also the science behind technology so they can develop a more complete picture of technological developments and be more critical about the data they receive. Informed journalists can help their readers better understand the hopes, problems, and arguments of the debate.

The media affect the debate. First, they help focus public attention on gene technology. Second, the choices that journalists and editors make in handling material affect the information that consumers receive. The financial community and investors use news reports of companies and industries in making market analyses and investment choices. Leaders in business, politics, the church, or the community also follow the news in an effort to stay current with a shifting social environment. In the 1993 Eurobarometer survey (Marlier, 1993), television, newspapers, magazines, and radio rank among the top information sources on new developments affecting people's lives. The main source of information for most of those interviewed was either television (56 percent) or newspapers (20 percent).

The way the media report on gene technology influences people's views. If they portray developments as miracles, they risk setting up unrealistic expectations that may be disappointments. If they portray developments as dangerous, they risk raising people's anxiety and possibly causing panic. Sensational stories that stress high hopes or strong fears will not create a realistic picture of developments. By contrast, the media can help present a broad, multifaceted picture of gene technology, including its many positive and negative implications. Critical journalists can verify the information they receive from stakeholders and by cross-referencing to a variety of sources present the wide range of opinions and interests involved. Even their best work, of course, depends on the time available and the cooperation of their sources.

POLICY INTEGRATORS

The difference between legislators (elected politicians) and administrators (career civil servants) is important. Legislators propose public policies and laws that reflect the views and interests of their parties, the people they represent. Because of their time-limited terms, many tend to have a short-run view of policies. Most have an interest in getting reelected. Administrators, by contrast, advise legislators on policy and legislative proposals. They are usually responsible for objectively formulating policies, interpreting legislation, and enforcing regulation. As professionals not subject to election, they tend to have a long-run view of politics. One of their interests is creating stable legislation that will survive changes in government.

Many legislators and administrators probably see gene technology as a controversial issue filled with political mine fields. Yet legislators in most countries are supposed to take a stance, setting social priorities by supporting one set of interests over another—otherwise there would be no need for different political parties. Legislators are the subject of lobbying efforts from the various players in the debate. Administrators face the task of answering the challenges of gene technology within the framework of existing legislation. If new laws are passed, administrators must enforce them.

From a political standpoint, the debate over gene technology involves at least three distinct but related conflicts. First, it is a conflict about values and interests. Second, it is a conflict over the degree of social acceptance of a new technology. Finally, it is a conflict over future directions for society. For any political initiative to succeed in a pluralistic society, it will have to address the values and interests of the majority. In the gene technology debate, one of the tasks facing legislators is to balance different values and interests: economic prosperity and environmental sustainability, social order and individual rights. Public policies, legislation, and regulation can set the necessary level of social control for the different applications of gene technology and the guidelines for future research, development, and production.

At least two factors could affect government policies on gene technology. First, is concern for the economy. Without sufficient economic resources, provided by a healthy economy, governments may have difficulty maintaining the standard of living, providing employment, maintaining an educational system, running public medical facilities, and operating other public services. More and more governments are looking at gene technology as an investment opportunity and a source of solutions to some of the problems their nations face. Some governments, for example, look to gene technology to solve problems in health care, agriculture, and environmental management. The pressures of a growing population in many parts of the world require the sound use of existing resources, including biological resources. Gene technology is not the only way to solve socioeconomic problems, but it is one option.

A second factor affecting government policy on gene technology is the need for some degree of social control to prevent abuse or misuse of the technology and to encourage growth in certain areas and restrict it in others. For example, because the insurance industry in the United Kingdom had not developed any policy guidelines on the use of genetic information, Parliament gave it a year to propose such guidelines before imposing its own set of regulations. That government initiative seemed to recognize the growing importance of genetic data in the insurance industry and the need to protect the rights of the individual over third-party access to personal information.

Many people fear that gene technology will bring about major changes in attitude with unforeseeable effects on individuals, society, and the environment. This fear has led to calls to legislators and administrators to propose measures that would minimize negative effects. The way governments respond to these calls will have an impact on the debate.

INDUSTRIALIZING NATIONS

"The purpose of human development is to increase people's range of choices. If they are not free to make those choices, the entire process becomes a mockery (UNDP, 1992, p. 26)." In discussions on gene technology, the question of how it will affect industrializing nations comes up time and again. Some argue that it will destroy the economies of countries that depend on cash crops (such as sugar cane, cocoa beans, coffee beans, vanilla, and other natural flavoring agents). Others argue that it will solve the problems of hunger and malnutrition and such serious diseases as measles, malaria, hepatitis, and AIDS. For yet others, especially nongovernmental organizations working closely with industrializing nations, the issues are far more complicated. Gene technology has a tremendous potential for both good and harm for the industrializing world.

> Biotechnology is neither demon nor angel. It should not be attacked as entirely a scourge of the poor, or as an unmitigated environmental disaster. Neither should it be uncritically embraced as a panacea, an instant provider of food, medicine and wealth. (Walgate, 1990)

At the same time, there is a sense of urgency that the lessons of the past with technology not be forgotten. In his preface to R. Walgate's book, Jon Tinker writes: "For the technologies based on physics and chemistry, most of the Third World has been a bystander, receiving leftovers from western tables, with little opportunity to influence research or innovation" (Walgate, 1990). There is a sense that the technologies of biology should be different: the applications of gene technology are wide ranging enough to satisfy the needs of both that industrialized and industrializing nations.

It is useful to take a moment here to understand the assumptions of this section. First, it assumes that government and the populace do not always have the same interests. In many industrializing nations, power is in the hands of an influential minority. This section will put greater emphasis on the interests of the people.

Second, it assumes there is a real need to distinguish among the many different nations of the industrializing world. Not all have the same problems or place priority on the same needs. The problems facing sub-Saharan Africa are not the same as those facing South America or Southeast Asia. Even within the same region, nations react differently to similar situations.

For example, Malaysia is focusing on economic development by using its forests as a source of timber, while Thailand has banned commercial logging in order to protect its forests (Kawai, 1995).

Finally, this section assumes that the problems facing industrializing countries are not "simply" the problems of low-income countries. Many of them have repercussions on industrialized countries, for example, disappearing tropical rainforests and global warming. Similarly, poverty may lead to economic instability in industrializing countries, resulting in a change in migratory patterns, not only in the region but worldwide. In the 1990s, for example, there has been a rise in the number of "economic refugees," people who find no hope in their own lands and are not wanted elsewhere.

On the basis of these assumptions, this section will first outline some of the most pressing needs of industrializing countries and then examine the impact these countries can have on the debate in industrialized countries. In the poorest countries, most people struggle to survive. They need to overcome the following:

- malnutrition and hunger
- illiteracy
- diseases
- poverty
- the turbulence of a developing economy
- ecological destruction

The following tables (6.1, 6.2, 6.3) provide a basis of comparison in various areas, including life expectancy at birth, adult literacy, mean years of schooling, and real purchasing power parities (PPP). The tables are based on the UNDP human development index, which ranks 160 nations according to life expectancy, education, and income.

Most if not all of the challenges listed above have deep-rooted causes and are also often linked with sociocultural patterns or sociopolitical structures, some long established, others more recent: the subordinate role of women, limited access to education, limited access to essential goods and services, uneven distribution of wealth, increasing migration to urban areas, rapid population growth, and lack of respect for human rights. There is a need to break away from old paradigms that bind people to systems that no longer work.

To some extent, individuals have started to change in response to new realities. A good example is the role of women. In the frequently drought-stricken sub-Sahara, as men move to cities or coastal regions to find work, women have to take on the responsibilities traditionally belonging to men. "The old division of labour based on sex is no longer valid. In many places, 40 percent or more of the households and production units are headed by women" (Leisinger, Schmitt, and ISNAR, 1995, p. 68). Solutions for complex social, cultural, and political problems cannot come from technology, *least of all* gene technology. At best, technology is equipped to deal with chal-

Table 6.1 Top Five Countries in the 1992 UNDP Human Development Index

High Human Development Countries (UNDP ranking)	Human Develop-ment Index	Life Expectancy at Birth (in years) in 1990	Adult Literacy Rate (in percent) in 1990	Mean Years of Schooling in 1990	PPP* (in inter-national dollars) in 1989
1. Canada	0.982	77.0	99.0	12.1	18 635
2. Japan	0.981	78.6	99.0	10.7	14 311
3. Norway	0.978	77.1	99.0	11.6	16 838
4. Switzerland	0.977	77.4	99.0	11.1	18 590
5. Sweden	0.976	77.4	99.0	11.1	14 817

Source: UNDP, 1992 no. 76, p. 127.

Table 6.2 Middle Five Countries in the 1992 UNDP Human Development Index

Medium Human Development Countries (UNDP ranking)	Human Develop-ment Index	Life Expectancy at Birth (in years) in 1990	Adult Literacy Rate (in percent) in 1990	Mean Years of Schooling in 1990	PPP* (in inter-national dollars) in 1989
68. Saint Kitts and Nevis	0.686	67.5	92.0	6.0	3 150
69. Thailand	0.685	66.1	93.0	3.8	3 569
70. South Africa	0.674	61.7	70.0	3.9	4 958
71. Turkey	0.671	65.1	80.7	3.5	4 002
72. Syria	0.665	66.1	64.5	4.2	4 348

Source: UNDP, 1992 no. 76, p. 128.

Table 6.3 Bottom Five Countries in the 1992 UNDP Human Development Index

Low Human Development Countries (UNDP ranking)	Human Develop-ment Index	Life Expectancy at Birth (in years) in 1990	Adult Literacy Rate (in percent) in 1990	Mean Years of Schooling in 1990	PPP* (in inter-national dollars) in 1989
156. Niger	.078	45.5	28.4	0.1	634
157. Burkina Faso	.074	48.2	18.2	0.1	617
158. Afghanistan	.065	42.5	29.4	0.8	710
159. Sierra Leone	.062	42.0	20.7	0.9	1 061
160. Guinea	.052	43.5	24.0	0.8	602

Source: UNDP, 1992 no. 76, p. 129.

* Purchasing power parties. PPP is a means of comparison developed by the UN to measure "GDP on an internationally comparable scale . . . expressed in international dollars" (UNDP, 1992, no. 76, p. 208).

lenges in tangible areas such as health, agriculture, and the environment.

People in industrializing countries share two overriding interests: attaining self-sufficiency and doing it their own way. Self-sufficiency, as individuals and as nations, includes the ability to satisfy the basic needs for food and health. Self-sufficiency is linked with sustainable development in the sense of responsible management of limited natural resources. In the struggle to feed a growing population, overproduction on the same piece of land leads to the depletion of valuable minerals and nutrients in the soil, causing soil erosion and even desertification. This process reduces the soil's ability to meet future agricultural needs. The reversal or prevention of this destructive process is important for the self-sufficiency of individuals, but it is critical for the self-sufficiency of nations. It should not be forgotten that the importance of sustainable development for industrializing nations is closely linked with the wealth of genetic resources found in most parts of the South. The genetic resources they manage are a vital part of their cultural and economic assets.

Regarding the second major interest of industrializing nations, choosing their own way to development, as K. M. Leisinger explains, during the 1950s and 1960s the countries of the Third World wanted to set out on their own route—following neither the road of capitalism nor that of communism. The rising importance of genetic resources will probably play a role in this third route to development.

This third route is a chance for most industrializing nations to capitalize on the assets of their own region: the wildlife that flourishes there and maybe nowhere else (Kawai, 1995; Walgate, 1990). "Developing nations such as those situated in tropical regions, which possess an abundant array of species, are now starting to re-evaluate their species as 'genetic resources' which have economic value" (Kawai, 1995, p. 443).

At the same time, development must also include the preservation of traditional knowledge of local plants and animals. In the past, tradition and development often came into conflict. For example, indigenous peoples living in rain forests and jungles have long made use of the organisms in those forests and probably understand their habitat better than anyone else. Up to now, however, development has often taken the forms of logging and mining, migration of younger people to cities, or deforestation to make new farmland. Such contacts with industrialization have destroyed not only the environment that supported these people but also the skills, knowledge, and way of life that they inherited from their ancestors.

> These "forest people" possess a remarkable amount of knowledge concerning the useful plants and animals of the tropical forest. However, changes in their way of life are occurring along with the wave of development that has been happening, and they are

increasingly coming into contact with surrounding cultures. As a result, there is the danger that the valuable traditional knowledge which has been passed down from generation to generation is disappearing along with the tropical forests. (Kawai, 1995, p. 438)

This example from the rain forests underlines the problems of development in developing nations. Discussions on the future of gene technology must take them into consideration.

The first problem is not that tradition and development have to be mutually exclusive. Indeed traditional knowledge of local plants and animals can be the starting point for research in gene technology. The problem is agreeing on how the benefits can be fairly distributed between the owners of this knowledge (the industrializing South) and the owners of this technology (the industrialized North).

The second problem is not whether gene technology is the right solution for the problems of industrializing nations. No technology can solve all the difficulties facing any society. The problem is recognizing what areas technology can address (technological problems) and areas where it can play only a minor role (political, social, or cultural problems).

Again, it must be stressed that the problems facing industrializing nations and those facing industrialized nations are interconnected. Discussions on the dilemmas facing the industrialized North must involve consideration of the problems facing the industrializing South because the South will be affected by what the North decides.

Gene technology developed in the North, where much research and development comes from business and industry rather than governments under fiscal restraint. In health care, for example, the high costs of developing new drugs makes it difficult for government agencies and research institutions to commit themselves to such undertakings (Tzotzos and Leopold, 1995, p. 357). Thus, much of R&D is left to the private sector, which focuses on products that will earn a profit. Since profit is made mostly in industrialized countries, facilities for research, development, and production tend to be located there and to focus on their concerns. As a result, debates seldom if ever consider the needs of industrializing nations. For example, agricultural research in industrialized countries focuses mainly on crops of importance to the North, such as wheat instead of on millet or cassava, which are important in the South. These latter crops are called **orphan commodities**, crops of little commercial interest to industrialized countries (Tzotzos and Leopold, 1995; Walgate, 1990).

If the concerns of industrializing nations do enter public debate in the North, it is rarely in the appropriate context. For example, in chapter 2, it was suggested that resistance to genetically engineered crops may stem in part from overproduction of certain crops using conventional farming methods. By contrast, in many areas of Southeast Asia one of the most urgent problems is how to increase agroproduction *without* any increase in arable land or other resources (such as water or fertilizer).

Finally, and perhaps most important, many industrializing countries lack the necessary skills, knowledge, and funds to develop their own technical expertise and infrastructure in gene technology. As noted earlier, the speed of technical advances in gene technology means that there is an ever growing gap between industrialized and industrializing countries, unless there is a real commitment from both sides to close this distance.

> In 1960, the richest 20% of the world's population had incomes 30 times greater than the poorest 20%. By 1990, the richest 20% were getting 60 times more. And this comparison is based on the distribution between rich and poor *countries*. Adding the maldistributions within countries, the richest 20% of the world's *people* get at least 150 times more than the poorest 20%. (UNDP, 1992, p. 1)

Although UN agencies helped sponsor a number of biotechnology-research programs in industrializing countries in the mid-1980s, these programs still have to overcome a number of obstacles. In a review of such programs in three countries—Egypt, Thailand, and Venezuela—R. A. Zilinskas identified six common problems. The most important is perhaps limited access to information. Some reasons are the high cost of creating and maintaining a resource base, a limited communications infrastructure, and the lack of contact between researchers in industrialized and industrializing countries. Other reasons are that little applied research in biotechnology is being carried out at universities in industrializing countries, and what little there is, is often not applicable to the situation in those countries (Zilinskas, 1995).

This problem of limited access makes it likely that the gap in technology between industrializing and industrialized countries will increase—and that the interests of the South will not be properly represented—much less taken into consideration—in the debate in the North. One common argument for gene technology is that it will help eradicate deadly diseases and improve nutrition in industrializing nations. This may be true in an absolute sense, but in practice, lack of finances and knowledge makes it hard for industrializing nations to use gene technology to meet their needs. As a remedy, several authors propose greater investments from nongovernmental organizations and international research centers (Walgate, 1990; Zilinskas, 1995).

One common argument against gene technology is that the substitutes it creates will devastate the economies of countries that depend on cash crops such as cocoa, coffee, or vanilla. This threat is serious (Ahmed, 1995), but other applications of gene technology (for example, crops resistant to drought or tolerant of salt) might in fact increase crop production.

> Biotechnology's role in income generation could be two-fold: to improve existing cash crops and develop new uses for them; and to generate entirely new forms of income for developing countries, based on establishing their ownership and control over the vast resources of genetic material locked in their fields and forests. (Walgate, 1990, p. 9)

As has been pointed out, technology is only part of the solution: there is also a need for fundamental changes to existing structures. First, everyone must have access to the right resources—germ plasm, medicine, or information—because access is just as important as the ability to produce them. One of the problems of the Green Revolution was that not all farmers in industrializing nations had access to the additional water, fertilizer, and sophisticated tools that the new crops required. Second, the legitimate interests of industrializing nations should be considered in the context of their own situation, not in the context of the industrialized world. As Maslow points out: "For our chronically and extremely hungry person, Utopia can be defined simply as a place where there is plenty of food" (Maslow, 1970, p. 17). That is, the priorities of industrializing nations are different from those of industrialized ones. Nutrition, health, and self-sufficiency take on a different sense of urgency where hunger, disease, and poverty are widespread.

Third, the impetus for change must come from those who will be affected. The peoples of industrializing countries must have the right and opportunity to make their own choices, to decide which—if any—techniques of gene technology could help them fulfill their needs. "Biotechnology can be good for developing countries; but only if they and their friends make it so" (Walgate, 1990, p. 182).

SUGGESTIONS FOR DIALOGUE AND ACTION
The following discussion builds on the traditional approaches to resolving clashes of values and interests (see "Conventional Approaches" above), especially issue management and conflict management. At the same time, it points out the particular contributions of the different players to the discussion.

GENERAL STRATEGY
At the beginning of this chapter, it was proposed that a shift in paradigm creates conflict because it is an opportunity for satisfying the interests of some and a threat to the interests of others. The resolution requires a three-part approach that gives meaning to the contributions of different partici-

pants: 1) Recognize the legitimate role of all segments of society in the debate. 2) Respond to the immediate concerns surrounding gene technology. 3) Acknowledge the underlying conflicts provoked by the paradigm shift.

Recognition of All Segments of Society

Each segment of society—stakeholders, value advocates, problem interpreters, and policy integrators—has different interests or functions in the debate. Although these differences can cause conflict, they can also be part of the solution. Because each segment sees gene technology from a different angle, it can offer a unique insight into the dilemmas that the technology raises. By contributing to a broad range of options to be explored, each segment plays a role in helping society solve the dilemmas.

In a choice-based society, **stakeholders** in a debate, both individuals and groups, have the freedom to speak out for their interests and the responsibility to take the consequences of their actions. Because there is always a scarcity of time, money, and information, society is unable to satisfy all the interests of all parties at all times. The result is competition for priority. In defining the common good, society has to set priorities by making decisions based on its underlying values.

By championing particular causes, **value advocates** make explicit to the rest of society the values that underlie social conflicts. Taking on the role once filled by philosophers and clergy, they point out inconsistencies in value systems and the consequences of specific social decisions. They also alert the rest of society to problems and dangers. They have often been at the forefront of efforts to stimulate debates over the nonscientific and noneconomic implications of gene technology.

Problem interpreters, who also focus society's attention on inconsistencies in value systems, do not necessarily defend a particular cause but may concentrate on a number of problems at the same time. Journalists, editors, lobbyists, and advertising consultants help shape public opinion because they are still the main source of information for most of the population.

As **policy integrators**, legislators and administrators are entrusted with the management of the public good. Legislators, in particular, have two main responsibilities: visionary leadership based on their own values and representation of society's values and interests. Sometimes these responsibilities come into conflict. In such situations, for example the paradigm change caused by gene technology, they have the additional responsibility to consult with the public on sensitive public questions of priorities. Such consultation can take various forms, including legislative enquiries, parliamentary commissions, plebiscites, and referendums.

Response to Technological Concerns

Resistance to gene technology stems in part from concerns about its negative effects. Some of these concerns may be exaggerated (from a scientist's point of view), but some are legitimate. As Postman reminds us, the inventor of a technology is not always the best judge of the good and harm that it will produce for the society that uses it. No single perspective can provide a solid basis for making informed, balanced, social decisions.

One of the problems surrounding gene technology is that large parts of the population are unfamiliar with its concepts and tend to rely on images from popular entertainment, such as the film *Jurassic Park,* to fill in the gaps in their knowledge. Communications between **scientists** and nonscientists play an important part in bridging the worlds of the science community and the community at large. Such communications should be viewed as two-way learning opportunities. Sometimes, especially where judgments about risk are involved, expertise depends at least as much on wisdom as on technical knowledge. Through such two-way communications, nonscientists can perhaps better appreciate that scientific understanding changes with new knowledge, that data are provided by different methods, and that scientists may interpret results in different ways. Scientists, for their part, may learn more about the concerns of their nonscientific neighbors. As one scientist comments:

> There isn't enough contact between the scientific and the public worlds. Scientists work in private places, behind closed doors, with little public exposure. The task of the scientific community will be to increase opportunities for contact whenever possible, by inviting the public in, and by going out and getting more involved with the public, in schools, in community activities, etc. Because just as we must enable members of the public to become more familiar with science, so science must also become more familiar with the public. (Thomas, 1993, p. 28)

DARAs and the health-care industry, because they enjoy a high degree of public trust, can take a leading role in public discussions of medical applications of gene technology. In situations where the public accepts many such applications but also feels uncertain about the inherent risks, there is an opportunity for discussions on the capabilities and limits of current medical knowledge.

The pharmaceutical and gene technology industries often lack the trust of the population because of their failure to communicate openly and the gaps between their words and their actions. Open communication means a willingness to consider other perspectives and not dismiss them out of hand, especially because *no technology* is without risks. As sectors that will benefit from the new technology, the pharmaceutical and gene technology industries have a particular responsibility to discuss the concerns of all sides openly. These industries should first make clear their own needs—new products, better R&D tools, and more efficient techniques—without any threats.

If they can show both the intellectual *and* emotional factors behind their decisions, most people are probably prepared to listen. They do not have to agree with a decision, but at least they can understand why it was made. To earn the public's trust, these industries must be able to show that they trust the public, with whom they are in dialogue. All too often, these industries have demonstrated a lack of confidence in other segments of society. Building trust includes acknowledging the limits of one's own knowledge and demonstrating willingness to learn from the experiences of others. If the general population were aware of the industries' long experience with using chemicals and radiation to alter microorganisms, it would have more confidence in genetic alteration.

The pharmaceutical and gene technology industries must also take care to match action to words. They must be careful not to raise false hopes and expectations. Public announcements, especially to the media, must be responsible communications. If a certain experiment carries low risks, the safety measures taken should reflect that. As H. Otway and B. Wynne point out, a paradox in communications about risk is that disproportionate emphasis on safety serves only to imply that the technology is inherently unsafe. "The reassurance-arousal paradox arises from the contradiction between siting and emergency plan communications—vivid and memorable messages about emergency procedures could accentuate anxiety, perhaps even causing demands that the facility be closed" (1989, p. 142).

Like the pharmaceutical and gene technology industries, the **farming and food industries** stand to benefit from gene technology and face resistance to it. The farming industry faces resistance from small farmers, who feel that they will not be able to afford genetically altered germ plasm or animals, although government or bank loans might be arranged. Other farmers fear that a successful breed of animal or variety of plant may come to dominate the market, creating uniformity rather than diversity. Both industries are opposed by public opinion, which, as noted in chapter 2, gives little support to research in gene technology to improve food or farm animals. The public is concerned about the side effects of novel foods on health and about labeling such foods to protect the interests of consumers. All those affected, led by farmers and consumer organizations, should take part in public discussions on this subject.

The **financial and investment community** should invest in public discussions of gene technology. Ernst and Young, for example, already makes active contributions in such discussions by releasing annual reports on the gene technology industry in the United States and Europe. The reports look at the impact of various influences, including the regulatory environment, public opinion, and legal protection for products. The expertise of financial analysts and industry observers lies in their ability to spot trends, including the possibility of new employment opportunities. At the same time, they must address the public's concerns for health, safety, and the environment because negative perceptions discourage investment and may lead to costly litigation.

Acknowledgment of Underlying Values and Interests

One of the most important components of successful conflict resolution lies in differentiating between stated positions and underlying interests. This difference was underlined, for example, in the dispute between Israel and Egypt over the Sinai Peninsula, which both claimed after the 1967 conflict.

> As the Camp David negotiations proceeded, however, it emerged that the seemingly irreconcilable positions of Israel and Egypt reflected underlying interests that were not incompatible. Israel's underlying interest was security. . . . Egypt was primarily interested in sovereignty. (Puitt and Rubin, 1986, p. 1)

As this book has repeatedly pointed out, part of the controversy over gene technology stems from the paradigm shift that it has triggered. As noted in chapter 5, this shift affects the rights of the individual (autonomy) versus the rights of society (control), technological development versus ecological balance, and life seen as biological process versus life seen as an irreducible whole. Stakeholders, value advocates, problem interpreters, and policy integrators have a responsibility to ensure dialogue that will address these concerns as well as persuading the rest of the population of the benefits, many self-evident, that gene technology will bring.

Right to Life—A major concern is the right to life. Gene technology makes it possible to diagnose genetic disorders in fetuses and embryos and aims to eliminate these disorders. Genetic counseling aims to provide expectant parents with the information on which to base their decision to continue or to terminate pregnancy. In a society where there are financial restraints on health care, will parents receive the moral, financial, or medical support needed for the care of a disabled child? Behind this dilemma loom such moral questions as, What does "quality of life" mean? What is "normal" in human terms? Can a person with disabilities lead a fulfilling life? Will society become less accepting of "imperfections"? When is a human life not worth living?

These are not new questions. They lie behind dilemmas posed by prenatal biopsies and abortion, artificial life support and euthanasia, even blood transfusion or surgery and the patient's right to refuse medical treatment. One of the effects of modern medical technology is that it changes society's understanding of life and death, as well as health and sickness. To some degree, all medical tools and techniques "intervene" in life's natural processes. Gene technology is different chiefly because it intervenes at the level of genes rather than organs and tissues. There is an ever finer distinction between genetic disorder and genetic variation. As more and more traits are linked to one or more genes, there is the concern that seeking a medical solution for learning disabilities or behavioral problems might outpace efforts to seek a social solution.

Social discrimination against people with disabilities is probably the biggest problem. As more and more genetic disorders are diagnosed and made targets of therapy, will individuals who have them still have a place in modern society? Do such people not contribute to society? Is the music of Beethoven less moving because he was deaf? Are the scientific contributions of Stephen Hawking less significant because he has Lou Gehrig's disease?

DARAs can probably speak on this matter with more authority than other stakeholders. They can present in human terms the dilemma between hope for some that gene therapy may hold the key to a cure and anxiety for others that gene therapy will result in greater social pressure to conform. Are there lives that are not worth living? The answer depends largely on the values of society. In that area, value advocates such as religious bodies can play an important role in the debate.

Right to Information—One of the most important concerns is the question of consumer choice. The right of the individual to information and the freedom to choose are not in dispute. Most people would probably agree that accurate labeling can help consumers choose. What is in dispute is the kind of information that should appear on the label. Some labels can be misleading: a label declaring that "this product does not contain . . ." implies that other products do contain that ingredient, which may not be true. Likewise, a label "not genetically altered" implies that products without this label have been.

The debate over labeling genetically altered food products is part of the broader debate over labels for technologically treated food items. Most food products today fall under this category, especially those involving cross-bred plant germ plasm, cloned animal embryos, artificial insemination, chemical fertilizers, pesticides or herbicides, antibiotics, irradiation to improve shelf life, chemical preservatives, and coloring and flavor enhancers. Critics of technological processing continue to press for special labeling in three areas: genetically altered food products, chemical residues on produce, and irradiated produce.

Beyond the question of consumer rights, the debate draws attention to the pervasive influence of technology on virtually all aspects of human life in modern technological society. Most urban dwellers are not even aware of how much they depend on technology. George Grant, the technological nihilist, calls this unawareness the loss of the sense of loss (Kroker, 1996). In a society where most people are no longer aware of the influence of technology on their lives, value advocates, especially so-called **technology critics**, such as antibiotechnology activists, act as society's early warning system. They raise uncomfortable questions about human dependency on technology. By focusing attention on how technology affects individual lives, value advocates help establish an ethical framework in which society can come to understand technology and its consequences. Such a framework allows society to arrive at an informed decision about gene technology and enables policy integrators to establish consistent measures of social control.

Duty to Care for the Planet—For environmental groups and some other segments of society, a major concern with gene technology is the impact that genetically altered organisms could have on the environment. Opponents of field trials fear that they may unleash effects that science cannot yet understand and may not be able to halt.

   This concern is not merely for safety but stems from a desire to minimize the damaging impact of human activities on the elements that support life on earth. Since at least the 1960s, accidents and disasters have provided mounting evidence of the destructive effect of human activities on the environment. Rachel Carson and others drew attention to the negative side effects of chemical pesticides on the environment. The oil crisis of the 1970s drove home the point that energy is a nonrenewable resource. The increase in nuclear weapons and reactors raised anxiety about their effect on the environment. Changes in weather patterns and signs of ozone depletion focused greater attention on the need to manage the earth's resources for future generations. The continuing support for Greenpeace and other environmental organizations, the rise of the Green Party in Germany and elsewhere, the Rio Conference, the Montreal Protocol, international protests against the French testing of atomic weapons on the Murarao Atoll, and the multilateral agreement on nuclear test bans are all evidence that concern for the environment was strong in the mid-1990s. In many industrialized countries, emphasis shifted from cleaning up polluted land or water to preventing pollution. This trend is summed up by the three "Rs" of the 1990s: reduce, re-use, and recycle. Both the environmental movement and the New Age movement of the 1980s, with its view of Earth as Gaia, were born out of the realization that all life on this planet is connected. If human beings continue to destroy the systems that support life, then they will end up destroying themselves.

> Although the dinosaurs disappeared, they did not, as we may well be doing, bring about their own extinction. . . . We are shortsighted and egocentric, little realising that our survival is intimately related to and depends upon the survival of 30 million other species. This behaviour may, in the long run, be a kind of suicide. (Caldicott, 1992, pp. 96-97)

   Gene technology has deepened the schism between the scientific and the holistic views of life. The discovery of the structure of DNA led to the realization that all cellular life on this planet is based on the same four nucleotides that form an organism's genetic code. There is consensus that all life is the same. But this statement has different practical meanings. For the scientists and gene technology industries it means that genes can be transferred across the traditional scientific classifications of species and even kingdoms, as indeed some species of plants and animals have done for centuries: for example, horses and donkeys producing mules. For the advocates of Gaia, it means that due care must be taken to protect all life so that changes to one species may not affect other species, as might happen with transgenic crops .

This schism between worldviews is not a simple split between industry and environmentalists over environmental questions. Scientists, industry leaders, environmentalists, and legislators have a responsibility to take discussions on biosafety, biodiversity, and legislative and social controls to a deeper level to explore the underlying differences in values. The facts that industry participated at the Rio Conference and that many companies have made voluntary moves to reduce pollution and include such efforts in their financial plans show that industry has been listening to the demands of environmentalist groups, consumers, and government. They also suggest that many managers realize that pollution control can make financial sense. Finally, they suggest that many individuals in industry share the same concerns as environmental activists over the future of this planet. The dilemma is rather how to reconcile the needs of a growing and increasingly technology-dependent society with the duty to care for a planet that human beings share with millions of other organisms. Everyone shares the responsibility for finding a solution.

SPECIFIC ACTIONS
The various segments of society involved in the debate over gene technology can take specific actions to help them reach an informed decision. The aim of this book is not to tell them what to do but to suggest what they can do.

Stakeholders
Scientists could provide opportunities for people to visit laboratories to see what is involved in genetic alteration and perhaps even try first hand some simple experiments. Such opportunities would allow the public to see for themselves what scientists do. At the same time, scientists should make themselves available to talk with school classes and community groups outside the laboratory. They might maintain a speaker's bureau, where schools, the media, and other groups could find speakers on various themes. These speaking engagements should be treated as opportunities for mutual learning by both scientists and the public.

Representatives of DARAs could make themselves available for public discussions and speaking engagements. The public trust they enjoy makes them valuable participants but also places responsibility on them to be accurate.

The pharmaceutical and gene technology industries could sponsor or take part in round-table public discussions. To see beyond their own horizons, they need input from a wide range of sources. Multilateral encounters may give them new ideas and perhaps facilitate future collaboration as well as a better understanding of the underlying values and interests of other parties. A fruitful encounter means that balance in communication is essential. No single opinion is sufficient. Unlike marketing and advertising, communication requires openness, mutual respect, and two-way exchanges. These industries as a whole can take a stance in public debate but they should also listen.

Value Advocates

Value advocates have a dual role in public debates. On one hand, they voice concerns related directly to gene technology, such as its effect on human health and the environment. On the other hand, they focus attention on the values underlying the positions taken by different segments of society, positions they themselves represent. Like other segments of society, value advocates are responsible for presenting government, the media and, ultimately, the rest of society with accurate information. False or misleading information undermines the reputation of the organization that provides it and so is as much a disservice to the organization itself as it is to society. Society depends on value advocates—for example, environmental groups, antibiotechnology activists, religious organizations, and animal-rights activists—to provide a counterbalance to the views of industries and even governments.

Problem Interpreters

Ordinary citizens and decision makers—in industry, government, and nonprofit organizations—generally rely on the media for information and for their opinions. How the media interpret events and developments is as important as the events themselves. In the gene technology debate, there is emphasis on the hopes, dreams, and benefits it can realize and just as much emphasis on the fears, nightmares, and costs. Stories of success—gene therapy worked for a sick child—are offset by stories of failure—the first transgenic pig was severely arthritic. The media have an opportunity—perhaps even a responsibility—to provide some balance between these extremes. Editors can play an important role by allowing reporters to spend time in the environment—academic or industrial—in which scientists work. Research institutes, following the lead of the Max-Planck-Institute in Germany or the Novartis Foundation in the United Kingdom can organize programs and symposiums that allow journalists and scientists to spend time in each other's working environment gaining insight about each other's work. Science journalists can place stories—successes and failures—in context.

They can place the triumph of a discovery against the backdrop of the long years of research behind and the work still ahead, and a failure in the context of the trial-and-error approaches of science, of the need to keep on looking. Science journalists can give their audience a point of reference that does not raise false hopes or cause unnecessary anxiety.

Policy Integrators

Legislators and administrators, who manage the common good, hold office only so long as they have the consent of the electorate. Their key functions include leadership (setting policies), representation (understanding the will of the people), administration (distributing resources where needed), and integration (reconciling different social forces). Where the fundamental values and interests of different segments of society are in conflict, representation and integration are critical. For this reason, most parliamentary states have consultative mechanisms that allow policy integrators to go to the people on important questions. Switzerland, for example, held a plebiscite in 1998 on a set of propositions made by a citizen's group to curb further developments in some areas of gene technology such as genetically altered animals and genetically altered organisms that could put human health or the environment at risk.

As leaders, policy integrators must help society come to decisions in conflict. Governments could, for example, develop policies that would provide students with more information about gene technology. They could create a curriculum that would bring together information about scientific developments and the social issues.

KEY POINTS

- Technology, as a motor of change, adds to the uncertainty of life in two ways: by contributing to the stress of the change itself and by arousing anxiety as a result of the paradigm shift.

- Gene technology is no different from other technologies that cause a paradigm shift. Lack of familiarity with its applications raises concerns about risks to human health and the environment. Moreover, it has the potential to change the way people view one another, the environment, and even life itself, thus threatening the status quo.

- When the fundamental values and interests of different segments of society collide, the result is social conflict. Resolution depends on the ability of those segments to understand the interests and values behind stated positions.

- Traditional approaches to addressing conflict tend to look at the problem in a narrow framework. Technology assessment looks at it in terms of public policies. Issue management looks at its impact on a particular organization. Conflict management looks at it in the context of the particular crisis situation.

• Gene technology creates a paradigm shift in society that is social, technological, ethical, legal, economic, environmental, and political. This shift requires a new model of analysis that looks at the way gene technology affects the underlying values and interests of different parts of society.

• Stakeholders have a vital interest in the outcome of the conflict. They include the scientific community, disease-awareness and research organizations, and a number of industries with long-term interests in the new technology. Value advocates have no direct interests at stake, but the changes brought about by gene technology clash with their values and worldviews. This group includes environmentalists, animal-welfare activists, human-rights groups, and consumer-advocacy groups. Problem interpreters by focusing on a particular problem or interpreting information, influence the way others perceive a particular situation. Policy integrators are supposed to represent the values and interests of different sections of society and develop policies, that reflect them.

• The resolution of the social conflict over gene technology requires a three-pronged approach: 1) Recognize that all segments involved in the debate have a legitimate role to play in it. 2) Respond to the immediate concerns and problems surrounding gene technology itself. 3) Acknowledge the underlying conflicts of values and interests that the paradigm shift has provoked.

• The debate over gene technology is a measure of the way society copes with change. Gene technology presents a challenge—both opportunity and threat—that requires redistribution of society's resources and rethinking of its values.

REFERENCES

Ahmed, I. 1995. The Employment Impact of Biotechnology. In *The Biotechnology Revolution?*, edited by M. Fransman, G. Junne, and A. Roobeek, pp. 368–384. Oxford: Blackwell Scientific Publications.

Ansoff, H. I. 1980. Strategic Issue Management. *Strategic Management Journal* 1: 131–148.

Austrom, D. R., and L. Lad. 1989. Collaborative Approaches to Turbulence in the Sociopolitical Environment: The Emergence of Issues Management Alliances. *Futures Research Quarterly* 5: 22–42.

Bercovitch, J. 1984. *Social Conflict and Third Parties*. Boulder, Colo.: Westview Press.

Berg, P., and M. Singer. 1995. The Recombinant DNA Controversy: Twenty Years Later. *Bio/Technology* 13: 1132.

Bigelow, B., L. Fahey, and J. Mahon. 1993. A Typology of Issue Evolution. *Business and Society* 32 (1): 18–29.

Burton, J. W. 1987. *Resolving Deep-Rooted Conflict*. Lanham, Md: University Press of America.

Caldicott, H. 1992. *If You Love This Planet: A Plan to Heal the Earth*. New York: W. W. Norton and Co.

Cammillus, J. C., and D. K. Datta. 1991. Managing Strategic Issues in a Turbulent Environment. *Long Range Planning* 24 (2): 67–74.

Canibol, H.-P. 1994. Forscher gegen Bürokraten. *Focus*, 2 May, pp. 220–222.

Cantley, M. 1995. The Regulation of Modern Biotechnology: A Historical and European Perspective. In *Legal, Economic and Ethical Dimensions*, edited by D. Brauer, 2d ed., vol. 12, pp. 508–681. Weinheim, Germany: VCH Verlagsgesellschaft mbH.

Chase, W. H. 1984. *Issue Management: Origins of the Future*. Stamford, Calif.: Issue Actions Publication.

Dickson, D. 1995. UK Parliamentary Panel Calls for Human Genetics Authority. *Nature* 376: 202.

Drucker, P. F. 1992. The Post-Capitalist World. *Public Interest* 109: 89–100.

Ernst and Young. 1995. *European Biotech '95: Gathering Momentum—The Industry Annual Report*. London: Ernst and Young.

European Commission (Directorate General XII). 1997. *European Opinions on Modern Biotechnology*. Brussels: European Commission (Directorate General XII).

Ewing, R. P. 1980. Evaluating Issues Management. *Public Relations Journal* 36 (6): 14–16.

Freudenberg, W. R. 1992. Heuristics, Biases, and the Not-So-General Publics: Expertise and Error in the Assessment of Risks. In *Social Theories of Risk*, edited by S. Krimsky and D. Golding, pp. 215–228. Westport, Ct.: Praeger.

Greber, M. A., E. R. Frech, and J. A. Hillier. 1994. *The Disposal of Canada's Nuclear Fuel Waste: Public Involvement and Social Aspects* (AECL-10712, COG-93-2). Pinawa, Canada: Atomic Energy of Canada Ltd. Research.

Grunig, J. E., and F. C. Repper. 1992. Strategic Management, Publics and Issues. In *Excellence in Public Relations and Communications Management,* edited by J. E. Grunig, pp. 117–157. Hillsdale, N.J.: Lawrence Erlbaum Associates.

Hansen, L., and J. Grundahl. Undated. *Consensus Conferences: Public Debate on New Technology.* Copenhagen: TeknologiNævnet (The Danish Board of Technology).

Hudson, K. L., K. H. Rothenberg, L. B. Andrews, M. J. E. Kahn, and F. S. Collins. 1995. Genetic Discrimination and Health Insurance: An Urgent Need to Reform. *Science* 270: 391–393.

Joss, S., and J. Durant. 1994. *Consensus Conferences: A Review of the Danish, Dutch, and UK Approaches to This Special Form of Technology Assessment, and an Assessment of the Options for a Proposed Swiss Consensus Conference.* Basel: Agency for Biosafety Research and Assessment of Technology Impacts of the Swiss Priority Programme.

Kawai, M. 1995. Biotechnology and Biodiversity. In *Legal, Economic and Ethical Dimensions,* edited by D. Brauer, 2d ed., vol. 12, pp. 434–445. Weinheim Germany: VCH Verlagsgesellschaft mbH.

Kroker, A. 1996. *1984.* Montreal: New World Perspectives.

Lawless, E. W., M. V. Jones, and R. M. Jones. 1986. Methods for Comparing the Risks of Technologies. In *Risk Evaluation and Management,* edited by V. T. Covello, J. Menkes, and J. Mumpower, pp. 157–182. New York: Plenum Press.

Leisinger, K. M. 1990. *Wege aus Der Not—Die Dritte Welt: Probleme-Hoffnungen-Chancen.* Franfurt am Main: Bundesverband der Pharmazeutischen Industrie e.V.

Leisinger, K. M., K. Schmitt, and ISNAR, eds. 1995. *Survival in the Sahel.* The Hague: International Service for National Agricultural Research.

Leiss, W., and C. Chociolko. 1994. *Risk and Responsibility.* Montreal: McGill-Queen's University Press.

Lowrance, W. W. 1985. *Modern Science and Human Values.* New York: Oxford University Press.

Mahon, J. F., and S. A. Waddock. 1992. Strategic Issues Management. *Business and Society* 31 (1): 19–32.

Marlier, E. 1993. *Biotechnology and Genetic Engineering: What Europeans Think About It in 1993* (Survey Report Eurobarometer 39.1). Brussels: The European Commission.

Maslow, A. H. 1970. *Motivation and Personality*. 3d ed. New York: Harper and Row, Publishers.

Masood, E., S. Lehrman, Q. Shiermeier, D. Butler, and R. Nathan. 1996. Gene Tests: Who Benefits from Risk? *Nature* 379: 389–392.

Miller, S. K. 1993. To Catch a Killer Gene. *New Scientist* 138: 37–40.

Nelkin, D. 1985. Introduction: Analyzing Risk. In *The Language of Risk: Conflicting Perspectives on Occupational Health,* edited by D. Nelkin, pp. 11–24. Beverly Hills, Calif.: Sage Publications.

———. 1993. *Selling Science: How the Press Covers Science and Technology*. New York: W. H. Freeman and Co.

Nelkin, D., and M. S. Lindee. 1995. *The DNA Mystique: The Gene as a Cultural Icon*. New York: W. H. Freeman and Co.

Nelkin, D., and L. Tancredi. 1989. *Dangerous Diagnostics: The Social Power of Biological Information*. New York: Basic Books.

Otway, H. 1992. Public Wisdom, Expert Fallibility. In *Social Theories of Risk,* edited by S. Krimsky and D. Golding, pp. 215–228. Wesport, Ct.: Praeger.

Otway, H., and P. Haastrup. 1989. On the Social Acceptability of Inherently Safe Technologies. *IEEE Transactions on Engineering Management* 36 (1): 57–60.

Otway, H., and B. Wynne. 1989. Risk Communication: Paradigm and Paradox. *Risk Analysis* 9 (2): 141–145.

Post, J. E. 1978. *Corporate Behavior and Social Change*. Reston, Va.: Reston Public Co.

Postman, N. 1992. *Technopoly: The Surrender of Culture to Technology*. New York: Vintage Books.

Puitt, D. G., and J. Z. Rubin. 1986. *Social Conflict: Escalation, Stalemate, and Settlement*. New York: Random House.

Rohwedder, C., M. M. Nelson, T. Kamm, and K. Pope. 1995. Changing Climate: Greenpeace Loses Some of Its Veneer During Double Blast. *Wall Street Journal Europe*, 7 September, pp. 1, 9.

Schwank, A. 1993. Von der Rassenhygiene zu den genetischen Utopien der Moderne. *Soziale Medezin*, no. 4: 16–20.

Schweizerischer Invalidenverband. 1991. *Behinderte zwischen Prävention und Integration: Anfrage an die Humangenetik.* Paper presented at the Behinderte zwischen Prävention und Integration: Anfrage an die Humangenetik, Basle, 16 November 1996. Basel: Schweizerischer Invalidenverband.

Shlaes, A. 1995. A Germany That Kills Science. *Wall Street Journal Europe,* 8 November.

Slovic, P. 1987. Perception of Risk. *Science* 236: 280–285.

———. 1992. Perception of Risk: Reflections on the Psychometric Paradigm. In *Social Theories of Risk,* edited by S. Krimsky and D. Golding, pp. 117–152 . Westport, Ct.: Praeger.

Thomas, G. 1993. *Science in the Public Mind: A Cause for Concern?* Paper presented at the Schering Lecture Series, Berlin.

Tzotzos, G. T., and M. Leopold. 1995. Commercial Biotechnology: Developing World Prospects. In *Legal, Economic and Ethical Dimensions,* edited by D. Brauer, 2d ed., vol. 12, pp. 339–367. Weinheim, Germany: VCH Verlagsgesellschaft mbH.

UNDP. 1992. *Human Development Report 1992.* New York: Oxford University Press.

Walgate, R. 1990. *Miracle or Menace? Biotechnology and the Third World.* Budapest: Panos Institute.

Zilinskas, R. A. 1995. Biotechnology and the Third World: The Missing Link Between Research and Applications. In *The Biotechnology Revolution?,* edited by M. Fransman, G. Junne, and A. Roobeek, pp. 501–520. Oxford: Blackwell Scientific Publication.

SUMMARY AND OUTLOOK

This book has attempted to analyze the emergence of gene technology and the resulting challenges and dilemmas for society. As with any new technology, the greatest challenge gene technology presents is not in controlling the technical risks but in controlling its power to change people's lives.

Technology is about power. Power in this context has two aspects. One is the influence and authority that technology gives to certain groups of individuals and institutions in society. A new technology redistributes resources and creates new wealth. Those who understand, manage, and use the new technology benefit from it and have the power to make decisions. Those who cannot deal with the new technology are at a disadvantage. The existing power structure is disrupted, and the delicate balance of power and interests is altered.

The other aspect of power is the ability of a new technology to change people's perception of the world and of themselves. It calls into question old values and assumptions, creating anxiety and unease. Thus the power of a new technology creates a paradigm shift in both the structure of society and people's minds.

A paradigm shift inevitably brings the interests and values of different segments of society into conflict. Society's decision whether or not to accept a new technology is a complex process that must allow different segments to be heard. It is vital to recognize that all segments have a legitimate part to play in the resolution of such conflicts, which will affect the future of society as a whole. Patent offices provide one framework in which people may voice their concerns. The media can also contribute to the debate.

Gene technology is not the first technology to change a paradigm, nor will it be the last. It has created a furor in modern, high tech, postindustrial society because it has raised issues that challenge the materialist worldview on which our society is based. It is forcing us to raise questions about the nature of life and reconsider ethics in a high tech world.

Three critical lessons emerge from the debate on gene technology. First, social control is more difficult than technical control. Social control cannot be a series of stop-gap measures but must be a long-range policy with a firm ethical basis.

Second, all segments of society must be involved in the debate. Without technological innovation and willingness to take risks, society would become economically stagnant. Without opponents of innovation and risk to remind us of the human dimension and the need for caution, society would become morally stagnant. Society can advance—in all senses of that word—only if it can draw on the best of all segments of society.

Third, no resolution of the debate is possible unless the concerns—specific fears and deep-seated values—of all segments are made clear. This process requires time for consideration of both rational and emotional factors and the development of trust on both sides.

It has been more than twenty-five years since the first successful experiment with recombinant DNA. Since then, gene technology has been applied to the needs of almost every aspect of society. It is here to stay; the question is to what extent and under what conditions. If experience with other new technologies is any guide, it is likely that some people will consider that the benefits outweigh the costs; others will consider the costs too high.

Gene technology is not the only high technology based on the life sciences. Bioengineering and biocatalysis use microorganisms to convert raw material into new substances, such as biodegradable plastic. Neuroinformatics applies information technology and neurology to medicine and computer science. Bioelectronics focuses on the development of artificial biosensors made of biological and electronic components for the transmission of signals. New reproductive technology uses artificial insemination and in vitro fertilization to enable sterile couples to conceive. These new biotechnologies will not have the same diversity of application that gene technology has, nor will they have as far-reaching consequences; but they will raise similar questions that will force our high tech society to think about the value we place on human and other life.

Again and again society will have to make decisions about the role of technology in preserving and ending human life, the rights of the individual versus the interests of society, and who will have access to new medical technologies. This book offers no ready-made solutions, but perhaps it will allow decision makers to see these dilemmas from fresh perspectives.